yoshoku

A cookbook is the result of an amalgamation of talent, skill and passion.

First of all, I would like to thank Kay Scarlett and Juliet Rogers for believing in the project; Zoë Harpham, Kim Rowney and Marylouise Brammer for their editorial and design expertise; and all the behind-the-scenes stars at Murdoch Books who make it all happen.

Thanks also to Mikkel Vang and Christine Rudolph for doing an amazing job with the photography, and a huge hug to Ross Dobson for making the food look so beautiful. To Vicky Harris and Lee Husband, thank you for all your help and discriminating palates. Thank you also to Hannah Yiu and Cindy Buitenhuis from Oriental Merchant for supplying such wonderful Japanese food products.

And, finally, a very big thank you to my Japanophile mum (who still allows me to take over her fantastic kitchen from time to time), Adam, Ness, Andrew and all the rest of my wonderful family and friends for your love, support, encouragement and willing taste buds.

My dad loved his food, as I do—this is for you.

Published by Murdoch Books Pty Limited.

Murdoch Books Australia
Pier 8/9, 23 Hickson Road, Millers Point NSW 2000
Phone: +61 (0)2 8220 2000 Fax: +61 (0)2 8220 2558

Murdoch Books UK Limited
Erico House, 6th Floor North, 93–99 Upper Richmond Road
Putney, London SW15 2TG
Phone: +44 (0)20 8785 5995 Fax: +44 (0)20 8785 5985

Chief Executive: Juliet Rogers
Publisher: Kay Scarlett

Photographer: Mikkel Vang
Stylist: Christine Rudolph
Art direction and design: Marylouise Brammer
Project manager: Zoë Harpham
Editor: Kim Rowney
Editorial director: Diana Hill
Food preparation: Ross Dobson
Recipe testing: Grace Campbell, Lee Husband, Jennifer Tolhurst
Production: Monika Vidovic
Photographer's assistant: Andrew Wilson
Stylist's assistant: Nina Ross

National Library of Australia Cataloguing-in-Publication Data
Lawson, Jane. Yoshoku. Includes index. ISBN 1 74045 396 4
1. Cookery, Japanese. I. Title.
641.5952

Printed by 1010 Printing Limited in 2005. PRINTED IN CHINA.
First published 2005.
©Text Jane Lawson.
©Design and photography Murdoch Books Pty Limited 2005.
All rights reserved.
No part of this publication may be reproduced, stored in a retrieval system or transmitted in any form or by any means, electronic, mechanical, photocopying, recording or otherwise without the prior written permission of the publisher.

IMPORTANT: Those who might be at risk from the effects of salmonella poisoning (the elderly, pregnant women, young children and those suffering from immune deficiency diseases) should consult their doctor with any concerns about eating raw eggs.

CONVERSION GUIDE: You may find cooking times vary depending on the oven you are using. For fan-forced ovens, as a general rule, set the oven temperature to 20°C (70°F) lower than indicated in the recipe. We have used 20 ml (4 teaspoon) tablespoon measures. If you are using a 15 ml (3 teaspoon) tablespoon, for most recipes the difference will not be noticeable. However, for recipes using baking powder, gelatine, bicarbonate of soda (baking soda) or small amounts of cornflour (cornstarch), add an extra teaspoon for each tablespoon specified.

The Publisher thanks Archaeos, Bison Homewares, Kris Coad, Moss Melbourne, Mud Australia, Simon Johnson and The Essential Ingredient for their assistance with the photography for this book.

yoshoku

japanese food western style

jane lawson

photography by Mikkel Vang
styling by Christine Rudolph

MURDOCH BOOKS

contents

japanese food western style

Writing this book has enabled me to combine two of my greatest passions—food and Japan. I've been travelling to Japan for over 20 years and it never ceases to amaze me how dramatically and quickly things there can change—yet, at the same time, there is such awe-inspiring and humbling respect for tradition. Old and new stand side by side in all facets of life. Although this could suggest confusion and contradiction, the Japanese have successfully mastered the skill of unifying the old world with the new.

Japanese cuisine is no exception: at one end of the scale is the very formal and exquisite *kaiseki* cuisine in which food is painstakingly prepared for special occasions; and at the opposite end of the spectrum lie the fast-food joints. In between these two extremes resides an eclectic mix of Buddhist vegetarian specialities; street food; *izakaya*, the Japanese version of the tapas bar; super-fresh sushi and sashimi turned out by hole-in-the-wall vendors; simple, rustic homestyle fare; and the most fantastic array of foreign food restaurants I have ever seen. Incredibly, no matter where you dine you can be assured that, in every instance, flavour, appearance, freshness and texture are of utmost importance.

Although I love the dining diversity of Japan, I am most intrigued by *yoshoku* —a magical blend of Japanese and Western ingredients and cookery methods, resulting in an array of exciting and delicious new dishes.

My aim in this book is to show just how comfortably Japanese and Western flavours can be blended. Traditional Japanese cuisine can be a little intimidating for some; however, this gentle introduction to Japanese foods will allow you to explore some less familiar ingredients with a buffer of better known flavours and cookery methods. To help familiarize you with these ingredients I have included a comprehensive glossary, which lists both the English and Japanese names, as well as suggestions for substitutes, where applicable.

Another of the really lovely aspects of Japanese cuisine is that as well as being delicious it is often very good for you. Soy and seaweed products are already highly regarded in health arenas but within these pages you will find some wonderful new ingredients, many of which are loaded with antioxidants, vitamins and minerals.

The recipes in *yoshoku* range from homey comfort food to fabulous party fare. Start in the *small plates* chapter for a range of dishes for sharing, either as a snack or en masse at a cocktail party; or select just a few for an interesting, casual dinner. Each chapter moves from lighter foods through to more substantial fare, so you can choose dishes to suit your mood. If you make a hearty selection from the *main plates* or *bowl food* chapters, perhaps start with something from the lighter end of *small plates*. *Side plates* will provide you with a little something extra to go with your mains. And finally, *sweet plates*, dedicated to a group of Japanese co-workers who once tried to convince me that we all have a second stomach reserved exclusively for dessert.

I hope you enjoy discovering *yoshoku*, and that my recipes inspire you to experiment and develop your own.

Jane Lawson

small plates

Green soya beans in the pod, known as *edamame* in Japanese, are available fresh when in season, and frozen when not. I always keep a packet in the freezer as they are so quick to prepare when unexpected friends drop in. Here, the *edamame* are served while still warm; in summer, try them chilled and serve with an ice-cold Japanese beer.

edamame

1 teaspoon dashi granules

3 teaspoons Japanese soy sauce

2 teaspoons mirin

1 teaspoon sesame oil

3 small red chillies, cut in half lengthways

4 garlic cloves, bruised

2 star anise

500 g (1 lb 2 oz) frozen soya beans in the pod

sea salt flakes

serves 4–6 as a snack

Put the dashi granules, soy sauce, mirin, sesame oil, chilli, garlic, star anise and 1 litre (35 fl oz/4 cups) water in a large saucepan and bring to the boil over high heat. Cook for 5 minutes to infuse the flavours.

Add the soya beans and cook for 2–3 minutes, or until tender. Drain well, remove the chilli, garlic and star anise, reserving some chilli and star anise for garnish, if desired. Sprinkle with sea salt and toss to combine. Serve warm in a bowl, topped with the garnishes, if using. To eat, simply squeeze the beans straight from the pod into your mouth. Supply an extra bowl for the empty pods.

hint: If using fresh soya bean pods, prepare them by rubbing the pods with salt between your hands to remove the fine hairy fibres. You will need to increase the cooking time to 6–8 minutes.

Forget the potato chips—hand around a bowl of these crunchy, nutty snacks. Lotus root is thought to increase stamina and make your skin glow—the perfect party food.

zen party mix

vegetable oil, for deep-frying

125 ml (4 fl oz/½ cup) sesame oil

200 g (7 oz) fresh lotus root

2 x 85 g (3 oz) tins ginkgo nuts, drained well and patted dry

300 g (10½ oz) tin cooked soya beans, drained well and patted dry

2 tablespoons dried wakame pieces

2 sheets of kombu, each 5 x 18 cm (2 x 7 in), wiped with a damp cloth, cut widthways into 1 cm (½ in) strips

caster (superfine) sugar, to sprinkle

serves 4 as a snack

Fill a deep-fat fryer or large saucepan one-third full with vegetable oil and add the sesame oil. Heat to 180°C (350°F), or until a cube of bread dropped into the oil browns in 15 seconds.

Peel the lotus, then slice it very thinly using a Japanese mandolin or a sharp knife and steady hand. Deep-fry the lotus in three batches until golden, stirring occasionally—this will take about 2 minutes per batch. Drain well on paper towels, sprinkle with salt and set aside.

Prick the ginkgo nuts with a skewer or halve them, as they have a tendency to 'explode' when fried, then deep-fry all at once for 3–4 minutes, or until golden. Remove from the oil, drain well, and set aside in a bowl. Add the soya beans to the oil and

cook in three batches for 5 minutes, or until crisp and golden. Remove, drain well, sprinkle with salt and add to the ginkgo.

Add the wakame and kombu and cook for about 30 seconds, or until the oil stops bubbling, then remove, drain well and sprinkle with a little salt and caster sugar. Allow to cool slightly, then add to the ginkgo and soya beans. Add the lotus and toss gently to combine. Taste for seasoning and add a little more salt, if needed. Serve immediately.

If making ahead of time, allow to cool completely, then store in an airtight container. If they lose their crispness, spread out on a baking tray and heat for 10 minutes in a 180°C (350°F/Gas 4) oven until crisp again.

hint: If fresh lotus root is unavailable, it is also sold thickly sliced and frozen, and in vacuum packs. Cut into 5 mm (¼ in) thick slices and increase the cooking time to 8 minutes.

The following three dressings each make enough for 24 oysters, so if you choose to serve two or three dressings at once you'll need to decrease the quantity of each.

oysters with japanese flavours

24 freshly shucked oysters, chilled

ponzu dressing
2 teaspoons lemon juice
2 teaspoons lime juice
2 teaspoons Japanese rice vinegar
1½ tablespoons Japanese soy sauce
2 teaspoons mirin
1½ tablespoons drinking sake
½ teaspoon caster (superfine) sugar
5 x 2 cm (2 x ¾ in) piece of kombu, wiped with
   a damp cloth, cut into strips
2 teaspoons bonito flakes
tiny slivers of lemon or lime zest, to garnish

wasabi dressing
2 teaspoons wasabi paste
60 ml (2 fl oz/¼ cup) Japanese rice vinegar
½ teaspoon caster (superfine) sugar
2 teaspoons mirin
1 tablespoon cream
flying fish roe, to garnish

ginger and sesame dressing
1½ teaspoons finely grated ginger
1 teaspoon caster (superfine) sugar
1 tablespoon Japanese soy sauce
1½ tablespoons Japanese rice vinegar
1½ tablespoons drinking sake
½ teaspoon sesame oil
toasted sesame seeds, to garnish

makes 24

To make the ponzu dressing, put all the ingredients, except the zest, in a non-metallic bowl and stir until the sugar has dissolved. Cover with plastic wrap and refrigerate for 24 hours. Strain through muslin (cheesecloth) or a fine sieve before using.

To make the wasabi dressing, combine all the ingredients, except the fish roe, in a bowl, whisk until smooth, then chill.

To make the ginger and sesame dressing, combine all the ingredients, except the sesame seeds, in a bowl, whisk until smooth, then chill.

Serve the oysters chilled, drizzle with one of the dressings and top with the appropriate garnish. Alternatively, serve all three dressings in separate bowls and with little spoons so guests can then select their preferred dressing.

hint: If flying fish roe, *tobiko*, is unavailable, use the larger salmon roe.

If you like nori-wrapped rice crackers, you'll absolutely love these. They are so easy to make and deliciously crisp and savoury.

nori, sesame and parmesan pastries

2 sheets frozen butter puff pastry

2 tablespoons nori flakes

2 tablespoons toasted sesame seeds

100 g (3½ oz/1 cup) finely grated
  Parmesan cheese

½ teaspoon caster (superfine) sugar

½ teaspoon sea salt flakes

50 g (1¾ oz) butter, melted

makes about 32

Lay the pastry sheets out on a bench and allow them to thaw. Combine the nori flakes, sesame seeds, Parmesan, sugar, sea salt and a little freshly ground black pepper, then divide the mixture between two small bowls.

Put one sheet of pastry on a piece of baking paper and brush the pastry with melted butter, then sprinkle with two-thirds of the mixture from one of the bowls. Press down to adhere then, using the baking paper, fold the pastry in half, from left to right, and press down again. Brush the top of this with a little more butter and sprinkle with the remaining third of the topping mixture so it covers the pastry evenly. Fold in half again lengthways so that you have a long rectangular log, and press down to adhere.

Repeat with the remaining pastry sheet and the remaining mixture. Lay the two pastry logs on a tray and refrigerate for 30 minutes. Meanwhile, preheat the oven to 200°C (400°F/Gas 6).

Remove the pastry logs from the refrigerator and, using a sharp knife, trim the ends, then cut across into 1 cm (½ in) slices. Place the slices, cut-side up, on three baking trays lined with baking paper, spacing them a little apart to allow for expansion.

Cook for 15 minutes, or until puffed and golden. Serve warm with drinks such as the Dirty ninja saketini (page 47), or as an accompaniment to Corn potage (page 69).

This dressing is quite piquant but still allows the lovely fresh flavour of the fish to shine through.

salmon sashimi with caper dressing

500 g (1 lb 2 oz) sashimi-grade salmon
   (in one piece)
1½ tablespoons salted capers, rinsed well and
   drained
2 small handfuls mitsuba or flat-leaf (Italian) parsley
½ teaspoon wasabi paste
1 teaspoon caster (superfine) sugar
1½ tablespoons drinking sake
1½ tablespoons mirin
1½ tablespoons lemon juice
mustard cress, to garnish (optional)
salmon roe, to garnish (optional)

serves 4–6 as a starter

Using a sharp knife, and carefully wiping the blade with a damp cloth between each slice, cut the fish along its length into two even rectangular blocks, then cut into 5 mm (¼ in) slices across the width. The rectangles should be about 6 x 2–3 cm (2½ x ¾–1¼ in).

Arrange the sashimi in a single line on a platter, with the pieces overlapping slightly or, alternatively, divide the sashimi between individual bowls. Cover and refrigerate while you make the dressing.

To make the dressing, finely chop the capers and mitsuba, then add the wasabi, sugar, sake, mirin, lemon juice and a pinch of salt and mix to combine well. Pour the dressing over the salmon and top with a few sprigs of mustard cress and little clumps of roe, if using. Serve immediately.

Wonderfully garlicky and rich with salty miso, this dip is perfectly complemented by crisp, cooling cucumber.

miso garlic dip with cucumber

1 tablespoon red miso

1½ tablespoons white miso

2 garlic cloves, crushed

2 teaspoons caster (superfine) sugar

½ teaspoon sesame oil

1 tablespoon sake

2 teaspoons mirin

large pinch of dashi granules, dissolved in
   60 ml (2 fl oz/¼ cup) hot water

4 small, chilled Lebanese (short) cucumbers, cut
   lengthways into eighths, seeds removed

serves 4–6 as a snack

Combine the red and white miso, garlic, sugar, sesame oil, sake, mirin and dashi and whisk until smooth. Refrigerate for 1 hour to thicken slightly and to allow the flavours to develop.

Serve in a small bowl with the cucumbers for dipping. (You can use other vegetables such as blanched baby carrots, asparagus spears, snow peas (mangetout) and sticks of daikon, but cucumbers are the most refreshing.)

hint: Add 40 g (1½ oz/¼ cup) finely chopped toasted almonds or peanuts to the dip for extra crunch.

Simply cooked in the shell with butter and soy sauce, the delicate flavour of these scallops is enhanced by a fresh herb and lemon dressing.

scallops with herb dressing

40 g (1½ oz) butter, melted

3 teaspoons Japanese soy sauce

¼ teaspoon sesame oil

24 large white scallops without roe, on the shell, beards removed

herb dressing

3 handfuls mitsuba or flat-leaf (Italian) parsley, finely chopped

4 shiso leaves, finely shredded

2 teaspoons finely grated lemon zest

2 garlic cloves, finely chopped

1 tablespoon toasted sesame seeds

1 tablespoon Japanese soy sauce

1 tablespoon mirin

2 tablespoons lemon juice

2 tablespoons Japanese rice vinegar

makes 24

To make the herb dressing, use a *suribachi* (ribbed mortar) or a mortar and pestle to grind the mitsuba, shiso, lemon zest, garlic and sesame seeds to a rough paste, then stir in the soy sauce, mirin, lemon juice and vinegar. Preheat the griller (broiler) to high.

Combine the melted butter, soy sauce and sesame oil and brush it liberally over the scallops, being careful not to get any on the shell. Put the scallops under the hot griller for 1½–2 minutes, or until they are just cooked and the butter is a little browned— the scallops should still yield slightly to the touch. Remove from the griller and top each scallop with the herb dressing. Serve immediately.

hint: The herb dressing can also be served over grilled chicken or steak, or over other seafood.

Although they look similar to frittata, these are based on the traditional Japanese recipe, *chawan mushi*, steamed savoury custard cups. The steaming promotes a silken texture and is normally done in bamboo steamer baskets, but the method used here is also effective.

steamed mushroom custards

20 g (¾ oz) butter

1 teaspoon sesame oil

1 leek, thinly sliced

150 g (5½ oz/3 cups) shiitake mushrooms, stems discarded, caps thinly sliced

100 g (3½ oz/1⅓ cups) enoki mushrooms, ends trimmed, then lengths halved

½ teaspoon dashi granules

4 eggs

3 egg yolks

185 ml (6 fl oz/¾ cup) cream

1½ tablespoons mirin

2 teaspoons Japanese soy sauce

ground white pepper

Japanese mayonnaise, to garnish

snipped chives, nori flakes or bonito flakes, to garnish

soy caramel (optional)

1 tablespoon mirin

1½ tablespoons caster (superfine) sugar

1½ tablespoons Japanese soy sauce

makes 24

Put the butter and sesame oil in a small frying pan over medium heat. Add the leek and cook for 3 minutes, or until the leek has softened. Add the shiitake and a pinch of salt and cook for 8 minutes, or until softened. Add the enoki and cook for a further 1 minute to wilt. Sprinkle the dashi into the pan and mix until dissolved. Allow to cool.

Put the eggs, egg yolks, cream, mirin and soy sauce in a bowl and beat until combined. Season with a little salt and white pepper, then strain into a bowl with a pouring lip. Place a roasting tin half-filled with water on the bottom shelf of the oven and preheat to 140°C (275°F/Gas 1).

Divide the mushrooms between 24 non-stick mini muffin holes, then carefully pour over the egg mixture. Lightly tap the tray on the bench to bring any air bubbles to the surface. Leave the custards to sit for 10 minutes then, using a fine skewer, pop any obvious bubbles.

To make the soy caramel, if using, combine the mirin, sugar and 1 tablespoon water in a small saucepan over medium–high heat. Stir until the sugar has dissolved, then bring to the boil. Cook for 2–3 minutes, or until slightly syrupy, then add the soy sauce and cook for a further 3–4 minutes until syrupy again. Cool to room temperature.

Place the custards on the middle shelf of the oven and cook for 13–15 minutes, or until just set. They should still be slightly wobbly to the touch but there should not be wet patches on top. Remove from the oven and allow to cool slightly in the tin before carefully removing.

Allow the custards to cool to room temperature, then top with a small dollop of the mayonnaise, drizzle with the soy caramel and sprinkle with chives, nori flakes or bonito flakes, or alternate with two or more toppings.

yoshoku

melon frost

½ honeydew melon
125 ml (4 fl oz/½ cup) Midori melon liqueur
125 ml (4 fl oz/½ cup) drinking sake
4 long strips of lemon zest, tied into knots

serves 4

Peel the melon and cut the flesh into small cubes.
Put the melon in the freezer for 20 minutes, or until
frozen, then put the frozen melon in a blender,
along with the Midori and sake and blend until
smooth. Divide between four cocktail glasses and
serve with a little knot of lemon zest.

cherry blossom

185 ml (6 fl oz/¾ cup) chilled plum wine
125 ml (4 fl oz/½ cup) chilled drinking sake
250 ml (9 fl oz/1 cup) peach juice
250 ml (9 fl oz/1 cup) sour cherry juice

serves 4

Combine all the ingredients, then divide between
four tall glasses filled with some ice cubes.

hint: If you can't find sour cherry juice, double the
amount of peach juice.

citrus sawaah

1 pink grapefruit
1 lime
1 orange or blood orange
125 ml (4 fl oz/½ cup) shochu or drinking sake
chilled soda

serves 4

Juice the grapefruit, lime and orange, then divide
between four tall glasses filled with some ice cubes.
Add the shochu to each glass, then top up with
chilled soda and stir gently.

hint: A popular way of serving this refreshing drink
is to give guests a selection of halved citrus fruits
and a hand juicer, and they simply add as much of
the juice of their choice as they like. Lemons are
also a popular ingredient.

lychee muddle

40 fresh lychees
125 ml (4 fl oz/½ cup) shochu or drinking sake
½ vanilla bean, split in half lengthways and
    finely chopped, or a few drops of pure
    vanilla extract
1 small handful mint leaves, torn if large
chilled soda (optional)

serves 4

Peel the lychees and remove the seeds over a
bowl to catch any juices. Divide the lychees between
four sturdy tumblers. Divide the shochu, vanilla and
mint leaves between the glasses, then crush the
lychees with a wooden spoon or muddler until the
lychees are pulpy and the juice has released. Add a
little crushed ice to each and serve as is or top up
with soda. This is also great with a dash of pure
ginger cordial.

From left: Lychee muddle, Cherry blossom.

This recipe is loosely based on two recipes: Italy's *insalata caprese*—a mozzarella, tomato and basil salad; and Japan's *hiyayakko tofu*—a chilled tofu dish. The flavour of the rich, sweet tomatoes teams beautifully with the creamy, cold tofu.

chilled tofu with roasted tomatoes

350 g (12 oz) cherry tomatoes on the vine

6 garlic cloves, unpeeled

60 ml (2 fl oz/¼ cup) olive oil

sea salt flakes

½ teaspoon caster (superfine) sugar

600 g (1 lb 5 oz) silken firm tofu

good-quality balsamic vinegar, to drizzle

sesame oil, to drizzle

3 shiso leaves, finely shredded

serves 4–6 as a starter

Preheat the oven to 160°C (315°F/Gas 2–3). Leaving the tomatoes on the vine, put them, along with the garlic cloves, in a small baking dish. Pour over the oil and sprinkle with sea salt and sugar. Put in the oven and cook for 30–35 minutes, or until the tomatoes start to shrivel slightly. Remove from the oven and cool to room temperature.

Cut the tofu into eight even slices and arrange the slices on a serving platter. Top with the roasted tomatoes and garlic and spoon over any olive oil left in the baking dish. Drizzle with a little balsamic vinegar and sesame oil and scatter the shiso over the top. Serve immediately and ask your guests to squeeze over a little of the roasted garlic, straight from its skin, if they desire.

This tempura strays a little from conventional style in that it uses a combination of two ingredients: prawns and mushrooms. Lightly cloaked in a delicately crisp tempura batter they are very hard to resist.

shiitake and prawn tempura

400 g (14 oz) raw prawns (shrimp), peeled and
    deveined
1 egg white
¼ teaspoon finely grated ginger
1 teaspoon Japanese soy sauce
1 teaspoon mirin
1 spring onion (scallion), finely chopped
pinch of ground white pepper
20 g (¾ oz/⅓ cup) Japanese breadcrumbs
24 medium shiitake mushrooms
vegetable oil, for deep-frying
125 ml (4 fl oz/½ cup) sesame oil

tempura batter
325 ml (11 fl oz) iced water
50 g (1¾ oz/¼ cup) potato starch, sifted
90 g (3¼ oz/¾ cup) plain (all-purpose) flour, sifted
¼ teaspoon baking powder
¼ teaspoon salt

dipping sauce
⅛ teaspoon dashi granules, dissolved in
    2 tablespoons boiling water
2 teaspoons mirin
3 teaspoons Japanese soy sauce

makes 24

Roughly chop the prawns and place in a food processor, along with the egg white, ginger, soy sauce, mirin, spring onion and white pepper and process until minced. Stir in the breadcrumbs, then cover and chill for 1 hour to allow the flavours to develop and the mixture to firm up.

Discard the stems from the shiitake and fill the caps with the prawn mixture, smoothing over the top with the side of a butter knife. Place in a single layer on a tray lined with paper towels, cover with plastic wrap and refrigerate until ready to use.

To make the dipping sauce, combine all the ingredients and leave to cool to room temperature.

Fill a deep-fat fryer or large saucepan one-third full with vegetable oil and add the sesame oil. Heat to 180°C (350°F), or until a cube of bread dropped into the oil browns in 15 seconds.

The delicate tempura batter must be made quickly just before cooking. Put the iced water in a chilled bowl, add the sifted flours, baking powder and salt, all at once, and give just a few light strokes with a pair of chopsticks to loosely combine. There should be flour all around the edges of the bowl and the batter should be lumpy but not thick.

Sprinkle the prawn side of the mushrooms with a little flour and dip each mushroom into the batter to coat, then lower into the oil. Cook in batches—you'll need to do it in about six batches—so you don't crowd the pan. Cook for 2–3 minutes, or until lightly golden and cooked through. Thin the batter with a little more iced water if necessary—you should have a crisp, lacy, almost see-through batter. Serve immediately with the dipping sauce.

hint: Instead of serving the tempura with dipping sauce, serve with small lemon wedges and sprinkle with green tea salt made from ½ teaspoon green tea powder mixed with 2 teaspoons table salt.

This refreshing Japanese vinegared crab salad is a wonderful filling for these Vietnamese-style rice paper rolls. If crabs are not available, prawns are just as delicious.

rice paper rolls filled with crab salad

1 kg (2 lb 4 oz) cooked blue swimmer crab or other small, sweet crab—you'll need about 400 g (14 oz/2⅔ cups) cooked meat
2 small Lebanese (short) cucumbers
30 g (1 oz) bundle of harusame noodles
3 teaspoons dried wakame pieces
80 ml (2½ fl oz/⅓ cup) Japanese rice vinegar
1 tablespoon mirin
1½ teaspoons Japanese soy sauce
1 teaspoon finely grated ginger and its juice
1 teaspoon caster (superfine) sugar
1 small handful mitsuba or flat-leaf (Italian) parsley, shredded
3 shiso leaves, finely shredded
1 spring onion (scallion), thinly sliced
12 rice paper wrappers, 20 cm (8 in) in diameter

dipping sauce
½ teaspoon dashi granules
125 ml (4 fl oz/½ cup) Japanese rice vinegar
1 tablespoon caster (superfine) sugar
1 small red chilli, seeded and very thinly sliced

makes 12

Remove the meat from the crabs, cover and refrigerate. Halve the cucumbers lengthways, scoop out the seeds with a teaspoon, then slice the flesh thinly. Sprinkle liberally with salt and allow to rest for 30 minutes. Rinse and drain well, squeezing out any excess moisture, then chill. Meanwhile, soak the harusame in warm water for 10 minutes to soften. Drain well and cut into short lengths using scissors. Soak the wakame in cold water for 5 minutes, then drain well and slice. Add to the cucumber and chill.

To make a dressing, combine the rice vinegar, mirin, soy sauce, grated ginger and juice, sugar and a pinch of salt and stir until the sugar dissolves. Put the crabmeat, cucumber, noodles, wakame, mitsuba, shiso and spring onion in a bowl, then pour over the dressing, mixing well. Chill well.

To make the dipping sauce, combine the dashi granules, rice vinegar, sugar, chilli and 60 ml (2 fl oz/¼ cup) water in a small saucepan and bring to the boil. Cook for 4–5 minutes, or until slightly syrupy. Cool to room temperature.

When you are ready to make the rolls, dip the rice paper wrappers in a bowl of cold water to soften. Lay them flat on a tea towel and put 2 tablespoons of the crab mixture near the end closest to you, then roll up, tucking the ends in about halfway. Serve immediately with the dipping sauce.

hint: You can make these rolls a few hours in advance. Store the rolls between layers of plastic wrap and refrigerate until you are ready to serve.

Tataki, a method of preparing beef by briefly searing it, is considered by the Japanese to be a form of sashimi. Here the beef is served with fresh, peppery salad leaves and a gingery soy dressing.

beef tataki salad

2 large handfuls mizuna or baby rocket (arugula)
2 x 250 g (9 oz) eye fillet steaks (cut from the
    middle part of the fillet)
ground white pepper
1 tablespoon vegetable oil
1 spring onion (scallion), thinly sliced on the
    diagonal

dressing
2 tablespoons Japanese soy sauce
1 tablespoon Japanese rice vinegar
1 tablespoon sake
½ teaspoon Japanese mustard
1 garlic glove, crushed
1 teaspoon finely grated ginger and its juice
1 teaspoon caster (superfine) sugar
½ teaspoon sesame oil
1 tablespoon vegetable oil

serves 4 as a starter

Cut the mizuna into 3 cm (1 ¼ in) lengths, rinse and drain, then chill in the refrigerator.

Season the steaks with salt and white pepper. Heat the oil in a heavy-based frying pan, add the steaks and sear on each side for about 2 minutes, or until well browned, then plunge immediately into a bowl of iced water to stop the cooking process. Remove the steaks and pat dry with paper towels. Set aside.

To make the dressing, put the soy sauce, vinegar, sake, mustard, garlic, ginger and juice, sugar, sesame and vegetable oils in a small bowl and whisk well to combine.

Slice the beef thinly across the grain, then arrange the slices, slightly overlapping each slice, on a plate. Pile the chilled mizuna on top of the beef, pour over the dressing, then sprinkle with the spring onion.

hint: Make this a light summery main course for two by serving it with some rice or noodles.

You can be as creative as you like with the coating on these fried prawns. Try sesame seeds, flaked almonds or *panko*, Japanese breadcrumbs, which are larger than traditional breadcrumbs and make a very light and crisp coating for deep-fried foods.

crispy prawns with japanese tartare

20 raw king prawns (shrimp), peeled and deveined, tails intact
plain (all-purpose) flour, to coat
ground white pepper
1 egg, lightly beaten with a dash of cold water
sesame seeds, flaked almonds or Japanese breadcrumbs, to coat
vegetable oil, for deep-frying
60 ml (2 fl oz/¼ cup) sesame oil
lemon wedges, to serve

japanese tartare
175 g (6 oz) Japanese mayonnaise
1½ tablespoons Japanese cucumber pickles or dill pickles, finely chopped
1 tablespoon Japanese rice vinegar
1 spring onion (scallion), white part only, finely chopped
1 small handful mitsuba or flat-leaf (Italian) parsley, chopped
1 garlic clove, crushed
ground white pepper

serves 4 as a starter

To make the Japanese tartare, put the mayonnaise, pickles, vinegar, spring onion, mitsuba and garlic in a small bowl and stir to combine. Season to taste with salt and white pepper. Chill until ready to serve.

Lightly score the belly, or underside, of the prawns. Turn them over and, starting from the tail end, press down gently at intervals along the length of the prawn—this helps to break the connective tissue, preventing the prawns from curling up too much when cooked.

Season the flour with salt and white pepper. Lightly coat the prawns in the flour, avoiding their tails, then dip into the egg, allowing any excess to drip off. Coat with your choice of sesame seeds, almonds or breadcrumbs, pressing to help them adhere. Refrigerate while you heat the oil.

Fill a deep-fat fryer or large heavy-based saucepan one-third full with vegetable oil and add the sesame oil. Heat the oil to 180°C (350°F), or until a cube of bread dropped into the oil browns in 15 seconds. Deep-fry the prawns in batches for 2 minutes, or until golden. Drain on paper towels and serve immediately, accompanied by the tartare and lemon wedges.

hint: Experiment with other crispy coatings for the prawns. Try chopped nuts, dried noodles such as harusame or soba cut into short lengths, or even finely chopped seaweed, such as wakame. Instead of prawns, try squid or calamari. Oysters are also a favourite, deep-fried in Japanese breadcrumbs.

This free-form sushi allows you to experiment with non-Japanese fillings— the suggestions given below will get you started. The only two essential Japanese ingredients you'll need are sushi rice and nori.

sushi hand rolls

sushi rice

550 g (1 lb 4 oz/2½ cups) Japanese
   short-grain white rice
5 x 5 cm (2 x 2 in) piece of kombu, wiped with a
   damp cloth (optional)
2 tablespoons sake (optional)
80 ml (2½ fl oz/⅓ cup) Japanese rice vinegar
1½ tablespoons caster (superfine) sugar
½ teaspoon salt

6 sheets of nori, cut in half

mediterranean fillings

basil leaves, prosciutto, asparagus, cooked or raw
   tuna, aïoli, salami, mozzarella or bocconcini,
   capers, artichokes, olives, sun-dried tomatoes

mexican fillings

raw tuna or salmon, avocado, coriander (cilantro)
   leaves, finely sliced red or green chilli, spring
   onion (scallion), cucumber, tomato, pickles,
   jalapeños

chinese fillings

barbecued duck, barbecued pork, spring onion
   (scallion), hoisin sauce, capsicum (pepper),
   cucumber

makes 12

To make the sushi rice, rinse the rice several times in cold water, or until the water runs clear, then drain in a colander for 1 hour.

Put the rice in a saucepan with 750 ml (26 fl oz/ 3 cups) cold water and, if using them, the kombu and sake. Bring to the boil, then discard the kombu. Cover with a tight-fitting lid, reduce the heat to low and simmer for 15 minutes. Turn off the heat but leave the pan on the hotplate. Remove the lid and place a clean tea towel across the top to absorb excess moisture, then put the lid on and rest for 15 minutes. Alternatively, cook the rice in a rice cooker, following the manufacturer's instructions.

Tip the rice into a wide, shallow non-metallic container and spread it out. Combine the vinegar, sugar and salt, stirring until the sugar has dissolved, then sprinkle over the warm rice. Using quick, short strokes mix the rice and liquid together with a damp wooden rice paddle or thin wooden spoon, being careful not to mush the rice. (Traditionally the rice is cooled with a hand-held fan while mixing the liquid into the rice.)

When cooled, cover with a clean, damp tea towel. For best results, use the rice immediately and do not refrigerate it. However, if you are not making your sushi within 1–2 hours, the rice must be refrigerated or bacteria may develop.

Choose your selection of fillings, and cut the larger ingredients into small strips or lengths. Place the filling ingredients on a platter and the sushi rice in a bowl. Hold a piece of nori in your hand, put a small amount of rice into the centre of the nori, then top with a few of the filler ingredients. Roll up and enjoy with accompaniments of your choice.

hint: Fill some small bowls with water and mix in a little rice vinegar. Dip your fingers into the water before assembling the hand rolls, as this prevents the rice from sticking to your fingers.

Although I love the smooth creaminess of plain tofu, it's also great when cooked with other ingredients—its soft, porous texture absorbs flavours so easily. These tofu fries have a spicy, crisp shell and a soft, fluffy centre.

spicy tofu fries

2 x 500 g (1 lb 2 oz) blocks cotton (firm) tofu
2 teaspoons Japanese chilli sesame oil
60 ml (2 fl oz/¼ cup) Japanese soy sauce
3 teaspoons finely grated ginger
4 garlic cloves, crushed
2 tablespoons white miso
vegetable oil, for deep-frying
175 g (6 oz/1 cup) potato starch
1½–2 tablespoons seven-spice mix
ground white pepper
seven-spice mix, to serve (optional)

serves 6–8 as a snack

Wrap each block of tofu in a clean tea towel and put in separate large bowls. Put a plate on the top of each block, sit a heavy tin on top and weigh down for 2 hours to extract any excess moisture. Unwrap and pat dry. Cut each block into 1.5 cm (⅝ in) thick slices, then cut the slices into fingers, 1.5–2 cm (⅝–¾ in) wide.

To make a marinade for the tofu, combine the chilli sesame oil, soy sauce, ginger, garlic and miso in a bowl and stir until smooth. Pour half into a large, shallow non-metallic dish. Add the tofu, then pour over the remaining marinade, carefully shaking the dish to help coat the tofu fingers. Cover tightly and refrigerate overnight to allow the flavours to absorb into the tofu, shaking the dish occasionally to help disperse the marinade.

When ready to cook, fill a deep-fat fryer or deep heavy-based saucepan one-third full with oil and heat to 180°C (350°F), or until a cube of bread dropped into the oil browns in 15 seconds. Combine the potato starch and seven-spice mix and season with a little salt and white pepper. Gently scrape any excess marinade from the tofu fingers, then dip them into the seasoned flour and shake off any excess. Cook in four batches for 5–6 minutes each batch, or until golden. Drain well on paper towels, sprinkle with salt, to taste, and serve immediately with extra seven-spice mix, if desired.

hint: To make a dip for the tofu fries, combine some Japanese mayonnaise with a little lemon juice and some freshly chopped mitsuba or parsley. Sprinkle with black sesame seeds and serve with the fries. They are also good with sweet chilli sauce.

yakitori plate

yakitori sauce

500 g (1 lb 2 oz) chicken wings, cut into 3 pieces
  at the joints
375 ml (13 fl oz/1½ cups) mirin
250 ml (9 fl oz/1 cup) sake
375 ml (13 fl oz/1½ cups) Japanese soy sauce
55 g (2 oz/¼ cup) caster (superfine) sugar
3 teaspoons kuzu starch rocks or arrowroot

chicken

4 small bamboo skewers, soaked in water for 1 hour
1 large chicken thigh fillet, cut into 12 even pieces
2 baby leeks or thick spring onions (scallions), white
  part only, cut into 8 short lengths

asparagus

4 small bamboo skewers, soaked in water for 1 hour
4 streaky bacon rashers, cut in half
8 x 5 cm (2 in) lengths of asparagus

enoki

4 small bamboo skewers, soaked in water for 1 hour
4 small bundles of trimmed enoki, 2 cm (¾ in)
  in diameter
4 streaky bacon rashers

shiitake

4 small bamboo skewers, soaked in water for 1 hour
12 small shiitake mushrooms or 12 halves of larger
  shiitake mushrooms, stems discarded
sea salt flakes

makes 16 skewers (4 of each type)

To make the yakitori sauce, preheat the griller (broiler) to high. Cook the chicken wings, turning occasionally, for 15 minutes, or until dark golden and starting to blacken slightly. Remove and set aside. Pour the mirin and sake into a saucepan over high heat and bring to the boil. Add the soy sauce and sugar and stir until the sugar has dissolved. Add the wings and bring the liquid to the boil, then reduce to a simmer for 30 minutes.

Remove the pan from the heat and allow to cool for 30 minutes. Strain the sauce (you can serve the chicken wings as a snack). Pour a little of the sauce into a small dish and add the kuzu. Crush the rocks and stir into the liquid until dissolved, then return to the pan. Put the pan over high heat and stir until the mixture boils and becomes thick and glossy—about 20 minutes. Remove from the heat and allow to cool before using.

To make the chicken skewers, thread 3 pieces of chicken and 2 pieces of leek onto each skewer, starting with a piece of chicken and alternating with leek. Pour a little of the sauce into a small dish for basting and reserve some for serving. Heat a griller to high and cook the skewers, turning regularly, for 3–4 minutes, then baste with the sauce. Cook on each side for a further 1–2 minutes, basting again, until well glazed and the chicken is cooked through. Serve with a drizzle of the sauce.

To make the asparagus skewers, wrap a piece of bacon around each piece of asparagus. Thread 2 pieces onto each skewer. Put under a hot griller for 2 minutes on each side, then brush with a little sauce. Grill for a further 30 seconds on each side.

To make the enoki skewers, wrap a piece of bacon around a bundle of mushrooms, so their heads are poking out, and skewer to secure. Put under a hot griller for 2 minutes on each side, then brush with a little sauce. Grill for 30 seconds on each side.

To make the shiitake skewers, thread 3 shiitake onto each skewer. Sprinkle with sea salt, put under a hot griller for 2 minutes on each side, or until cooked. You can also baste these lightly with yakitori sauce during the last minute of cooking.

dirty ninja saketini

½ small Lebanese (short) cucumber
5 x 2 cm (2 x ¾ in) piece of kombu, wiped with a
    damp cloth
1 tablespoon Japanese rice vinegar
1 teaspoon caster (superfine) sugar
125 ml (4 fl oz/½ cup) well-chilled drinking sake
125 ml (4 fl oz/½ cup) well-chilled vodka

serves 4

Halve the cucumber lengthways, scoop out the
seeds with a teaspoon, and thinly slice the flesh.
Sprinkle liberally with salt and sit for 10 minutes.
Rinse off and squeeze out any excess moisture with
your hands. To make a cucumber vinegar, combine
the kombu, rice vinegar and sugar in a small bowl,
then add the cucumber and combine well. Allow to
sit for at least 1 hour. To serve, place a small mound
of cucumber in the base of four well-chilled large
martini glasses. Combine the sake and vodka and
divide between the glasses. Add a small splash of
the cucumber vinegar and serve.

ginger mizuwari

2 teaspoons fresh ginger juice
125 ml (4 fl oz/½ cup) Japanese malt whisky
4 long, thin, diagonal slices of ginger
chilled water

serves 4

Combine the ginger juice and whisky and divide
between four glasses filled with ice cubes. Add a
long slice of fresh ginger to each, then top with as
much chilled water as you like. Stir and serve.

bloody wasabi oyster shooter

½ teaspoon wasabi paste
1 tablespoon fresh lime juice
small pinch of dashi granules
small pinch of caster (superfine) sugar
125 ml (4 fl oz/½ cup) chilled tomato juice
60 ml (2 fl oz/¼ cup) shochu or drinking sake
4 freshly shucked small oysters

serves 4

Whisk together the wasabi, lime juice, dashi granules
and sugar until the dashi has dissolved, then mix in
the tomato juice and shochu. Place an oyster in
the base of four 60 ml (2 fl oz/¼ cup) chilled shot
glasses, then pour over the tomato mixture and
serve immediately.

green tea chuhai

2 teaspoons Japanese green tea powder
125 ml (4 fl oz/½ cup) shochu or drinking sake
4 long strips of lemon or lime zest, tied into knots
chilled lemonade

serves 4

Put the green tea powder in a small bowl and
whisk in 1 ½ tablespoons boiling water until smooth,
then allow to cool. Strain into a bowl and combine
with the shochu. Divide between four tall glasses
filled with some ice and add the lemon or lime
knots. Top up with the lemonade.

From left: Green tea chuhai, Dirty ninja saketini, Ginger mizuwari.

Gyoza, or dumplings, are traditionally pan-fried, but this deep-fried version goes best with the slightly sweet and tangy plum dipping sauce.

gyoza with pickled plum sauce

200 g (7 oz) packet gyoza wrappers (30 wrappers)
vegetable oil, for deep-frying

plum dipping sauce
8 Japanese pickled plums
185 ml (6 fl oz/¾ cup) plum wine
60 ml (2 fl oz/¼ cup) plum vinegar or Japanese
   rice vinegar
115 g (4 oz/½ cup) caster (superfine) sugar
2 teaspoons finely grated ginger and its juice

filling
200 g (7 oz) Chinese cabbage, stems removed,
   finely chopped
200 g (7 oz) minced (ground) pork
3 teaspoons finely grated ginger
3 garlic cloves, crushed
1½ tablespoons Japanese soy sauce
2 teaspoons sake
2 teaspoons mirin
¼ teaspoon ground white pepper
2 spring onions (scallions), finely chopped

makes 30

To make the plum dipping sauce, prick the plums all over with a fork, then soak them in several changes of cold water for 2 hours to remove the excess salt. Drain, pat dry, then remove the seeds and purée the flesh in a small food processor or using a stick blender. Put the puréed flesh in a small saucepan with the remaining ingredients and 185 ml (6 fl oz/¾ cup) water. Stir over high heat to dissolve the sugar, bring to the boil and cook for 15–20 minutes, or until the sauce is slightly syrupy. Cool to room temperature.

To make the filling, put the cabbage in a colander, sprinkle with salt and stand for 30 minutes. Squeeze well, then mix with the rest of the filling ingredients.

Lay a wrapper in the palm of your hand and put 2 teaspoons of the filling in the middle. Lightly dampen the edge of the wrapper with a little water, then fold the edges together to form a semicircle, pressing firmly to enclose the filling. Lightly dampen the curved edge of the wrapper, then overlap around the edge to form pleats. Put each gyoza on a tray lined with plastic wrap. Repeat with the remaining wrappers and filling. Refrigerate until ready to cook.

Fill a deep-fat fryer or deep heavy-based saucepan one-third full with vegetable oil and heat to 180°C (350°F), or until a cube of bread dropped into the oil browns in 15 seconds. Cook the gyoza in three batches for 3–4 minutes, or until golden and bubbly and the filling is cooked through. Drain well on paper towels and serve with the dipping sauce.

hint: If you prefer to pan-fry the gyoza, heat a little vegetable oil in a large non-stick frying pan over medium–high heat. Put the gyoza, flat-side down, in the pan in a single layer, leaving a little space between each. Cook them in batches for 2 minutes, or until the bottoms are crisp and golden. Combine 125 ml (4 fl oz/½ cup) boiling water with 2 teaspoons each of vegetable oil and sesame oil and add to the pan. Cover, reduce the heat to low and cook for about 10 minutes. Remove the lid, increase the heat to high and cook until the liquid has evaporated, making sure the dumplings don't catch on the base of the pan and burn. Remove from the pan and sit them flat on paper towels to drain. Serve with a simple dipping sauce of equal parts soy sauce and rice vinegar.

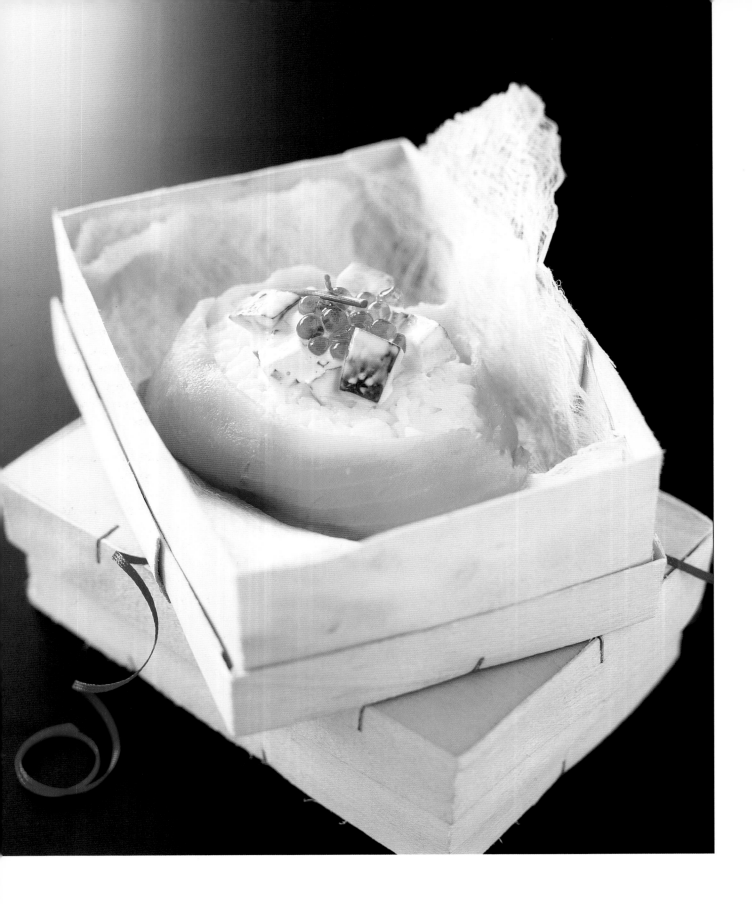

This appetizer is great for those new to the sushi experience because, unlike regular sushi or sashimi, the fish is not raw. This sushi is quite large and is best eaten with a knife and fork rather than with your fingers.

smoked salmon sushi

sushi rice
175 g (6 oz/¾ cup) Japanese
    short-grain white rice
5 x 2 cm (2 x ¾ in) piece of kombu, wiped with a
    damp cloth (optional)
3 teapoons sake (optional)
1½ tablespoons Japanese rice vinegar
2 teaspoons caster (superfine) sugar
¼ teaspoon salt

2 Lebanese (short) cucumbers, unpeeled, halved
    lengthways, seeded and cut into 1 cm (½ in) dice
3 tablespoons Japanese mayonnaise
1 tablespoon thinly sliced chives, plus extra
    to garnish
½ teaspoon lemon juice
100 g (3½ oz) smoked salmon slices
½ teaspoon wasabi paste
2 tablespoons salmon roe or flying fish roe

serves 4 as a starter

To make the sushi rice, rinse the rice several times in cold water, or until the water runs clear, then drain in a colander for 1 hour.

Put the rice in a saucepan with 250 ml (9 fl oz/ 1 cup) cold water and, if using them, the kombu and sake. Bring to the boil, then discard the kombu. Cover with a tight-fitting lid, reduce the heat to low and simmer for 15 minutes. Turn off the heat but

leave the pan on the hotplate. Remove the lid and place a clean tea towel across the top to absorb excess moisture, then put the lid on and rest for 15 minutes. Alternatively, cook the rice in a rice cooker, following the manufacturer's instructions.

Tip the rice into a wide, shallow non-metallic container and spread it out. Combine the vinegar, sugar and salt, stirring until the sugar has dissolved, then sprinkle over the warm rice. Using quick, short strokes mix the rice and liquid together with a damp wooden rice paddle or thin wooden spoon, being careful not to mush the rice. (Traditionally the rice is cooled with a hand-held fan while mixing the liquid into the rice.) When cooled, cover with a clean, damp tea towel. For best results, use the rice immediately and do not refrigerate it. However, if you are not making your sushi within 1–2 hours, the rice must be refrigerated or bacteria may develop.

Combine the cucumber, mayonnaise, chives and lemon juice in a small bowl and season.

Using all the rice, wet your hands and then mould the rice into four large ovals. Line up the four ovals along the bench in front of you, with one of the short sides towards the end of the bench. Lightly press your hand down onto the rice to slightly flatten the ovals. Using a tablespoon, make a slight indentation on the top of each oval—this hollow is where the cucumber salad will sit.

Trim the edges of the salmon to neaten. Using your finger, smear one side of each salmon slice with a little wasabi, then neatly wrap it around the outside edge of each rice oval, wasabi-side in. The salmon should come just up to, or a little above, the rim of the rice. Top each oval with one-quarter of the cucumber mixture, then add one-quarter of the salmon roe. Garnish with a few snipped chives.

hint: These could also be made as bite-sized versions, perfect for serving at cocktail parties.

Remove the bone from the chicken cutlets and cut the chicken into 4 cm (1 ½ in) squares. Combine the soy sauce, mirin, sake, ginger and juice, and garlic in a non-metallic bowl and add the chicken. Stir to coat, cover with plastic wrap, and marinate in the refrigerator for 1 hour only (the flavour becomes too strong if left for longer than this).

Fill a deep-fat fryer or large saucepan one-third full with vegetable oil and add the sesame oil, if using. Heat to 180°C (350°F), or until a cube of bread dropped into the oil browns in 15 seconds.

Combine the potato starch with the nori flakes, sansho pepper and a large pinch of salt. Drain the chicken well, discarding the marinade. Lightly coat the chicken with the potato starch mixture and shake off any excess.

Deep-fry in batches for 6–7 minutes, or until golden and crisp and the chicken is just cooked through. Drain well on paper towels and sprinkle with salt. Serve with lemon wedges.

hint: Try this recipe with white fish fillets, prawns (shrimp) or squid, but you won't need to marinate or cook them for as long.

To make Japanese-style fried chicken, the chicken is marinated in soy sauce, garlic and ginger, then dusted with potato starch and quickly fried, leaving it meltingly tender and with the crispiest of coatings.

crispy nori chicken

1 kg (2 lb 4 oz) chicken thigh cutlets, skin on
60 ml (2 fl oz/¼ cup) Japanese soy sauce
60 ml (2 fl oz/¼ cup) mirin
1 tablespoon sake
2 teaspoons finely grated ginger and its juice
3 garlic cloves, crushed
vegetable oil, for deep-frying
80 ml (2½ fl oz/⅓ cup) sesame oil (optional)
85 g (3 oz/½ cup) potato starch
2 tablespoons nori flakes
⅛ teaspoon sansho pepper
lemon wedges, to serve

serves 6–8 as a snack

The Japanese have taken the gourmet pizza to new heights—there is even a website devoted to the topic—and most pizza joints have an incredible, if not bizarre, array of topping combinations.

blue cheese, prawn and shimeji pizza

20 g (¾ oz) butter

1 large onion, thinly sliced

60 ml (2 fl oz/¼ cup) mirin

1 ready-made 250 g (9 oz) pizza base, about 26 cm (10½ in) in diameter

1 tablespoon white miso

12 raw king prawns (shrimp), peeled and deveined

1 garlic clove, crushed

2 teaspoons olive oil

70 g (2½ oz/¾ cup) shimeji mushrooms, pulled apart into small clumps

150 g (5½ oz/1 cup) crumbled mild blue cheese

serves 4–6 as a snack

Melt the butter in a saucepan over low heat, add the onion and mirin and cook, stirring regularly, for 1 hour, or until deep golden and caramelized. Remove from the heat.

Preheat the oven to 220°C (425°F/Gas 7). Spread the miso on the pizza base, then top with the onion. Toss the prawns with the garlic and olive oil and evenly distribute over the onion. Scatter the shimeji and blue cheese over the top and place in the preheated oven for 25 minutes, or until the base is crisp and the top is golden and bubbling.

Remove from the oven, slice and serve. Make it a meal by serving with a green salad and Chilled tofu with roasted tomatoes (page 31).

japanese-style cabbage rolls

3 dried shiitake mushrooms

1 tablespoon vegetable oil

1 teaspoon sesame oil

5 spring onions (scallions), thinly sliced

2–3 teaspoons finely grated ginger

2 garlic cloves, crushed

½ teaspoon sansho pepper

400 g (14 oz) minced (ground) pork

115 g (4 oz/½ cup) Japanese short-grain rice

4 tablespoons finely chopped mitsuba or
    flat-leaf (Italian) parsley

ground white pepper

1 large whole Chinese cabbage (about 1.6 kg/
    3 lb 8 oz)

1 teaspoon dashi granules

2 tablespoons Japanese soy sauce

2 tablespoons sake

2 tablespoons mirin

60 ml (2 fl oz/¼ cup) Japanese rice vinegar

80 ml (2½ fl oz/⅓ cup) vegetable oil

Japanese mustard, to serve (optional)

dipping sauce

60 ml (2 fl oz/¼ cup) Japanese soy sauce

1½ tablespoons Japanese rice vinegar

2 teaspoons mirin

2 teaspoons caster (superfine) sugar

½ teaspoon chilli sesame oil

makes 16

Soak the shiitake in boiling water for 30 minutes to soften. Drain, discard the stems and finely chop the caps. Set aside. Heat the vegetable and sesame oils in a small saucepan, add the spring onions, ginger, garlic and sansho and cook, stirring over medium heat, for about 1½ minutes, or until the spring onions have softened and the mixture is fragrant. Allow to cool.

Combine the pork with the cooled spring onion mixture, the reserved shiitake, and the rice and mitsuba. Season well with salt and white pepper and mix thoroughly. Set aside.

Bring a large saucepan of water to the boil. Trim 5 cm (2 in) from the white base of the cabbage. Put the remaining cabbage in the water and boil for 5 minutes. As the leaves start to come away from the cabbage, gently pull them away from the head and allow to wilt completely. Remove to a colander to drain. Continue until you have removed all the large leaves and only a small head is left, then add it to the other leaves. Take 750 ml (26 fl oz/3 cups) of the cooking liquid and, while still hot, add the dashi granules and stir until dissolved. Add the soy sauce, sake, mirin, rice vinegar and oil and set aside.

Lay one of the larger cabbage leaves, vein-side down, on the work surface. Put a heaped tablespoon of pork mixture at the base and roll up the leaf, tucking in the sides halfway. Continue in this way, using the larger leaves—you should have about 16 rolls.

Line a large heavy-based saucepan or flameproof casserole dish with three-quarters of the remaining cabbage leaves, then snugly put the rolls in a single layer on top, seam-side down. Cover with more cabbage leaves. Pour over enough of the reserved cooking liquid mixture to just cover the leaves, then place over high heat and bring to the boil. Cover, reduce to a simmer, and cook for 1 hour, or until the pork and rice are cooked through.

To make the dipping sauce, combine all ingredients in a bowl and stir until the sugar has dissolved.

Remove the rolls with a slotted spoon and serve with the sauce and the Japanese mustard on the side, if using. If you are not serving straight away, cool slightly, then place the rolls in a ceramic dish, pour over the cooking liquid, cover and refrigerate. Reheat gently in a large saucepan.

I first tried these at a popular Japanese fast-food chain where they serve all kinds of burgers with rice 'buns' instead of bread.

teriyaki chicken riceburger

800 g (1 lb 12 oz/4 cups) freshly cooked Japanese short-grain rice, slightly cooled—you will need 325 g (11½ oz/1½ cups) raw rice

2 teaspoons sesame seeds

1½ tablespoons vegetable oil

60 ml (2 fl oz/¼ cup) Japanese soy sauce

2 tablespoons mirin

2 tablespoons sake

1½ tablespoons caster (superfine) sugar

4 x 150 g (5½ oz) chicken thigh fillets, skin on (or buy thigh cutlets and remove the bone)

1 handful mizuna leaves

2 small Lebanese (short) cucumbers, thinly sliced into ribbons (using a vegetable peeler)

Japanese mayonnaise, to serve

serves 4

Spread the warm rice into a lightly oiled 40 x 25 cm (16 x 10 in) tin, then press down and smooth over the surface so that it is flat and even. Dampen your hands to do this, as this will prevent the rice from sticking to your hands. Sprinkle over the sesame seeds and press down to adhere. Allow to cool to room temperature. Using a 9 cm (3½ in) round cookie cutter, stamp out rounds of rice and carefully set aside. Dip the cutter in hot water between each stamping so the rice doesn't stick.

Put a large non-stick frying pan over medium–high heat, brush with a little of the vegetable oil and, working in two batches, cook the rice rounds on both sides for 5 minutes each side, or until lightly golden and a little crispy. Drain on paper towels, then place on a baking tray lined with baking paper and keep warm in a low oven.

Combine the soy sauce, mirin, sake and sugar. Put the remaining oil in a large frying pan (do not use a non-stick pan this time or the sauce won't glaze properly) and heat over medium–high heat. Add the chicken, skin-side down, and cook for 4–5 minutes, or until the skin is golden. Turn over and cook for 3–4 minutes, or until lightly golden and the chicken is almost cooked through. Remove from the pan.

Discard any excess fat from the pan and pour in the soy sauce mixture, increase the heat to high and bring to the boil. Cook for 1 minute, or until the sauce is slightly glazy. Return the chicken to the pan and turn to coat well in the glaze. Take the pan off the heat.

Place a rice round on a serving plate as your 'bun' base and top with mizuna, a few cucumber ribbons, a piece of chicken, skin-side up, and a dollop of the mayonnaise. Top with a rice 'lid', sesame-side up. Repeat with the remaining ingredients to make four burgers. Serve immediately.

hint: If you don't have time to make the rice 'buns', use lightly toasted bread rolls, or simply serve the chicken and salad with cooked rice.

bowl food

Comforting and cleansing, this soup is packed with vitamins and minerals and tastes way too good to be as healthy as it is.

mushroom and wakame broth

5 dried shiitake mushrooms

5 x 20 cm (2 x 8 in) piece of kombu, wiped with a
    damp cloth, cut into strips

3 tablespoons dried wakame pieces

1 tablespoon vegetable oil

½ teaspoon sesame oil

1 onion, very finely chopped

1 celery stalk, very finely chopped

1 garlic clove, crushed

60 ml (2 fl oz/¼ cup) mirin

300 g (10½ oz/6 cups) shiitake mushrooms, stems
    discarded, caps sliced

150 g (5½ oz/1⅔ cups) shimeji mushrooms, pulled
    apart

150 g (5½ oz/2 cups) whole baby oyster
    mushrooms, or sliced if larger

2 tablespoons tamari

100 g (3½ oz/1⅓ cups) enoki mushrooms, ends
    trimmed, pulled apart

1 teaspoon finely grated ginger and its juice

seven-spice mix, to serve (optional)

serves 4–6 as a light meal

Put the dried shiitake and kombu in a large saucepan with 2 litres (70 fl oz/8 cups) cold water. Bring to the boil over high heat, reduce to a simmer and cook for 5 minutes, then discard the kombu. Increase the heat and bring to the boil for another 15 minutes, then turn off the heat and allow to sit for 10 minutes to allow the mushroom flavour to infuse. Remove the shiitake with a slotted spoon and, when cool enough to handle, remove and discard the stems, thinly slice the caps and return them to the stock.

Put the wakame in a bowl and pour in enough cold water so it is just covered. Soak for 5 minutes, then drain well and set aside.

Heat the vegetable and sesame oils in a frying pan over medium–high heat, add the onion and celery and cook for 10 minutes, or until the onion is lightly golden. Add the garlic and mirin and cook for a further minute. Add the fresh shiitake and a pinch of salt and cook for 3–4 minutes, or until softened. Add the shimeji and oyster mushrooms and cook for 2 minutes.

Add the cooked mushrooms to the pan filled with the stock, then pour in the tamari. Bring to the boil, cook for 2 minutes, then remove the pan from the heat and stir in the drained wakame, enoki and the ginger and juice. Ladle into bowls and sprinkle with some seven-spice mix, if desired.

hint: Add some cooked soba noodles for a more substantial meal.

This light soup has a wonderful fresh colour and taste. Here it is served warm, although it also makes a refreshing chilled soup for summer. If you can't find *edamame*, green soya beans in their pods, try broad (fava) beans, but be sure to slip them out of their skins after cooking.

edamame and asparagus soup with mizuna pesto

650 g (1 lb 7 oz) fresh or frozen soya beans in the pod

20 g (¾ oz) butter

2 teaspoons soya bean oil or olive oil

1 bay leaf

1 onion, chopped

1 celery stalk, chopped

250 g (9 oz) all-purpose potatoes, such as desiree, peeled and cut into 1 cm (½ in) dice

2 tablespoons mirin

2 teaspoons dashi granules, dissolved in 1 litre (35 fl oz/4 cups) hot water

250 g (9 oz) thin asparagus, chopped

mizuna pesto

2 handfuls mizuna or rocket (arugula) leaves

1 handful mitsuba or flat-leaf (Italian) parsley, chopped

40 g (1½ oz/¼ cup) toasted whole almonds, chopped

¼ teaspoon finely chopped lemon zest

1 garlic clove, chopped

¼ teaspoon salt

80 ml (2½ fl oz/⅓ cup) soya bean oil or olive oil

25 g (1 oz/¼ cup) grated Parmesan cheese

serves 4–6 as a starter

Bring a large saucepan of water to the boil, add the soya beans, allow to come to the boil again and cook for 2–3 minutes if using frozen soya beans, or 4–5 minutes if using fresh. Drain and leave until cool enough to handle, then remove the beans from the pods. You should have about 200 g (7 oz/2 cups) of beans. Set 25 g (1 oz/¼ cup) of beans aside for garnish.

Meanwhile, to make the mizuna pesto, put the mizuna, mitsuba, almonds, lemon zest, garlic, salt and oil in a blender and process until smooth. Stir in the Parmesan. Set the pesto aside.

Put the butter, soya bean oil and bay leaf in a large saucepan over medium heat. Add the onion and celery and cook until softened but not browned— about 6 minutes—then add the potato and cook for a further minute. Add the mirin and bring to the boil. Pour in the dashi, increase the heat to high, bring to the boil again and cook for 6 minutes. Add the soya beans and asparagus and cook for 5 minutes, or until everything is very tender.

Remove from the heat, discard the bay leaf and blend until as smooth as possible using a stick blender, or wait until the mixture has cooled slightly and carefully process in batches in an upright blender. Strain through a fine sieve, scraping and pressing down on the mixture with the back of a soup ladle to extract all the liquid. You should have about 1.25 litres (44 fl oz/5 cups). Season to taste and heat gently before serving, topped with a dollop of the pesto and a few of the reserved soya beans.

hint: Add a little extra oil to any leftover pesto and stir it through pasta.

Based on a traditional Japanese dish of seaweed and shellfish dressed in vinegar, this fine noodle salad makes a lovely starter or light meal. The fresh flavours of the sea are brought to life by a slightly sweet, zippy vinaigrette.

chilled prawn, cucumber and noodle salad

12 cooked king prawns (shrimp)

2 Lebanese (short) cucumbers

1 tablespoon dried wakame pieces

100 g (3½ oz) somen noodles

3 spring onions (scallions), thinly sliced on
   the diagonal

seven-spice mix (optional)

dressing

½ teaspoon dashi granules

125 ml (4 fl oz/½ cup) Japanese rice vinegar

60 ml (2 fl oz/¼ cup) mirin

1 teaspoon Japanese soy sauce

2 teaspoons very finely grated ginger and its juice

pinch of sugar

½ teaspoon sesame oil

serves 4 as a starter

Peel and devein the prawns, cut them in half lengthways, then refrigerate until ready to use. Halve the cucumbers lengthways, scoop out the seeds with a teaspoon, then slice very thinly on a slight diagonal. Put in a colander, sprinkle with salt and rest for 10 minutes, then rinse and squeeze out as much water as you can. Chill in the refrigerator.

Soak the wakame in cold water for 5 minutes—it should be rehydrated and glossy but not mushy. Drain, then chill.

Meanwhile, to make the dressing, mix the dashi granules with 1 tablespoon hot water and stir until dissolved. Add the rice vinegar, mirin, soy sauce, grated ginger and juice, the sugar and sesame oil. Stir to combine, then chill.

Bring a large saucepan of water to the boil, then reduce to a simmer. Add the somen and cook for 2 minutes, or until tender, then quickly drain and rinse under cold running water until the noodles are completely cooled.

Combine the noodles, prawns, cucumber, wakame and half the spring onions with the dressing and toss well. Serve immediately, garnished with the remaining spring onions and sprinkled with the seven-spice mix, if desired.

The Japanese have such a fondness for corn potage that it is available in packet form—just add water or milk. While this version may take a little more time, the results are well worth the effort. Surprisingly rich, this soup is best served in small bowls as a starter.

corn potage

5 x 10 cm (2 x 4 in) piece of kombu, wiped with
   a damp cloth, cut into strips
4 cobs sweet corn
20 g (¾ oz) butter
1 teaspoon sesame oil
1 leek, thinly sliced
1 celery stalk, finely chopped
1 garlic clove, crushed
1 teaspoon finely grated ginger
60 ml (2 fl oz/¼ cup) mirin
125 ml (4 fl oz/½ cup) cream
ground white pepper
sesame oil, to serve
Japanese soy sauce, to serve (optional)
nori flakes or thinly sliced spring onion (scallion),
   to garnish

serves 4–6 as a starter

To make a stock, put the kombu and 1 litre (35 fl oz/4 cups) cold water in a large saucepan. Slowly bring to the boil, cook for 30 seconds, then remove the kombu. Cut the kernels from the corn cobs, then add both the corn kernels and the cobs to the pan and return to the boil. Reduce to a simmer and cook for 10 minutes, then remove from the heat and set the saucepan aside.

In a clean saucepan, add the butter and sesame oil and melt over medium heat. Add the leek and cook, stirring regularly, for 6 minutes, or until lightly golden. Add the celery, garlic and ginger and cook for 1 minute, or until fragrant.

Remove the corn cobs, but not the kernels, from the stock and discard. Add the corn stock and the mirin to the leek mixture and bring to the boil over high heat, then reduce to a simmer and cook for 15 minutes. Remove from the heat and, using a stick blender, purée the soup until as smooth as possible, or wait until cooled slightly and carefully process in batches in an upright blender.

Push the mixture through a fine sieve into a clean saucepan, pressing down on the solids to help extract more liquid. Discard the solids. Stir in the cream and heat gently over low heat—do not allow to boil. Season to taste with salt and white pepper. Serve in small bowls dotted with a little sesame oil and soy sauce, if using, and sprinkle with nori flakes or spring onion. Great with Nori, sesame and parmesan pastries (page 19).

hint: Add a little more cream to the soup if you find it is too thick.

Here's a wonderful Japanese version of soul-warming chicken soup. It's light, fresh and flavoursome and very good for you.

chicken and vegetable broth

350 g (12 oz) daikon, peeled, cut into
    5 cm (2 in) lengths
1 large carrot, peeled, cut into 5 cm (2 in) lengths
1 celery stalk, cut into 5 cm (2 in) lengths
1 leek, cut into 5 cm (2 in) lengths
80 g (2¾ oz) snow peas (mangetout), trimmed
50 g (1¾ oz/¼ cup) drained, sliced tinned bamboo
    shoots
1.5 kg (3 lb 5 oz) whole chicken
8 spring onions (scallions), bruised
110 g (3¾ oz/1 cup) sliced ginger
8 garlic cloves, bruised
5 x 20 cm (2 x 8 in) piece of kombu, wiped with a
    damp cloth
2 teaspoons dashi granules
4 small dried shiitake mushrooms
ground white pepper
4 long strips of lemon zest, tied into knots
Japanese chilli sesame oil (optional)

serves 4–6 as a light meal

Finely julienne the daikon, carrot, celery and leek, using either the coarse-tooth blade on a Japanese mandolin or a sharp knife. Cut the snow peas and bamboo shoots into matchsticks.

Rinse the cavity of the chicken, then put it into a large, deep saucepan, breast-side down. Add the spring onions, ginger, garlic, kombu, dashi, shiitake and 3 litres (105 fl oz/12 cups) cold water. Bring to the boil over high heat, then reduce to a simmer and cook for 5 minutes. Remove the kombu. Continue to simmer for 12 minutes, skimming any foam off the surface, then carefully turn the chicken over and simmer for a further 15–20 minutes, or until the thigh juices run clear when pierced.

Remove the shiitake and chicken from the broth, tipping any liquid in the cavity of the chicken back into the pan. Cover the chicken with foil and set aside to cool slightly. Strain the stock into a clean saucepan. Remove and discard the shiitake stems, slice the caps and return them to the pan with the stock. Bring the stock to a boil, reduce the heat and simmer for 10 minutes. Add the julienned and matchstick vegetables and cook for 8–10 minutes, or until just tender. Season to taste with salt and white pepper and remove from the heat.

Remove the breasts and legs from the chicken. Discard the skin and cut the meat into short, neat strips.

Place a little breast and leg meat into the base of each soup bowl, along with a knot of lemon zest, then ladle over the broth and vegetables. Pass around some chilli sesame oil for drizzling, if desired. Serve with chopsticks and a spoon.

hint: As a variation, add 200 g (7 oz) silken firm tofu, cut into dice, to each bowl before ladling over the broth.

Burdock has a wonderful earthy flavour —to me, it tastes like a cross between Jerusalem artichokes and bamboo shoots. Combined with prosciutto and sage, it develops a rich, savoury accent. If you can't find fresh burdock, it is available frozen in Asian grocery stores, peeled and ready for cooking.

burdock cream soup with crispy prosciutto and sage

800 g (1 lb 12 oz) fresh burdock root

1 tablespoon Japanese rice vinegar

1½ tablespoons olive oil

a few drops of sesame oil

1 large onion, finely chopped

1 celery stalk, finely chopped

1 carrot, finely chopped

2 garlic cloves, finely chopped

3 teaspoons finely chopped sage

2 tablespoons mirin

700 g (1 lb 9 oz) floury potatoes, such as russet (Idaho), peeled and diced

1.25 litres (44 fl oz/5 cups) chicken broth or chicken stock

10 g (¼ oz) butter

12 whole large sage leaves

6 long slices prosciutto

250 ml (9 fl oz/1 cup) cream

serves 4–6 as a starter

Lightly scrape the burdock with a knife to remove its thin brown skin, then dice and put in a bowl of water with the rice vinegar. This maintains the pale colour of the burdock and also helps to remove any bitterness.

Put 1 tablespoon of the olive oil and the sesame oil in a large saucepan over medium heat. Add the onion, celery and carrot and cook until softened and lightly golden. Add the garlic, sage and mirin and cook for 1 minute. Drain the burdock and add it to the pan, along with the potato and stock. Bring to the boil over high heat, then reduce to a simmer and cook for 1 hour, or until the burdock is tender.

Remove from the heat and, using a stick blender, purée the soup, or wait until cooled slightly and carefully process in batches in a food processor or an upright blender. Strain twice through a fine sieve into a clean saucepan to remove any tough fibrous matter, pushing down with a wooden spoon to extract all the liquid.

Put the butter and remaining oil in a frying pan over medium–high heat, then add the sage leaves and cook, stirring occasionally, for a few minutes, or until crispy and aromatic. Remove and drain on paper towels. Add the prosciutto and cook for about 3 minutes, or until crispy. Drain on paper towels, then break into small pieces.

Stir the cream into the soup and place on a gentle heat to warm through. Season to taste, then ladle into bowls. Garnish with a little prosciutto and some fried sage leaves. Serve with crusty bread.

Green tea soba noodles, made with buckwheat flour and finely ground green tea, look and taste spectacular when combined with bright, fresh vegetables, crispy bacon and a velvety sesame soy dressing.

green tea noodle salad

200 g (7 oz) green tea soba noodles, cut in half

3 teaspoons dried hijiki or wakame pieces

2 teaspoons vegetable oil

4 bacon rashers, thinly sliced

150 g (5½ oz/1 cup) cherry tomatoes,
    cut in half

70 g (2½ oz/1½ cups) baby English spinach leaves,
    rinsed and drained well

1 ripe avocado, cut into 1.5 cm (⅝ in) cubes

sesame seeds, to serve

sesame soy dressing

2 tablespoons Japanese soy sauce

60 ml (2 fl oz/¼ cup) Japanese rice vinegar

1½ tablespoons mirin

2½ teaspoons sesame oil

2 garlic cloves, crushed

1 teaspoon caster (superfine) sugar

1½ teaspoons finely grated ginger and its juice

1 tablespoon toasted sesame seeds

serves 4 as a starter

Bring a large saucepan of salted water to the boil over high heat, then gradually lower the soba noodles into the water. Stir so the noodles don't stick together. Add 250 ml (9 fl oz/1 cup) cold water and return to the boil. Repeat this step another two or three times, or until the noodles are tender. This method helps to cook this delicate noodle more evenly. The noodles should be *al dente*—there should be no hard core in the centre, but they should not be completely soft all the way through either.

Drain, then rinse well under cold running water, rubbing together lightly with your hands to remove any excess starch. Put the noodles in a bowl filled with water and ice cubes until they are completely chilled. Drain well.

Meanwhile, put the hijiki in a bowl and cover with cold water. Lightly rub the pieces between your fingers to break up and to loosen any dirt, then lift the hijiki out of the water and put in a clean bowl filled with cold water. Soak for 8 minutes, then drain and pour boiling water over them. Drain well. If using wakame, put it in a bowl and pour in enough cold water to just cover. Soak for 5 minutes, then drain well and set aside.

To make the sesame soy dressing, combine all the ingredients in a bowl and set aside.

Heat the oil in a frying pan, add the bacon and cook over medium–high heat for 4–5 minutes, or until crispy. Drain on paper towels and set aside.

Combine the noodles with two-thirds of the dressing, then fold in the hijiki or wakame, bacon, tomatoes, spinach and avocado. Place in a mound in a bowl and drizzle over the remaining dressing. Sprinkle with extra sesame seeds and serve immediately.

This hearty, filling dish is similar to a Middle Eastern chickpea soup. You can, in fact, substitute chickpeas if preferred, but the cooking time will be shorter. Prepare this ahead of time as soya beans need to be soaked overnight.

soya bean and cumin soup

500 g (1 lb 2 oz/2⅔ cups) dried soya beans

5 x 10 cm (2 x 4 in) piece of kombu, wiped with a damp cloth

2 tablespoons soya bean oil or olive oil

1 large onion, chopped

1 bay leaf

1 carrot, chopped

2 celery stalks, chopped

4 garlic cloves, crushed

2 teaspoons ground cumin

1 teaspoon ground cinnamon

1 teaspoon seven-spice mix

large pinch of bicarbonate of soda (baking soda)

1 tablespoon dashi granules

1½ tablespoons soya bean oil or extra virgin olive oil, extra

1½ tablespoons lemon juice

2 tablespoons finely chopped mitsuba or flat-leaf (Italian) parsley

serves 6 as a starter, or 4 as a main

Soak the soya beans and kombu overnight in cold water, then drain, discarding the kombu. Put the soya beans in a large saucepan filled with water, bring to the boil and cook for 5 minutes, then drain and rinse well.

Heat the soya bean oil in a large saucepan and add the onion and bay leaf and cook over medium heat for 5 minutes, or until lightly golden. Add the carrot and celery and cook for 10 minutes, or until softened and slightly caramelized. Add the garlic, cumin, cinnamon and seven-spice mix and cook for 30 seconds, or until fragrant. Add the soya beans, bicarbonate of soda and 3.5 litres (122 fl oz/ 14 cups) cold water (don't add salt or the beans won't soften properly). Bring to the boil over high heat, then reduce to a simmer and cook for about 4 hours, or until the beans are very soft, skimming occasionally to remove any foam from the surface.

Add the dashi and stir to dissolve. Take the pan off the heat, remove the bay leaf and purée the soup using a stick blender, or wait until cooled slightly and process in a food processor until smooth. Season to taste. The soup will thicken on standing so you may need to add a little extra water if reheating.

Combine the extra soya bean oil with the lemon juice and mitsuba. Ladle the soup into bowls and drizzle the mitsuba and oil mixture over the top.

hint: The time it takes to cook soya beans depends on the age of the beans and storage conditions, so it may take more or less than the times given.

This chunky soup is really a meal in a bowl—a warming, aromatic broth brimming with tender, fresh seafood and vegetables.

spicy miso seafood hotpot

250 g (9 oz) baby clams (vongole)

12 black mussels

12 raw medium prawns (shrimp)

12 large scallops without roe

400 g (14 oz) salmon fillet

2 small squid tubes (about 100 g/3½ oz each), cleaned

1 tablespoon vegetable oil

1 teaspoon sesame oil

2 leeks, thinly sliced

1–2 small red chillies, seeded and finely chopped

1 bay leaf

5 garlic cloves, finely chopped

1 tablespoon very finely chopped ginger

80 ml (2½ fl oz/⅓ cup) sake

60 ml (2 fl oz/¼ cup) mirin

2 teaspoons dashi granules, dissolved in 2 litres (70 fl oz/8 cups) hot water

5 x 10 cm (2 x 4 in) piece of kombu, wiped with a damp cloth

1 tablespoon Japanese soy sauce

12 small new potatoes, peeled

200 g (7 oz/2½ cups) sliced Chinese cabbage

3 tablespoons white or red miso

1 log of kamaboko, about 160 g (5½ oz), cut into 12 even slices

1 small handful mitsuba or flat-leaf (Italian) parsley

lemon wedges, to serve

Japanese chilli sesame oil (optional)

serves 6 as a main

Soak the clams in several changes of cold water for about 2 hours to rid them of sand. Drain well. Scrub the mussels, remove their beards, and discard any mussels that are cracked or open. Peel and devein the prawns, leaving the tails intact. Remove the muscle from the scallops. Remove any bones from the salmon and cut into 3 cm (1¼ in) pieces. Cut the squid into 1 cm (½ in) thick rings. Put all the seafood in the refrigerator, in separate groups.

Heat the vegetable and sesame oils in a very large saucepan over medium heat, then add the leek, chilli and bay leaf and cook for 10 minutes, or until the leek is golden. Add the garlic and ginger and cook for 1 minute.

Increase the heat to high and add the sake, mirin, clams and mussels and cook, shaking the pan, for 4–6 minutes. When the shells open, remove from the pan and set aside (still in their shells). Discard any shells that remain closed.

Add the dashi mixture, kombu, soy sauce and potatoes to the pan. Bring to the boil, remove the kombu, and cook for 15 minutes, or until the potato is quite tender. Skim any foam from the surface. Reduce to a simmer, add the cabbage and cook for 4 minutes, or until the cabbage is wilted. Add the prawns, scallops, salmon and squid, bring to a simmer again and cook for 2–3 minutes, or until everything is just cooked through. Remove the solids from the broth with a slotted spoon and divide the ingredients equally between six deep, wide bowls. Cover with foil to keep warm.

Increase the heat to high. Mix a little of the hot broth into the miso to form a paste, then add to the pan with the kamaboko, the clams and mussels (and any juices) and heat for 1–2 minutes. Divide the solids between the bowls, then ladle over the remaining soup. Scatter with a few mitsuba leaves and serve with lemon wedges and chilli sesame oil for drizzling over, if desired.

Sweet potatoes are popular in Japan, and in the cooler months street vendors roast them over hot coals and serve them topped with a knob of butter, which melts into the soft smoky flesh—the aroma is irresistible. Not quite so aromatic but just as delicious are these delicate gnocchi—the pancetta and butter adding rich, nutty flavours.

sweet potato gnocchi with pickled ginger brown butter

2 x 600 g (1 lb 5 oz) orange sweet potatoes

2 egg yolks

2 tablespoons finely grated Parmesan cheese, plus extra to serve

300 g (10½ oz/2½ cups) plain (all-purpose) flour

2 teaspoons vegetable oil

150 g (5½ oz) pancetta, finely diced

125 g (4½ oz) butter

60 g (2¼ oz/¼ cup) pickled ginger, rinsed, squeezed dry, finely shredded

3 garlic cloves, crushed

90 g (3¼ oz/2 cups) chopped mizuna, baby rocket (arugula) or spinach leaves

serves 6 as starter, or 4 as main

Preheat the oven to 200°C (400°F/Gas 6). Prick the sweet potatoes all over, then cook for 2 hours, or until very tender. Set aside until cool enough to handle, then peel and mash well. Put the mashed sweet potato in a clean tea towel and twist and squeeze out any excess moisture.

Mix the mashed sweet potato with the egg yolks and Parmesan, then gradually stir in the flour. When it forms a soft dough, remove to a lightly floured work bench and knead gently for a minute to just bring it together—add a little extra flour if needed. You should have a soft, pliable dough that is slightly damp but not sticky. Do not overwork the dough or it will toughen.

Heat the oil in a frying pan and cook the pancetta over medium–high heat for 4–5 minutes, or until frizzled and crispy. Drain on paper towels.

Bring a large saucepan of salted water to the boil. Divide the dough into quarters and roll each into smooth 1.5 cm (⅝ in) thick ropes, then cut each rope into 2 cm (¾ in) lengths with a sharp knife. You should end up with about 85 gnocchi.

Cook the gnocchi in four batches for 1–2 minutes, or until they rise to the surface. Lift them out with a slotted spoon, transfer to a bowl and toss with 1–2 teaspoons olive oil.

Meanwhile, put the butter and pickled ginger in a saucepan over medium heat and cook, stirring regularly, for 3–4 minutes, or until the butter foams, then turns golden brown and has a nutty aroma. Stir in the garlic and remove the pan from the heat immediately to make sure the garlic doesn't burn. Add to the gnocchi, along with the mizuna and pancetta and toss to combine. Season to taste with a little salt and freshly ground black pepper and serve with extra Parmesan to sprinkle over.

Fans of garlicky vongole, or baby clams, need look no further. This aromatic version uses sake, ginger and dashi granules. Dashi is made from dried bonito, a type of tuna, and its addition helps boost the overall seafood flavour. Slurp them one by one from the shells, or serve over freshly cooked udon noodles or linguine for pasta vongole, Japanese style.

sake-steamed clams with garlic and chilli

1 kg (2 lb 4 oz) baby clams (vongole)

80 ml (2½ fl oz/⅓ cup) vegetable oil

1 teaspoon sesame oil

6 garlic cloves, thinly sliced lengthways

2 small red chillies, seeded and thinly sliced

1 small leek, very thinly sliced

60 ml (2 fl oz/¼ cup) drinking sake

ground white pepper

1 teaspoon finely chopped ginger

large pinch of dashi granules

15 g (½ oz) butter

3 tablespoons chopped mitsuba or flat-leaf (Italian) parsley

lemon wedges, to serve

450 g (1 lb) udon noodles, freshly cooked (optional)

serves 6 as a starter, or 4 as a main

Soak the clams in several changes of cold water for about 2 hours to rid them of sand. Drain well.

Heat the vegetable and sesame oils in a large saucepan over low heat, add the garlic and chilli and cook, stirring regularly, until the garlic is golden and crisp (do not allow the garlic to burn or it will become bitter). Remove with a slotted spoon and drain on paper towels.

Add the leek to the pan and cook for 5 minutes, or until softened. Increase the heat to high and add the sake and clams, a pinch each of salt and white pepper, the ginger and dashi granules. Cover and cook for 5 minutes, shaking the pan occasionally, until all the clams are open. Discard any that remain closed. Stir in the garlic and chilli, the butter and mitsuba and serve immediately with lemon wedges on the side for squeezing over. If you like, serve with udon noodles.

As Japanese rice is quite glutinous you will notice that this recipe calls for a little more liquid than a regular risotto. If you can't find all the fantastic Japanese mushrooms used here, simply substitute with funghi of your choice.

japanese mushroom risotto

4 dried shiitake mushrooms
5 x 5 cm (2 x 2 in) piece of kombu, wiped with a
    damp cloth
2½ tablespoons Japanese soy sauce
80 ml (2½ fl oz/⅓ cup) mirin
40 g (1½ oz) butter
100 g (3½ oz/2 cups) shiitake mushrooms, stems
    discarded, caps sliced
150 g (5½ oz/1⅔ cups) shimeji mushrooms, pulled
    apart
150 g (5½ oz/2 cups) oyster mushrooms, sliced
1 tablespoon vegetable oil
1 teaspoon sesame oil
1 onion, finely chopped
1 celery stalk, finely chopped
2 garlic cloves, crushed
2 teaspoons grated ginger
450 g (1 lb/2 cups) Japanese short-grain rice
100 g (3½ oz/1⅓ cups) enoki mushrooms, ends
    trimmed, pulled apart
2 handfuls mitsuba or flat-leaf (Italian) parsley,
    finely chopped
25 g (1 oz/1 bunch) chives, chopped
shaved Parmesan cheese, to serve

serves 6 as a starter, or 4 as a main

Put the dried shiitake and kombu in a saucepan with 1.875 litres (65 fl oz/7½ cups) water and bring to the boil over high heat. Turn off the heat and sit for 15 minutes. Discard the kombu. Discard the mushroom stems, thinly slice the caps and set aside. Bring the stock back to the boil, then reduce to a simmer and add the soy sauce and mirin.

Melt half of the butter in a saucepan over medium–high heat, then add the fresh shiitake, shimeji and oyster mushrooms and a pinch of salt and cook for 8–10 minutes, or until the mushrooms are wilted and any liquid has cooked off. Set aside.

Melt the remaining butter with the vegetable and sesame oils in a large saucepan over medium–high heat. Add the onion and celery and cook for about 5 minutes, or until the onion is lightly golden. Add the garlic and ginger and cook for 30 seconds, or until aromatic.

Add the rice and stir to coat in the butter and onion mixture. Cook, stirring, for 2 minutes, or until the rice is slightly translucent. Gradually stir in 125 ml (4 fl oz/½ cup) of the simmering liquid, stirring until it has almost been absorbed, then continue to add the remaining stock, 125 ml (4 fl oz/½ cup) at a time, stirring constantly until the stock has been absorbed. This should take about 25 minutes. With the last 125 ml (4 fl oz/½ cup) of liquid, add the cooked mushrooms, the sliced shiitake, and the enoki, stirring to heat through.

Remove from the heat, scatter over the mitsuba and chives and season, to taste. Serve immediately with Parmesan. Great with Green salad with Japanese dressing (page 142).

Confusingly, this recipe is called 'yakisoba'—in fact, it does not use soba noodles but a soft Chinese-style egg noodle, sold in Japanese stores as yakisoba. If you can't find them, use thin hokkien (egg) or udon noodles.

yakisoba with prawns

4 dried shiitake mushrooms

1 kg (2 lb 4 oz) raw medium prawns (shrimp), peeled and deveined

3 garlic cloves, finely chopped

1½ teaspoons finely chopped ginger

3 rashers streaky bacon, cut into 3 cm (1¼ in) lengths

1 tablespoon vegetable oil

1 teaspoon sesame oil

1 carrot, thinly julienned

1 small green capsicum (pepper), cut into thin strips

200 g (7 oz) Chinese cabbage, cut into 3 cm (1¼ in) squares

100 g (3½ oz/½ cup) drained, sliced tinned bamboo shoots, thinly sliced lengthways

6 spring onions (scallions), cut into 3 cm (1¼ in) lengths

500 g (1 lb 2 oz) yakisoba noodles, separated

1 tablespoon thinly sliced pickled ginger

lemon wedges, to serve (optional)

yakisoba sauce

2 tablespoons Japanese soy sauce

60 ml (2 fl oz/¼ cup) Worcestershire sauce

1 tablespoon Japanese rice vinegar

1½ tablespoons sake

1 tablespoon tomato sauce (ketchup)

1 tablespoon oyster sauce

3 teaspoons black sugar or dark brown sugar

½ teaspoon dashi granules

serves 4–6 as a main

Soak the shiitake in hot water for 30 minutes. Drain, reserving 2 tablespoons of the liquid, discard the mushroom stems and slice the caps. Combine the prawns with half the garlic and half the ginger.

To make the yakisoba sauce, combine all the sauce ingredients in a bowl, along with the reserved mushroom soaking liquid, and set aside.

Heat a wok over medium–high heat, add the bacon and stir-fry for 2–3 minutes, or until lightly browned. Remove and set aside. Combine the vegetable and sesame oils, add half to the wok and increase the heat to high. Add the prawns and stir-fry for 1–2 minutes, or until they just turn pink. Remove and add to the bacon.

Add a little more of the combined oils to the wok, then add the carrot, capsicum, cabbage, bamboo shoots and shiitake and stir-fry for 4–5 minutes. Add the spring onions and remaining garlic and ginger and stir-fry for a further minute. Remove from the wok and set aside.

Add the remaining oil to the wok and stir-fry the noodles for 1 minute. Add the vegetables, sauce and pickled ginger and stir-fry for 3 minutes, then add the prawns and bacon and cook for a further 2–3 minutes, or until the prawns are cooked through and the sauce glazes the noodles. Serve with lemon wedges to squeeze over if desired.

hint: This dish is also good sprinkled with nori flakes or bonito flakes.

87

This brothy stew is light on the stomach but big on flavour and texture.

chicken and eight vegetable stew

200 g (7 oz) fresh burdock root

1 teaspoon Japanese rice vinegar

200 g (7 oz) fresh lotus root

1 tablespoon vegetable oil

2 teaspoons sesame oil

2 kg (4 lb 8 oz) whole chicken, cut into
10 even-sized pieces, lightly seasoned

200 g (7 oz) taro, peeled and cut into
3 cm (1¼ in) cubes

2 carrots, thickly sliced

100 g (3½ oz/2 cups) small shiitake mushrooms,
stems discarded

100 g (3½ oz/½ cup) drained, sliced tinned
bamboo shoots

2 teaspoons dashi granules, dissolved in
1 litre (35 fl oz/4 cups) hot water

125 ml (4 fl oz/½ cup) Japanese soy sauce

1½ tablespoons caster (superfine) sugar

80 ml (2½ fl oz/⅓ cup) mirin

100 g (3½ oz) snow peas (mangetout), trimmed

3 spring onions (scallions), cut into 4 cm (1½ in)
lengths on the diagonal

serves 6–8 as a main

Gently scrape the thin skin from the burdock root, then rinse. Starting at the thin end and using a small sharp knife, shave off pieces as if you are sharpening a pencil with a knife. Put the shavings in a small bowl of vinegared water and set aside. This not only helps to remove any bitterness but also prevents the burdock from turning brown. Peel the lotus, then cut into 5 mm (¼ in) slices and put into a bowl of cold water.

Heat the vegetable and sesame oils in a large saucepan over medium–high heat. Add the chicken pieces in two batches and cook until golden—about 10 minutes per batch. Set aside.

Add the taro and carrot to the saucepan and cook, stirring regularly, for 2 minutes, then add the well-drained burdock and lotus and cook for 2 minutes, or until lightly golden. Add the shiitake and bamboo shoots and cook for 2 minutes.

Add the dashi, soy sauce, sugar, mirin and chicken pieces (along with any juices) and bring to the boil. Reduce to a simmer and cook for 12–15 minutes, or until the chicken is just cooked through and the vegetables are tender. The breast pieces may cook more quickly than the others—if so, remove from the pan and return to the heat just before serving. Add the snow peas and spring onions and cook for 1 minute, or until tender. Serve with rice.

hint: If fresh burdock and lotus are not available, you can find them in the freezer compartment of Japanese or Asian grocery stores.

This dish, originally Chinese, uses soba noodles. Soba, or buckwheat, noodles are made from wheat flour and ground buckwheat seeds, which gives them their distinctive brown colouring and slightly nutty flavour.

soba with sautéed pork, eggplant and chilli

60 ml (2 fl oz/¼ cup) vegetable oil

1 teaspoon sesame oil

3 long, slender eggplants (aubergines), sliced
    1.5 cm (⅝ in) thick

3 garlic cloves, crushed

1½ teaspoons finely grated ginger

6 spring onions (scallions), sliced on the diagonal,
    white and green parts kept separate

600 g (1 lb 5 oz) minced (ground) pork

2 tablespoons chilli bean sauce

1 tablespoon tomato paste (purée)

½ teaspoon dashi granules

2 tablespoons mirin

1 tablespoon Japanese soy sauce

1 teaspoon soft brown sugar

250 g (9 oz) soba noodles

extra sesame oil, to drizzle (optional)

serves 4 as a main

Put 2 tablespoons of the vegetable oil and the sesame oil in a wok over medium–high heat (do not use a non-stick wok for this recipe). Add the eggplant slices and cook, stir-frying until golden on both sides, for about 4–5 minutes. Drain on paper towels and set aside.

Add the remaining vegetable oil to the wok, then add the garlic, ginger and the white part of the spring onions and cook for 30 seconds, then remove and set aside. Add the pork and brown well all over, using a fork to break up any lumps— this should take 6–8 minutes.

Add the chilli bean sauce, tomato paste, dashi granules, mirin, soy sauce, sugar and 250 ml (9 fl oz/1 cup) water to the wok, along with the spring onion and garlic mixture. Allow to come to the boil, then reduce to a simmer and cook for 5 minutes. Add the eggplant and most of the spring onion greens, reserving some for garnish, and cook for 3 minutes, or until the eggplant is cooked through. Increase the heat to high and cook until most of the liquid has evaporated and the mixture is slightly glazy—about 4–5 minutes.

Bring a large saucepan of salted water to the boil over high heat. Add the soba, stirring so they don't stick together, and return to the boil. Add 125 ml (4 fl oz/½ cup) cold water and return to the boil. Repeat this procedure twice more, or until the noodles are *al dente*. Drain, then rinse well under cold running water, rubbing the noodles lightly between your hands to remove any excess starch.

Pile the noodles into a 'nest' in the centre of the plate. Top with the meat and eggplant sauce and garnish with the reserved spring onions. Serve with sesame oil for drizzling over, if desired.

hint: Brands of chilli bean sauce differ in flavour and heat, so use with caution. One of my favourites is the Chinese brand, Pun Chun.

This simple recipe is based on a Japanese home-style dish, *niku jaga*, which traditionally uses beef. Lamb is rarely used in Japanese cuisine but in this dish it really works.

lamb shank and potato stew

700 g (1 lb 9 oz) all-purpose potatoes, such as
    desiree, peeled
2 tablespoons vegetable oil
1 large onion, cut into thin wedges
6 large lamb shanks (about 1.5 kg/3 lb 5 oz)
ground white pepper
1 teaspoon sesame oil
2 teaspoons dashi granules
125 ml (4 fl oz/½ cup) Japanese beer, such as Kirin,
    Asahi or Sapporo
60 ml (2 fl oz/¼ cup) Japanese soy sauce
125 ml (4 fl oz/½ cup) sake
2 tablespoons black sugar or dark brown sugar
60 g (2¼ oz/⅓ cup) drained, sliced tinned bamboo
    shoots

serves 4–6 as a main

Cut the potatoes into 3–4 cm (1¼–1½ in) chunks, then bevel the edges by running a sharp knife or vegetable peeler along the sharp edges so the shape is softened and slightly rounded. This also prevents them from breaking up too much during cooking. Soak in cold water for 30 minutes, then drain well and thoroughly pat dry with paper towels.

Heat 2 teaspoons of the vegetable oil in a large saucepan over medium–high heat. Add the onion and cook, stirring occasionally, for 5 minutes, or until lightly browned. Remove and set aside. Add another 2 teaspoons of oil to the pan, add the potatoes and toss well to coat. Cook, shaking the pan regularly, for about 7 minutes, or until the potatoes are lightly golden, then set aside.

Season the lamb shanks with a little salt and white pepper. Add the remaining vegetable oil and the sesame oil to the pan, then cook the shanks in batches for 5 minutes, or until they are well browned on all sides.

Return the onions to the pan, along with the dashi granules, beer, soy sauce, sake, sugar and 1 litre (35 fl oz/4 cups) cold water and stir to combine. Increase the heat and bring to the boil, removing any foam that rises to the surface. Cover, reduce to a simmer and cook for 1¼ hours.

Add the potatoes and bamboo shoots and cook, uncovered, continuing to remove any foam, for a further 45 minutes, or until both the potato and meat are very tender but not falling apart.

Serve in bowls with a little of the broth poured over. Alternatively, for a richer dish, remove the lamb shanks and potato from the pan, cover and set aside. Increase the heat to high and boil the liquid for 20–25 minutes to reduce slightly. Carefully return the lamb and potato to the pan and turn to coat in the sauce, then reduce the heat to low and gently heat through. Serve a shank in a shallow bowl with a few pieces of potato and spoon over the sauce. Great with a bowl of hot, lightly buttered mixed greens.

This is the Japanese version of spaghetti and meatballs. Ginger and tomato are a surprisingly great combination and make for a light, zesty sauce.

chicken meatballs in gingery tomato sauce

chicken meatballs

700 g (1 lb 9 oz) chicken thigh fillets, minced (ground)
4 spring onions (scallions), finely chopped
1 large garlic clove, crushed
1 egg
1 egg yolk
2 tablespoons sake
2 tablespoons Japanese soy sauce
60 g (2¼ oz/1 cup) Japanese breadcrumbs
ground white pepper
1 tablespoon vegetable oil
1 teaspoon sesame oil

sauce

1 tablespoon vegetable oil
1 small onion, finely chopped
1 small red chilli, seeded and finely chopped
1 garlic clove, crushed
1 tablespoon finely grated ginger and its juice
60 ml (2 fl oz/¼ cup) mirin
2 x 400 g (14 oz) tins crushed tomatoes
1 tablespoon tomato paste (purée)
¼ teaspoon dashi granules
1½ teaspoons Japanese soy sauce
½ teaspoon caster (superfine) sugar
3 tablespoons finely chopped mitsuba or flat-leaf (Italian) parsley

450 g (1 lb) udon noodles, freshly cooked, to serve

serves 4–6 as a main

To make the meatballs, put the chicken, spring onions, garlic, egg, egg yolk, sake, soy sauce and breadcrumbs in a bowl, season lightly with salt and white pepper and mix thoroughly. Cover and refrigerate until ready to use.

To make the sauce, heat the vegetable oil in a large saucepan over medium heat, then add the onion and cook, stirring regularly, for 5 minutes, or until lightly golden. Add the chilli, garlic and ginger and juice and stir for 30 seconds, or until fragrant.

Add the mirin, tomatoes, tomato paste, dashi granules, soy sauce, sugar and 250 ml (9 fl oz/ 1 cup) cold water to the pan, then increase the heat and allow to come to the boil. Reduce to a simmer and cook for 40 minutes, or until slightly thickened and pulpy. Set aside.

Form the chicken mixture into walnut-sized balls (about 1 level tablespoon for each). Heat the vegetable and sesame oils over medium–high heat in a non-stick frying pan and cook the balls in batches for 5 minutes, or until lightly golden all over.

Return the sauce to medium–high heat and add the chicken balls. When the mixture comes to the boil, reduce to a simmer and cook for 5 minutes, or until the balls are cooked through. Stir through the mitsuba or parsley and season, to taste. Serve with freshly cooked udon noodles.

Based on the French favourite, beef bourguignon, this adaptation contains fresh shiitake mushrooms, peppery sansho, dry sake and rich, earthy miso. *Bon appétit*, or, as the Japanese would say—*itadakimasu*.

beef, shiitake and red wine stew

60 ml (2 fl oz/¼ cup) vegetable oil

6 baby leeks, cut into 4 cm (1½ in) lengths

300 g (10½ oz/6 cups) shiitake mushrooms, stems discarded, caps cut in half if large

1 large onion, chopped

1 large carrot, chopped

4 streaky bacon rashers, chopped

2 tablespoons plain (all-purpose) flour

1 teaspoon sansho pepper

pinch of sea salt flakes

1 kg (2 lb 4 oz) stewing beef, cut into large cubes

3 garlic cloves, crushed

375 ml (13 fl oz/1½ cups) red wine

375 ml (13 fl oz/1½ cups) sake

2 tablespoons red miso

serves 6 as a main

Heat 1 tablespoon of the oil in a large saucepan over medium heat. Add the leeks and cook until lightly golden, then remove them to a plate and set aside. Add the shiitake and cook for a few minutes, or until softened and lightly browned, then remove to the plate with the leeks. Set the leeks and mushrooms aside until ready to use.

Add the onion, carrot and bacon to the pan and cook for 10 minutes, or until lightly browned, then remove and set aside, separate from the leeks.

Combine the flour, sansho pepper and sea salt in a large bowl. Toss with the beef to coat well.

Add a little more oil to the pan and brown the beef in batches. Remove and set aside. Add the garlic to the pan and stir for a few seconds, then add the red wine and sake and stir, scraping up any sediment stuck to the base of the pan.

Return the beef to the pan, along with the onion, carrot and bacon, the miso and 250 ml (9 fl oz/ 1 cup) water. Increase the heat to high, stir until the miso dissolves, then bring to the boil. Reduce the heat to low, cover and simmer for 1½ hours, then add the leeks and shiitake to the pan and cook, uncovered, for a further 30 minutes, or until the beef is very tender and the sauce has thickened. Serve with Mitsuba mash (page 158).

main plates

Sometimes the most simple of cooking methods can yield the best results. Japanese cooks have a fondness for steaming, which helps to retain flavours and nutrients, and keeps the food tender and moist. The subtle 'ocean flavour' of wakame brings out the natural sweetness of the fish.

steamed snapper with wakame

2 tablespoons dried wakame pieces

4 x 175 g (6 oz) snapper fillets

2 spring onions (scallions), thinly sliced on the diagonal

2 tablespoons drinking sake

20 g (¾ oz) butter

1 teaspoon finely grated ginger and its juice

2 teaspoons Japanese soy sauce

1 tablespoon lemon juice

¼ teaspoon sesame oil

serves 4

Put the wakame in a bowl, pour in enough cold water to just cover the wakame, and allow to soak for 2–3 minutes to soften slightly. Drain well. Put each snapper fillet on a piece of baking paper or foil approximately 30 cm (12 in) square.

Mix together the wakame and the spring onions. Drizzle the sake over the fish, then sprinkle lightly with salt. Divide the wakame mixture between the fish, then dot the butter over the top. Fold up the edges of the paper, seal tightly and put the parcels in a large bamboo steamer and cover with the lid.

Bring a wok or large saucepan filled with water to the boil. Place the steamer over the top and steam for 10–12 minutes, or until the fish is just cooked through and the flesh is opaque.

While the fish is cooking, combine the ginger and juice, soy sauce, lemon juice and sesame oil in a small serving bowl.

Place each parcel of fish on a serving platter and ask each guest to open the parcels at the table. Serve with the sauce for drizzling over.

Niçoise salad, Japanese style.

nihon niçoise

500 g (1 lb 2 oz) kipfler (fingerling) potatoes, peeled
    and sliced on the diagonal, 1 cm (½ in) thick
400 g (14 oz) fresh or frozen soya beans
    in the pod
12 cherry tomatoes, cut in half
2 spring onions (scallions), sliced on the diagonal
40 g (1½ oz/¼ cup) small black olives
1 large handful mitsuba or flat-leaf (Italian) parsley
1 tablespoon vegetable oil
4 x 175 g (6 oz) sashimi-grade tuna fillets

dressing
2 teaspoons Japanese soy sauce
2 tablespoons Japanese rice vinegar
1½ tablespoons lemon juice
1 garlic clove, crushed
80 ml (2½ fl oz/⅓ cup) extra virgin olive oil
½ teaspoon sesame oil
¼ teaspoon Japanese mustard

serves 4

Put the potatoes in a saucepan and cover with
water. Place over high heat and bring to the boil.
Cook for 8–10 minutes, or until tender, then drain,
rinse and drain well again.

Bring a small saucepan of water to the boil, add
the soya beans and cook for 2–3 minutes if frozen,
and for a further 2 minutes if fresh, or until tender.
Drain and refresh with cold water, then drain well
again. When cool enough to handle, slip the beans
from their pods.

To make the dressing, combine all the ingredients
and whisk until smooth. Combine the potatoes,
soya beans, cherry tomatoes, spring onions, olives
and mitsuba with the dressing and toss lightly.

Heat the vegetable oil in a large heavy-based frying
pan over medium–high heat. Season the tuna
steaks, then cook for 1–2 minutes each side, or
until cooked to your liking (ideally the inside should
still be rare and pink).

Divide the salad between four plates, top with a
piece of tuna and serve immediately.

The richness of the duck meat marries well with the flavours in this salad— sweet citrus, fresh daikon and slightly peppery salad leaves, all brought together with a tart but smoky soy dressing. The ponzu dressing is best made the day before to allow the flavours to develop.

crisp duck breast with orange and daikon salad

3 oranges
300 g (10½ oz) daikon
80 g (2¾ oz/2½ cups) mizuna or baby rocket
    (arugula)
4 x 175–200 g (6–7 oz) duck breast fillets
oil, for brushing
1½ tablespoons vegetable oil
1 teaspoon sesame oil
1 tablespoon drinking sake

ponzu dressing
1 teaspoon lemon juice
1 teaspoon lime juice
1 teaspoon Japanese rice vinegar
1 tablespoon Japanese soy sauce
1 teaspoon mirin
1 tablespoon sake
¼ teaspoon sugar
5 x 1 cm (2 x ½ in) piece of kombu, wiped with
    a damp cloth, julienned
1 teaspoon bonito flakes

serves 4

To make the ponzu dressing, put all the ingredients in a non-metallic bowl and stir until the sugar has dissolved. Cover with plastic wrap and refrigerate for 24 hours.

Remove the skin from the oranges and carefully remove all the pith. Segment the oranges into a bowl, then squeeze the juice from the membranes over the top. Chill.

Peel the daikon, cut in half lengthways and slice very thinly into half moons using a Japanese mandolin or a very steady hand and a sharp knife. Rinse and drain the mizuna well, then put it, along with the daikon, in the refrigerator to chill.

Lightly score through the skin and fat of the duck breasts using a sharp knife, being careful not to cut into the flesh. Season with salt, rubbing into the skin. Put a large heavy-based frying pan over medium heat and brush with a little oil. Place the seasoned duck breasts skin-side down and cook for 6 minutes to render the fat, then remove the duck from the pan.

Discard the fat, return the frying pan to the heat and increase the temperature to high. When hot, put the duck, skin-side up, in the pan and cook for 2 minutes to seal, then turn over and cook, skin-side down, for 4–5 minutes, or until crisp and golden. The flesh should still be pink inside. Remove to a plate, lightly cover and rest for a few minutes.

Strain the ponzu through muslin (cheesecloth) or a fine sieve into a bowl and add the vegetable and sesame oils and sake, along with 1 tablespoon orange juice from the bowl of oranges.

Drain the orange segments, toss together with the daikon, mizuna and the dressing and divide between four plates. Arrange the duck breasts over the top and serve immediately.

Heat the vegetable and sesame oils in a large heavy-based saucepan over high heat and brown the pork well on all sides. Remove from the pan and rinse the pork under hot water to remove any excess oil. Discard the fat from the pan, then return the pork to the pan and add enough cold water to cover well. Add the ginger slices and bring to the boil over high heat. Reduce to a simmer, cover and cook for 2½ hours, topping up the water if needed.

Remove the pork and 750 ml (26 fl oz/3 cups) of the cooking liquid from the pan and put into a clean saucepan, along with the dashi granules, sake, mirin, rice vinegar, sugar, tamari and soy sauce. Return to the heat and bring to the boil, then reduce to a simmer and cook, uncovered, for 1–1¼ hours, or until the pork is very tender but not falling apart. Carefully turn the pork a couple of times while it is cooking to help promote more even cooking.

Remove from the heat and allow the pork to rest in the liquid for 20 minutes, then remove and cut into slices approximately 2 cm (¾ in) thick. Serve the pork with rice and steamed green vegetables, such as bok choy (pak choi), choy sum, snow peas (mangetout) and asparagus. Spoon over some of the cooking liquid and serve. Try it with some hot Japanese mustard, *karashi*, if desired.

Hailing from Okinawa, and of Chinese influence, is this very rich, tender pork dish. Only small amounts are needed but it makes for a hearty meal when accompanied by rice and steamed green vegetables.

sweet simmered pork

2 teaspoons vegetable oil
½ teaspoon sesame oil
1 kg (2 lb 4 oz) boneless pork belly
150 g (5½ oz/1¼ cups) sliced ginger
2 teaspoons dashi granules
170 ml (5½ fl oz/⅔ cup) sake
60 ml (2 fl oz/¼ cup) mirin
60 ml (2 fl oz/¼ cup) Japanese rice vinegar
55 g (2 oz/⅓ cup) black sugar or dark brown sugar
60 ml (2 fl oz/¼ cup) tamari
60 ml (2 fl oz/¼ cup) Japanese soy sauce

serves 4

hint: For a more aromatic and spiced version, add a star anise and a cinnamon stick to the saucepan when you add the other flavourings during the second stage of cooking.

Salmon is one of the few fish that benefits from a flavoursome sauce—with most white-fleshed fish you can end up masking the natural flavour. The sauce used here is similar to teriyaki, but it is not as sweet because of the addition of citrus juice. This recipe is also great with tuna or swordfish.

salmon with citrus soy glaze

4 x 200 g (7 oz) salmon fillets, skin on

1 tablespoon vegetable oil

1 teaspoon sesame oil

1½ tablespoons Japanese soy sauce

60 ml (2 fl oz/¼ cup) sake

1 tablespoon mirin

1 tablespoon lemon or lime juice, or a combination
of both

2 teaspoons caster (superfine) sugar

40 g (1½ oz) unsalted butter

¼ teaspoon finely grated ginger

black sesame seeds, to garnish

serves 4

Carefully check the salmon for bones, pulling any out with clean tweezers. Season lightly with salt.

Heat the vegetable and sesame oils in a large heavy-based frying pan over medium–high heat and add the salmon pieces, skin-side down. Cook for 4 minutes, or until the skin is golden. Reduce the heat to medium, turn the fish over and cook for 2–3 minutes, or until almost cooked through. Remove from the pan, cover and set aside.

Remove any excess oil from the pan, then add the soy sauce, sake, mirin, lemon juice, sugar, butter and ginger to the pan, increase the heat to high and stir to dissolve the sugar. Bring to the boil and cook for 4–5 minutes, or until the sauce is quite glazy.

Garnish with the sesame seeds and serve the sauce on the side, for drizzling over the salmon. Serve with rice and a mix of steamed green vegetables, such as asparagus, bok choy (pak choi), sugarsnap peas, snow peas (mangetout) or green soya beans.

Although the eggplant in this recipe is prepared, cooked and dressed in the traditional Japanese manner, I've strayed from tradition by pairing it with lamb, a meat introduced to Japan only in recent years. The smoky flavour of the eggplant is perfectly partnered with lamb.

lamb with grilled eggplant

6 long, slender eggplants (aubergines)

1½ tablespoons Japanese soy sauce

½ teaspoon grated ginger and its juice

1 garlic clove, crushed

⅛ teaspoon dashi granules, dissolved in
60 ml (2 fl oz/¼ cup) hot water

pinch of caster (superfine) sugar

2 tablespoons vegetable oil

½ teaspoon sesame oil

4 x 200 g (7 oz) lamb backstraps or loin fillets

seven-spice mix, to season (optional)

shiso leaves, to garnish

serves 4

Preheat the griller (broiler) to high. Brush the eggplants with a little oil, prick them a few times with a skewer, then place under the griller and cook for about 12 minutes, turning regularly until the skin is slightly blackened and wrinkled and the flesh feels soft to the touch. Immediately remove from the heat and plunge into iced water. Leave until just cool enough to handle, then remove all blackened and blistered skin. Cut each eggplant into 4 cm (1½ in) lengths and put into a bowl.

Combine the soy sauce, ginger and juice, garlic, dashi and sugar and stir until the sugar dissolves. Pour over the eggplant and turn to coat well.

Heat the vegetable and sesame oils in a large frying pan over medium–high heat. Season the lamb with salt, pepper and the seven-spice mix, if using, and cook on each side for 3 minutes for rare, or a little longer if preferred. Remove from the pan and rest for 5 minutes. Slice off the ends on the diagonal and discard them, then slice the backstrap into two pieces, again on the diagonal and in the same direction.

Place a few shiso leaves on each plate, then arrange the eggplant and lamb on top. Drizzle over any dressing left in the bowl and serve immediately.

This dish is a little French, a little Italian and, of course, a little Japanese. I love the combination of the veal with the sweetness of the vegetables and the earthy, savoury mayonnaise. Mirin, rice vinegar and shiitake mushrooms give an extra dimension to what is basically ratatouille.

veal cutlets with japanese ratatouille and soy mayonnaise

60 ml (2 fl oz/¼ cup) vegetable oil

1 teaspoon sesame oil

1 leek, chopped

2 teaspoons grated ginger

2 garlic cloves, crushed

3 long, slender eggplants (aubergines), halved lengthways and thickly sliced

2 zucchini (courgettes), halved lengthways and thickly sliced

1 red capsicum (pepper), cut into 2 cm (¾ in) squares

100 g (3½ oz/2 cups) shiitake mushrooms, stems discarded, caps quartered

60 ml (2 fl oz/¼ cup) mirin

60 ml (2 fl oz/¼ cup) Japanese rice vinegar

185 ml (6 fl oz/¾ cup) ready-made puréed tomatoes

pinch of caster (superfine) sugar

4 x 225 g (8 oz) veal cutlets

ground white pepper

1 tablespoon finely shredded shiso or basil leaves

soy mayonnaise

2 teaspoons white miso

½ teaspoon Japanese soy sauce

1 garlic clove, crushed

125 g (4½ oz/½ cup) Japanese mayonnaise

serves 4

Heat 2 tablespoons of the combined vegetable and sesame oils in a large deep-sided frying pan over medium heat. Add the leek and cook for 5 minutes, or until lightly golden. Add the ginger and garlic and cook for a few seconds, then add the eggplant, zucchini, capsicum and shiitake and sauté for about 10 minutes, or until lightly golden. Add the mirin and cook for 1 minute, then add the vinegar, tomato purée, sugar and 60 ml (2 fl oz/¼ cup) water and stir to combine. Bring to the boil, then reduce to a simmer and cook for about 20 minutes, or until the vegetables are very tender but not falling apart. Season to taste.

To make the soy mayonnaise, mix the miso, soy sauce and garlic until smooth, then whisk into the mayonnaise and set aside.

Season the veal with salt and white pepper. Put the remaining oil in a large heavy-based frying pan over high heat. Add the veal and cook for 4 minutes on each side, or until cooked to your liking. Remove from the heat, cover and rest for a few minutes.

Stir the shiso through the vegetables, then divide between four plates, top with a veal cutlet and a dollop of soy mayonnaise and serve immediately.

This simple dish hints of Thailand, with its combination of salty, sweet, hot and sour flavours, frequently used in Thai stir-fries, dressings and dipping sauces.

caramel chicken with shiso

1 tablespoon vegetable oil

½ teaspoon sesame oil

4 garlic cloves, thinly sliced lengthways

2 small red chillies, seeded and julienned

4 x 150 g (5½ oz) chicken breast fillets,
   skin on

60 ml (2 fl oz/¼ cup) Japanese rice vinegar

60 ml (2 fl oz/¼ cup) mirin

3 tablespoons caster (superfine) sugar

⅛ teaspoon dashi granules

2 teaspoons Japanese soy sauce

4 shiso leaves, finely shredded

serves 4

Heat the vegetable and sesame oils in a large frying pan over low heat (don't use a non-stick pan for this recipe). Add the garlic and chilli and stir for 3 minutes, or until the garlic is evenly golden and crisp. Remove with a slotted spoon and set aside.

Increase the heat to medium–high and place the seasoned chicken, skin-side down, in the pan. Cook for 5 minutes, then turn and cook for 5 minutes on the other side, or until just cooked through. Remove and set aside.

Combine the vinegar, mirin, sugar, dashi and soy sauce with 60 ml (2 fl oz/¼ cup) water and slowly add to the pan, being careful as it may splatter. Stir to dissolve the sugar, then add the garlic and chilli and continue to stir, scraping up any cooked sediment from the base of the pan. Bring to the boil and cook for 3–5 minutes, or until slightly glazy. Return the chicken to the pan, add the shredded shiso, and turn the chicken to coat in the sauce. Remove from the heat and drizzle with any sauce left in the pan. Serve with rice and steamed greens.

hint: If you can't find shiso, try Thai basil.

In Japan, 'borrowed' words are used for many Western items, particularly food, and *hambaagaa* is one of them (read it slowly, pronouncing the 'aa' as 'ah'). Although Japanese *hambaagaas* are usually served drizzled with a mixture of soy sauce and grated daikon, which I highly recommend, I have opted here for a lovely creamy mushroom sauce.

japanese hambaagaa with mushroom sauce

300 g (10½ oz) minced (ground) pork

300 g (10½ oz) minced (ground) beef

1 small onion, finely chopped

80 g (2¾ oz/1¼ cups) Japanese breadcrumbs

2 garlic cloves, crushed

2 teaspoons finely grated ginger and its juice

1 egg, lightly beaten

60 ml (2 fl oz/¼ cup) Japanese soy sauce

60 ml (2 fl oz/¼ cup) mirin

2 teaspoons vegetable oil

½ teaspoon sesame oil

20 g (¾ oz) butter

100 g (3½ oz/2 cups) shiitake mushrooms, stems discarded, caps thinly sliced

150 g (5½ oz/1⅔ cups) shimeji mushrooms, pulled apart

200 g (7 oz/2⅔ cups) enoki mushrooms, ends trimmed, pulled apart in small clumps

¼ teaspoon dashi granules

170 ml (5½ fl oz/⅔ cup) cream

serves 4

Combine the pork, beef, onion, breadcrumbs, garlic, ginger and juice, egg, 2 tablespoons of the soy sauce and 1 tablespoon of the mirin, and season. Shape into eight equal-sized oval patties, about 2.5 cm (1 in) thick, place on a tray in a single layer, cover and refrigerate for 2 hours to allow the flavours to develop.

Heat the vegetable and sesame oils in a large non-stick frying pan over high heat and cook the patties in batches for 1–2 minutes on each side, or until browned. Reduce the heat to medium and cook for a further 3–4 minutes on each side, or until just cooked through. Remove from the pan, cover and set aside.

Add the butter to the pan, then add the shiitake, shimeji and a pinch of salt and cook for about 4 minutes, or until softened and starting to colour. Add the enoki, the remaining soy sauce and mirin, the dashi granules and cream and bring to the boil. Cook for 2 minutes, or until the sauce has thickened slightly and is of a coating consistency. Stir in any juices from the resting meat, season to taste, then add the patties and turn to coat. Cook for a further minute to heat through.

Place two patties on each plate, spoon on the mushroom sauce and serve immediately. Great with steamed greens or Green salad with Japanese dressing (page 142).

This chicken schnitzel is first marinated, then coated in breadcrumbs spiced with *shichimi togarashi*, a seven-flavour spice mix. The base of the spice mix is chilli, along with six other possible flavours—often sesame seeds, sansho pepper, shiso, mustard, nori flakes or poppy seeds. Regional variations are found at local Japanese markets.

shichimi schnitzel

4 x 175 g (6 oz) chicken thigh fillets
1½ tablespoons Japanese soy sauce
1½ tablespoons mirin
2 teaspoons finely grated ginger
3 garlic cloves, crushed
1 tablespoon seven-spice mix
60 g (2¼ oz/½ cup) plain (all-purpose) flour
½ teaspoon salt
125 g (4½ oz/2 cups) Japanese breadcrumbs
2 eggs, lightly beaten
vegetable oil, for deep-frying
125 ml (4 fl oz/½ cup) sesame oil, for deep-frying
   (optional)
chopped mitsuba or flat-leaf (Italian) parsley, to serve
lemon wedges, to serve

serves 4

Place a piece of chicken between two pieces of plastic wrap and pound with a meat mallet or the back of a heavy knife to flatten to 5 mm (¼ in) thick. Continue with the remaining chicken to make four schnitzels.

Combine the soy sauce, mirin, ginger, garlic and half the seven-spice mix in a non-metallic dish, add the chicken and turn to coat. Cover with plastic wrap and refrigerate for 1 hour.

Combine the flour with the salt in a bowl. In another bowl, combine the remaining seven-spice mix with the breadcrumbs. Lift the schnitzels out of the marinade, allowing the excess to drip off. Lightly coat the chicken in the flour, then dip into the egg and coat with the spiced breadcrumbs, pressing the breadcrumbs to help them adhere. Refrigerate for 30 minutes.

Fill a deep-fat fryer or large saucepan one-third full with vegetable oil and add the sesame oil, if using. Heat to 170°C (325°F), or until a cube of bread dropped into the oil browns in 20 seconds. Lower one or two schnitzels at a time into the oil and cook for about 5 minutes, or until golden and cooked through. Drain well on paper towels and keep warm in a very low oven while you cook the rest. Sprinkle with the mitsuba and serve immediately with lemon wedges. Great with Japanese coleslaw (page 145) and Potato salad (page 150).

hint: Make a great chicken schnitzel sandwich with some lettuce, Lebanese (short) cucumber, Japanese mayonnaise and tonkatsu sauce. Both the mayonnaise and tonkatsu sauce are available at Japanese grocery stores.

Seaweed paste is a rather unattractive black paste made from kelp, but it has a divine sweet yet salty, mellow flavour that is absolutely delicious with steak.

beef fillet steak with seaweed butter

100 g (3½ oz) unsalted butter, softened

3 teaspoons prepared seaweed paste, or to taste

1 tablespoon nori flakes

1 garlic clove, crushed

1 tablespoon vegetable oil

½ teaspoon sesame oil

4 x 200 g (7 oz) fillet steaks

1 tablespoon finely chopped chives

serves 4

Combine the softened butter with the prepared seaweed paste, nori flakes and garlic and season. Shape the butter into a small squarish log, about 4 cm (1½ in) in diameter, then wrap it in a large piece of plastic wrap. Refrigerate the butter for 20 minutes, or until firm.

When ready to start cooking the steaks, remove the butter from the fridge to soften slightly. Heat the vegetable and sesame oils in a frying pan over medium heat. Season the steaks with salt and pepper and cook for 4–5 minutes on each side for rare to medium, or until cooked to your liking.

Remove the steaks from the pan and rest for 5 minutes before topping with a couple of slices of the softened butter and a sprinkling of chives. Great with boiled new potatoes and Asian greens or a green salad.

hint: Prepared seaweed paste, *nori tsukudani*, is available in Asian grocery stores. The labels of some call it 'prepared', and others, 'seasoned', but they are the same thing. Different brands may vary in strength. The paste can be also added to sauces or soups for a boost of flavour.

Nashi, a type of Japanese pear that actually looks more like an apple, stays quite crisp when cooked this way and makes for a refreshing balance with the rich pork and mustard cream sauce. Brown nashi have a more caramel flavour than the pale green yellow-skinned variety.

pan-fried pork cutlets with nashi

2 nashi
20 g (¾ oz) butter
1 teaspoon vegetable oil
1 teaspoon sesame oil
4 x 200 g (7 oz) pork cutlets
1 small garlic clove, crushed
60 ml (2 fl oz/¼ cup) mirin
80 ml (2½ fl oz/⅓ cup) chicken stock
1 tablespoon Japanese rice vinegar
½ teaspoon Japanese mustard
170 ml (5½ fl oz/⅔ cup) cream
2 shiso leaves, finely shredded

serves 4

Trim the ends off the top and bottom of the nashi and discard them. Slice the remaining nashi into 1.5 cm (⅝ in) thick discs so that you can see the cross-section and a little star in the centre of each (you will need eight slices in total). Put the butter in a large frying pan over medium heat and fry the nashi, in batches if necessary, for about 2 minutes on each side, or until golden and slightly tender. Remove the nashi from the pan, cover to keep warm, and set aside.

Add the vegetable and sesame oils to the pan and heat over medium–high heat. Season the pork cutlets and cook on each side for 4–5 minutes, or

until just cooked through. Remove from the pan and cover to keep warm.

Add the garlic, mirin, stock and vinegar and bring to the boil, scraping up any cooked sediment on the base of the pan. Over high heat, add the mustard and cream to the pan, along with any juices from the resting pork, season to taste and bring to the boil again. Cook for 2 minutes, or until the sauce has thickened slightly.

Arrange a pork cutlet with two nashi slices on each plate and spoon over the sauce. Sprinkle the shiso over the top and serve immediately. Great with Daikon hash browns (page 153) and steamed greens or a green salad.

Although one of my absolute favourite foods is a simply seasoned, perfectly roasted chicken, I have recently become extremely fond of a different method of preparation. For this dish, you will need to start the day before, as overnight marinating allows the flavours to develop and the meat to tenderize, but it's well worth the little extra effort for succulent, flavoursome chicken.

soy roast chicken

2 kg (4 lb 8 oz) whole chicken
125 ml (4 fl oz/½ cup) Japanese soy sauce
60 ml (2 fl oz/¼ cup) mirin
60 ml (2 fl oz/¼ cup) sake
100 g (3½ oz/⅓ cup) white miso
2 tablespoons soya bean oil or vegetable oil
5 garlic cloves, bruised
80 g (2¾ oz) ginger, sliced
1 teaspoon soft brown sugar

serves 4–6

Rinse the chicken inside and out and pat dry. Put the soy sauce, mirin, sake, miso and soya bean oil in a non-metallic dish, large enough to easily fit the chicken, then mix until smooth. Add the chicken and turn to coat well in the marinade. Loosen the skin covering the breast and spoon some of the marinade under the skin and some into the cavity. Cover and refrigerate overnight, occasionally turning the chicken in the marinade.

Preheat the oven to 190°C (375°F/Gas 5). Remove the chicken from the dish, reserving the marinade, and place on a rack in a roasting tin. Stuff the cavity with the garlic and ginger and pour 500 ml (17 fl oz/2 cups) water into the base of the tin.

Sprinkle the chicken with salt, then put in the preheated oven and cook for 1–1¼ hours, or until the juices run clear when a skewer is pierced through the thickest part of the thigh. Allow to rest for 15 minutes before carving.

Meanwhile, put the reserved marinade in a small saucepan with the brown sugar and boil for about 5 minutes, or until thickened slightly. Add any resting juices from the chicken and boil until reduced again. Carve the chicken and serve with the sauce on the side. Great with Honey soy roast vegetables (page 157) and steamed Asian greens.

Marinating or preserving foods in miso has been a popular practice in Japan dating back as far as the 12th century. Although miso is used to make wonderful pickles and condiments, it also renders meat particularly tender and flavoursome. I love the slightly sweet, earthy hint that miso gives to the lamb.

lamb racks in miso

2 x 8 racks of lamb
2 tablespoons white miso
2 tablespoons red miso
2 garlic cloves, crushed
80 g (2¾ oz/1¼ cups) Japanese breadcrumbs
1 teaspoon finely chopped lemon zest
2 small handfuls mitsuba or flat-leaf (Italian) parsley, finely chopped
60 g (2¼ oz) butter, melted
ground white pepper

serves 4

Trim any excess fat from around the bones of the lamb racks. Combine the white and red miso with the garlic, then rub the mixture all over the meat. Place in a ceramic dish and cover tightly with plastic wrap so the miso doesn't dry out too much. Refrigerate overnight.

When ready to cook, preheat the oven to 190°C (375°F/Gas 5). To make a breadcrumb crust for the lamb, combine the breadcrumbs, lemon zest, mitsuba and melted butter in a bowl and season with a little salt and white pepper.

With a clean, damp cloth, wipe the top bones of the rack to remove any miso, as it may burn. Place the racks together so their bones interlock, then stand the racks upright in the dish (this helps to promote even cooking).

Evenly pat the breadcrumb mixture onto the outside of the rack, pressing down to adhere the crumbs. Place the rack in a roasting tin, put in the preheated oven and cook for 35 minutes, or until pink to medium–rare, or until cooked to your liking. Serve with Roast pumpkin and ginger mash (page 154) and steamed greens.

soya beans and vegetables with roasted garlic aïoli

425 g (15 oz/2¼ cups) dried soya beans

5 x 10 cm (2 x 4 in) piece of kombu, wiped with a
   damp cloth

3 bay leaves

2 garlic cloves, bruised

60 ml (2 fl oz/¼ cup) soya bean oil or olive oil

40 g (1½ oz) butter

2 large onions, chopped

3 carrots, cut into 3 cm (1¼ in) lengths

2 celery stalks, cut into 3 cm (1¼ in) lengths

250 g (9 oz) daikon, cut into 2 cm (¾ in) cubes

3 long, slender eggplants (aubergines), cut into
   3 cm (1¼ in) lengths

125 g (4½ oz/1½ cups) peeled and shaved fresh
   burdock root (see page 188)

1½ tablespoons plain (all-purpose) flour

185 ml (6 fl oz/¾ cup) mirin

125 ml (4 fl oz/½ cup) sake

400 g (14 oz) tin crushed tomatoes

750 ml (26 fl oz/3 cups) vegetable stock, or
   1¼ teaspoons dashi granules, dissolved in
   750 ml (26 fl oz/3 cups) water

2 tablespoons red miso

2 tablespoons Japanese soy sauce

1 tablespoon finely chopped thyme

2 teaspoons finely grated ginger

1 teaspoon lemon zest, very finely chopped

90 g (3¼ oz/1½ cups) Japanese breadcrumbs,
   seasoned

2 tablespoons finely chopped mitsuba
   or flat-leaf (Italian) parsley

roasted garlic aïoli

1 head of garlic

olive oil, to drizzle

150 g (5½ oz/⅔ cup) Japanese mayonnaise

serves 6–8

Soak the soya beans and kombu overnight in cold water. Drain, discard the kombu, and put the beans in a large saucepan with 2 of the bay leaves and the garlic cloves and cover with water by 10 cm (4 in). Bring to the boil, then reduce to a simmer and cook for 2½ hours, or until tender. Rinse and drain.

Preheat the oven to 170°C (325°F/Gas 3). Heat half the oil and half the butter with the remaining bay leaf in a large, deep-sided frying pan over medium heat, add the onions and cook for 15 minutes, or until deep golden. Remove and set aside. Pour in a little more oil, if needed, then add the carrots, celery and daikon and cook, stirring occasionally, for 15 minutes, or until golden. Add to the onions. Pour in the remaining oil and add the eggplant and burdock and cook for 5 minutes, or until lightly golden, then set aside with the other vegetables.

Add the remaining butter to the pan, then add the flour and cook for 1 minute. Gradually whisk in the mirin and sake until smooth. Stir in the tomatoes, stock or dashi, miso, soy sauce, thyme, ginger and lemon zest. Bring to the boil, then reduce to a simmer for 10 minutes, or until thickened slightly.

Combine the soya beans with the vegetables and sauce. Season well. Put in a 4 litre (140 fl oz/16 cup) casserole dish and cover. Cook for 2 hours, or until the beans are tender, then uncover and sprinkle with the combined breadcrumbs and mitsuba. Cook, uncovered, for 30 minutes, or until the top is golden and crisp.

To make the aïoli, slice the top off the whole garlic head. Place in a small baking dish, drizzle with olive oil and season. Cover tightly with foil and put on a separate shelf in the oven. Cook for 25 minutes, or until the cloves are very soft. Allow to cool, then squeeze each clove from its skin and mash to a paste. Mix with the mayonnaise and season. Serve the casserole with the aïoli on the side to dollop over as desired. Great with a green salad.

Pork belly is a standard cut in Japan and other Asian countries and is now becoming increasingly popular in Western cooking. This tender meat is wonderful for roasting and the boneless, regular-shaped slabs make for shorter but more even cooking and very easy carving. Fuji apples hold together well during cooking, so are great when making a chunky-style apple sauce.

roast pork belly with fuji apple sauce

1 kg (2 lb 4 oz) boneless pork belly
1½ teaspoons sea salt flakes
vegetable oil
1 leek, sliced
1 large carrot, chopped
1 celery stalk, chopped
4 garlic cloves, bruised
2 bay leaves, crumbled
1½ tablespoons plain (all-purpose) flour
185 ml (6 fl oz/¾ cup) chicken stock

fuji apple sauce
2 Fuji apples, peeled and diced
2 teaspoons finely grated ginger and its juice
1½ tablespoons Japanese rice vinegar
80 ml (2½ fl oz/⅓ cup) mirin
pinch of sugar

serves 4

Preheat the oven to 200°C (400°F/Gas 6). Rub the pork skin with the salt flakes and a little vegetable oil. Combine the leek, carrot, celery, garlic and bay leaves and place in the centre of a roasting tin. Sit the pork on top of the vegetables and put in the oven. Pour 375 ml (13 fl oz/1½ cups) water into

the base of the tin and cook for 1 hour, or until the skin is crispy and the meat is cooked through.

While the meat is cooking, make the apple sauce. Combine the apples, ginger and juice, rice vinegar, mirin, sugar and a pinch of salt with 60 ml (2 fl oz/¼ cup) water in a small saucepan. Cook over low heat, stirring regularly so the apples don't stick to the pan, for about 40 minutes, or until the apples are very soft but not mushy—there should still be a few chunks of apple.

When the pork is cooked, remove from the heat, cover lightly with foil and rest for 10–15 minutes before carving.

While the meat is resting, tip the vegetables and juices from the roasting tin into a fine sieve over a bowl. Press down to extract as much flavour and juice as possible—you should have about 125 ml (4 fl oz/½ cup). Allow the juices to sit so the fat rises to the top. Spoon off 1½ tablespoons of fat and put into a small saucepan over medium–high heat, then stir in the flour and cook for 1 minute.

Discard any remaining fat on top of the juices, then gradually whisk the juices and the chicken stock into the flour mixture until a smooth gravy is formed. Bring to the boil and cook for 1–2 minutes, or until thickened slightly. Season to taste.

Carve the pork into thick slices and serve with gravy and apple sauce. Serve with Daikon and potato gratin (page 161), and steamed greens or Green beans with sesame miso dressing (page 146).

This slow method of cooking duck results in the crispiest of skin and a melt-in-the-mouth tender flesh. The dried zest of the yuzu, a large Japanese citrus fruit, adds an exotic flavour and aroma to the delicious savoury meat and sweet caramelized peaches.

slow-roasted duck with yuzu peaches

2.5 kg (5 lb 8 oz) whole duck

sea salt flakes

a few drops of sesame oil

1 head of garlic

80 g (2¾ oz/⅔ cup) sliced ginger

2 teaspoons dried yuzu pieces, or lemon zest

800 g (1 lb 12 oz) kipfler (fingerling) potatoes, sliced in half lengthways

2 bay leaves

3 peaches

2 tablespoons sugar

60 ml (2 fl oz/¼ cup) Japanese rice vinegar

serves 4

Preheat the oven to 120°C (230°F/Gas ½). To prepare the duck, discard the parson's nose and a small amount of the surrounding area to remove the oil glands. Discard the neck and giblets, if intact. Rinse the duck well, then thoroughly pat dry with paper towels. Carefully prick the skin all over by inserting a thin skewer in and under the skin at an angle almost parallel to the duck—this will prevent you from piercing the flesh.

Rub the duck all over, inside and out, with sea salt flakes and the sesame oil. Separate the garlic cloves from the head and place the unpeeled cloves inside the duck cavity, along with the ginger

slices and 1½ teaspoons of the yuzu. Place the duck, breast-side up, on a 'V' rack in a roasting tin, tucking the wings under, and roast on the middle shelf of the oven for 2½ hours. There is no need to baste during the cooking time.

Remove the duck from the oven. Increase the oven temperature to 200°C (400°F/Gas 6). Spoon the fat from the duck's roasting tin into a second roasting tin. Add the potatoes and bay leaves, toss to coat in the fat, then sprinkle with sea salt.

Pour 500 ml (17 fl oz/2 cups) water into the base of the duck's roasting tin and return to the top shelf of the oven, only when the oven has reached 200°C (400°F/Gas 6). At the same time, put the potatoes on the shelf below. Cook for 1¼ hours.

Meanwhile, cut the peaches into quarters, discarding the stone. Put the sugar, vinegar, 2 tablespoons water and the remaining yuzu pieces in a frying pan over high heat and stir until the sugar has dissolved. Bring to the boil and cook for 1 minute, or until pale gold in colour, then add the peach pieces and cook for 5 minutes, occasionally stirring carefully, until the peaches are soft but not mushy.

When the duck is crisp and golden all over, remove from the oven, cover lightly with foil and leave to rest for 10–15 minutes. Move the potatoes up to the top shelf and continue to cook for 15 minutes while you rest and carve the duck. Serve the duck with the potatoes and peaches.

This is a modern twist on an old classic. I love Béarnaise any way it is served, but this one is lighter and sweeter in flavour than the traditional version due to the addition of rice vinegar and mirin.

sansho beef with rice vinegar béarnaise

1.8 kg (4 lb) whole fillet of beef

2 teaspoons sansho pepper

½ teaspoon ground black pepper

½ teaspoon ground white pepper

2 teaspoons salt

2 tablespoons vegetable oil

350 g (12 oz/2 bunches) spring onions (scallions), cleaned and trimmed to a uniform length

béarnaise

60 ml (2 fl oz/¼ cup) Japanese rice vinegar

60 ml (2 fl oz/¼ cup) sake

60 ml (2 fl oz/¼ cup) mirin

2 spring onions (scallions), finely chopped

3 stems (not leaves) from mitsuba or flat-leaf (Italian) parsley, chopped

¼ teaspoon whole black peppercorns

4 large egg yolks

200 g (7 oz) chilled butter, cut into small dice

1 tablespoon finely chopped mitsuba or flat-leaf (Italian) parsley

serves 8–10

Tuck under the small end of the beef fillet so the end is about as thick as the large end, then tie up with kitchen string. This will promote more even cooking. Combine the sansho pepper and black and white peppers with the salt, then rub the mixture all over the beef.

Preheat the oven to 190°C (375°F/Gas 5). Heat the oil in a large frying pan over high heat and brown the beef well on all sides—cook each side for about 2 minutes, then turn. Arrange the spring onions over the base of a roasting tin and sit the beef on top of them. Cook in the preheated oven for 35–40 minutes for medium–rare, or until cooked to your liking. Rest for 10–15 minutes before slicing.

While the beef is cooking, make the Béarnaise. Combine the rice vinegar, sake, mirin, chopped spring onions, mitsuba stems and peppercorns in a small saucepan and bring to the boil over high heat. Cook for 6–7 minutes, or until reduced to about 1½ tablespoons.

Remove from the heat and strain into a heatproof bowl, then whisk in the egg yolks until smooth. Place over a small saucepan of simmering water, ensuring the water is not touching the bowl, and whisk until thick and frothy—about 2–3 minutes. Gradually whisk in the butter, piece by piece, until you have a thick, creamy sauce. Don't rush this process—it should take 8–10 minutes.

Remove from the heat, season to taste with a little salt and add a dash more vinegar if you like. Stir through the mitsuba and serve with the sliced beef and spring onions. Serve this dish with boiled baby potatoes and steamed Asian greens, green beans or asparagus.

hint: You can make the Béarnaise ahead of time and refrigerate it. Just make sure you reheat it very gently, whisking as you do so, until it is just heated, otherwise it will separate and become oily.

chicken pot pies

pastry

325 g (11½ oz/2½ cups) plain (all-purpose) flour

½ teaspoon sugar

90 g (3¼ oz) chilled butter, cut into small dice

2 tablespoons nori flakes

filling

1 teaspoon dashi granules

60 ml (2 fl oz/¼ cup) mirin

1 bay leaf

750 g (1 lb 10 oz) chicken thigh fillets, cut into
    bite-sized pieces

1 streaky bacon rasher, finely chopped

50 g (1¾ oz) butter

1 leek, thinly sliced

60 g (2¼ oz/½ cup) plain (all-purpose) flour

375 ml (13 fl oz/1½ cups) cream

½ teaspoon Japanese mustard

1 tablespoon white miso

1 garlic clove, crushed

1 teaspoon sesame oil

200 g (7 oz) daikon, cut into 1 cm (½ in) dice

1 carrot, cut into 1 cm (½ in) dice

1 celery stalk, cut into 1 cm (½ in) dice

100 g (3½ oz/2 cups) shiitake mushrooms, stems
    discarded, caps chopped

50 g (1¾ oz/⅓ cup) frozen peas, thawed

1 egg, beaten

makes 6

To make the pastry, sift the flour, sugar and a large pinch of salt into a bowl. Rub the butter in with your fingertips until the mixture resembles breadcrumbs. Using a flat-bladed knife, mix in the nori flakes, then gradually mix in 5–7 tablespoons iced water, using a cutting action, until the mixture forms small clumps. Gather into a ball and flatten into a disc. Cover with plastic wrap and refrigerate for about 30 minutes.

To make the filling, put the dashi granules, mirin, bay leaf and 375 ml (13 fl oz/1½ cups) water in a saucepan and bring to the boil. Add the chicken and allow to just come to the boil again. Cook for 2 minutes, or until almost cooked through, then remove with a slotted spoon, cool slightly, cover and refrigerate. Strain and reserve the cooking liquid and the bay leaf.

Sauté the bacon in a saucepan over medium heat for 1 minute, or until starting to brown. Set aside. Add half the butter and the leek and cook for 8 minutes, or until golden. Add the flour and cook for 1 minute. Gradually stir the reserved cooking liquid into the flour to form a smooth sauce. Add the cream and bay leaf and bring to the boil. Reduce to a simmer and cook for 30 minutes, stirring occasionally, until it becomes a thick white sauce. Stir in the mustard, miso and garlic. Discard the bay leaf.

Put the remaining butter and the sesame oil in a frying pan over medium–high heat, add the daikon, carrot, celery and shiitake and cook, stirring regularly, for 10–12 minutes until golden. Add the vegetables to the white sauce, along with the peas, chicken and bacon. Divide the mixture between six 375 ml (13 fl oz/1½ cup) ramekins or small ovenproof ceramic dishes and refrigerate until chilled.

Preheat the oven to 180°C (350°F/Gas 4). Divide the pastry into six equal portions, then roll out each separately between two pieces of baking paper so that they are larger in diameter than the tops of the ramekins. Remove one piece of baking paper and invert the pastry onto the top of the ramekins. Peel off the top layer and gently press the overhanging edges around the side of each dish to help adhere. Trim to neaten. Pierce the lid to form an air vent. Refrigerate for at least 20 minutes.

Brush the tops of the pies with beaten egg, avoiding the air vent, then bake for 35–40 minutes, or until the pastry is golden and the filling is heated through.

137

I have enjoyed many versions of this dish during my travels throughout Japan. It is basically an Italian recipe that is quite similar to lasagne, but made with rice instead of pasta. It's no wonder then that a rice-loving country like Japan would embrace it with such enthusiasm.

seafood doria

béchamel sauce
50 g (1¾ oz) butter
60 g (2¼ oz/½ cup) plain (all-purpose) flour
large pinch of freshly grated nutmeg
600 ml (21 fl oz) milk
1 bay leaf
125 ml (4 fl oz/½ cup) cream

1 tablespoon olive oil
20 g (¾ oz) butter
1 onion, finely chopped
2 streaky bacon rashers, chopped
1 garlic clove, crushed
1 small red capsicum (pepper), cut into small dice
150 g (5½ oz/1⅔ cups) shimeji mushrooms, pulled apart
16 raw medium prawns (shrimp), peeled and deveined
16 large white scallops without roe, muscle removed
2 tablespoons mirin
¼ teaspoon dashi granules
60 g (2¼ oz/¼ cup) tomato paste (purée)
1 kg (2 lb 4 oz/6 cups) cooked Japanese short-grain rice, cooled to room temperature—you will need 550 g (1 lb 4 oz/2½ cups) raw rice
3 teaspoons nori flakes
225 g (8 oz/1½ cups) grated mozzarella cheese
100 g (3½ oz/1 cup) grated Parmesan cheese

serves 6–8

To make the béchamel sauce, heat the butter in a saucepan over medium heat, add the flour and nutmeg and cook, stirring, for 1 minute. Remove from the heat and slowly whisk in the milk until smooth. Add the bay leaf and return to the heat, then stir for 10 minutes, or until the sauce thickens and coats the back of a spoon. Remove from the heat, stir in the cream and cool to room temperature. Discard the bay leaf. Season to taste.

Preheat the oven to 180°C (350°F/Gas 4). Heat half the olive oil and half the butter in a deep-sided frying pan over medium heat, add the onion and cook for 5 minutes, or until soft and lightly golden. Add the bacon, garlic, capsicum and shimeji and cook for 6–7 minutes, or until softened. Remove from the pan and set aside.

Add the remaining oil and butter to the pan and increase the heat to high. Add the prawns and sauté for 30–40 seconds, or until the prawns just turn pink. Remove and set aside with the vegetables. Allow the pan to heat up again and add a little more oil, if needed. Add the scallops and sear on each side for 30 seconds, then set aside. Add the mirin, dashi granules, tomato paste and 250 ml (9 fl oz/1 cup) water to the pan, stirring to scrape up any cooked sediment on the base of the pan, then bring to the boil. Remove from the heat and add the rice, seafood, vegetables and nori flakes and stir to combine well. Season.

Spoon the rice mixture into a greased 3 litre (105 fl oz/12 cup) gratin or ceramic baking dish and smooth over with the back of a spoon. Spoon the béchamel over the top. Sprinkle with the combined mozzarella and Parmesan cheeses and bake in the preheated oven for about 50 minutes, or until the rice is heated through and the top is golden and bubbling. Serve with Green salad with Japanese dressing (page 142).

side plates

Western-style green side salads are very popular in Japan today and they are almost always served with this addictive vinaigrette.

green salad with japanese dressing

100 g (3½ oz/3 cups) mixed salad leaves

175 g (6 oz/1 bunch) asparagus, lightly blanched and refreshed

8 snow peas (mangetout), lightly blanched and refreshed

1 small Lebanese (short) cucumber

1 small ripe avocado

dressing

1½ tablespoons Japanese rice vinegar

2 tablespoons Japanese soy sauce

1 tablespoon mirin

¼ teaspoon finely grated ginger

1 garlic clove, bruised

1 teaspoon caster (superfine) sugar

1½ tablespoons vegetable oil

½ teaspoon sesame oil

serves 4–6

Rinse and drain the salad leaves well, and cut large or long leaves into small bite-sized pieces. Cut the asparagus and snow peas into 3 cm (1¼ in) lengths. Cut the cucumber in half lengthways, scoop out the seeds with a teaspoon, then slice the flesh into half moons. Put in the refrigerator to chill.

Meanwhile, put all the dressing ingredients in a jar and shake well. Leave for 15 minutes to allow the flavours to develop.

When ready to serve, cut the avocado into 2 cm (¾ in) dice, then gently toss together with the salad leaves, asparagus, snow peas and cucumber. Pour over the dressing and serve immediately.

hint: Add some halved cherry tomatoes for colour or add some extra crunch by garnishing with small Japanese rice crackers or crispy wasabi peas (you can find these in your local Asian food store). To make the salad a meal, add some sliced poached or barbecued chicken.

Refreshing and tart with crisp apple
and a light soy and ginger dressing,
this coleslaw is a welcome change
from the usual heavily mayonnaise-
laden versions.

japanese coleslaw

200 g (7 oz) Chinese cabbage
1 carrot, peeled
150 g (5½ oz) daikon, peeled
2 spring onions (scallions), thinly sliced
2½ teaspoons toasted black sesame seeds
1 large Fuji apple

dressing
2 tablespoons Japanese rice vinegar
1½ tablespoons sake
¼ teaspoon Japanese mustard
½ teaspoon sesame oil
1 tablespoon Japanese soy sauce
1½ teaspoons caster (superfine) sugar
½ teaspoon finely grated ginger and its juice

serves 4–6

Combine all the dressing ingredients and whisk
until smooth. Pour over the coleslaw, season to
taste and toss well to combine. Chill for 1 hour
before serving. Great with fried foods.

hint: If you can't resist a creamy coleslaw dressing,
add 90 g (3¼ oz/⅓ cup) Japanese mayonnaise to
the dressing and stir until smooth.

Finely shred the cabbage and place in a large bowl.
Cut the carrot and daikon into 5 cm (2 in) lengths,
then either julienne using a Japanese mandolin
with the coarse-toothed comb, or coarsely grate.
Put the daikon in a colander, sprinkle with salt and
rest for 15 minutes. Use your hands to squeeze
out any excess moisture from the daikon.

Add the daikon and carrot to the cabbage, along
with the spring onions and sesame seeds. Core
the apple (if preferred, you can leave the skin on for
colour and extra nutrients) and julienne with the
Japanese mandolin or coarsely grate. Add to the
other vegetables.

Miso has many uses other than in soups. Here, this versatile ingredient is used in a delicious dressing for crisp green beans.

green beans with sesame miso dressing

250 g (9 oz) green beans, trimmed and cut into
    5 cm (2 in) lengths

dressing
50 g (1¾ oz/⅓ cup) sesame seeds
1 teaspoon sugar
2 tablespoons red or white miso
2 tablespoons mirin

serves 4–6

Bring a saucepan of lightly salted water to the boil, then add the beans and cook for 2 minutes, or until just tender. Drain, plunge into iced water until cool, then drain well.

To make the dressing, dry-fry the sesame seeds over medium heat, stirring regularly, for 5 minutes, or until lightly golden and aromatic. Immediately scoop into a mortar or *suribachi* (ribbed mortar), reserving 1 teaspoon of whole seeds for garnish, and grind until finely crushed. Gradually incorporate the sugar, miso and mirin to form a thickish paste.

Put the beans in a bowl, pour over the dressing and toss to combine. Serve in a bowl and sprinkle with the reserved sesame seeds.

hint: A *suribachi* is a Japanese mortar made from sturdy pottery. It has a ridged or textured interior designed for efficient grinding of ingredients such as sesame seeds.

Sweet corn, brushed with soy sauce and butter—what could be more simple? Great as a healthy, delicious snack and kids love them, so you might want to make a second batch.

corn batayaki

3 corn cobs, halved
30 g (1 oz) butter, melted
3 teaspoons Japanese soy sauce
2 teaspoons mirin
1 teaspoon caster (superfine) sugar

makes 6 pieces

Put the corn in a large saucepan and cover with water. Bring to the boil over high heat and cook for 3 minutes. Drain well, then put the cobs on a baking tray lined with aluminium foil.

Preheat the griller (broiler) to high. Combine the butter, soy sauce, mirin and sugar and brush liberally over the corn. Place under the griller and cook for 2–3 minutes, turning and basting regularly, until golden and slightly blistered. Brush any remaining butter mixture over the corn before serving. Sprinkle with salt and serve immediately.

hint: Try grilling (broiling) other vegetables this way. Make sure you partially cook them first if they are large pieces; smaller vegetables such as asparagus or mushrooms can go straight under the griller.

The Japanese have very successfully adopted and then adapted the humble potato salad. In Japan you find it served at the most unexpected times—at breakfast; or at lunch, neatly tapped from an ice cream scoop into a perfect mound to accompany a sandwich.

potato salad

500 g (1 lb 2 oz) all-purpose potatoes, such as
   desiree, peeled
50 g (1¾ oz) sliced ham
1 Lebanese (short) cucumber

dressing
175 g (6 oz/¾ cup) Japanese mayonnaise
½ teaspoon Japanese mustard
2 tablespoons Japanese rice vinegar
a few drops of sesame oil
2 spring onions (scallions), finely chopped
2 large handfuls mitsuba or flat-leaf (Italian) parsley,
   finely chopped, plus extra to garnish
ground white pepper

serves 6–8

Cut the potatoes into 2 cm (¾ in) dice. Bring a saucepan of salted water to the boil and add the potatoes. Cook for 8–10 minutes, or until tender. Drain, rinse under cold running water, then drain again. Crush the potatoes lightly with a fork but do not mash—there should still be some lumps.

Cut the ham into thin strips, about 3 cm (1¼ in) in length. Cut the cucumber in half lengthways, scoop out the seeds with a teaspoon, and slice the flesh very thinly.

To make the dressing, combine the mayonnaise, mustard, vinegar and sesame oil in a small bowl and mix until smooth, then stir in the spring onions and chopped mitsuba. Season with salt and ground white pepper.

Put the warm potato, ham, cucumber and dressing in a bowl and toss to combine well. Allow to sit for 15 minutes so the potato can absorb some of the dressing and the flavours can develop. Garnish with the extra mitsuba and serve.

Because daikon is so nutritious, it makes you feel a little less guilty about eating something fried and crispy.

daikon hash browns

600 g (1 lb 5 oz) daikon, peeled
1½ teaspoons grated ginger
1 small onion, very finely chopped
1 small handful mitsuba or flat-leaf (Italian) parsley,
    roughly chopped
1 egg, lightly beaten
ground white pepper
60 g (2¼ oz/⅓ cup) potato starch
30 g (1 oz/¼ cup) plain (all-purpose) flour
1½ teaspoons salt
vegetable oil, for shallow-frying

makes 10–12

Cut the daikon into three even pieces, then put the pieces in a saucepan and cover with water. Bring to the boil and cook for 25–30 minutes, or until just tender. Drain well and, when cool enough to handle, coarsely grate into a bowl lined with a tea towel. Gather the tea towel up to enclose the daikon and squeeze out any excess moisture.

Put the squeezed daikon into a clean bowl, then add the ginger, onion, mitsuba and egg, season with white pepper and combine. Mix in the potato starch, flour and the salt.

Pour enough vegetable oil into a deep-sided frying pan to come 5 mm (¼ in) up the side of the pan, then place over medium–high heat. When the oil is hot, add the mixture to the pan in heaped tablespoons, working in batches and flattening the mixture down with the back of the spoon. Cook for 2 minutes on each side, or until crisp and golden. Drain well on paper towels and serve hot as a side dish or as a snack.

Jap pumpkin has a naturally sweet flavour, which is enhanced by roasting. When mashed together with fresh ginger, it makes a wonderful accompaniment to rich roast meats such as lamb, pork or duck.

roast pumpkin and ginger mash

1.5 kg (3 lb 5 oz) jap (kent) pumpkin, seeded and
    cut into 4 even pieces
vegetable oil
sea salt flakes
100 g (3½ oz) butter, cut into small dice
¼ teaspoon sesame oil
2 teaspoons Japanese soy sauce
1½ teaspoons finely grated ginger and its juice
ground white pepper

serves 6

Preheat the oven to 200°C (400°F/Gas 6). Put the pumpkin, skin-side down, in a roasting tin, drizzle with vegetable oil and sprinkle with sea salt. Roast for 1 hour 20 minutes, or until very tender.

Scoop the flesh from the skin and place it in a bowl. Add the butter and sesame oil and mash until very smooth and lump-free. Stir in the soy sauce and ginger and juice and season with a little salt and white pepper, to taste. Reheat gently if necessary.

The addition of honey, soy sauce and a little butter to roast vegetables gives them a slight glaze and sweetness. Although daikon is normally simmered or served raw, it is a welcome addition to the roasted vegetables, giving the dish a real Japanese flavour, perfect for matching with other foods in this book.

honey soy roast vegetables

300 g (10½ oz) white sweet potato

300 g (10½ oz) orange sweet potato

300 g (10½ oz) all-purpose potatoes,
    such as desiree

600 g (1 lb 5 oz) daikon

450 g (1 lb) jap (kent) pumpkin

60 ml (2 fl oz/¼ cup) vegetable oil

1 teaspoon sesame oil

1 teaspoon sea salt flakes

1½ tablespoons honey

10 g (¼ oz) butter

3 teaspoons Japanese soy sauce

1 tablespoon sesame seeds

serves 6

Preheat the oven to 200°C (400°F/Gas 6). Peel all the vegetables except the pumpkin. Remove any seeds from the pumpkin. Cut the vegetables into even-sized pieces, about 4 x 4 cm (1½ x 1½ in). Put the pumpkin in a single layer in one roasting tin and put the other vegetables in a single layer in a second tin. Drizzle with the vegetable and sesame oils and sprinkle with sea salt. (It is a good idea to put the pumpkin in one tin as it may need to be removed from the oven earlier than the other vegetables.) Use your hands to mix the vegetables so they are lightly coated in the oil.

Put the vegetables in the oven and cook for 1 hour, or until golden and just cooked through, shaking the tins occasionally during cooking time. As the pumpkin may cook faster than the other vegetables, check after 35 minutes of cooking, remove it from the oven if cooked, and return to the oven for the last 5 minutes of cooking to heat through. Swap the tins halfway through to ensure even cooking.

Combine the honey, butter, soy sauce and sesame seeds in a small saucepan and heat over medium heat until the butter is melted and the honey is liquid. Combine all the vegetables, put them onto one of the roasting tins and drizzle with the honey mixture. Return to the oven for 10–15 minutes, shaking the tin occasionally, until the vegetables are slightly glazed and the sesame seeds are toasted. Serve with green beans to accompany a roast, or as part of a vegetarian buffet.

Creamy mash with a hint of garlic and mitsuba is perfect for accompanying richly flavoured stews and casseroles. Mitsuba, which translates as 'three leaves', is a type of Japanese parsley with a fresh, slightly peppery flavour.

mitsuba mash

1 kg (2 lb 4 oz) all-purpose potatoes, such as
    desiree, peeled and chopped
60 g (2¼ oz) butter
250 ml (9 fl oz/1 cup) cream
2 garlic cloves, crushed
3 handfuls mitsuba or flat-leaf (Italian) parsley,
    chopped

serves 6

Cook the potatoes in a large saucepan of salted boiling water for 12–15 minutes, or until tender, then drain well. Combine the butter, cream and garlic in a small saucepan and heat gently until the butter melts.

Mash the potatoes while you gradually pour in the cream mixture. Continue mashing until smooth. Stir in the mitsuba and season, to taste.

hint: Add chives or spring onions (scallions) for added flavour.

A perfect accompaniment to roasts and other savoury mains, this creamy gratin is a little lighter in texture than you might expect, thanks to the combination of daikon and potato.

daikon and potato gratin

800 g (1 lb 12 oz) daikon, peeled

1½ tablespoons salt

500 g (1 lb 2 oz) all-purpose potatoes, such as desiree, peeled

600 ml (21 fl oz) cream

5 x 10 cm (2 x 4 in) piece of kombu, wiped with a damp cloth, cut into strips

3 spring onions (scallions), bruised

2 bay leaves

2 garlic cloves, crushed

ground white pepper

serves 6–8

Using a Japanese mandolin or a very steady hand and a sharp knife, slice the daikon into very thin rounds. Toss with the salt and put in a colander over a bowl and allow to drain for 45 minutes. Slice the potatoes in the same manner, put them in a bowl and cover with cold water.

Meanwhile, put the cream, kombu strips, spring onions, bay leaves and garlic in a large saucepan and slowly bring to the boil. Remove the kombu and discard it. Boil for 2 minutes, then discard the spring onions and bay leaves and season well with salt and a little white pepper.

Rinse the daikon well, then drain again and squeeze out any excess moisture with your hands. Drain the potatoes well. Pat dry the daikon and potato slices with paper towels or a clean tea towel.

Preheat the oven to 180°C (350°F/Gas 4). Combine the daikon, potatoes and cream mixture in a bowl, then neatly layer the vegetable slices into a lightly buttered 2 litre (70 fl oz/8 cup) non-metallic gratin or baking dish. Pour over any remaining cream left in the bowl. Cover the dish tightly with foil and cook for 50 minutes, then remove the foil and cook for a further 20 minutes, or until the vegetables are tender and the top is bubbling and golden. Rest for 10 minutes before cutting into slices.

hint: Although you might be tempted, don't skip the salting step (this draws out excess liquid from the water-rich daikon), or you may end up with a rather watery mess. The starch in the potatoes helps to thicken any remaining liquid.

sweet plates

This glistening green jelly with lush fruit salad is great on its own but I can't resist teaming it with green tea ice cream for my own rendition of jelly and ice cream.

midori jelly with green fruit salad

green tea ice cream
250 ml (9 fl oz/1 cup) milk
625 ml (22 fl oz/2½ cups) cream
1 vanilla bean, roughly chopped
9 egg yolks
150 g (5½ oz/⅔ cup) caster (superfine) sugar
3 teaspoons Japanese green tea powder

jelly
150 g (5½ oz/⅔ cup) caster (superfine) sugar
a strip of lemon or lime zest
5 teaspoons gelatine powder
250 ml (9 fl oz/1 cup) Midori or other green, melon-flavoured liqueur

green fruit salad
3 kiwi fruit, peeled
¼ small ripe honeydew melon, peeled and seeds removed
175 g (6 oz/1 cup) green grapes, halved

serves 8

To make the green tea ice cream, pour the milk and cream into a saucepan, add the chopped vanilla bean, and bring just to the boil over medium–high heat. Remove the pan from the heat and allow the vanilla to infuse into the milk mixture for 15 minutes.

Put the egg yolks and sugar in a bowl and beat until creamy. Slowly pour in the milk mixture, whisking as you pour, until smooth. Pour into a clean saucepan and put the pan over medium heat. Stir for 10 minutes, or until the custard is just thick enough to coat the back of a spoon.

Put the green tea in a small bowl, stir in enough of the hot custard to form a paste, then add to the rest of the custard, whisking until smooth and an even green colour. Strain through a fine sieve and cool slightly. Cover and refrigerate until chilled.

Meanwhile, make the jelly. Put the sugar, zest and 625 ml (22 fl oz/2 ½ cups) water in a saucepan and stir over high heat until it boils. Reduce to a simmer and cook for 10 minutes. Turn off the heat.

Put the gelatine in a small bowl and stir in 60 ml (2 fl oz/¼ cup) of the hot liquid to form a smooth paste. Return to the pan and whisk until the gelatine has dissolved. Strain through a fine sieve and allow to cool. Stir in the Midori until well combined, then divide among eight tumblers or small glass bowls. Refrigerate for about 3 hours, or until set.

Remove the chilled ice cream mixture from the refrigerator and pour into an ice cream machine, then churn according to the manufacturer's instructions. Place in the freezer until ready to use. If making by hand, pour the mixture into a metal container and freeze until frozen around the edges but not in the centre, then whisk with electric beaters to break down any ice crystals. Return to the freezer and repeat this process at least twice more. The more times it is beaten while freezing, the finer and silkier the finished ice cream will be.

To make the fruit salad, cut the kiwi fruit and melon into 1.5 cm (⅝ in) dice. Place in a bowl, add the grapes and toss to combine. Spoon the fruit on top of the jelly and serve immediately with green tea ice cream.

Combine the sugar, lemon zest, ginger and 375 ml (13 fl oz/1½ cups) water in a saucepan. Stir over high heat until the sugar has dissolved, then bring to the boil. Reduce the heat to low and simmer for 10 minutes. Cool completely and strain.

Purée the plum flesh in a food processor, then strain through a fine sieve to extract the juice— about 250 ml (9 fl oz/1 cup). Add to the cooled syrup, along with the plum wine, then pour into a shallow 30 x 20 cm (12 x 8 in) metal container. Place in the freezer until the mixture begins to freeze around the edges—this will take 1½–2 hours. Scrape the frozen sections back into the mixture with a fork. Repeat every 30 minutes until the mixture has even-sized ice crystals. Just before serving, beat the mixture with a fork, then spoon into six glasses or small bowls. Serve with sliced fresh ripe plums, if desired.

hint: For a refreshing summer cocktail, serve the granita in tall glasses topped up with extra plum wine and soda, or serve in martini glasses topped with Champagne.

Japanese plum wine, *ume shu*, is a sweet wine that has an almondish flavour. It is made from *ume*, a fruit often called a plum, but actually a member of the apricot family. This sparkling pink granita is light and refreshing, perfect for the warmer summer months.

plum wine granita

115 g (4 oz/½ cup) caster (superfine) sugar
a few strips of lemon zest
2 cm (¾ in) piece young ginger, thinly sliced
500 g (1 lb 2 oz) ripe plums, seeded
500 ml (17 fl oz/2 cups) Japanese plum wine
sliced plums, extra to serve (optional)

serves 6

Melons in Japan are often seen with price tags equating to a few hundred dollars and, although exorbitantly priced, they are always beautifully gift boxed and perfect in every way—shape, colour, texture, flavour and aroma. The wonderful perfume of yuzu, a Japanese citrus, adds an exotic touch to the rockmelon, which, for most of us living outside of Japan, is an everyday food.

rockmelon and lychees with yuzu syrup

1 teaspoon dried yuzu pieces, or ½ teaspoon
    each lemon and lime zest
½ vanilla bean, thinly sliced
80 g (2¾ oz/⅓ cup) caster (superfine) sugar
½ small ripe rockmelon or other orange-fleshed
    melon, peeled and seeded
375 g (13 oz/2 cups) peeled and seeded fresh
    lychees (do this carefully to retain their shape)

serves 4

Put the yuzu, vanilla bean, sugar and 185 ml (6 fl oz/¾ cup) water in a small saucepan over high heat and stir until the sugar has dissolved. Bring to the boil, then reduce the heat and simmer for about 8 minutes, or until you have reached a thin syrup consistency. Remove from the heat and allow to cool completely.

Cut the rockmelon into 2.5 cm (1 in) cubes and carefully toss with the lychees, then pour the cooled syrup over the top. (There's no need to remove the vanilla bean as it softens in the syrup, and has a nice subtle flavour.) Refrigerate for 2–3 hours, or until well chilled. Gently stir every so often. Serve by itself or with Ginger ice cream (page 184).

ginger custard tart with toffeed strawberries

pastry

225 g (8 oz/1¾ cups) plain (all-purpose) flour

40 g (1½ oz/⅓ cup) icing (confectioners') sugar

125 g (4½ oz) frozen unsalted butter, grated

2 tablespoons black sesame seeds

1 egg yolk, beaten

custard

500 ml (17 fl oz/2 cups) cream

125 ml (4 fl oz/½ cup) milk

1 vanilla bean, split in half lengthways, seeds scraped

50 g (1¾ oz/⅓ cup) peeled, thinly sliced young ginger

8 egg yolks

80 g (2¾ oz/⅓ cup) caster (superfine) sugar

2 tablespoons plain (all-purpose) flour

2 tablespoons cornflour (cornstarch)

toffee

280 g (10 oz/1¼ cups) caster (superfine) sugar

750 g (1 lb 10 oz) strawberries, unhulled

serves 6–8

To make the pastry, sift the flour and icing sugar into a bowl. Rub the butter into the mixture until it resembles breadcrumbs. Combine the sesame seeds, egg yolk and 2½ tablespoons iced water and, using a flat-bladed knife, 'cut' into the flour mixture until it clumps. Add a little more iced water if needed. Gather into a ball and flatten slightly. Cover with plastic wrap and refrigerate for 1 hour.

To make the custard, put 375 ml (13 fl oz/1½ cups) of the cream, the milk, vanilla bean and seeds, and ginger into a saucepan and bring to the boil over medium heat. Set aside to infuse for 15 minutes. Combine the egg yolks, sugar, flour and cornflour in a large heatproof bowl and whisk until smooth.

Return the cream mixture to a medium heat, bring just to the boil again, then strain onto the eggs, whisking until smooth. Place the bowl over a saucepan of simmering water and stir continuously for 15 minutes, or until smooth and thick. Cool slightly, then press plastic wrap onto the surface of the custard and chill completely. Whip the remaining cream and fold it through the chilled custard. Chill until ready to serve.

Meanwhile, sprinkle the pastry with flour and roll out between two pieces of baking paper to 5 mm (¼ in) thick and 36 cm (14½ in) round. Trim the edges to neaten. Peel off the top layer of baking paper and invert the pastry over a 2.5 cm (1 in) deep, 28 cm (11 in) diameter loose-based tart tin and carefully press the pastry into the base. Patch any holes with excess pastry. Allow the pastry to come up 5 mm (¼ in) above the edge of the tin and pinch the edges to neaten. Refrigerate for 20 minutes.

Preheat the oven to 180°C (350°F/Gas 4). Prick the base of the pastry all over, line with baking paper and fill with baking beads or raw rice. Cook for 10 minutes, then remove the paper and weights and cook for 25 minutes, or until golden and dry to touch. Cool thoroughly in the tin on a wire rack. Only remove the tart shell from the tin when you are about to fill it with the custard.

To make the toffee, combine the sugar and 80 ml (2½ fl oz/⅓ cup) water in a saucepan. Stir with a metal spoon over medium heat until the sugar has dissolved, then bring to the boil and cook, without stirring, for 6 minutes, or until deep golden in colour (swirl the pan occasionally). Remove the pan from the heat and, holding each strawberry by the stem, carefully dip it into the hot toffee. Place the toffeed strawberries on a tray lined with baking paper to set. In humid weather the toffee will start to dissolve, so don't prepare them too far in advance. To serve, spoon the custard cream into the pastry shell, smooth over, and decorate with the strawberries.

The crisp cinnamon wafers in this recipe were inspired by a cookie, local to Kyoto, called *yatsuhashi*. These, combined with the flavour and texture of chestnuts and mandarins, make for an unusual but delicious dessert.

cinnamon wafers with chestnut cream

wafers

40 g (1½ oz/¼ cup) blanched almonds

90 g (3¼ oz/½ cup) brown rice flour

60 g (2¼ oz/½ cup) plain (all-purpose) flour

3 tablespoons roasted soya bean flour

2 tablespoons arrowroot

60 g (2¼ oz/½ cup) icing (confectioners') sugar

5 teaspoons ground cinnamon

100 g (3½ oz) chilled unsalted butter, chopped

1½ tablespoons black sugar syrup or molasses

½ teaspoon pure vanilla extract

chestnut cream

440 g (15½ oz) tin unsweetened chestnut purée

2½ tablespoons caster (superfine) sugar

2 teaspoons pure vanilla extract

1 tablespoon cognac or brandy

1 tablespoon black sugar syrup or molasses

300 ml (10½ fl oz) thickened cream, whipped

235 g (8½ oz/1 cup) tinned mandarin segments

extra black sugar syrup, for drizzling (optional)

serves 6

To make the wafers, finely grind the almonds in a food processor. Add the rice flour, plain flour, soya bean flour, arrowroot, icing sugar and cinnamon and process to combine. Add the butter and pulse until the mixture resembles breadcrumbs, then add the black sugar syrup and vanilla and pulse again until it comes together to form a smooth dough. Add a little water if needed, but only add 1 teaspoon at a time. Wrap in plastic wrap and refrigerate for 1 hour.

Preheat the oven to 180°C (350°F/Gas 4). Remove the pastry from the fridge 5 minutes before rolling it out. Meanwhile, line two baking trays with baking paper. On a lightly floured work surface, roll out the dough to about 3 mm (⅛ in) thick, sprinkling a little flour on top if the dough is a bit sticky. Using an 8 cm (3¼ in) round cookie cutter, cut out 12 circles from the dough.

Place on the lined trays (they don't spread much so you don't need to leave much space between them) and bake for 12–15 minutes, or until dark golden, but be careful as they can burn quickly at this point. Cool on the tray on a wire rack.

To make the chestnut cream, mash the chestnut purée with the sugar, vanilla, brandy and black sugar syrup until smooth, then fold through the cream and chill.

To serve, place a wafer on a serving plate and top with a large dollop of the chestnut cream and 2 tablespoons of the mandarin segments. Drizzle with the extra sugar syrup, if using, and top with a wafer 'lid'. Repeat with the remaining ingredients to make six stacks.

hint: The wafers are also great on their own and store well in sealed containers.

172

Japanese green tea powder, or *matcha*, is made by grinding a high-grade green tea to a fine powder. Its most common use is in traditional tea ceremonies but it is also used to flavour Japanese confectionery and desserts. It can be expensive but a little goes a long way.

green tea panna cotta with rhubarb

panna cotta
1½ teaspoons Japanese green tea powder
600 ml (21 fl oz) cream
175 g (6 oz/¾ cup) caster (superfine) sugar
3 teaspoons gelatine powder
125 ml (4 fl oz/½ cup) milk
½ teaspoon pure vanilla extract

6 large rhubarb stalks
80 g (2¾ oz/⅓ cup) caster (superfine) sugar
25 g (1 oz) unsalted butter

serves 6

To make the panna cotta, put the green tea powder in a saucepan with a little of the cream and mix to form a paste. Whisk in the remaining cream, ensuring there are no lumps. Add the sugar to the saucepan, stirring to dissolve the sugar, then slowly bring to the boil over medium heat. Turn off the heat.

Put the gelatine in a small bowl and whisk in 60 ml (2 fl oz/¼ cup) of the hot cream to form a smooth paste. Return the mixture to the saucepan, stirring until the gelatine has completely dissolved. Rest for 10 minutes to infuse the flavours and colour from the tea.

Strain into a large bowl with a pouring lip and then pour in the milk and vanilla and stir until combined. Pour the mixture into six 125 ml (4 fl oz/½ cup) moulds and chill for at least 3 hours, or until set.

Preheat the oven to 200°C (400°F/Gas 6). Remove any tough strings from the rhubarb, then cut into 5 cm (2 in) lengths. Arrange the rhubarb in a single layer in a baking dish, then sprinkle with the sugar and dot with the butter. Bake for 12–15 minutes, or until the rhubarb is slightly glazed and tender but not mushy. Remove from the heat and cool to room temperature.

If you would like to unmould the panna cotta, dip the bottom of the mould briefly into hot water, then invert the mould onto a serving plate. It should be quite wobbly. Serve with the rhubarb and spoon over some syrup.

This dish is not overly sweet, so you can really enjoy the nutty toasted sesame seeds and the lovely malty flavour of *kinako*, ground soya bean flour. Sesame seeds are believed to help reduce cholesterol, high blood pressure and stress—what better excuse do you need for dessert?

toasted sesame semi freddo

300 ml (10½ fl oz) cream

4 eggs, separated

40 g (1½ oz/⅓ cup) icing (confectioners') sugar

2 tablespoons honey

25 g (1 oz/¼ cup) roasted soya bean flour

80 g (2¾ oz/½ cup) toasted sesame seeds, lightly crushed

3 bananas, sliced on the diagonal

honey, to drizzle

serves 6–8

Whip the cream to firm peaks, then cover with plastic wrap and refrigerate until chilled. Combine the egg yolks, icing sugar and honey in a bowl and whisk for 3 minutes, or until pale and creamy. Stir in the soya bean flour and crushed sesame seeds. Fold in the chilled whipped cream.

Beat the egg whites to firm peaks, stir a large spoonful into the cream mixture, then gently fold in the rest of the whites until smooth and lump-free.

Line a 10 x 21 cm (4 x 8¼ in) loaf tin with plastic wrap, using enough plastic so that the wrap hangs over the long sides. Carefully pour the mixture into the tin, then fold the plastic over the top to cover. Freeze for 4 hours, or until frozen but not rock hard. If you make this ahead of time, remove it from the freezer about 10 minutes before cutting. Slice and serve with bananas and drizzle with honey.

hint: This is also great drizzled with chocolate sauce. Make your own sauce by gently heating 150 g (5½ oz) dark chocolate and 250 ml (9 fl oz/ 1 cup) cream until the chocolate just melts, then stir until smooth. Use Japanese chocolate if you can find it; otherwise use your favourite brand.

Azuki beans, or red beans, might seem like an unusual choice for dessert but they are used all over Japan in confectionery, often as a ready-made bean paste. These rolls are very rich, so one per person should be enough.

azuki bean, banana and chocolate spring rolls

6 large spring roll wrappers
150 g (5½ oz/½ cup) sweet azuki bean paste
3 small bananas, sliced
85 g (3 oz) good-quality dark chocolate, preferably Japanese, cut into 6 fingers
1 egg, lightly beaten
vegetable oil, for deep-frying

makes 6

Place a spring roll wrapper on your work surface, with a corner towards you. Put 1 tablespoon of bean paste in the lower third of the diamond and flatten slightly into a horizontal mound. Place a few slices of banana on top, slightly overlapping, then top with a finger of chocolate.

Starting at the end closest to you, roll the spring roll up and away from you, tucking in the ends halfway. Brush the final flap with a little of the beaten egg and seal. Refrigerate while you heat the oil.

Fill a deep-fat fryer or large saucepan one-third full with oil and heat to 180°C (350°F), or until a cube of bread dropped into the oil browns in 15 seconds. Cook the spring rolls for 3 minutes, or until golden. Drain on paper towels. Cool slightly, then serve with a scoop of ice cream, such as Green tea ice cream (page 164).

179

This sweet steamed custard was inspired by the Japanese savoury custard, *chawan mushi*. Steaming over simmering water gives the custard a silken texture, but if the water boils you will end up with a grainy mass, so take care. Like the sake that flavours it, this dish is great served warm or cold.

steamed vanilla custard cups

300 g (10½ oz/2 cups) blueberries

1½ tablespoons drinking sake

3 teaspoons caster (superfine) sugar

½ teaspoon finely grated lemon zest

4 eggs

4 egg yolks

500 ml (17 fl oz/2 cups) cream

80 g (2¾ oz/⅓ cup) caster (superfine) sugar, extra

1 teaspoon pure vanilla extract

serves 6

Toss the blueberries with the sake, sugar and lemon zest, then divide among six *chawan mushi* cups, Japanese teacups or small Chinese rice bowls, about 250 ml (9 fl oz/1 cup) capacity.

Lightly beat the eggs and egg yolks, then stir in the cream, sugar and vanilla, combining well—do not overbeat or you will aerate too much. Strain into a large bowl with a pouring lip, then pour into the teacups or bowls. Allow to sit for 10 minutes, then prick any air bubbles with a fine skewer.

Bring a wok or large saucepan filled with water to the boil, then reduce to a simmer. Put the cups in a large bamboo steamer. Wrap a clean tea towel around the steamer lid (this will collect the steam and stop any condensation from dripping onto the custards) and firmly place the lid on the steamer. Put the steamer on top of the wok and leave the custards to steam for 15–20 minutes, or until just set. If you can fit all the custards in the steamer at once, they will take the longer cooking time; if you have to do them in two batches, they will cook more quickly.

Remove from the heat and allow to cool slightly before serving. The custards can also be served chilled, but they will not have the silky texture that they have when warm.

hint: Meaning 'steamed teacups', *chawan mushi* is the name given not only to the recipe but also to the specially designed lidded, ceramic cup in which it is cooked. These may be difficult to find outside of Japan, but may be substituted with Japanese teacups or small Asian rice or soup bowls.

At one time in Tokyo, tiramisu was featured on the menu of almost every café, restaurant and fast-food chain. Like many other Italian dishes that have been adopted by the Japanese, it has been made their own by substituting flavours that are more familiar to them. This version is quite a leap from the original.

tokyo tiramisu

300 g (10½ oz) good-quality white chocolate, chopped
500 ml (17 fl oz/2 cups) cream
¾ teaspoon Japanese green tea powder, plus extra to serve
55 g (2 oz/¼ cup) caster (superfine) sugar
325 ml (11 fl oz) drinking sake
22 large savoiardi biscuits, cut in half lengthways
500 g (1 lb 2 oz/1½ cups) sweet azuki bean paste
extra white chocolate

serves 8–10

Combine the chocolate and cream in a saucepan and stir over low heat until almost melted. Remove from the heat and stir until completely lump-free. Add a little of the mixture to the green tea powder in a small bowl and stir to make a smooth runny paste. Pour this back into the chocolate mixture and stir until smooth and evenly coloured. Pour through a very fine sieve into a bowl, pressing down on any lumps of tea with the back of a spoon to extract the flavour and colour. The cream may still be slightly speckled, which is fine. Cover and refrigerate for 4 hours, or until completely cold.

When cold, whip the chocolate cream until just spreadable—be careful not to overbeat the mixture as it may split—then refrigerate until ready to use.

Combine the sugar with 170 ml (5½ fl oz/⅔ cup) water and stir over high heat until the sugar has dissolved. Allow to boil for 2 minutes, then remove the pan from the heat, cool completely and mix in the sake. Dip half the sponge fingers into the syrup, one at a time, and use them to line the base of a 6–7 cm (2½–2¾ in) deep, 2.5 litre (87 fl oz/10 cup) capacity serving dish.

Using half the azuki bean paste, drop spoonfuls over the sponge fingers and gently spread out with the back of a spoon, trying not to move the savoiardi. Spread half the green tea chocolate cream over this and smooth over.

Repeat the layering with the sponge, syrup, bean paste and chocolate cream and smooth the top with a palette knife so that it is as flat as possible. Finely grate the extra white chocolate over the top, ensuring the surface is evenly and completely covered. Carefully cover with plastic wrap and refrigerate overnight to allow the flavours to develop. Do not store in the refrigerator with any other strong flavours. Sprinkle with the extra green tea powder. Serve in small portions as this is a very sweet dessert.

hint: If you prefer, layer the tiramisu using fresh raspberries instead of the bean paste, which will help to cut the sweetness.

Nashi is a type of pear with a crisp flesh, similar to that of an apple. Its sweet, refreshing flavour blends beautifully with the slightly spicy ice cream.

nashi strudel with ginger ice cream

ginger ice cream

250 ml (9 fl oz/1 cup) milk

630 ml (22 fl oz) cream

1 vanilla bean, split, seeds scraped and reserved

150 g (5½ oz/1¼ cups) thinly sliced young ginger

9 egg yolks

140 g (5 oz/⅔ cup) caster (superfine) sugar

4 nashi, peeled and quartered, core removed, then cut into 5 mm (¼ in) thick slices

2 teaspoons lemon juice

2 teaspoons finely grated ginger

235 g (8½ oz/1 cup) caster (superfine) sugar

30 g (1 oz/½ cup) Japanese breadcrumbs

80 g (2¾ oz/½ cup) toasted sesame seeds, lightly ground

80 g (2¾ oz/¾ cup) walnuts, finely chopped

2 teaspoons ground cinnamon

1 teaspoon ground ginger

18 sheets filo pastry

150 g (5½ oz) unsalted butter, melted

3 tablespoons icing (confectioners') sugar

3 tablespoons roasted soya bean flour

serves 6

To make the ginger ice cream, put the milk, cream, vanilla bean and seeds and ginger in a saucepan over medium–high heat. Bring just to the boil, then remove from the heat and set aside for 20 minutes to allow the vanilla to infuse into the milk. Strain, reserving the vanilla bean.

Put the egg yolks and sugar in a bowl and beat until the eggs are light and creamy. Whisk in the cream mixture until smooth, then pour into a clean saucepan and return to a medium heat. Add the reserved vanilla bean and stir for 10 minutes, or until the mixture just coats the back of a spoon. Strain through a fine sieve and cool slightly. Cover and refrigerate until cold, then churn in an ice cream machine, according to the manufacturer's instructions. Freeze until ready to use.

If making the ice cream by hand, pour the mixture into a metal container and freeze until it is frozen around the edges but not in the centre, then whisk with electric beaters to break down any ice crystals. Return to the freezer and repeat this process at least twice more.

Preheat the oven to 180°C (350°F/Gas 4). Put the nashi in a bowl with the lemon juice, ginger, half the sugar, and the breadcrumbs and stir. Combine the sesame seeds, remaining sugar, walnuts, cinnamon and ground ginger in a small bowl.

Lay one sheet of filo on the work surface, with the short end towards you, and brush lightly with the melted butter, then butter another sheet and place it directly on top of the first. Repeat with a third sheet, brushing the top as well. Sprinkle one-sixth of the sesame mixture over the top, then, leaving a 5 cm (2 in) border on the edge of the pastry closest to you and on both sides, put one-sixth of the nashi mixture in a neat bundle. Gently roll it up, folding in the sides about halfway, brushing more butter down each folded side. Carefully transfer to a lightly greased baking tray, seam-side down, and brush all over with melted butter. Repeat with the remaining filo and filling to form six strudels. Bake for 35 minutes, or until crisp and golden. Allow to cool slightly, then slice the ends off to expose the filling. Sift over the combined icing sugar and soya bean flour and serve with the ginger ice cream, or with lightly whipped cream.

Jap pumpkin has a rich sweet flesh, so it is little wonder the Japanese have such a fondness for it in desserts. *Kabocha*, or pumpkin, is found in many sweet foods such as puddings, pies and ice creams. Here I have used it to flavour cheesecake, which is now a staple on most Japanese café and restaurant menus.

pumpkin cheesecake

500 g (1 lb 2 oz) jap (kent) pumpkin, peeled and
    roughly chopped
175 g (6 oz) hard ginger biscuits
40 g (1½ oz/¼ cup) toasted sesame seeds, crushed
50 g (1¾ oz/½ cup) walnuts, chopped
2 tablespoons caster (superfine) sugar
80 g (2¾ oz) unsalted butter, melted
1½ tablespoons gelatine powder
600 g (1 lb 5 oz) cream cheese, softened
300 g (10½ oz) sour cream
175 g (6 oz/1 cup) loosely packed soft brown sugar
2 teaspoons pure vanilla extract
1½ teaspoons ground cinnamon
1½ teaspoons finely grated orange zest
lightly whipped cream, to serve

pumpkin and sesame seed toffee (optional)
30 g (1 oz/¼ cup) toasted unsalted pepitas
    (pumpkin seeds)
2 tablespoons toasted sesame seeds
350 g (12 oz/1½ cups) caster (superfine) sugar

serves 10–12

Cook the pumpkin in a saucepan of boiling water for 20 minutes, or until very tender. Drain well, mash and cool completely.

Break the biscuits into small pieces, then pulse with the sesame seeds, walnuts and sugar in a food processor until even crumbs are formed. Add the melted butter and mix until combined. Press into the greased and lined base of a 23 cm (9 in) springform tin and smooth over with the back of a spoon. Refrigerate until needed.

Sprinkle the gelatine over 60 ml (2 fl oz/¼ cup) warm water in a small bowl. Leave until spongy—do not stir. Bring a small saucepan of water to the boil, remove from the heat and put the bowl in the pan. The water in the pan should come only halfway up the side of the bowl—tip out a little water if necessary. Stir the gelatine until clear and dissolved.

Put the cream cheese, sour cream, brown sugar, vanilla, cinnamon and orange zest in a food processor and mix until smooth and lump-free, then add the pumpkin and gelatine and process again until smooth. Pour the mixture into the prepared tin and smooth the top. Refrigerate for 6 hours, or overnight, until set.

To make the pumpkin and sesame seed toffee, if using, line a baking tray with baking paper and sprinkle over the toasted seeds. Put the sugar and 60 ml (2 fl oz/¼ cup) water in a small saucepan, place over high heat, stir until the sugar dissolves, then bring to the boil. Cook for 8 minutes, or until deeply golden, swirling occasionally to help distribute the colour, then immediately and carefully pour over the seeds on the tray. Using protection from the heat for your hands, gently tilt and swirl the tray so that the toffee covers the seeds. Allow to cool completely before breaking into small shards. To serve, top the cheesecake with whipped cream and the toffee.

glossary

azuki bean A small red bean often used to make *an*, a sweet bean paste made by slowly cooking azuki beans in a sugar syrup.

bamboo shoots *(takenoko)* The young, pale shoots of certain bamboo, which have a mellow flavour. Sometimes available fresh, but require preparation. The precooked, tinned ones only need to be drained and rinsed before use.

black sugar *(kurozato)* A dark brown sugar with a rich molasses flavour, sold in small lumps or crushed. Used mainly in confectionery, particularly for making a sweet black sugar syrup called *kuromitsu*.

bonito flakes *(katsuobushi)* Shavings of dried, smoked and cured bonito, a type of tuna. The large flakes are used for making stock (dashi); smaller flakes are used as a garnish. It has a strong aroma but a smoky, mellow flavour.

burdock root *(gobo)* A long, brown-skinned root with a creamy coloured flesh. Available fresh when in season. To prepare, scrape off the skin, then rinse. Slice and soak in acidulated water to remove any bitterness. Some recipes ask for the root to be shaved. To do this, start at the thin end of the root and, using a sharp knife, shave off pieces as if sharpening a pencil. Frozen lengths are sold in Asian food stores. These are scraped and ready to cook.

daikon A giant radish resembling a very large white carrot. Its flavour when raw is fresh and mild, and it is used in salads or grated into dipping sauces. When cooked, it becomes a little sweet and is great in stews and stir-fries, or roasted. Daikon have a high water content and become soft and bitter with age. As they are very porous, wrap in plastic wrap and refrigerate to store.

dashi granules Dehydrated granules of the essential Japanese base stock, dashi. Also available in powdered form. Made from kombu (kelp) and dried, smoked bonito tuna, dashi forms the base for many dishes, most famously miso soup but also stews, hotpots, noodle soups and salad dressings.

enoki These mushrooms have long, thin, creamy white stems and tiny caps. They grow in clumps, attached by a spongy root that needs to be cut off before use, and can be pulled apart. They require very little cooking, if any.

ginkgo nuts *(ginnan)* Native to China, this pale yellow fruit from the *Ginkgo biloba* tree has a crisp shell when fresh, which must be removed before cooking. Commonly found ready-prepared in tins, vacuum-packed or frozen. When cooked, they develop a creamy, nutty flavour and slightly chewy texture.

harusame noodles Meaning 'spring rain', these thin, clear noodles are authentically made from bean starch, but can also be made from potato or sweet potato starch.

hijiki A porous seaweed, high in fibre and calcium. Sold dried in short lengths, which need to be reconstituted before eating.

Japanese breadcrumbs *(panko)* Crisp breadcrumbs available in fine and coarse grades. Usually larger than traditional breadcrumbs, they make a very crisp coating for deep-fried foods. The coarser grade is used for the recipes in this book.

Japanese green tea powder *(matcha)* A fine powder made by grinding high-grade green tea. It is the essential element of the Japanese tea ceremony, and is whisked with hot water before drinking. Also used to flavour desserts and some soba noodles.

Japanese mayonnaise A creamy mayonnaise with a slightly salty, sweet flavour, containing soya bean oil and rice vinegar. A popular brand is QP (for 'kewpie', the name of the doll on the label). Sold in a soft squeeze bottle for easy use.

Japanese mustard *(karashi)* A very hot and spicy yellow mustard, similar to English mustard. Use sparingly.

Japanese pickled plum *(umeboshi)* Made from *ume*, which is actually not a plum but a member of the apricot family. The fruit is pickled in salt and vinegar and coloured a deep pink-red by the red shiso leaf. Served as a tart accompaniment to rice and other foods, or desalted and used in dressings.

Japanese rice vinegar *(komesu)* Made from vinegar and a natural rice extract, this refreshing vinegar is less sharp than other types. Japanese rice vinegar has a milder, sweeter flavour than other rice vinegars, so choose a Japanese brand when cooking Japanese food.

Japanese soy sauce *(shoyu)* A high-grade soy sauce used in cooking and as a condiment. There are several good brands available and some versions are saltier or sweeter than others. The recipes in this book generally use the less sweet, lighter version, which has a more savoury flavour, but you can substitute the Japanese soy sauce of your choice.

kamaboko A small loaf of steamed fish paste made from a variety of mild-fleshed fish and tasting a little like crab sticks. It is sometimes coloured bright pink for festival foods; the regular version is a creamy white colour. Used in soups and stews.

kombu Also called konbu, this dried kelp is essential for making dashi. It can turn bitter if cooked for too long, so is often soaked overnight in the cooking liquid and then discarded. Sold in strips about 5 cm (2 in) wide from which lengths can be cut with scissors. Wipe over it with a damp cloth to remove any grit before cooking but do not rub off the white powdery substance that coats the surface.

kuzu A thickening starch added to sauces to help them glaze well, also used to set foods and to make certain noodles. Sold as a powder or as small rocks, which need to be crushed before use. Kuzu is often labelled, or substituted with, arrowroot.

lotus root *(renkon)* A rhizome rather than a root, with a crisp texture and delicate flavour. It has small holes throughout its length, which, when sliced into rounds, look like a flower. Fresh lotus root must be peeled and cooked before eating. Also available prepared and ready for cooking in tins, vacuum packs and frozen.

mirin A pale gold spirit-based rice liquid sometimes referred to as sweet rice wine. Manufactured for cooking, not drinking, and used in sauces, dressings and simmered dishes. To avoid imitations, look for bottles labelled *hon mirin*, meaning 'true mirin'.

miso A rich, earthy paste made from fermented soya beans, available in different grades, colours and strengths. Generally, the lighter the paste the sweeter and less salty the taste. Used in miso soup, but also added to other soups, marinades, dressings and simmered dishes. Two types are used in this book: white, or *shiro*, miso has a mild, sweet flavour; and red, or *aka*, miso has more earthy, salty characteristics. Often confusingly labelled, so please note that white miso is actually pale gold in colour and red miso is more a caramel brown.

mitsuba Translated as 'three leaves', this herb is a type of Japanese parsley. Similar in appearance to a cross between coriander (cilantro) and flat-leaf (Italian) parsley. If not in season, substitute flat-leaf (Italian) parsley.

mizuna A large-leafed herb with a slight peppery mustard flavour, used in salads and sometimes in simmered dishes. If not in season it can sometimes be substituted with rocket (arugula).

nashi A type of Japanese pear, more closely resembling the shape of an apple. The flesh is crisp, refreshing and sweet, and the skin is slightly rough and either pale yellow-green or brown. Browner-skinned nashi have a richer, more caramel flavour.

nori Crisp paper-like sheets of compressed seaweed, commonly used to wrap sushi, and sold in pre-cut toasted sheets for this purpose. Small strips and flakes of nori, *aonori*, are frequently used as a condiment or garnish.

pickled ginger *(gari)* Thinly sliced fresh, young ginger that turns pale pink during the pickling process. It has a sharp yet sweet and refreshing flavour, which is great as a palate cleanser for rich foods such as sashimi, which uses fatty fish, or deep-fried foods. Avoid the inferior darker pinkish-red strips that are tinted with food colouring as these have a less refined flavour.

plum wine *(umeshu)* A sweet liquor with a bitter almond flavour made from a type of Japanese apricot, *ume*.

ponzu A dressing or dipping sauce made from citrus juice, soy sauce and bonito flakes that is available commercially. To make your own, see page 16.

potato starch A starch used to thicken sauces and to coat deep-fried foods for a very crisp result.

sake An alcoholic liquid made from the fermenting of cooked, ground rice. It has a clean, dry flavour, somewhere between vodka and dry sherry. There are various grades: the more refined, clear liquid is for drinking; the less refined form, pale amber in colour, is for cooking. In this book, recipes using sake refer to cooking sake unless specified as drinking sake. Served chilled in summer and warmed in winter.

sansho pepper The ground seeds of the Japanese prickly ash. Its spicy aroma and flavour and slightly numbing quality demonstrate its close relation to Chinese Sichuan pepper. It is one of the spices that make up seven-spice mix.

soba noodles Made from buckwheat flour, these grey-brown noodles have a slightly nutty flavour and are often served chilled with a soy-based dipping sauce, or hot in broth. Available in dried form and sometimes flavoured with green tea, *cha soba*.

seaweed paste *(nori tsukudani)* A black paste made from kelp with a sweet, yet salty, mellow flavour.

seven-spice mix *(shichimi togarashi)* A spice mix containing seven flavours. It always includes *togarashi*, a hot red Japanese chilli. The remaining ingredients are flexible but often include mustard seeds, sesame seeds, poppy seeds, sansho pepper, shiso and nori flakes.

sesame oil Strongly flavoured oil extracted from toasted sesame seeds. A spicy version infused with chilli is popular for sprinkling over noodle soups. Use sparingly.

sesame seeds *(goma)* Usually white or cream, but also black. The oil-rich seeds are often toasted to enhance their flavour. To toast the seeds, put them in a small frying pan over low heat for 10 minutes, shaking the pan, or until golden and fragrant.

shiso Also known as perilla or beefsteak plant, this large-leafed, aromatic herb has slightly ragged edges and a flavour similar to basil or Thai basil, with which it can be substituted if unavailable. Usually dark green in colour, or with a purplish red hue. Used in salads, soups and as a garnish, it is also a popular tempura ingredient.

shiitake This mushroom has a unique, relatively strong flavour and is available both fresh and dried. The more pungent dried version is similar in appearance to the Chinese dried mushroom with which it may be substituted.

shimeji This mushroom grows in a cluster of long stems and has small grey-brown caps. It is often pulled apart before use. Delicately flavoured, it is eaten raw in salads, or briefly cooked in soups, stews or stir-fries.

shochu A distilled spirit with a high alcohol content, made from potato, sweet potato or various grains. Quality shochu is very smooth with a vodka-like flavour.

somen Fine, white wheat-flour noodles most commonly eaten chilled with a dipping sauce or warm in a light broth.

soya bean flour, roasted *(kinako)* A flour made from ground, roasted soya beans, it has a slightly sweet, nutty flavour. Commonly used when making traditional Japanese confectionery or desserts.

soya beans Available dried as small yellowish oval beans that require soaking before use, precooked in tins, or fresh or frozen in the pod *(edamame)*. Rich in protein and used in the manufacture of tofu, miso and soy sauce.

tamari A naturally fermented, thick, dark and sweet Japanese soy sauce. True tamari is wheat-free, but there are some lesser quality brands that have misapplied the name, so check labels carefully if this is an important consideration.

taro A starchy tuber with a creamy, slightly nutty flavour when cooked. It must be cooked before eating.

tofu Also known as bean curd, this creamy flavoured, high-protein food is made by setting the 'milk' that results when soya beans and water are ground together. Available in a variety of textures: silken, a very soft, fragile tofu used in dressings or desserts; silken firm is slightly more set and added to light soups or salads; cotton (firm) tofu is a dense, textured tofu that holds together well for stir-fries and stews.

udon Thick, white, wheat-flour noodles available in various widths, fresh and dried. Usually served in soups, hotpots or stir-fries.

wakame A curly-leafed seaweed, usually dehydrated and broken into very small pieces. It swells considerably and quickly when added to water and has a soft texture, which can become slimy if left to soak for too long. Use in soups and salads.

wasabi Wasabi paste is a hot, pungent mixture made from the knobbly green root of the Japanese wasabi plant. It is also available in powdered form to be mixed to a paste when needed. Also available fresh when in season. The root can be finely grated and has better flavour and less heat than the paste. Use sparingly as a condiment for sushi and sashimi, and in dipping sauces for noodles.

yakisoba Chinese-style yellow egg noodles that are partially cooked and ready for use in the stir-fried noodle dish of the same name. You can substitute with thin hokkien (egg) noodles.

yuzu An aromatic Japanese citrus fruit. It is the rind, either fresh or dried, which is used more frequently than other parts of the fruit. Yuzu is used in soups and simmered dishes for added flavour and aroma. The juice is added to dipping sauces or dressings.

index

essential PASTA

MURDOCH BOOKS

Published in 2011 by Murdoch Books Pty Limited

Murdoch Books Australia
Pier 8/9
23 Hickson Road
Millers Point NSW 2000
Phone: +61 (0) 2 8220 2000
Fax: +61 (0) 2 8220 2558
www.murdochbooks.com.au

Murdoch Books UK Limited
Erico House, 6th Floor
93–99 Upper Richmond Road
Putney, London SW15 2TG
Phone: +44 (0) 20 8785 5995
Fax: +44 (0) 20 8785 5985
www.murdochbooks.co.uk

Publisher: Kylie Walker
Project Editor: Melody Lord
Food Editor: Anneka Manning
Editor: Anna Scobie
Concept Design: Vivien Sung
Designer: Susanne Geppert

Photographers: Jared Fowler, Julie Renouf
Stylist: Cherise Koch
Food preparation: Alan Wilson

Text copyright © Murdoch Books Pty Limited 2011
Based on The essential Pasta cookbook, first published by Murdoch Books in 1997.
Recipes developed in the Murdoch Books Test Kitchen.
Design copyright © Murdoch Books Pty Limited 2011

National Library of Australia Cataloguing-in-Publication entry

Title: Essential pasta.
ISBN: 978-1-74266-091-2 (pbk.)
Series: New essential.
Notes: Includes index.
Subjects: Cooking (Pasta)
Dewey Number: 641.822

A catalogue record for this book is available from the British Library.

Printed by 1010 Printing International Limited, China

IMPORTANT: Those who might be at risk from the effects of salmonella poisoning (the elderly, pregnant women, young children and those suffering from immune deficiency diseases) should consult their doctor with any concerns about eating raw eggs.

CONVERSION GUIDE: Cooking times may vary depending on the oven you are using. For fan-forced ovens, as a general rule, set the oven temperature to 20°C (35°F) lower than indicated in the recipe. We have used 20 ml (4 teaspoon) tablespoon measures. If you are using a 15 ml (3 teaspoon) tablespoon, add an extra teaspoon for each tablespoon specified. We have used 60 g (Grade 3) eggs in all recipes.

a feast for the gods

The world has finally discovered a cookery secret the Italians knew for centuries ... it is difficult to go wrong with pasta. What could be simpler or more appealing than butter and shavings of parmesan melting over a bowl of fresh tagliatelle? As comfort food, pasta is unbeatable. It is warming, filling and, above all, mouthwateringly delicious.

It was said that Marco Polo brought pasta noodles to Italy from China in 1295, a rumour that does great disservice to the people of the Italian peninsula, who had been tucking into it since the days of Ancient Rome. Cicero himself, so legend has it, was inordinately fond of laganum, the flat, ribbon pasta we now call tagliatelle. And, from the Middle Ages, comes the story of how an innkeeper invented tortellini in the image of Venus' navel, which he glimpsed through a keyhole. So, if you're enjoying your pasta, you're in good company. Buon appetito.

contents

classic bolognese (page 22)

pasta secrets

There are good reasons why pasta is such a popular food: it's cheap, it's quick and easy to prepare (you'll notice most of our recipes have an 'easy' rating of one star), it's delicious, it's nutritious and, as this book demonstrates, it's amazingly versatile. You can dress up pasta for a dinner party with a creamy smoked salmon sauce, or serve it simply, with parmesan or bacon and eggs. You can serve it cold in salads, warm in soups or piping hot from the oven, stuffed with spinach and ricotta. You can even serve it as a hangover cure … according to the Italians, spaghetti with garlic and chilli oil, eaten before going to sleep, will ward off the after-effects of too much *vino*. You can eat pasta every day of the week (as indeed many Italians do) and never tire of it. Pasta goes well with anything, including breads, vegetables and salads, which is why we have also included ideas for these throughout the book. They are all listed in the index under Side dishes.

And of course, there is the traditional accompaniment to some pasta dishes, parmesan. Although small amounts of grated parmesan, or little shavings, do look attractive, resist the temptation to serve it with everything. Avoid it with seafood sauces, in particular, as the flavours do not always mix well. If you can't resist garnishing your pasta, try sprinkling it with the gremolata suggested on page 89.

dried or fresh?

Many people think that fresh pasta must be better than dried. This is not always the case — some sauces are better teamed with fresh pasta and some are best with dried. Fresh pasta works well with rich sauces made from cream, butter and cheese, because its soft texture absorbs the sauce. Alfredo is one of the nicest sauces to serve on fresh homemade pasta, as is a simple topping of butter and grated parmesan. Dried pasta is the one to choose if you're serving a heartier, tomato-based

sauce. If your sauce has olives, anchovies, chilli, meat or seafood, you'll almost certainly need dried.

Pasta is a combination of flour, water and sometimes eggs and oil. Pasta made with wholemeal (whole-wheat) flour is darker and nuttier in flavour. If dried pasta is made with durum wheat flour, it is considered to be of superior quality. Other dried pastas that are available include those made from different flours and cereals such as buckwheat, corn, rice and soy beans. Pastas are sometimes flavoured with a purée of herbs, tomato, spinach or other vegetables. Dried pasta will last up to six months, stored in an airtight container in a cool, dark place. However, dried wholemeal pasta will only last for one month before turning rancid. Fresh pasta can be wrapped in a double layer of plastic wrap and frozen for up to four months. There is no need to thaw it before cooking.

which pasta shape?

There are good reasons for matching one pasta shape with a particular sauce. Apart from the traditional regional preference for a local shape, its ability to hold and support the sauce is all important. Tubular shapes, such as penne, capture thick sauces, while flat or long pastas are traditionally served with thin, smooth sauces. But there are no hard and fast rules and part of the fun of pasta is trying out all those fabulous colours, flavours and shapes. See the following pages for photographs of some of the many fresh and dried pasta shapes now available.

A lot of information about the pasta can be gleaned from its name. A name ending in -ricce means the pasta has a wavy edge; -nidi indicates that the lengths are formed into nests; -rigate means ridged; and -lisce, smooth surfaced. And, if your Italian is up to scratch, you can pretty much visualise your pasta from its name … although sometimes you may find this a little offputting. Orecchiette are little ears; eliche (a type of spiral pasta) are propellers; ditali (small, short tubes) are thimbles; conchiglie, conch shells; linguine, little tongues; and vermicelli, little worms. If the name of the pasta ends with -oni, this indicates a larger size: for example, conchiglioni are large conchiglie. Likewise, -ini and -ette mean smaller versions, as in farfallini. However, before we become too embroiled in the importance of names, let us point out that they do vary from manufacturer to manufacturer and book to book … one man's tortelloni can be another man's agnolotti. Luckily, if a little commonsense is used, this isn't going to pose problems of life-threatening importance.

how much pasta?

Another highly charged subject, as far as pasta aficionados are concerned, is how much pasta each person should be served and, even more controversially, how much sauce should be served on that pasta. As a general guide, use 90 g (3¼ oz) of fresh pasta per person for a starter, and 150 g (5½ oz) for a main dish. Dried pasta contains less moisture and is lighter, so allow a little less: about 60 g (2¼ oz) each for a starter and 125 g (4½ oz) per person for a main.

How much sauce is obviously a matter of personal taste, but the biggest mistake non-Italian cooks make is to use too much sauce: the pasta should be lightly coated, not drenched. When the pasta and sauce are tossed, there shouldn't be any extra sauce swimming around at the bottom.

cooking your pasta

Unsalted water will come to the boil faster than salted water, so add the salt once the water is boiling. Use a large saucepan of water, enough to ensure the pasta has plenty of room to move around, and only add the pasta when the water has reached a rapid boil. Some people like to add a tablespoon of olive oil to help prevent the water boiling over or the pasta sticking together. After the pasta has been added, cover the pan to help bring the water back to the boil as quickly as possible, then remove the lid as soon as the water returns to the boil.

Perfectly cooked pasta should be *al dente*, tender but still firm 'to the tooth'. It is important to drain the pasta and then turn it immediately into a heated dish, into the pan with the sauce, or back into its cooking pan. It should never be overdrained, as it needs to be slippery for the sauce to coat it well. Never leave it sitting in the colander or it will become a sticky mass. A little oil or butter tossed through drained pasta will stop it sticking together. Alternatively, lightly spray the pasta with boiling water and toss it gently (keep a little of the cooking water for this).

Timing can make all the difference between a good pasta meal and a great one, so always read the recipe through first and then coordinate your cooking times. Try to have the sauce ready to dress the pasta as soon as it is cooked, especially if the pasta is fresh (it will continue to cook if it is left to sit around). Pasta that is to be used in cold pasta salads should be rinsed under cold water to remove excess starch and tossed with a small amount of oil, then covered and refrigerated until ready to use.

Our star rating:
When we test recipes, we rate them for ease of preparation. The following cookery ratings are used in this book:

☀ A single star indicates a recipe that is simple and generally quick to make, perfect for beginners.

☀☀ Two stars indicate the need for a little more care or a little more time.

☀☀☀ Three stars indicate special dishes that need more investment in time, care and patience, but the results are worth it. Even beginners can make these dishes as long as the recipe is followed carefully.

dried pasta

Traditionally, long dried pastas, such as spaghetti, are served with thin, oily sauces, while shorter pasta shapes hold chunky sauces better.

fettuccine

cappellini or
angel hair pasta

fusilli or
bucati lunghi

cannelloni

lasagne

spaghetti

farfalle

giant
conchiglie

gnocchi

rigatoni

fusilli or
eliche

anelli

lasagnette or
mafaldini

lumaconi or
pipe rigate

fettuccine

casarecce

risoni

orecchiette

conchiglie

macaroni

stellini

dried pasta

continued

spaghettini

orecchio

penne

tagliatelle

cavatielli

ziti

fresh pasta

Fresh pastas are wonderful with butter- or cream-based sauces, as the soft texture absorbs the flavours. Make your own or buy it at the supermarket or delicatessen.

spaghetti

agnolotti

ravioli

pappardelle

spinach ravioli

gnocchi

fettuccine

tagliatelle

lasagne

making pasta

What could be more satisfying? With just a little practice and good-quality ingredients, you'll soon be creating fabulous fresh pasta in a variety of shapes, flavours and textures.

Making pasta isn't difficult — in fact, it can be extremely relaxing — but there are a few tips that will help. One important element that is often overlooked is a well-ventilated kitchen without breezes or air-conditioning. Also, humidity can cause unruly dough, so don't make pasta on a rainy day.

Kneading is an important part of the process, as it is necessary to work the gluten content of the flour to give a firm but tender dough. Knead the dough until it is pliable, adding small amounts of flour at a time if it is too soft.

Homemade pasta can be refrigerated for up to 48 hours, loosely packed in an airtight container. Turn it over once to check for moisture. Freezing works quite well, but sometimes the pasta becomes brittle. Don't defrost frozen pasta before cooking, just put it straight into boiling water. Lasagne sheets store best if blanched first, then drained and stacked between layers of waxed paper before being refrigerated or frozen.

equipment

No special equipment is necessary to make pasta, but some will save time. Set yourself up at a large work area or a board with a hard, even surface. Wood or marble is ideal. If making the dough by hand, a long rolling pin gives an evenly-rolled dough and requires less strokes, and a large bowl makes mixing tidier. A food processor will mix the dough quickly and reduce kneading time. For cutting, you'll need a long, sharp knife, perhaps a pastry wheel, and a dough scraper is handy. The hand-cranked pasta machines are highly recommended. They knead the dough as it is being rolled, give even sheets of pasta with good texture and are easy to handle. The better brands are sturdy, with a strong holding clamp and rollers that adjust easily as well as crank smoothly.

ingredients

All the ingredients for pasta dough should be brought to room temperature before you start. The proportion of flour to eggs depends on the weather, the quality of the flour and the age and size of the eggs. Oil makes the dough easier to work with but you don't have to add it.

Use plain (all-purpose) or unbleached flour, as it gives a well-textured and light dough with good manageability. A percentage of durum wheat semolina is favoured by some pasta makers as it improves flavour, colour and texture. However, its hard wheat qualities can make it hard to work, particularly on a hand-cranked machine, and any proportion greater than equal parts durum wheat semolina to plain flour can cause problems.

basic plain dough

To make enough pasta dough to serve six as a first course or four as a main course, you will need 300 g (10½ oz) plain (all-purpose) flour, 3 large (60 g/2¼ oz) eggs, 30 ml (1 fl oz) olive oil (optional), and a pinch of salt.

1 To mix by hand, mound the flour on a work surface or in a large bowl and then make a well in the centre.

2 Break the eggs into the well and add the oil, if using, and a large pinch of salt. Using a fork, begin to whisk the eggs and oil together, incorporating a little of the flour as you do so.

3 Gradually blend the flour with the eggs, working from the centre out. Use your free hand to hold the mound in place and stop leakage if any of the egg escapes. This step can be done in a food processor if desired.

4 Knead the dough on a lightly floured surface with smooth, light strokes, turning it as you fold and press. It should be

▶

soft and pliable, but dry to the touch. If it is sticky, knead in a little extra flour.

5 It will take at least 6 minutes kneading to achieve a smooth, elastic texture with a slightly glossy appearance. If durum wheat semolina is used, kneading will take at least 8 minutes. Put the dough in a plastic bag without sealing, or cover with a tea towel (dish towel) or upturned bowl. Allow it to rest for 30 minutes.

rolling and cutting by hand

1 Divide the dough into three or four manageable portions and cover them to prevent drying out.

2 Lightly flour a large work surface. Flatten one portion of dough, then use a long, floured rolling pin to roll out the dough from the centre to the outer edge to form a rectangle.

3 Continue rolling, always away from you, and rotating the dough often. Keep the work surface dusted with just enough flour to prevent sticking. When you have rolled a well-shaped rectangle, fold the dough in thirds and roll it out again. Continue in this way seven or eight times to give a smooth rectangle of pasta about 5 mm (¼ inch) thick.

4 Roll the sheet quickly and smoothly to a thickness of 2.5 mm (⅛ inch). Patch any tears with a piece of dough from the edge and a little water to help it stick.

5 As each sheet is done, transfer it to a dry tea towel (dish towel). If the pasta is to be used to make filled pasta, keep it covered, but if they are to be cut into lengths or shapes, leave them uncovered while the others are being rolled so that the surface moisture will dry slightly.

6 For lasagne sheets, simply cut the pasta into the sizes required. The best way to cut lengths such as fettuccine is to roll each pasta sheet up like a swiss (jelly) roll, then cut this into uniform widths with a long, sharp knife. For fettuccine, cut at 5 mm (¼ inch) intervals, 8 mm (⅜ inch) for tagliatelle, or about 2.5 cm (1 inch) for pappardelle. Discard the offcuts. Place the lengths in a single layer on a tea towel to surface dry for no more than 10 minutes. Or, hang long pasta strips to surface dry on broom handles or long wooden spoons between two chairs. Don't dry pasta in a cold place or in a draught as it may become brittle. It is better if it dries slowly. Lengths can also be cut from the flat sheet using a long, sharp knife or pastry wheel. You may find it easier to run the wheel beside a ruler for straight cutting. A fluted pastry wheel will give an interesting edge to pasta shapes such as lasagnette and farfalle.

using a hand-cranked pasta machine

1 Clamp the machine securely onto the edge of your work surface. Divide the dough into three or four portions and shape each into a rough log. Keeping the unworked portions covered, take one and flatten it by one or two rolls with a rolling pin. Dust lightly with flour.

2 With the machine's rollers at their widest setting, crank the dough through two or three times. Fold it in thirds, turn the dough 90 degrees and feed through again. If the dough feels damp or tends to stick, lightly flour the outside surfaces each time it is rolled until it passes through cleanly. Repeat this folding and rolling process eight to 10 times, or until the dough is a smooth and elastic sheet with a velvety appearance. From now on the dough is not folded.

3 Reduce the width of the rollers by one setting and pass the dough through. Repeat, setting the rollers one notch closer each time until you have rolled the desired thickness. Some machines may roll the sheets too thinly on their last setting, tearing them. A way around this is to stop at the second last setting and roll the dough through several times. It will come out a little thinner each time. This step also applies to machines that don't roll the pasta thinly enough on the last setting.

4 As each pasta sheet is completed, place it on a dry tea towel (dish towel) and then leave them, uncovered, to surface dry for 10 minutes if the sheets are to be cut, but cover them if they are going to be used for filled pasta.

5 For lasagne sheets, cut the pasta to the desired size. For narrower lengths, select the appropriate cutters on the machine and crank each pasta sheet through it. Spread them on the tea towel until ready to be cooked, only covering them if they appear to be drying too much. Long pasta, such as tagliatelle, can be hung to surface dry on broom handles or long wooden spoons between two chairs.

making shapes

To make farfalle, you will need sheets of pasta dough freshly rolled to a standard thickness of 2.5 mm (⅛ inch). Use a fluted pastry wheel rolled against a ruler to cut rectangles about 2.5 x 5.5 cm (1 x 2¼ inches). Pinch the centres to form a bow-tie shape and spread them on a dry tea towel (dish towel) for 10–12 minutes to surface dry. After 5 minutes, re-pinch any that are looking a little wayward.

To make orecchiette, start with unrolled, but rested, dough. Divide into manageable portions and use your hands to roll each into a long, thin log about 1 cm (½ inch) in diameter. Working with one log at a time, cut slices about 2.5 mm (⅛ inch) wide. Roll each slice between your thumb and a lightly floured wooden board to form little ear-like shells, thicker than most pasta shapes and with an obvious hand-made look. Spread over a tea towel (dish towel) to surface dry.

classic sauces

Sometimes it's difficult to determine whether you're eating pasta with your sauce or sauce with your pasta. While the difference is subtle, the Italians always intend their pasta to be evenly dressed by its sauce, rather than swimming in it. Prepare these classic sauces using the freshest ingredients and toss them through a bowl of pasta. And remember the Italian philosophy regarding sauce. To eat your pasta any other way is to do it a great injustice.

classic bolognese

Preparation time: **25 minutes**
Cooking time: **at least 2½ hours**
Serves **4**

50 g (1¾ oz) butter
180 g (6¼ oz) bacon slices or speck,
    rind removed and finely chopped
1 large onion, finely chopped
1 carrot, finely chopped
1 celery stalk, finely chopped
400 g (14 oz) lean minced (ground) beef
150 g (5½ oz) chicken livers, trimmed,
    finely chopped
500 ml (17 fl oz/2 cups) beef stock
250 ml (9 fl oz/1 cup) tomato passata
    (puréed tomatoes)
125 ml (4 fl oz/½ cup) red wine
¼ teaspoon freshly grated nutmeg
500 g (1 lb 2 oz) pasta
freshly grated parmesan cheese,
    to serve

1 Heat half the butter in a heavy-based
frying pan. Add the bacon and cook until
golden. Add the onion, carrot and celery
and cook over low heat for 8 minutes,
stirring occasionally.
2 Increase the heat, add the remaining
butter and, when the pan is hot, add the
beef. Break up any lumps with a fork and
stir until browned. Add the chicken livers
and stir until they change colour. Add the
stock, passata, wine, nutmeg, and salt and
pepper, to taste.
3 Bring to the boil and simmer, covered,
over very low heat for 2–5 hours, adding
a little more stock if the sauce becomes
too dry. The longer the sauce is cooked,
the more flavour it will have.
4 Cook the pasta in a large saucepan of
rapidly boiling salted water until *al dente*.
Drain and divide among warmed serving
bowls. Serve the sauce over the top and
sprinkle with freshly grated parmesan.

NOTE: Traditionally, bolognese was served
with tagliatelle, but it is now commonly
served with spaghetti.

Finely chop the bacon slices or
speck, after removing any rind.

Grate a little of the whole nutmeg
using a fine grater.

alfredo

Preparation time: **10 minutes**
Cooking time: **15 minutes**
Serves **4–6**

500 g (1 lb 2 oz) pasta
90 g (3¼ oz) butter
150 g (5½ oz/1½ cups) freshly grated
  parmesan cheese
310 ml (10¾ fl oz/1¼ cups) pouring
  (whipping) cream
3 tablespoons chopped flat-leaf (Italian)
  parsley

1 Cook the pasta in a large saucepan of rapidly boiling salted water until *al dente*. Drain and return to the pan.
2 While the pasta is cooking, melt the butter in a pan over low heat. Add the parmesan and cream and bring to the boil, stirring constantly. Reduce the heat and simmer, stirring, until the sauce has thickened slightly. Add the chopped parsley, salt and pepper, to taste, and stir until well combined.
3 Add the sauce to the pasta and toss well to coat. This dish can be garnished with chopped herbs or sprigs of herbs such as thyme.

NOTE: Traditionally, plain fettuccine, as shown in the picture, is used with this sauce, but you can use any style of pasta. It is a very simple sauce to make and should be prepared just before the pasta has finished cooking.

Ideally, parmesan is grated just before using. This prevents loss of flavour and drying out.

Use a large, sharp knife to chop the parsley. A swivel action is easiest, holding the point of the knife in one place.

napolitana

✵

Preparation time: 20 minutes
Cooking time: 25 minutes
Serves 4–6

2 tablespoons olive oil
1 onion, finely chopped
2–3 garlic cloves, finely chopped
1 small carrot, finely diced
1 celery stalk, finely diced
800 g (1 lb 12 oz) tin chopped
    tomatoes or 1 kg (2 lb 4 oz) ripe
    tomatoes, peeled and chopped
1 tablespoon tomato paste
    (concentrated purée)

3 tablespoons shredded basil
500 g (1 lb 2 oz) pasta
freshly grated parmesan cheese,
    to serve (optional)

1   Heat the oil in a large frying pan.
Add the onion and garlic and cook for
2 minutes, or until golden. Add the carrot
and celery and cook, stirring often, for
a further 2 minutes.
2   Add the tomatoes and tomato paste.
Simmer for 20 minutes, or until the sauce
thickens, stirring occasionally. Stir in the
basil and season with salt and freshly
ground black pepper, to taste.
3   While the sauce is cooking, cook the
pasta in a large saucepan of rapidly

boiling salted water until *al dente*. Drain
well and return to the pan.
4   Add the sauce to the pasta and mix
well. Serve with freshly grated parmesan
cheese, if desired.

NOTE: Traditionally, spaghetti is used with
this sauce, but you can use any pasta. We
have shown penne rigate. The sauce can
be reduced to a concentrated version by
cooking it for a longer period. Store it in
the refrigerator and add water or stock to
thin it, if necessary, when reheating.

For this sauce, the vegetables need
to be chopped into small pieces
before adding to the hot oil.

carbonara

Preparation time: **10 minutes**
Cooking time: **20 minutes**
Serves **6**

500 g (1 lb 2 oz) pasta
8 bacon slices
4 eggs
50 g (1¾ oz/½ cup) freshly grated
 parmesan cheese
310 ml (10¾ fl oz/1¼ cups) pouring
 (whipping) cream
snipped chives, to garnish

1 Cook the pasta in a large saucepan of rapidly boiling salted water until *al dente*. Drain and return to the pan.
2 While the pasta is cooking, discard the bacon rind and cut the bacon into thin strips. Cook in a heavy-based frying pan over medium heat until crisp. Remove and drain on paper towels.
3 Beat the eggs, parmesan and cream in a bowl until well combined. Add the bacon and pour the sauce over the warm pasta. Toss gently until the pasta is well coated in the sauce.
4 Return the pan to the heat and cook over low heat for 1 minute, or until slightly thickened. Season with freshly ground black pepper and serve garnished with snipped chives.

NOTE: Traditionally, fettuccine is used with this dish, but you can use any pasta of your choice. We have used spaghetti.

Cook the bacon strips in a heavy-based frying pan, stirring until crisp, being careful not to let them burn.

Drain the bacon on paper towels. After beating the eggs, freshly grated parmesan and cream together, mix in the bacon.

Stir the parmesan into the pesto and season to taste.

When storing pesto, cover the surface with a layer of oil.

pesto

✹

Preparation time: 15 minutes
Cooking time: 15 minutes
Serves 4–6

100 g (3½ oz) basil
2 garlic cloves, crushed
40 g (1½ oz/¼ cup) pine nuts, toasted
185 ml (6 fl oz/¾ cup) olive oil
50 g (1¾ oz/½ cup) freshly grated parmesan cheese, plus extra, to serve
500 g (1 lb 2 oz) pasta

1 Process the basil, garlic and pine nuts together in a food processor. With the motor running, add the oil in a steady stream until mixed to a smooth paste. Transfer to a bowl, stir in the parmesan and season to taste.
2 Cook the pasta in a large saucepan of rapidly boiling salted water until *al dente*.

Drain and return to the pan. Toss enough of the pesto through the pasta to coat it well. Serve sprinkled with parmesan.

NOTE: Traditionally, linguine, as shown, is used with pesto but you can serve it with any pasta of your choice. Refrigerate any leftover pesto in an airtight jar for up to a week. Cover the surface with a layer of oil. Freeze for up to 1 month.

amatriciana (spicy bacon and tomato sauce)

Preparation time: 45 minutes
Cooking time: 20 minutes
Serves 4–6

6 thin pancetta slices or 3 bacon slices
1 kg (2 lb 4 oz) very ripe tomatoes
500 g (1 lb 2 oz) pasta
1 tablespoon olive oil
1 small onion, very finely chopped
2 teaspoons very finely chopped fresh chilli
parmesan cheese shavings, to serve
   (optional)

1   Finely chop the pancetta or bacon.
Score a cross in the base of each tomato.
Soak in boiling water for 1–2 minutes,
drain and plunge into cold water briefly.
Peel back the skin from the cross. Halve,
remove the seeds and chop the flesh.
2   Add the pasta to a large saucepan of
rapidly boiling salted water and cook until
al dente. Drain and return to the pan.
3   About 5 minutes before the pasta is
cooked, heat the oil in a heavy-based
frying pan. Add the pancetta or bacon,
onion and chilli and stir over medium
heat for 3 minutes. Add the tomato and
salt and pepper, to taste. Reduce the heat
and simmer for another 3 minutes. Add
the sauce to the pasta and toss until well
combined. Serve garnished with shavings
of parmesan, if desired, and freshly
ground black pepper, to taste.

NOTE: It is believed this dish originated
in the town of Amatrice, where bacon
is a prized local product. For a change
from regular tomatoes, you can try roma
(plum) tomatoes. They are firm-fleshed,
with few seeds and have a rich flavour
when cooked. Traditionally, bucatini is
used with this sauce, but you can use any
pasta you prefer, such as casarecce.

Remove the tomatoes from the
cold water and peel the skin
down from the cross.

Halve the tomatoes and use
a teaspoon to scrape out the
seeds before chopping the flesh.

creamy boscaiola

Preparation time: **15 minutes**
Cooking time: **25 minutes**
Serves **4**

500 g (1 lb 2 oz) pasta
1 tablespoon olive oil
6 bacon slices, roughly chopped
200 g (7 oz) button mushrooms, sliced
625 ml (21½ fl oz/2½ cups) pouring
    (whipping) cream
2 spring onions (scallions), sliced
1 tablespoon chopped flat-leaf
    (Italian) parsley

1 Cook the pasta in a large saucepan of rapidly boiling salted water until *al dente*. Drain, return to the pan and keep warm.
2 While the pasta is cooking, heat the oil in a large frying pan, add the bacon and mushroom and cook, stirring, for 5 minutes, or until golden brown.
3 Stir in a little of the cream and scrape the wooden spoon on the bottom of the pan to dislodge any bacon that has stuck.
4 Add the remaining cream, bring to the boil and cook over high heat for 15 minutes, or until the sauce is thick enough to coat the back of a spoon. Stir the spring onion through the mixture. Pour the sauce over the pasta and toss to combine. Serve sprinkled with the parsley.

NOTE: This sauce is normally served with spaghetti, but you can use any pasta. We have shown it with pappardelle. If you are short on time and don't have 15 minutes to reduce the sauce, it can be thickened with 2 teaspoons of cornflour (cornstarch) mixed with 1 tablespoon of water. Stir until the mixture boils and thickens. 'Boscaiola' means woodcutter — collecting mushrooms is part of the heritage of the woodcutters.

Add a little cream and scrape the bottom of the pan with a wooden spoon to dislodge any bacon that has stuck.

Cook the sauce over high heat until it is thick enough to coat the back of a wooden spoon.

puttanesca

Preparation time: **15 minutes**
Cooking time: **25 minutes**
Serves **4**

80 ml (2½ fl oz/⅓ cup) olive oil
2 onions, finely chopped
3 garlic cloves, finely chopped
½ teaspoon chilli flakes
6 large ripe tomatoes, diced
4 tablespoons capers, rinsed and
   squeezed dry
8 anchovy fillets in oil, drained and chopped
150 g (5½ oz) kalamata olives
3 tablespoons chopped flat-leaf (Italian)
   parsley
375 g (13 oz) pasta

1 Heat the olive oil in a saucepan, add the onion and cook over medium heat for 5 minutes. Add the garlic and chilli flakes to the saucepan and cook for 30 seconds. Add the tomato, capers and anchovies. Simmer over low heat for 10–15 minutes, or until the sauce is thick and pulpy. Stir the olives and parsley through the sauce.

2 While the sauce is cooking, cook the pasta in a large saucepan of rapidly boiling salted water until *al dente*. Drain and return to the pan.
3 Add the sauce to the pasta and stir it through. Season to taste and serve.

NOTE: Traditionally, spaghetti is served with this sauce, but you can use other pasta if you prefer.

To make peeling easier, squash each clove of garlic with the flat side of a knife, pressing with the palm of your hand.

Chop the garlic with a little salt, then scrape the knife at an angle to finely crush the garlic.

soups

Soup is food for the soul — spreading warmth and comfort and memories of winter suppers. The best kind of soup is made by simmering all your favourite ingredients in a tasty stock, and what better way to beef it up than by throwing in a handful of pasta? Conchiglie and fusilli make a soup almost a stew, while tortellini or ravioli make a meal of any elegant clear consommé. There are even special tiny pastas for floating in your soup. In fact, pasta and soup go together like, well, like macaroni and minestrone.

lemon-scented broth with tortellini

Preparation time: **10 minutes**
Cooking time: **20 minutes**
Serves **4–6**

1 lemon
125 ml (4 fl oz/½ cup) white wine
440 g (15½ oz) tin chicken consommé
375 g (13 oz) fresh or dried veal or
   chicken tortellini
4 tablespoons chopped flat-leaf (Italian)
   parsley
freshly grated parmesan cheese, to serve

1 Using a vegetable peeler, peel wide strips from the lemon. Remove the white pith with a small sharp knife. Cut three of the wide pieces into fine strips and set aside for a garnish.
2 Combine the remaining wide strips of lemon zest, wine, consommé and 750 ml (26 fl oz/3 cups) water in a large saucepan. Cook for 10 minutes over low heat. Remove the lemon zest from the pan and bring the mixture to the boil. Add the tortellini and parsley and season with black pepper. Cook for 6–7 minutes, or until the pasta is *al dente*. Garnish with fine strips of zest and grated parmesan.

chicken, leek and chickpea soup

Preparation time: **15 minutes**
Cooking time: **20 minutes**
Serves **4**

1 litre (35 fl oz/4 cups) chicken stock
125 g (4½ oz) miniature pasta shapes
20 g (¾ oz) butter
1 leek, white part only, sliced
1 garlic clove, crushed
110 g (3¾ oz/½ cup) drained tinned
   chickpeas, lightly roasted
1 tablespoon plain (all-purpose) flour
2 tablespoons finely chopped flat-leaf
   (Italian) parsley
pinch of cayenne pepper
200 g (7 oz) chopped cooked chicken meat

1 Bring the stock to the boil in a large saucepan. Add the pasta and cook until just tender. Remove the pasta using a slotted spoon and set aside, keeping the stock on the heat and just boiling.
2 Meanwhile, melt the butter in a large saucepan, add the leek and garlic and stir until golden, but not brown. Add the chickpeas, toss for a minute and then sprinkle with the flour. Fry for about 10 seconds, then gradually blend in the boiling stock.
3 Add the parsley and cayenne, and season to taste. Add the pasta and the chicken to the pan and return to the boil before serving in individual bowls.

minestrone

Preparation time: **25 minutes**
   + overnight soaking time
Cooking time: **2 hours**
Serves **6**

125 g (4½ oz) dried borlotti (cranberry)
   beans
60 ml (2 fl oz/¼ cup) olive oil
1 large onion, finely chopped

lemon-scented broth with tortellini

2 garlic cloves, crushed

60 g (2¼ oz) pancetta, finely chopped

1 celery stalk, halved lengthways and thinly sliced

1 carrot, halved lengthways and thinly sliced

1 potato, diced

2 teaspoons tomato paste (concentrated purée)

400 g (14 oz) tin chopped tomatoes

6 basil leaves, roughly torn

2 litres (70 fl oz/8 cups) chicken or vegetable stock

2 zucchini (courgettes), thinly sliced

115 g (4 oz/¾ cup) shelled fresh peas

60 g (2¼ oz) green beans, cut into short lengths

80 g (2¾ oz) silverbeet (Swiss chard) leaves, shredded

3 tablespoons chopped flat-leaf (Italian) parsley

70 g (2½ oz) ditalini or other small pasta

PESTO

30 g (1 oz) basil leaves

20 g (¾ oz) lightly toasted pine nuts (see Note)

2 garlic cloves

100 ml (3½ fl oz) olive oil

25 g (1 oz/¼ cup) freshly grated parmesan cheese

1 Soak the borlotti beans in plenty of cold water overnight. Drain and rinse thoroughly under cold water.

2 Heat the oil in a large, heavy-based saucepan, add the onion, garlic and pancetta and cook over low heat, stirring occasionally, for 8–10 minutes, or until softened. Add the celery, carrot and potato and cook for 5 minutes. Stir in the tomato paste, tomatoes, basil and borlotti beans. Season with freshly ground black pepper, to taste. Add the stock and bring slowly to the boil. Cover and simmer, stirring occasionally, for 1½ hours. Add the zucchini, peas, green beans, silverbeet, parsley and the pasta. Simmer for 8–10 minutes, or until the vegetables and pasta are *al dente*. Check for seasoning and adjust if necessary.

3 To make the pesto, place the basil, pine nuts and garlic with a pinch of salt in a

borlotti beans

Borlotti beans, also known as cranberry or red haricot, are the large, beautifully marked kidney beans so loved in northern and central Italy. They have a nutty flavour and creamy flesh that is especially fine in soups and stews, but they are also well suited to salads and puréeing. They can be found fresh in the spring and summer. Otherwise, the dried or pre-cooked tinned beans are used, the latter having the advantage of greater convenience.

food processor and process until finely chopped. With the motor running, pour in the oil in a slow, steady stream. Transfer the pesto to a bowl and stir in the parmesan and some ground black pepper, to taste. Serve the soup with a dollop of pesto spooned over the top.

NOTE: Toast the pine nuts in a frying pan over medium heat, stirring constantly, until they are golden brown and aromatic. Watch carefully as they will burn easily.

leeks

Like onions, leeks are a member of the *Allium* family. They are favoured for their delicate, mildly sweet flavour and are used both raw and cooked. Leeks have cylindrical, not rounded, bulbs and the leaves are flattened and solid. These leaves are tightly compacted and grit tends to stick between the layers, so careful rinsing is necessary after the green tops have been discarded. Only the tender white part is used.

bean soup with sausage

Preparation time: 25 minutes
Cooking time: 40 minutes
Serves 4–6

4 Italian sausages, skin removed
2 teaspoons olive oil
2 leeks, white part only, sliced
1 garlic clove, crushed
1 large carrot, chopped
2 celery stalks, sliced
2 tablespoons plain (all-purpose) flour
2 beef stock (bouillon) cubes, crumbled
2 litres (70 fl oz/8 cups) boiling water

125 ml (4 fl oz/½ cup) white wine
125 g (4½ oz) conchiglie (shell pasta)
440 g (15½ oz) tin mixed beans, drained
chopped parsley, to serve (optional)

1 Cut the sausages into small pieces. Heat the oil in a large heavy-based saucepan and add the sausage pieces. Cook over medium heat for 5 minutes, or until golden, stirring regularly. Remove from the pan, set aside and drain on paper towels.
2 Add the leek, garlic, carrot and celery to the pan and cook for 2–3 minutes or until soft, stirring occasionally. Add the flour and stir for 1 minute. Gradually stir in the combined stock cubes, water and

wine. Bring to the boil, reduce the heat and simmer for 10 minutes.
3 Add the pasta and beans to the saucepan. Increase the heat and cook for 8–10 minutes, or until the pasta is *al dente*. Return the sausage to the pan and season to taste. Serve sprinkled with chopped parsley, if desired.

NOTE: You can use dried beans, if preferred. Put them in a bowl, cover with water and soak overnight. Drain and add to a large saucepan with enough water to cover the beans well. Bring to the boil, reduce the heat and simmer for 1 hour. Drain well before adding to the soup.

tomato soup with pasta and basil

Preparation time: 25 minutes
Cooking time: 35–40 minutes
Serves 4

3 very ripe, large tomatoes
  (about 750 g/1 lb 10 oz)
2 tablespoons olive oil
1 onion, finely chopped
1 garlic clove, crushed
1 small red capsicum (pepper), finely chopped
1 litre (35 fl oz/4 cups) chicken or
  vegetable stock

60 g (2¼ oz/¼ cup) tomato paste
  (concentrated purée)
1 teaspoon sugar
15 g (½ oz/¼ cup) basil leaves
155 g (5½ oz/1 cup) conchiglie
  (shell pasta) or macaroni

1 Score a small cross in the base of each tomato. Place the tomatoes into boiling water for 1–2 minutes, then plunge into cold water. Peel the skin away from the cross. Remove the seeds and roughly chop the tomatoes. Heat the oil in a large heavy-based saucepan and cook the onion, garlic and capsicum, stirring, for 10 minutes, or until soft. Add the tomato and cook for another 10 minutes.

2 Add the stock, tomato paste, sugar and salt and pepper, to taste. Cover and simmer for 15 minutes. Remove from the heat and add the basil. Cool slightly before blending or processing the mixture, in batches, until smooth. Return the mixture to the pan and reheat gently.
3 Meanwhile, add the pasta to a large saucepan of rapidly boiling salted water and cook until *al dente*. Drain, add to the soup and heat through. Garnish with basil leaves if you wish.

NOTE: Basil is added at the end of cooking so its flavour is not impaired.

basil

There are many varieties of this spicy, aromatic herb, but sweet basil is the most commonly used. Basil plays an important role in Italian and Asian, especially Indonesian, cuisine. It is most often used fresh and added at the last minute, the dried form only being successful in dishes of complex flavours needing long cooking. Basil leaves have a high moisture content and bruise easily. They are best if shredded, not chopped, and the less they are cut, the less blackening will occur.

broccoli

Broccoli belongs to the cabbage family. It is so closely related to the cauliflower that they both have the same varietal name, *botrytis*, from the Greek meaning 'formed in a cluster' like a bunch of grapes. Broccoli adds not only colour and flavour to a meal, but nutritional value as well, as it has high levels of vitamins and essential minerals. It boils or steams well and, if trimmed and cut into separate florets, will cook quickly and evenly. Broccoli is also suitable for puréeing and the bulk of the florets can be used to give volume to salads and stir-fries.

broccoli soup

broccoli soup

Preparation time: **15 minutes**
Cooking time: **20 minutes**
Serves **4**

2 tablespoons olive oil
1 large onion, thinly sliced
50 g (1¾ oz) diced unsmoked ham or
  prosciutto
1 garlic clove, crushed
1.25 litres (44 fl oz/5 cups) chicken
  stock
50 g (1¾ oz) stellini or other small
  pasta shapes
250 g (9 oz) broccoli, tops cut into
  small florets and the tender stems
  cut into thin batons
freshly grated parmesan cheese,
  to serve (optional)

1 Heat the oil in a large saucepan over low heat, add the onion, prosciutto and garlic and cook for 4–5 minutes. Add the stock and bring to the boil, then reduce the heat slightly and simmer for 10 minutes with the lid three-quarters on.
2 Add the pasta and broccoli and cook until the pasta is *al dente* and the broccoli is crisp but tender. Season to taste. Serve sprinkled with parmesan, if desired.

prawn and basil soup

Preparation time: **45 minutes**
Cooking time: **15–20 minutes**
Serves **4**

500 g (1 lb 2 oz) raw prawns
  (shrimp)
2 tablespoons olive oil
20 g (¾ oz) butter
2 garlic cloves
1 small red onion, thinly sliced
2 celery stalks, cut into thin batons
3 small carrots, cut into thin batons
1 tablespoon finely chopped flat-leaf
  (Italian) parsley
1½ tablespoons finely chopped basil
pinch of cayenne pepper
125 ml (4 fl oz/½ cup) dry sherry
1 litre (35 fl oz/4 cups) chicken stock
70 g (2½ oz) conchiglie (shell pasta)
60 ml (2 fl oz/¼ cup) pouring (whipping)
  cream

1 Peel the prawns and gently pull out the dark vein from each prawn back, starting at the head end.
2 In a large saucepan, heat the oil and butter. Add the garlic cloves and onion and cook over low heat for 2–3 minutes. Add the celery and carrot and fry until the vegetables are golden, but not brown. Add the parsley, basil and cayenne. Stir briefly, add the prawns and toss to combine. Remove the garlic cloves. Pour in the sherry, increase the heat and cook for 2–3 minutes. Add the stock, bring back to the boil, reduce the heat and simmer for 5 minutes. Add the pasta and simmer until it is *al dente*. Stir in the cream and season with salt and pepper, to taste.

bacon and pea soup

Preparation time: **20 minutes**
Cooking time: **15 minutes**
Serves 4–6

4 bacon slices
50 g (1¾ oz) butter
1 large onion, finely chopped
1 celery stalk, thinly sliced
2 litres (70 fl oz/8 cups)
   chicken stock
150 g (5½ oz/1 cup) frozen peas
250 g (9 oz) risoni
2 tablespoons chopped parsley

1 Trim the rind and excess fat from the bacon and chop into small pieces.
2 Melt the butter in a large heavy-based saucepan and cook the bacon, onion and celery over low heat for 5 minutes, stirring occasionally. Add the stock and peas and simmer, covered, for 5 minutes. Increase the heat, add the risoni and cook, uncovered, stirring occasionally, for 5 minutes, or until the risoni is tender. Add the parsley and season, to taste.

herb bread

Combine 125 g (4½ oz) softened butter with 30 g (1 oz/½ cup) chopped mixed herbs and a finely chopped garlic clove. Slice a baguette diagonally, almost all the way through, and spread each piece with the herb butter. Reshape into a loaf, wrap in foil and bake in a 180°C (350°F/Gas 4) oven for 30 minutes, or until the loaf is crisp and hot. If you don't want the garlic flavour, you can leave it out.

celery

An important flavouring vegetable for many dishes, celery is also delicious in its own right, whether it be braised, baked or served fresh in a salad. All the stalks are stringy, and the darker, outer ones might need to be stripped before use. These are more likely to be chopped for use in stews, while the pale, milder inner stalks can be eaten raw. Celery hearts do not need stringing and are ideal for braising. The dried seeds of the plant, aromatic and slightly bitter, are used as a seasoning.

ratatouille and pasta soup

Preparation time: 25 minutes
Cooking time: 40 minutes
Serves 6

1 eggplant (aubergine)
2 tablespoons olive oil
1 large onion, chopped
1 large red capsicum (pepper), chopped
1 large green capsicum (pepper), chopped
2 garlic cloves, crushed
3 zucchini (courgettes), sliced
800 g (1 lb 12 oz) tin chopped tomatoes
1 teaspoon dried oregano leaves
½ teaspoon dried thyme leaves
1 litre (35 fl oz/4 cups) vegetable stock
50 g (1¾ oz) fusilli (spiral pasta)
parmesan cheese shavings, to serve

1   Chop the eggplant. To remove any bitterness, spread the eggplant pieces in a colander and sprinkle generously with salt. Set aside for 20 minutes, then rinse thoroughly and pat dry with paper towels.

2   Heat the oil in a large heavy-based saucepan and cook the onion over medium heat for 10 minutes, or until golden. Add the capsicum, garlic, zucchini and eggplant and stir-fry for 5 minutes.

3   Add the tomatoes, herbs and stock. Bring to the boil, then reduce the heat and simmer for 10 minutes, or until the vegetables are tender. Add the pasta and cook for a further 15 minutes, or until it is *al dente*. Serve with shavings of parmesan scattered on top.

eggplant

The eggplant, or aubergine, comes in an amazing range of shapes and colours. It can be large and bulbous, thin and finger-like, or small and round like a cherry tomato. The colours range from deep purple to green or white and sometimes they are striped. Look for a glossy wrinkle-free skin, and firm, not hard, flesh.

chicken and pasta soup

Preparation time: **20 minutes**
Cooking time: **20 minutes**
Serves **4**

2 tablespoons olive oil
1 onion, finely diced
2 boneless, skinless chicken breasts, finely diced
90 g (3¼ oz) mushrooms, chopped
175 g (6 oz) spaghetti, broken into short lengths
1.5 litres (52 fl oz/6 cups) chicken stock
35 g (1¼ oz) torn basil leaves

1 Heat the olive oil in a saucepan and cook the onion until soft and golden. Add the chicken, mushroom, spaghetti pieces and chicken stock. Bring to the boil.
2 Reduce the heat and simmer for 10 minutes. Stir in the basil leaves. Season to taste and serve immediately.

NOTE: This is a chunky soup. If you prefer a thinner style of soup, add more stock.

garlic, pasta and fish soup

Preparation time: **30 minutes**
Cooking time: **40 minutes**
Serves **4–6**

80 ml (2½ fl oz/⅓ cup) olive oil
1 leek, white part only, trimmed and sliced
20–30 garlic cloves, thinly sliced
2 potatoes, chopped
2 litres (70 fl oz/8 cups) fish stock
70 g (2½ oz/½ cup) small pasta shapes
10 baby (pattypan) squash, halved
2 zucchini (courgettes), thickly sliced
300 g (10½ oz) firm white-fleshed fish fillets (such as ling), cut into large pieces

garlic, pasta and fish soup

1–2 tablespoons lemon juice
2 tablespoons shredded basil

1 Heat the oil in a large saucepan, add the leek, garlic and potato and cook over medium heat for 10 minutes. Add 500 ml (17 fl oz/2 cups) of the stock and cook for 10 minutes. Allow to cool slightly before transferring to a food processor or blender and blending, in batches, until smooth.
2 Pour the remaining stock into the pan and bring to the boil. Add the pasta, squash and zucchini. Add the purée, and simmer for 15 minutes. When the pasta is soft, add the fish and cook for a further 5 minutes, or until tender. Add the lemon juice and basil, and season with salt and freshly ground black pepper, to taste. Serve with lemon wedges, if desired.

NOTE: A large quantity of garlic cloves are used in this recipe to showcase the unique characteristic flavour of garlic.

country pumpkin and pasta soup

Preparation time: 25 minutes
Cooking time: 20 minutes
Serves 4–6

1 tablespoon olive oil
30 g (1 oz) butter
1 large onion, finely chopped
2 garlic cloves, crushed
700 g (1 lb 9 oz) pumpkin (winter squash),
    peeled, seeded and cut into small cubes
2 potatoes, cut into small cubes
3 litres (105 fl oz/12 cups) chicken stock
125 g (4½ oz) risoni or stellini
chopped parsley, to serve

1 Heat the oil and butter in a large saucepan. Add the onion and garlic and stir over low heat for 5 minutes.
2 Add the pumpkin, potato and stock. Increase the heat and cook, covered, for 10 minutes, or until the pumpkin and potato are tender.
3 Add the pasta and cook, stirring occasionally, for 5 minutes or until the pasta is just tender. Sprinkle with the parsley and serve immediately.

NOTE: Butternut and jap pumpkins will give the sweetest flavour. Be sure to use a good-quality chicken stock to give the best flavour and ensure the soup doesn't finish up too salty.

pumpkin

Pumpkins, or winter squash, are related to marrows and squash. Because of their relatively high moisture content, they cook more quickly than vegetables such as potatoes. When cooking pumpkin for a puréed soup, you can try baking the pumpkin instead of boiling it. The resulting texture is firmer and the flavour is richer and has a slightly nutty edge.

lamb and fusilli soup

Preparation time: **25 minutes**
Cooking time: **40 minutes**
Serves **6–8**

2 tablespoons oil
500 g (1 lb 2 oz) lean lamb meat, cubed
2 onions, finely chopped
2 carrots, diced
4 celery stalks, diced
400 g (14 oz) tin chopped tomatoes
2 litres (70 fl oz/8 cups) beef stock
500 g (1 lb 2 oz) fusilli (spiral pasta)
chopped flat-leaf (Italian) parsley, to serve

1 Heat the oil in a large saucepan and cook the lamb, in batches, until golden brown. Remove each batch as it is done and drain on paper towels. Set aside.
2 Add the onion to the pan and cook for 2 minutes or until softened. Return the meat to the pan, add the carrot, celery, tomatoes and stock. Stir to combine and bring to the boil. Reduce the heat to low and simmer, covered, for 15 minutes. Add the pasta and stir to prevent it sticking to the pan. Simmer, uncovered, for a further 10 minutes, or until the lamb and pasta are tender. Sprinkle with parsley, season with salt and freshly ground black pepper, and serve.

beef stock

Beef stock is the base of many soups and adds flavour to casseroles and stews. A good stock can be served as a light broth. When reduced to a concentrated form, it becomes a flavouring agent for sauces. Beef or chicken stock is used in recipes containing lamb and pork, as lamb gives a strong, muttony stock and pork has a thin, sweet flavour.

antipasto

What better way to whet the appetite? Literally translated as 'before the meal', the antipasto platter is a colourful reminder of the days of the Roman banquet. Excellent for serving at parties.

salami and potato frittata wedges

Fry 2 finely diced potatoes in about 2 tablespoons of oil in a 20 cm (8 inch) non-stick frying pan. Add 50 g (1¾ oz) roughly chopped spicy Italian salami and fry, stirring occasionally, for 10 minutes, or until the potato softens. Add 8 lightly beaten eggs and cook over medium heat for 10 minutes. Transfer the pan to a preheated grill (broiler) and cook for 3 minutes or until the frittata is set. Remove from the pan and allow to cool slightly before cutting into wedges. Serves 6–8.

stuffed mussels

Scrub 500 g (1 lb 2 oz) mussels and pull out the beards. Discard any open or damaged mussels. Cook in boiling water for 3 minutes, or until they open (discard any that don't open). Drain and cool. Remove the top shells and put the mussels in the shell in a baking dish. Preheat the oven to 200°C (400°F/ Gas 6). Fry 1 finely chopped onion in 1 tablespoon olive oil until golden. Add 2 chopped ripe tomatoes and 2 crushed garlic cloves. Remove from the heat and season. Spoon the sauce into the shells. Combine 80 g (2¾ oz/1 cup) fresh breadcrumbs and 20 g (¾ oz) finely grated parmesan cheese and sprinkle on top. Bake for 10 minutes, or until the crumbs are crisp. Serves 6–8.

polenta shapes with chorizo and salsa

Bring 750 ml (26 fl oz/3 cups) water to the boil in a saucepan. Gradually add 110 g (3¾ oz/¾ cup) polenta and stir constantly over medium heat until the mixture comes away from the side of the pan. Stir in 100 g (3½ oz) grated cheddar cheese, 50 g (1¾ oz/⅓ cup) grated mozzarella cheese and 1 tablespoon chopped oregano. Spread the mixture into a greased tin, about 18 x 28 cm (7 x 11 inches). Chill for 2 hours, or until set. Cut out shapes using pastry cutters about 5 cm (2 inches) in diameter. Brush lightly with oil and cook under a preheated grill (broiler) until golden. Thinly slice 4 chorizo sausages and brown on both sides in a non-stick frying pan. Top the polenta shapes with bottled tomato salsa and a piece of chorizo. Garnish with oregano leaves. Serves 6–8.

barbecued sardines

Combine 60 ml (2 fl oz/¼ cup) lemon juice, 2 tablespoons olive oil and 1–2 peeled and halved garlic cloves. Lightly oil a preheated barbecue or chargrill pan and brown 20 butterflied sardine fillets over high heat. Brush the sardines with the lemon mixture during cooking. Arrange the sardines on a serving platter. Makes 20.

antipasto

continued

grilled eggplant and capsicum

Cut 1 large eggplant (aubergine) into 1 cm (½ inch) slices. Cut 2 large red capsicums (peppers) in half and remove the seeds and membrane. Put the capsicum, skin side up, under a hot grill (broiler) and cook for 8 minutes, or until the skin blisters and blackens. Remove from the heat and place in a plastic bag. When cool enough to handle, peel away the skin and cut the flesh into thick strips. Brush the eggplant slices liberally with olive oil and cook under a medium grill until deep golden brown. Carefully turn the slices over, brush the other sides with oil and grill again until golden.

Do not rush this process by having the grill too hot, as slow cooking allows the sugar in the eggplant to caramelise. Combine the eggplant and capsicum in a bowl with 2 crushed garlic cloves, 2 tablespoons extra virgin olive oil, a pinch of sugar and about 2 tablespoons chopped flat-leaf (Italian) parsley. Cover and marinate in the refrigerator overnight. Bring to room temperature before serving. Serves 4–6.

pesto bocconcini balls

Blend 50 g (1¾ oz/1 cup) basil leaves, 3 tablespoons each of pine nuts and freshly grated parmesan cheese, and 2 garlic cloves in a food processor until finely chopped. With the motor running, gradually add 80 ml (2½ fl oz/⅓ cup) olive oil and process until a paste is formed. Transfer the pesto to a bowl and add 300 g (10½ oz) baby bocconcini. Mix very gently, cover and marinate in the refrigerator for 2 hours. Serves 4–6.

slow-roasted balsamic tomatoes

Preheat the oven to 160°C (315°F/Gas 2–3). Cut 500 g (1 lb 2 oz) roma (plum) tomatoes in half. Put them on a non-stick baking tray and brush lightly with extra virgin olive oil. Sprinkle with salt and drizzle with 2 tablespoons balsamic vinegar. Roast for 1 hour, basting every 15 minutes with another 2 tablespoons balsamic vinegar. Serves 6–8.

bruschetta

Thickly slice a loaf of Italian bread. Chop 500 g (1 lb 2 oz) ripe tomatoes into very small cubes. Finely dice 1 red onion. Combine the tomato and onion in a bowl with 2 tablespoons olive oil. Season with salt and freshly ground pepper, to taste. Lightly toast the bread and, while hot, rub both sides with a whole garlic clove. Top each piece with some tomato mixture and serve warm, topped with finely shredded basil. Serves 6–8.

cauliflower fritters

Cut 300 g (10½ oz) cauliflower into large florets. Cook the florets in a saucepan of boiling salted water until just tender. Do not overcook them, as they will fall apart. Drain thoroughly and set aside to cool slightly. Cut 200 g (7 oz) fontina cheese into small cubes and carefully tuck the cheese inside the florets. Lightly beat 3 eggs together in a bowl and dip each floret in the egg, then roll in 40 g (1¼ oz/½ cup) fresh breadcrumbs. When all the florets are crumbed, deep-fry them in hot oil, in batches, until they are crisp and golden. Serve hot. Serves 4–6.

pasta with meat

Undoubtedly the most famous pasta dish of all, and the most popular standby meal for many families, is spaghetti bolognese, the superb combination of minced meat sauce with pasta (see Classic sauces, page 22). Although most commonly made with beef, in Bologna pork is often added and sometimes lamb is used. All these meats, and many others, when flavoured with herbs, and married with tomatoes, vegetables and wine, turn a straightforward bowl of pasta into a hearty, nutritious and truly delicious meal.

tagliatelle with veal, wine and cream

Preparation time: **15 minutes**
Cooking time: **20 minutes**
Serves **4**

500 g (1 lb 2 oz) veal scaloppine or escalopes, cut into thin strips
plain (all-purpose) flour, seasoned
60 g (2¼ oz) butter
1 onion, sliced
125 ml (4 fl oz/½ cup) dry white wine
60 ml (2 fl oz/¼ cup) beef stock or chicken stock
170 ml (5½ fl oz/⅔ cup) pouring (whipping) cream
600 g (1 lb 5 oz) fresh plain or spinach tagliatelle (or a mixture of both)
1 tablespoon freshly grated parmesan cheese, plus extra, to serve (optional)
flat-leaf (Italian) parsley leaves, to garnish

1 Toss the veal strips in the seasoned flour until coated. Melt the butter in a frying pan. Add the veal and fry quickly until browned. Remove with a slotted spoon and set aside.

2 Add the onion to the pan and stir until soft and golden. Pour in the wine and cook rapidly to reduce the liquid. Add the stock and cream and season to taste. Reduce the sauce again, and add the veal towards the end.

3 Meanwhile, cook the pasta in a large saucepan of rapidly boiling salted water until *al dente*. Drain and transfer to a warm serving dish.

4 Stir the parmesan through the sauce and pour over the pasta. Sprinkle with extra parmesan, if desired, and parsley.

white wine

White wine contributes a delicate body to dishes. The taste should never be discernible and only a small amount should be used, which must then be completely cooked off to dispel the alcohol. The wine should be the same quality as a good drinking wine. Non-fruity dry white wines are used in savoury cooking, particularly with seafood, and for sweet dishes fortified wines or liqueurs are chosen, but not sweet white wine.

roast pumpkin with sage

Preheat the oven to 220°C (425°C/ Gas 7). Cut a pumpkin into small cubes and toss well in olive oil. Transfer to a baking dish and scatter with 2 tablespoons chopped sage and salt and pepper, to taste. Bake for 20 minutes, or a little longer, to brown the cubes a little more. Serve scattered with a little more chopped sage. Serve as a side dish.

rigatoni with braised oxtail and celery

✻

Preparation time: **25 minutes**
Cooking time: **2 hours**
Serves **4**

2 tablespoons olive oil
1.5 kg (3 lb 5 oz) oxtail, jointed
2 large onions, sliced
4 garlic cloves, chopped
2 celery stalks, sliced
2 carrots, thinly sliced
2 large rosemary sprigs, plus extra,
    for garnish
60 ml (2 fl oz/¼ cup) red wine
60 g (2¼ oz/¼ cup) tomato paste
    (concentrated purée)
4 tomatoes, peeled and chopped
1.5 litres (52 fl oz/6 cups) beef stock
500 g (1 lb 2 oz) rigatoni

1 Heat the oil in a large heavy-based saucepan. Brown the oxtail, then remove from the pan and set aside. Add the onion, garlic, celery and carrot to the pan and stir for 3–4 minutes, or until the onion is lightly browned.
2 Return the oxtail to the pan and add the rosemary and wine. Cover and cook for 10 minutes, shaking the pan occasionally to prevent the meat from sticking. Add the tomato paste, tomato

and 500 ml (17 fl oz/2 cups) of the stock and simmer, uncovered, for 30 minutes, stirring occasionally.
3 Add another 500 ml (17 fl oz/2 cups) of stock to the pan and cook for another 30 minutes. Add 250 ml (9 fl oz/1 cup) of stock and cook for 30 minutes more. Add the remaining stock and cook until the meat is falling from the bone. The liquid should have reduced to a thick sauce.
4 Just before the meat is cooked, cook the pasta in a large saucepan of rapidly

boiling salted water until *al dente*. Drain and serve with the meat and sauce, garnished with rosemary sprigs.

NOTE: For a different flavour, you can add 250 g (9 oz) bacon slices, rind removed and chopped, to the cooked onion, garlic and vegetables.

spaghetti with salami and capsicum

Preparation time: 15 minutes
Cooking time: 45 minutes
Serves 4–6

2 tablespoons olive oil
1 large onion, finely chopped
2 garlic cloves, crushed
150 g (5½ oz) sliced spicy salami,
  cut into strips
2 large red capsicums (peppers), chopped
800 g (1 lb 12 oz) tin chopped tomatoes
125 ml (4 fl oz/½ cup) dry white wine
500 g (1 lb 2 oz) spaghetti

1 Heat the oil in a heavy-based frying pan. Add the onion, garlic and salami and cook for 5 minutes, stirring, over medium heat. Add the capsicum, cover and cook for 5 minutes.
2 Add the tomatoes and wine and bring to the boil. Reduce the heat and simmer, covered, for 15 minutes. Remove the lid and cook for another 15 minutes, or until the liquid is reduced and the sauce is the desired consistency. Season with salt and pepper, to taste.
3 About 15 minutes before the sauce is ready, cook the spaghetti in a large

bean salad with vinaigrette

Toss cooked cannellini or haricot beans in a vinaigrette dressing made by thoroughly whisking together some walnut oil and balsamic vinegar with a crushed garlic clove. Add 2 tablespoons finely chopped parsley, 4 finely chopped spring onions (scallions) and a handful of torn basil leaves. Season well with salt and pepper. Before serving, allow to stand for about 10 minutes to allow the beans to soak up the flavour. Serve as a side dish.

salami

Salami, uncooked cured sausage, comes in numerous shapes, flavours and blends of meats. It can be mild or strong, fresh or mature, hard or soft, fine or coarse grained. The meats that are favoured are beef, pork and pork fat in varying proportions, and game meat is sometimes used. Most salamis are cured in salt, but there are some types that originated in mountainous regions which are air-cured. Salami should not be cooked for too long as this draws out the fat content.

saucepan of rapidly boiling salted water until *al dente*. Drain and return to the pan. Toss half the sauce with the pasta and divide among serving dishes. Top with the remaining sauce and serve.

baked pasta and mince

❋

Preparation time: **20 minutes**
Cooking time: **2 hours**
Serves **8**

2 tablespoons olive oil
1 large onion, chopped
1 kg (2 lb 4 oz) minced (ground) beef
60 ml (2 fl oz/¼ cup) red wine
700 ml (24 fl oz) chunky tomato pasta sauce
2 chicken stock (bouillon) cubes, crumbled
2 tablespoons finely chopped parsley
500 g (1 lb 2 oz) bucatini
2 egg whites, lightly beaten
2 tablespoons dry breadcrumbs

CHEESE SAUCE
50 g (1¾ oz) butter
2 tablespoons plain (all-purpose) flour
625 ml (21½ fl oz/2½ cups) milk
2 egg yolks, lightly beaten
125 g (4½ oz/1 cup) grated cheddar cheese

1 Heat the oil in a heavy-based saucepan. Add the onion and cook over medium heat for 2 minutes, or until soft. Add the beef and stir over high heat until well browned and almost all the liquid has evaporated.
2 Add the wine, sauce and stock cubes and bring to the boil. Reduce to a simmer and cook, covered, for 1 hour, stirring occasionally. Remove from the heat. Add the parsley and allow to cool.
3 To make the cheese sauce, heat the butter in a medium saucepan over low heat, add the flour and stir for 1 minute, or until golden and smooth. Remove from the heat and gradually stir in the milk. Return to the heat and stir constantly over medium heat for 5 minutes, or until the sauce boils and begins to thicken. Simmer

for another minute. Remove from the heat, allow to cool slightly and stir in the egg yolks and cheese.
4 Preheat the oven to 180°C (350°F/ Gas 4). Cook the bucatini in a large saucepan of rapidly boiling salted water until *al dente*. Drain, rinse under cold water and drain thoroughly, then mix with

the egg whites. Place half the bucatini over the base of a lightly oiled, ovenproof dish. Cover with the beef mixture.
5 Combine the remaining bucatini with the cheese sauce and spread over the mince. Sprinkle with the breadcrumbs. Bake for 45 minutes, or until the top is lightly golden.

rigatoni with chorizo and tomato

Preparation time: **15 minutes**
Cooking time: **25 minutes**
Serves **4**

2 tablespoons olive oil
1 onion, sliced
250 g (9 oz) chorizo sausage, sliced

400 g (14 oz) tin chopped tomatoes
125 ml (4 fl oz/½ cup) dry white wine
½–1 teaspoon chopped fresh chilli (optional)
375 g (13 oz) rigatoni
2 tablespoons chopped parsley
2 tablespoons freshly grated parmesan cheese

1 Heat the oil in a frying pan. Add the onion and stir over low heat until tender.
2 Add the sausage to the pan and cook, turning frequently, for 2–3 minutes. Add the tomatoes, wine, chilli, if using, and salt and pepper, to taste, and stir. Bring to the boil, then reduce the heat and simmer for 15–20 minutes.
3 Meanwhile, cook the rigatoni in a large saucepan of rapidly boiling salted water until *al dente*. Drain and return to the pan. Add the sauce to the hot pasta. Toss well to combine. Serve sprinkled with parsley and grated parmesan.

chorizo sausage

Chorizo is a firm, deep-red sausage from Spain. It is well spiced and coarsely grained and is made primarily from pork and pork fat with garlic and paprika. Some types are intended for eating raw, while others with less fat are suited to cooking in stews and soups. You can substitute Italian pepperoni or any other firm, spicy garlic sausage for chorizo.

ziti with vegetables and sausage

Preparation time: 30 minutes
Cooking time: 40 minutes
Serves 4

1 red capsicum (pepper)
1 green capsicum (pepper)
1 small eggplant (aubergine), sliced
60 ml (2 fl oz/¼ cup) olive oil
1 onion, sliced
1 garlic clove, crushed
250 g (9 oz) chipolatas, sliced
400 g (14 oz) tin chopped tomatoes
125 ml (4 fl oz/½ cup) red wine
35 g (1¼ oz/¼ cup) halved pitted
   black olives
1 tablespoon chopped basil
1 tablespoon chopped parsley
500 g (1 lb 2 oz) ziti
freshly grated parmesan cheese,
   to serve

1   Cut the capsicums into large flat pieces and discard the seeds and membrane. Put, skin side up, under a hot grill (broiler) and cook for 8 minutes, or until the skin is black and blistered. Remove from the heat and place in a plastic bag. When cool, peel away the skin, chop the flesh and set aside.

2   Brush the eggplant with a little of the oil. Grill until golden on each side, brushing with more oil as required. Set aside.

3   Heat the remaining oil in a frying pan. Add the onion and garlic and stir over low heat until the onion is tender. Add the chipolatas and cook until well browned.

4   Stir in the tomatoes, wine, olives, basil, parsley and salt and freshly ground black pepper, to taste. Bring to the boil, then reduce the heat and simmer for 15 minutes. Add the vegetables and heat until warmed through.

5   While the sauce is cooking, cook the ziti in a large saucepan of rapidly boiling salted water until *al dente*. Drain and return to the pan. Toss the vegetables and sauce through the hot pasta. Sprinkle with parmesan before serving.

NOTE: Ziti is a wide tubular pasta that is an excellent partner for this dish but you can substitute fettuccine or spaghetti, if you prefer.

cold meats

While Italy is famous for its pasta, cold meats and salamis are also close to the Italian cook's heart. Each region is passionately adamant about the superiority of its own speciality.

pancetta is the Italian version of bacon. The rind is removed and the meat is seasoned with salt, pepper and spices, which include nutmeg, juniper, cloves, cinnamon, depending on the person who is packing it. It is cured for two weeks, then tightly rolled and packed in a case similar to that used for salami. The flavour is less salty than prosciutto, though it can be eaten raw as you would prosciutto. It is prized for the flavour it imparts to cooked dishes where there is no real substitute for its savoury sweet taste.

prosciutto is the salt- and air-dried hind leg of a pig. The salt removes the moisture from the meat and the slow process of air-curing produces a soft delicate flavour. Prosciutto can be cured for up to 18 months and the most prized are judged against genuine Italian Parma ham. Sliced prosciutto should be consumed as soon as possible after cutting as it gradually loses its flavour. Remove it from the refrigerator 1 hour before you plan to serve it. Parma ham gets its unique flavour from the pigs being fed the whey left over from cheese-making. Traditionally served with melon or figs on an antipasto platter.

mortadella from Bologna takes its name from the mortar used to grind the pork. Flavoured with peppercorns, stuffed olives, pistachios and garlic and flecked with strips of fat, it can measure up to 40 cm (16 inches) in diameter. Mortadella is chopped and used on pizzas, in sandwiches or in tortellini.

salami is a cured dry sausage made from minced pork and seasoned with garlic, herbs and spices. Thought to have originated in Salamis in Cyprus, most Italian salamis take their names from the towns in which they are produced. Distinctive types of salami are also made in Denmark, Spain, Hungary, Austria and Germany.

cacciatore is made from pork and beef, garlic and spices, and can be mild or hot.

milano salami is a mildly flavoured Italian salami made with lean pork, beef and pork fat. It has a fine texture and is seasoned with garlic, pepper and wine.

finocchiona toscana is a salami made from pork and seasoned with fennel seeds that are distributed throughout the salami. Mild or hot.

pepperoni is a dried Italian sausage made from ground pork and beef, highly seasoned with pepper. It is used as a topping for pizzas and in pasta sauces.

coppa is made from the pork shoulder that has been cured. It is fattier than prosciutto and is sold rolled and cased like salami. Coppa is frequently served as a part of an antipasto platter.

speck is the fatty top part of a leg of bacon, which is usually smoked and salted. It is available in small pieces. Austrian in origin, speck can be sliced for a cold snack or chopped to use in cooked dishes.

chorizo is a coarsely textured Spanish sausage that comes in many varieties, although it is always made from pork and seasoned with pimiento. It is sliced, fried and used in pasta sauces or, as it is best known, in paella.

poppy seeds

These tiny seeds have a mild, sweet aroma that becomes stronger and nuttier when heated, with sweet and spicy undertones. Bluish-grey poppy seeds are mostly used in European cooking, sprinkled on breads and buns and used in a variety of cakes and pastries. When fried in butter, they can be added to savoury noodle and pasta dishes, providing a nice contrast of texture. Poppy seeds can also be used to give flavour and crunch to vegetables, salads, fish dishes and gratins.

pork, paprika and poppy seeds with pasta

Preparation time: 15 minutes
Cooking time: 20 minutes
Serves 4

500 g (1 lb 2 oz) pappardelle
20 g (¾ oz) butter
1½ tablespoons vegetable oil
1 onion, thinly sliced
1 garlic clove, crushed
2 teaspoons sweet paprika
pinch of cayenne pepper
500 g (1 lb 2 oz) lean pork (fillet or leg steaks), thinly sliced
1 tablespoon finely chopped parsley
1 tablespoon port or other dry fortified wine
1 tablespoon tomato paste (concentrated purée)
300 g (10½ oz) sour cream
150 g (5½ oz) button mushrooms, sliced
2 teaspoons poppy seeds
2 tablespoons chopped parsley, extra, for garnish (optional)

1 Cook the pasta in a large saucepan of rapidly boiling salted water until *al dente*. Drain and return to the pan.
2 Meanwhile, heat the butter and 2 teaspoons of oil in a frying pan and gently fry the onion for 6–8 minutes, or until soft. Add the garlic, paprika, cayenne, pork and parsley and season with freshly ground black pepper, to taste. Sauté quickly over high heat until the pork is just cooked through. Add the port, bring to the boil and stir briefly, for about 10 seconds. Add the tomato paste and sour cream and stir until combined. Stir in the mushrooms and poppy seeds. Taste and adjust the seasoning if necessary.
3 Stir the remaining oil through the warm pasta. Spoon the pork over the pasta and garnish with parsley, if desired.

turkish ravioli

Preparation time: 1 hour
Cooking time: 30 minutes
Serves 4–6

215 g (7½ oz/1¾ cups) plain (all-purpose) flour
50 g (1¾ oz/⅓ cup) wholemeal (whole-wheat) flour
125 ml (4 fl oz/½ cup) water
1 egg
1 egg yolk
½ cup mint leaves, finely chopped, for garnish

FILLING
1 tablespoon oil
1 small onion, finely grated

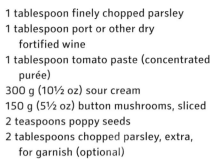

pork, paprika and poppy seeds with pasta

1 fresh red chilli, finely chopped
1 teaspoon ground cinnamon
1 teaspoon ground cloves
500 g (1 lb 2 oz) finely minced
    (ground) lamb
2 teaspoons finely grated lemon zest
2 teaspoons chopped dill
3 tablespoons chopped flat-leaf
    (Italian) parsley

SAUCE
250 ml (9 fl oz/1 cup) chicken stock
500 ml (17 fl oz/2 cups) plain yoghurt
4 garlic cloves, crushed

1 To make the filling, heat the oil in a
large frying pan, add the onion, chilli and
spices and cook over medium heat for
5 minutes, or until the onion is golden.
Add the lamb and cook over high heat
until browned, stirring constantly to
break up any lumps. Remove from the
heat, stir in the lemon zest and chopped
herbs. Set aside to cool.
2 To make the sauce, bring the stock to
the boil in a small saucepan and cook
until reduced by half. Remove from the
heat and whisk the stock into the yoghurt
and garlic. Season with salt and freshly
ground black pepper, to taste.
3 Combine the flours, water, egg and
yolk in a food processor until the mixture
comes together to form a smooth dough.
Turn the dough out onto a lightly floured
surface. If the dough is too sticky, you
may need to add a little extra flour.
(It is much easier to add more flour to
a wet dough than to add more egg to
a dry dough.)
4 Divide the dough into quarters, open
the rollers on your pasta machine to
the widest setting, sprinkle the rollers
generously with flour and roll the dough
through the machine. Fold the dough
into three, so that the width of the pasta
remains the same and the length should
now be one-third of what it was.
5 Pass the dough through the rollers
again, and repeat the folding and rolling
process, turning the dough to the right
on a 90 degree angle each time. Repeat
this at least 10 times, dusting the machine

plain yoghurt

Made by fermenting cow's or ewe's milk, yoghurt originated in the Balkans. It was initially used as a pharmaceutical remedy but is now enjoyed for its fresh, slightly sour flavour and is used in cooking for the complexity of tastes that its acidity creates. Yoghurt is produced when selected milk is treated with an active lactic culture. Under controlled temperatures, this action brings about a natural fermentation. The resulting curd is semi-set, smooth and a clean white colour. Fresh yoghurt keeps for 4–5 days, refrigerated, before deteriorating.

and dough lightly with flour if you need
to. When the pasta is smooth, set the
rollers in a groove closer, pass the pasta
through and keep setting the rollers closer
until the pasta is 1 mm (1/16 inch) thick.
Cover and set aside. Repeat with the
remaining dough.
6 Cut the dough into 12 cm (5 inch)
squares. Place 1 tablespoon of filling on
the centre of each square, brush the edges
lightly with water and fold each square

into a triangle. Press the edges together to
seal and place in a single layer on a lightly
floured baking tray. Keep covered while
making the rest of the ravioli.
7 Cook the ravioli, in batches, in a large
saucepan of rapidly boiling salted water
for 3 minutes, or until al dente. Drain
and serve with the sauce spooned over.
Garnish with the mint.

marjoram

Also known as sweet or knotted marjoram, common marjoram (*Majorana hortensis*) is very closely related to oregano. Sweet marjoram is milder and more subtle in flavour, and has a fresh, fragrant aroma. It is used in soups and with fish, and goes well with most vegetables. It is easy to grow and dries easily. For best results when drying, cut sprigs just before the flowers come into bloom, as this is when the herb is in full fragrance.

rigatoni with salami and herbs

Preparation time: 35 minutes
Cooking time: 40 minutes
Serves 4

20 g (¾ oz) butter
1 tablespoon olive oil
1 onion, thinly sliced
1 carrot, cut into julienne strips
1 bay leaf
75 g (2½ oz) bacon slices, cut into long thin strips

200 g (7 oz) spicy Italian salami, skinned and sliced
400 g (14 oz) tin whole tomatoes
125 ml (4 fl oz/½ cup) beef or chicken stock
400 g (14 oz) rigatoni
1 tablespoon oregano or marjoram leaves

1 Heat the butter and oil in a frying pan and cook the onion and carrot with the bay leaf until the onion is translucent and softened. Add the bacon and salami and cook, stirring often, until brown.
2 Squeeze half the tomatoes dry over the sink, pulp the flesh with your hand and add to the pan. Add the rest whole and break up loosely with the spoon while stirring. Season well with salt and pepper, to taste, and simmer for 30 minutes over low heat, gradually adding the stock as the sauce reduces.
3 When the sauce is nearly ready, cook the pasta in a large saucepan of rapidly boiling salted water until *al dente*. Drain and transfer to a warm serving dish. Add the oregano or marjoram and sauce, and gently toss together before serving.

NOTE: It's important to use good-quality salami and fresh herbs to produce the best flavour for this sauce.

meatballs with fusilli

Preparation time: **35 minutes**
Cooking time: **35 minutes**
Serves **4**

750 g (1 lb 10 oz) minced (ground) pork and veal or beef
80 g (2¾ oz/1 cup) fresh white breadcrumbs
3 tablespoons freshly grated parmesan cheese
1 onion, finely chopped
2 tablespoons chopped flat-leaf (Italian) parsley
1 egg, beaten
1 garlic clove, crushed
½ lemon, zest finely grated and juiced
30 g (1 oz/¼ cup) plain (all-purpose) flour, seasoned
2 tablespoons olive oil
500 g (1 lb 2 oz) fusilli

SAUCE
425 g (15 oz) tomato passata (puréed tomatoes)
125 ml (4 fl oz/½ cup) beef stock
125 ml (4 fl oz/½ cup) red wine
2 tablespoons chopped basil
1 garlic clove, crushed

1 Combine the meat, breadcrumbs, parmesan, onion, parsley, egg, garlic, lemon zest and juice in a large bowl and season to taste. Roll tablespoons of the mixture into balls and then roll the balls in the seasoned flour.

2 Heat the oil in a large frying pan and fry the meatballs until golden all over. Remove from the pan and drain on paper towels. Drain the excess fat and meat juices from the pan.

3 To make the sauce, in the same pan, combine the passata, stock, wine, basil, garlic, salt and pepper. Bring to the boil.

4 Reduce the heat and return the meatballs to the pan. Allow to simmer for 10–15 minutes.

5 Meanwhile, cook the pasta in a large saucepan of rapidly boiling salted water until *al dente*. Drain and serve with meatballs and sauce over the top.

seasoned flour

When plain (all-purpose) flour has salt added, it is called seasoned flour. Pepper, and sometimes other spices or herbs, may also be included. It is used to coat meats and vegetables before searing them for braising. The flour gives an even coating that colours well and helps to thicken sauce. It also enhances the overall flavour of the dish.

macaroni

Macaroni, or maccheroni, is short tubular lengths of pasta. It can be quite short and thin, or fat and as long as 4 cm (1½ inches), but it is always hollow. Various sizes are known by specific names, and different regions in Italy may have different names for the same shape and size. Along with many of the improbable stories regarding the origins of macaroni, one fact is known, and that is that it has been called maccheroni since at least 1041 when it was a word used to describe a man who was a bit of a dunce.

penne with prosciutto

Preparation time: **15 minutes**
Cooking time: **20 minutes**
Serves **4**

1 tablespoon olive oil
6 thin prosciutto slices, chopped
1 onion, finely chopped
1 tablespoon chopped rosemary
800 g (1 lb 12 oz) tin chopped tomatoes
500 g (1 lb 2 oz) penne or macaroni
50 g (1¾ oz/½ cup) freshly grated
   parmesan cheese

1 Heat the oil in a heavy-based frying pan. Add the prosciutto and onion and cook, stirring occasionally, over low heat for 5 minutes, or until golden.
2 Add the rosemary, tomatoes and salt and pepper. Simmer for 10 minutes.
3 While the sauce is cooking, add the pasta to a large saucepan of rapidly boiling salted water and cook until *al dente*. Drain. Divide the pasta among serving bowls and top with the sauce. Sprinkle with grated parmesan.

NOTE: Rosemary, commonly used in Mediterranean cookery, adds a distinctive flavour to this dish.

parsi lamb with cumin, eggs and tagliatelle

✸

Preparation time: 40 minutes
Cooking time: 1 hour 15 minutes
Serves 4

20 g (¾ oz) butter
1 large onion, finely chopped
2 garlic cloves, crushed
1 teaspoon finely chopped fresh ginger
¾ teaspoon each of chilli flakes, turmeric,
    garam masala and ground cumin
600 g (1 lb 5 oz) minced (ground) lamb
2 very ripe, large tomatoes, chopped
½ teaspoon sugar
1 tablespoon lemon juice
2 tablespoons finely chopped coriander
    (cilantro) leaves, plus extra leaves,
    to garnish
1 small fresh red chilli, finely chopped
    (optional)
350 g (12 oz) tagliatelle
1 tablespoon vegetable oil
3 hard-boiled eggs, chopped

1 Heat the butter in a frying pan and add the onion, garlic and ginger. Fry over low heat until the onion is soft but not browned. Stir in the chilli flakes, turmeric, garam masala and cumin.

2 Add the lamb, increase the heat and cook until well browned, stirring occasionally. Stir in the tomato, sugar, 250 ml (9 fl oz/1 cup) water and a good pinch of salt. Reduce the heat and simmer, covered, for 50–60 minutes, or until the sauce thickens and darkens. Increase the heat and add the lemon juice, the chopped coriander and the chilli, if using. Check the seasoning, add salt if required and cook, uncovered, for 2–3 minutes.

3 Cook the pasta in a large saucepan of rapidly boiling salted water until *al dente*. Drain, return to the pan and stir in the oil. Transfer to warmed serving dishes and spoon the lamb mixture on top. Sprinkle with hard-boiled eggs and coriander leaves before serving.

ginger

Ginger (*Zingiber officinale*) is a rhizome (underground stem). Buy firm pieces without any soft spots and make sure they aren't spongy when gently squeezed. Ginger becomes increasingly fibrous as it grows — this can make it difficult to chop finely, but the good news is that it also becomes hotter and more flavoursome. Ginger is best kept wrapped in foil in the crisper section of the refrigerator.

pasta with chicken

As tradition has it chicken would not, in days gone by, have been served with pasta, but we can now look back and wonder 'Why ever not?' With the added flavour of fresh herbs, spices, tomatoes or mushrooms, chicken combines perfectly with pasta, especially as a filling for tiny parcels such as tortellini or ravioli. The versatility of chicken is shown in dishes such as meatballs, lasagne and even bolognese: a new twist on recipes in which you would normally expect to find red meat.

spaghetti with chicken meatballs

✳

Preparation time: 45 minutes
  + 30 minutes chilling time
Cooking time: 1 hour 30 minutes
Serves 4–6

500 g (1 lb 2 oz) minced (ground) chicken
60 g (2¼ oz) freshly grated parmesan
  cheese, plus extra, for garnish
160 g (5¾ oz/2 cups) fresh white
  breadcrumbs
2 garlic cloves, crushed
1 egg
1 tablespoon chopped flat-leaf
  (Italian) parsley

1 tablespoon chopped sage
60 ml (2 fl oz/¼ cup) vegetable oil
500 g (1 lb 2 oz) spaghetti
2 tablespoons chopped oregano, to serve

TOMATO SAUCE
1 tablespoon olive oil
1 onion, finely chopped
2 kg (4 lb 8 oz) very ripe tomatoes, chopped
2 bay leaves
30 g (1 oz/1 cup) basil leaves, loosely
  packed
1 teaspoon coarsely ground black pepper

1 In a large bowl, combine the chicken, parmesan, breadcrumbs, garlic, egg and herbs. Season with salt and pepper. Shape tablespoonsful of the mixture into balls and chill for about 30 minutes, to firm.
2 Heat the oil in a shallow frying pan and cook the balls, in batches, until golden brown. Turn them often by gently shaking the pan. Drain on paper towels.
3 To make the tomato sauce, heat the oil in a large saucepan, add the onion and fry for about 1–2 minutes, until softened. Add the tomato and bay leaves, cover and bring to the boil, stirring occasionally. Reduce the heat to low, partially cover and cook for 50–60 minutes.
4 Add the meatballs to the sauce, along with the basil and pepper and simmer, uncovered, for 10–15 minutes.
5 While the sauce is simmering, cook the spaghetti in a large saucepan of rapidly boiling salted water until *al dente*. Drain and return to the pan. Add some sauce to the pasta and toss to distribute. Serve the pasta topped with sauce and meatballs, and sprinkled with chopped oregano and extra parmesan, if desired.

bay leaves

Bay or bay laurel is a symbol of fame and victory. Wreaths of laurel have been presented to honour achievement ever since the Ancient Greeks wove it into crowns for victorious athletes, poets and statesmen. The leaves have been used in the kitchen for just as long, although at first they were favoured as a flavouring for sweet dishes. Nowadays, they are used mainly in marinades and in pickling, and to enhance the taste of white sauces, soups and stews.

chicken tortellini with tomato sauce

✳ ✳

Preparation time: **1 hour**
  + 30 minutes resting time
Cooking time: **30 minutes**
Serves **4**

100 g (3½ oz) bocconcini, thinly sliced,
  to serve

PASTA
250 g (9 oz/2 cups) plain (all-purpose) flour
3 eggs
1 tablespoon olive oil

FILLING
20 g (¾ oz) butter
90 g (3¼ oz) boneless, skinless chicken
  breast, cubed
2 thin pancetta slices, chopped
50 g (1¾ oz/½ cup) freshly grated
  parmesan cheese
½ teaspoon freshly grated nutmeg
1 egg, lightly beaten

TOMATO SAUCE
80 ml (2½ fl oz/⅓ cup) olive oil
1.5 kg (3 lb 5 oz) very ripe tomatoes,
  peeled and chopped
10 g (¼ oz/¼ cup) chopped oregano
50 g (1¾ oz/½ cup) freshly grated
  parmesan cheese

1 To make the pasta, sift the flour and a pinch of salt into a bowl and make a well in the centre. In a jug, whisk together the eggs, oil and 1 tablespoon water. Add the egg mixture gradually to the flour, mixing to a firm dough. Gather into a ball, adding a little extra water if necessary.
2 Knead on a lightly floured surface for 5 minutes, or until the dough is smooth and elastic. Put in a lightly oiled bowl, cover with plastic wrap and set aside for 30 minutes.
3 To make the filling, heat the butter in a frying pan, add the chicken and cook, stirring, until golden brown. Drain and allow to cool slightly. Process the chicken

and pancetta in a food processor or mincer until finely chopped. Transfer to a bowl and add the parmesan, nutmeg, egg and salt and pepper. Set aside.
4 Roll out the dough very thinly on a lightly floured surface. Using a floured cutter, cut into 5 cm (2 inch) rounds and spoon ½ teaspoon of filling into the centre of each. Brush the edges with a little water. Fold in half to form semi-circles, pressing the edges together. Wrap each around your finger to form a ring and then press the ends of the dough together firmly.

5 To make the tomato sauce, put the oil, tomato and oregano in a frying pan and cook over high heat for 10 minutes. Stir the parmesan through and set aside.
6 Cook the tortellini, in two batches, in a large saucepan of rapidly boiling water for about 6 minutes each batch, or until *al dente*. Drain and return to the pan. Reheat the tomato sauce, add to the tortellini and toss to combine. Divide the tortellini among serving bowls, top with bocconcini and season with pepper.

bacon, lettuce and tomato salad

Grill (broil) or fry 4 bacon slices until crisp. Allow to cool on paper towels before roughly chopping. Combine in a bowl with the leaves of a cos (romaine) lettuce, 200 g (7 oz) halved cherry tomatoes and 1 chopped avocado. Toss gently to combine. Top with a dressing made by mixing together 125 g (4½ oz/ ½ cup) plain yoghurt, 1 tablespoon wholegrain mustard, 1 tablespoon lemon juice and 1 teaspoon honey. Serve as a side dish.

1 Preheat the oven to 180°C (350°F/ Gas 4). Remove and discard the stalks from the spinach. Plunge the leaves into a saucepan of boiling water for 2 minutes, or until tender. Remove, plunge immediately into a bowl of iced water and then drain.

2 Heat the oil in a heavy-based frying pan. Add the chicken, garlic and bacon. Cook over medium heat for 5 minutes, or until browned. Stir in the tomatoes, tomato paste, sauce and stock and bring to the boil. Reduce the heat and simmer, partially covered, for 10 minutes, or until the sauce is slightly thickened. Season with salt and pepper, to taste.

3 Melt the butter in a medium saucepan, add the flour and stir over low heat for 1 minute, or until the mixture is lightly golden and smooth. Remove from the heat and gradually stir in the milk. Return to the heat and stir constantly over medium heat for 4 minutes, or until the sauce boils and thickens. Remove from the heat and stir in half the cheese.

4 To assemble the lasagne, brush a 3 litre (105 fl oz/12 cup) baking dish with melted butter or oil. Spread one-quarter of the chicken mixture over the base. Top with 4 sheets of lasagne. Spread with a third of the cheese sauce, then another layer of the chicken filling. Top with all of the spinach, a layer of lasagne, a layer of cheese sauce and the remaining chicken

chicken and spinach lasagne

Preparation time: 30 minutes
Cooking time: 1 hour 10 minutes
Serves 8

500 g (1 lb 2 oz) English spinach
1 tablespoon olive oil
1 kg (2 lb 4 oz) minced (ground) chicken
1 garlic clove, crushed

3 bacon slices, chopped
425 g (15 oz) tin chopped tomatoes
125 g (4½ oz/½ cup) tomato paste (concentrated purée)
125 ml (4 fl oz/½ cup) tomato passata (puréed tomatoes)
125 ml (4 fl oz/½ cup) chicken stock
60 g (2¼ oz) butter
40 g (1¼ oz/⅓ cup) plain (all-purpose) flour
625 ml (21½ fl oz/2½ cups) milk
12 instant lasagne sheets
250 g (9 oz/2 cups) coarsely grated cheddar cheese

filling. Top with the remaining lasagne sheets, spread evenly with the remaining cheese sauce and sprinkle with remaining grated cheese. Bake for 50 minutes, until cooked through and golden brown on top.

chicken with lemon, parsley and pasta

✳ ✳

Preparation time: **10 minutes**
Cooking time: **20 minutes**
Serves **4**

375 g (13 oz) short pasta of your choice
1 tablespoon oil
60 g (2¼ oz) butter
4 small boneless, skinless chicken breasts
80 ml (2½ fl oz/⅓ cup) lemon juice
20 g (¾ oz/⅓ cup) finely chopped parsley, plus extra, to garnish
lemon slices, to garnish (optional)

1 Cook the pasta in a large saucepan of rapidly boiling salted water until it is *al dente*. Drain.
2 Meanwhile, heat the oil and half the butter in a large, heavy-based pan. Add the chicken and cook for 2 minutes each side; set aside. Add the lemon juice,

parsley and remaining butter to the pan. Stir to combine, return the chicken to the pan and cook over low heat for a further 3–4 minutes, turning once, or until cooked through. Season with salt and freshly ground black pepper, to taste.
3 Serve the pasta topped with a sliced chicken fillet and sauce. Garnish with lemon slices, if desired, and sprinkle with extra chopped parsley.

lemons

The zest, flesh and juice of lemons are all put to good use in savoury foods as well as desserts, cakes and sweets. The lemon is perhaps the most acid of citrus fruits and is highly scented. Bush lemons, with their thick and crinkly skins, are valued for their clean acid taste, which stays pure when blended with other flavours. The many types of smooth-skinned lemons tend to be sweeter and the fruit is more attractive for use as a decoration or garnish.

reheating pasta

Most sauced pasta dishes can be reheated. Dishes with a good amount of sauce or a lot of oil in the dressing, such as pesto, can be stirred over high heat in a pan or heated in a 180°C (350°F/Gas 4) oven in a greased ovenproof dish, covered with foil. Cooked pasta without sauce can be reheated by putting it in a colander and pouring boiling water over it, or immersing it in a saucepan of boiling water for about 30 seconds. A microwave is also ideal.

fettuccine with chicken and mushroom sauce

Preparation time: **20 minutes**
Cooking time: **20 minutes**
Serves **4**

400 g (14 oz) fettuccine
2 large boneless, skinless chicken
   breasts
1 tablespoon olive oil
30 g (1 oz) butter
2 bacon slices, cut into long thin strips
2 garlic cloves, crushed
250 g (9 oz) button mushrooms, sliced
80 ml (2½ fl oz/⅓ cup) white wine
170 ml (5½ fl oz/⅔ cup) pouring (whipping)
   cream
4 spring onions (scallions), chopped
1 tablespoon plain (all-purpose) flour
2 tablespoons water
35 g (1¼ oz/⅓ cup) freshly grated
   parmesan cheese, to serve

1 Cook the fettuccine in a large saucepan of rapidly boiling salted water until *al dente*. Drain and return to the pan.
2 Meanwhile, trim the chicken of excess fat and cut into thin strips. Heat the oil and butter in a heavy-based frying pan, add the chicken and cook over medium heat for 3 minutes, or until browned. Add the bacon, garlic and mushrooms and cook for 2 minutes, stirring occasionally.
3 Add the wine and cook until the liquid has reduced by half. Add the cream and spring onion and bring to the boil. Blend the flour with the water until smooth, add to the pan and stir until the mixture boils and thickens. Reduce the heat and simmer for 2 minutes. Season with salt and pepper, to taste.
4 Add the sauce to the pasta and stir over low heat until combined. Sprinkle with parmesan. Serve immediately with a green salad and perhaps herb bread.

roasted tomatoes with herbed goat's cheese

Brush halved roma (plum) tomatoes with a little olive oil, sprinkle with salt, sugar and pepper and bake in a 180°C (350°F/Gas 4) oven for 30 minutes, or until tender and slightly dried. Make a mixture of goat's cheese and chopped herbs and press a little onto each piece of cooked tomato. Cook under a grill (broiler) until the goat's cheese begins to soften and colour. Serve as a side dish.

pesto chicken pasta

Preparation time: 20 minutes
Cooking time: 20 minutes
Serves 4

250 g (9 oz) penne or fusilli
1 small barbecued chicken
125 g (4½ oz/1 cup) walnuts
4 bacon slices
250 g (9 oz) cherry tomatoes, halved
60 g (2¼ oz) pitted and sliced olives
125 g (4½ oz/½ cup) bottled
    pesto sauce
30 g (1 oz/½ cup) finely shredded basil

1   Cook the pasta in a large saucepan of rapidly boiling salted water until it is *al dente*. Drain.
2   While the pasta is cooking, discard the skin of the chicken. Remove the meat from the chicken, cut or shred it into bite-sized pieces and put in a large bowl.

3   Toast the walnuts for 2–3 minutes under a hot grill (broiler), allow to cool and then chop roughly.
4   Remove the rind from the bacon slices and grill them for 3–4 minutes, or until crisp. Allow to cool and then roughly chop. Add the nuts, bacon, tomato and olives to the chicken.
5   Add the pasta to the chicken mixture, along with the pesto sauce and basil. Toss until thoroughly mixed. Serve at room temperature.

cherry tomatoes with butter and dill

Pan-fry some cherry tomatoes in a little butter until the skins are beginning to split, season well with salt and cracked black pepper and sprinkle with chopped dill. Gently toss and serve immediately. Serve as a side dish.

chicken and macaroni bake

chicken and macaroni bake

Preparation time: **20 minutes**
Cooking time: **55 minutes**
Serves **6**

4 boneless, skinless chicken breasts
310 g (11 oz/2 cups) macaroni
60 ml (2 fl oz/¼ cup) olive oil
1 onion, chopped
1 carrot, chopped
3 bacon slices, chopped
2 zucchini (courgettes), chopped
440 g (15½ oz) tin tomato soup
90 g (3¼ oz/⅓ cup) sour cream
185 g (6½ oz/1½ cups) grated
    cheddar cheese

1 Trim the chicken of excess fat and sinew. Preheat the oven to 180°C (350°F/Gas 4). Cook the macaroni in a large saucepan of rapidly boiling salted water until *al dente*; drain.
2 Slice the chicken into long strips and then cut into cubes. Heat the oil in a heavy-based saucepan. Cook the chicken quickly over high heat until browned but not cooked through; drain on paper towels. Add the onion, carrot and bacon to the pan. Stir over medium heat for 10 minutes. Add the zucchini and soup, bring to the boil and simmer for 5 minutes. Remove from the heat.
3 Combine the pasta, chicken, tomato mixture and sour cream. Season with salt and pepper, to taste. Spread into a shallow ovenproof dish and top with cheese. Bake for 20 minutes, or until golden and cooked through.

lasagnette with mushrooms and chicken

Preparation time: **15 minutes**
Cooking time: **20 minutes**
Serves **4**

60 ml (2 fl oz/¼ cup) milk
½ teaspoon dried tarragon or 2 teaspoons
    chopped fresh tarragon
400 g (14 oz) lasagnette
25 g (¾ oz) butter
2 garlic cloves
200 g (7 oz) boneless, skinless chicken
    breast, sliced
100 g (3½ oz) button mushrooms, sliced
freshly grated nutmeg, to taste
500 ml (17 fl oz/2 cups) pouring (whipping)
    cream
tarragon sprigs, to garnish

1 Bring the milk and tarragon to the boil in a small saucepan. Remove from heat, strain and reserve the milk. Set aside.
2 Cook the lasagnette in a large saucepan of rapidly boiling salted water until *al dente*. Drain and return to the pan.
3 While the pasta is cooking, melt the butter in a frying pan and gently sauté

the garlic cloves, chicken and mushrooms until the chicken is golden and cooked through. Discard the garlic and add the nutmeg and salt and pepper, to taste. Stir for 10 seconds before stirring in the cream and tarragon milk. Bring to the boil, reduce the heat and simmer until the sauce thickens. Spoon the sauce over the pasta and garnish with tarragon sprigs.

chicken livers with penne

✹ ✹

Preparation time: **15 minutes**
Cooking time: **15 minutes**
Serves **4**

350 g (12 oz) chicken livers
500 g (1 lb 2 oz) penne
50 g (1¾ oz) butter
1 onion, diced
2 garlic cloves, crushed
2 teaspoons finely grated orange zest
2 bay leaves
125 ml (4 fl oz/½ cup) red wine
2 tablespoons tomato paste (concentrated purée)
2 tablespoons pouring (whipping) cream

1 Wash the chicken livers and use a small sharp knife to trim away any membrane. Cut each liver into six pieces.
2 Cook the penne in a large saucepan of rapidly boiling salted water until *al dente*. Drain and keep warm.

3 While the pasta is cooking, melt the butter in a frying pan and cook the onion until softened. Add the garlic, chicken livers, orange zest and bay leaves, and stir for 3 minutes. Remove the chicken livers with a slotted spoon. Stir in the wine, tomato paste and cream. Simmer until the sauce reduces and thickens.
4 Return the chicken livers to the pan and warm through. Season with salt and freshly ground pepper, to taste. Spoon the chicken liver sauce over the pasta.

chicken livers with penne

roast broccoli with cumin seeds

Gently boil or steam some evenly sized broccoli florets for a couple of minutes. Drain thoroughly and toss in a mixture of olive oil, crushed garlic and lightly toasted crushed cumin seeds. Put on a baking tray and bake in a 230°C (450°F/Gas 8) oven until the broccoli is browned at the edges. Serve as a side dish.

chicken ravioli with fresh tomato sauce

Preparation time: 40 minutes
Cooking time: 30 minutes
Serves 4

1 tablespoon oil
1 large onion, chopped
2 garlic cloves, crushed
90 g (3¼ oz/⅓ cup) tomato paste
   (concentrated purée)
60 ml (2 fl oz/¼ cup) red wine
170 ml (5½ fl oz/⅔ cup) chicken stock
2 very ripe tomatoes, chopped

1 tablespoon chopped basil
freshly grated parmesan cheese, to serve

RAVIOLI
200 g (7 oz) minced (ground) chicken
1 tablespoon chopped basil
25 g (1 oz/¼ cup) grated parmesan cheese
3 spring onions (scallions), finely chopped
50 g (1¾ oz) fresh ricotta cheese
250 g (9 oz) packet (48) gow gee wrappers

1   Heat the oil in a medium saucepan and add the onion and garlic. Cook for 2–3 minutes, then stir in the tomato paste, wine, stock and tomato. Simmer over low heat for 20 minutes. Stir in the basil and season, to taste.

2   Meanwhile, to make the ravioli, combine the chicken, basil, parmesan, spring onion, ricotta and some salt and pepper. Lay half the wrappers on a flat surface and brush with a little water. Place slightly heaped teaspoons of mixture in the centre of each wrapper. Place the remaining wrappers on top and press the edges firmly together.

3   Bring a large saucepan of water to the boil and cook the ravioli a few at a time for 2–3 minutes, or until tender. Drain well. Serve with the tomato sauce and freshly grated parmesan cheese.

beans with parsley butter

Cook green beans in salted boiling water until they are tender but still bright green. Drain and place in a bowl with some herbed butter, salt and black pepper. Toss well so that the beans are coated in the buttery mixture. Serve as a side dish.

panzanella

Tear 2 slices of day-old Italian bread into pieces and sprinkle with crushed garlic and oil. Toss it in a bowl with chopped cucumber, tomatoes, red onion and basil leaves. Drizzle with olive oil and red wine vinegar and season well. The bread should be slightly moist, but not too soggy. You can also add anchovies or hard-boiled eggs.

brandy chicken fettuccine

Preparation time: **40 minutes**
Cooking time: **25 minutes**
Serves 4–6

10 g (¼ oz) dried porcini mushrooms
2 tablespoons olive oil
2 garlic cloves, crushed
200 g (7 oz) button mushrooms, sliced
125 g (4½ oz) prosciutto slices, chopped
375 g (13 oz) fettuccine
60 ml (2 fl oz/¼ cup) brandy
250 ml (9 fl oz/1 cup) pouring (whipping) cream
1 barbecued chicken, shredded
155 g (5½ oz/1 cup) frozen peas
20 g (¾ oz/⅓ cup) finely chopped parsley

1 Put the porcini mushrooms in a bowl and cover with boiling water. Set aside for 10 minutes, then drain, squeeze dry and roughly chop.
2 Heat the oil in a large, heavy-based frying pan. Add the garlic and cook, stirring, for 1 minute over low heat. Add the button and porcini mushrooms, along with the prosciutto, and cook over low heat, stirring often, for 5 minutes.
3 Meanwhile, cook the pasta in a large saucepan of rapidly boiling salted water until *al dente*. Drain and keep warm.

4 Add the brandy and cream to the mushroom mixture. Cook, stirring, over low heat for 2 minutes. Add the chicken, peas and parsley. Cook, stirring, for 4–5 minutes, until heated through. Add the chicken mixture to the hot pasta and mix until well combined.

NOTE: Chop the slices of prosciutto separately, otherwise they will stick together. Use bacon instead, if preferred. If porcini mushrooms are not available, use 30 g (1 oz) dried Chinese mushrooms.

pasta with seafood

It is hardly a mystery why pasta and seafood go together so well.
Italy is surrounded on almost all sides by the tranquil blueness of
the Mediterranean Sea and the Italians have been reaping its fruits
since the dawn of their civilisation. It's only natural that they should
cook up their catch of fresh prawns, clams and succulent fish and
toss them together with their beloved pasta to come up with some
spectacular dishes.

spaghetti marinara

※

Preparation time: 40 minutes
Cooking time: 50 minutes
Serves 6

12 mussels
60 ml (2 fl oz/¼ cup) white wine
60 ml (2 fl oz/¼ cup) fish stock
1 garlic clove, crushed
375 g (13 oz) spaghetti
30 g (1 oz) butter
125 g (4½ oz) small squid tubes, sliced
125 g (4½ oz) boneless white fish fillets,
    cut into cubes
200 g (7 oz) raw prawns (shrimp), peeled
    and deveined, tails intact
30 g (1 oz/½ cup) parsley leaves, chopped
200 g (7 oz) tin clams (vongole), drained

TOMATO SAUCE
2 tablespoons olive oil
1 onion, finely diced
1 carrot, sliced
1 fresh red chilli, seeded and chopped
2 garlic cloves, crushed
400 g (14 oz) tin chopped tomatoes
125 ml (4 fl oz/½ cup) white wine
1 teaspoon sugar
pinch of cayenne pepper

1 Scrub the mussels with a stiff brush
and pull out the hairy beards. Discard any
open or damaged mussels. Rinse well.
2 To make the tomato sauce, heat the
oil in a medium saucepan, add the onion
and carrot and stir over medium heat
for about 10 minutes, or until lightly
browned. Add the chilli, garlic, tomatoes,
wine, sugar and cayenne and simmer for
30 minutes, stirring occasionally.
3 Meanwhile, heat the 60 ml (2 fl oz/
¼ cup) wine with the stock and garlic in
a large saucepan and add the mussels.
Cover the pan and shake it over high heat
for 3–5 minutes. After 3 minutes, start
removing any opened mussels and set
them aside. After 5 minutes, discard any
unopened mussels. Reserve the liquid.
4 Cook the pasta in a large saucepan of
rapidly boiling salted water until *al dente*.

calamari

Calamari, Italian for squid, is
a member of the cephalopod
family, along with octopus and
cuttlefish. Like the octopus,
the squid has eight limbs, but
also two longer tentacles with
suckers on the end. The body
sac is elongated and does
not contain a true skeleton,
and both this body and the
tentacles can be eaten. The
flesh is firm, mildly sweet and
doesn't have a 'fishy' flavour.
Calamari is eaten whole,
stuffed and stewed, or cut into
strips or rings and fried. It can
be rubbery and tasteless if
cooked without care.

Drain and keep warm. Meanwhile, melt the butter in a frying pan, add the calamari rings, fish and prawns and stir-fry for 2 minutes. Set aside. Add the reserved cooking liquid, mussels, calamari, fish, prawns, parsley and clams to the tomato sauce and reheat gently. Serve the marinara sauce spooned over the hot pasta.

farfalle with tuna, mushrooms and cream

✳

Preparation time: **10 minutes**
Cooking time: **15 minutes**
Serves **4**

60 g (2¼ oz) butter
1 tablespoon olive oil
1 onion, chopped
1 garlic clove, crushed
125 g (4½ oz) button mushrooms, sliced
250 ml (9 fl oz/1 cup) pouring (whipping) cream
425 g (15 oz) tin tuna in brine, drained and flaked
1 tablespoon lemon juice
1 tablespoon chopped flat-leaf (Italian) parsley
500 g (1 lb 2 oz) farfalle

1 Heat the butter and olive oil in a large frying pan. Add the onion and garlic and stir over low heat for 3–5 minutes, until the onion is soft. Add the mushrooms and cook for 2 minutes. Pour in the cream, bring to the boil, then reduce the heat and simmer until the sauce begins to thicken. Add the tuna, lemon juice and parsley and stir until heated through. Season to taste.

2 While the sauce is cooking, cook the farfalle in a large saucepan of rapidly boiling salted water until *al dente*. Drain well, then return to the pan. Add the sauce to the farfalle and toss to combine.

NOTE: You can use tinned salmon, drained and flaked, instead of tuna.

tinned tuna

Tuna is tinned in edible oils, salt water or spring water. The fish are cleaned and pre-cooked for anything from 45 minutes to three hours, then filleted, tinned and sealed. Its flavour, low cost, nutritional benefits and ease of use combine to make it a popular partner for pasta and numerous other savoury dishes.

creamy prawns with fettuccine

☀

Preparation time: 30 minutes
Cooking time: 20 minutes
Serves 4

500 g (1 lb 2 oz) fettuccine
30 g (1 oz) butter
1 tablespoon olive oil
6 spring onions (scallions),
    chopped
1 garlic clove, crushed
500 g (1 lb 2 oz) raw prawns (shrimp),
    peeled and deveined, tails intact
250 ml (9 fl oz/1 cup) pouring
    (whipping) cream
2 tablespoons chopped flat-leaf
    (Italian) parsley, to serve

1 Cook the fettuccine in a large saucepan of rapidly boiling salted water until it is *al dente*. Drain and return to the pan.
2 Heat the butter and oil in a frying pan, add the spring onion and garlic and stir over low heat for 1 minute. Add the prawns and cook for 2–3 minutes, or until the flesh changes colour. Remove the prawns from the pan and set aside.

marinated mushroom salad

Combine 500 g (1 lb 2 oz) halved button mushrooms, 4 thinly sliced spring onions (scallions), 1 finely diced red capsicum (pepper) and 2 tablespoons chopped flat-leaf (Italian) parsley. Make a dressing by combining 3 crushed garlic cloves, 3 tablespoons white wine vinegar, 2 teaspoons dijon mustard and 80 ml (2½ fl oz/⅓ cup) olive oil. Pour over the salad and toss to coat. Cover and refrigerate for 3 hours before serving as a side dish.

Add the cream to the pan and bring to the boil. Reduce the heat and simmer until the sauce begins to thicken. Return the prawns to the pan, season to taste, and simmer for 1 minute.

3 Add the prawns and sauce to the warm fettuccine and toss gently. Serve sprinkled with chopped parsley.

NOTE: For a variation on this recipe, in step 1 add 1 sliced red capsicum (pepper) and 1 very thinly sliced leek. Use scallops instead of prawns or a mixture of both.

spaghetti with chilli calamari

✹ ✹

Preparation time: 20 minutes
Cooking time: 20 minutes
Serves 4

500 g (1 lb 2 oz) calamari, cleaned
500 g (1 lb 2 oz) spaghetti
2 tablespoons olive oil
1 leek, chopped
2 garlic cloves, crushed
1–2 teaspoons chopped fresh chilli
½ teaspoon cayenne pepper
400 g (14 oz) tin chopped tomatoes
125 ml (4 fl oz/½ cup) fish stock
1 tablespoon chopped basil
2 teaspoons chopped sage
1 teaspoon chopped marjoram

1 Pull the tentacles from the body of the calamari. Using your fingers, pull the quill from the pouch of the calamari. Pull the skin away from the flesh and discard. Use a small sharp knife to slit the tubes up one side. Lay them out flat and score one side in a diamond pattern. Cut each tube into four pieces.

2 Cook the spaghetti in a large saucepan of rapidly boiling salted water until *al dente*. Drain and keep warm.

fish stock

Fish stock is available ready-made, but you may prefer to make your own and freeze it. Melt 1 tablespoon butter in a large saucepan and cook 2 finely chopped onions over low heat for 10 minutes, or until soft but not browned. Add 2 litres (70 fl oz/8 cups) water, 1.5 kg (3 lb 5 oz) fish bones, heads and tails and a bouquet garni. Simmer for about 20 minutes, skimming off any froth from surface. Strain the stock through a fine sieve before refrigerating. Use white-fleshed fish when making stock, as darker, oily fish tend to make the stock greasy.

3 While the pasta is cooking, heat the oil in a large frying pan. Add the leek and cook for 2 minutes. Add the garlic and stir over low heat for 1 minute. Stir in the chilli and cayenne. Add the tomatoes, stock and herbs and bring to the boil. Reduce the heat and simmer for 5 minutes.

4 Add the calamari to the pan. Simmer for another 5–10 minutes, or until the calamari is tender. Serve the chilli calamari spooned over the spaghetti.

fettuccine with caviar

fettuccine with caviar

Preparation time: 15 minutes
Cooking time: 15 minutes
Serves 4

2 hard-boiled eggs
4 spring onions (scallions)
150 g (5½ oz/1 cup) light sour cream
50 g (1¾ oz) red caviar or salmon roe
2 tablespoons chopped dill, plus dill sprigs,
    to garnish
1 tablespoon lemon juice
500 g (1 lb 2 oz) fettuccine

1 Peel the eggs and chop into small
pieces. Trim the spring onions, discarding
the dark-green tops, and chop finely.
2 In a small bowl, mix the sour cream,
egg, spring onion, caviar, dill, lemon juice
and pepper, to taste. Set aside.
3 Cook the fettuccine in a large saucepan
of rapidly boiling salted water until
al dente. Drain and return to the pan.
4 Toss the caviar mixture through the hot
pasta. Serve garnished with sprigs of dill.

NOTE: Use large red caviar or roe if
possible, as it has a far better flavour than
the small supermarket variety.

fragrant seafood pasta

Preparation time: 30 minutes
Cooking time: 20 minutes
Serves 4

500 g (1 lb 2 oz) conchiglie (shell pasta)
2–3 tablespoons light olive oil
4 spring onions (scallions), thinly sliced
1 small fresh chilli, finely chopped
500 g (1 lb 2 oz) raw prawns (shrimp),
    peeled and deveined, tails intact
250 g (9 oz) scallops, halved
15 g (½ oz/¼ cup) chopped coriander
    (cilantro) leaves
60 ml (2 fl oz/¼ cup) lime juice

2 tablespoons sweet chilli sauce
1 tablespoon fish sauce
1 tablespoon sesame oil
shredded lime zest, to garnish
    (optional)

1 Cook the conchiglie in a large saucepan
of rapidly boiling salted water until it is
al dente. Drain and keep warm.
2 While the pasta is cooking, heat the oil
in a frying pan and add the spring onion,
chilli, prawns and scallops. Stir constantly
over medium heat until the prawns curl
up and turn pink and the scallops are
lightly cooked. Remove from the heat
immediately. Stir in the coriander, lime
juice, sweet chilli sauce and fish sauce.
3 Drain the pasta and return to the pan.
Toss the sesame oil through, add the
prawn mixture and stir gently to combine.
Serve the pasta garnished with shredded
lime zest, if desired.

chilli seafood in tomato sauce

Preparation time: 25 minutes
Cooking time: 30 minutes
Serves 4

8 mussels
1 teaspoon olive oil
1 large onion, chopped
3 garlic cloves, finely chopped
2 small fresh red chillies, seeded
    and finely chopped
800 g (1 lb 12 oz) tin chopped tomatoes
2 tablespoons tomato paste
    (concentrated purée)
125 ml (4 fl oz/½ cup) vegetable stock
2 tablespoons Pernod
650 g (1 lb 7 oz) marinara mix

2 tablespoons chopped flat-leaf
    (Italian) parsley
1 tablespoon chopped dill
350 g (12 oz) bucatini

1 Scrub the mussels with a stiff brush
and pull out the hairy beards. Discard any
open or damaged mussels. Rinse well.
2 Heat the oil in a large saucepan. Add
the onion, garlic and chilli and cook for
1–2 minutes. Stir in the tomatoes, tomato
paste, stock, Pernod and ½ teaspoon
cracked black pepper. Reduce the heat
and simmer for 8–10 minutes. Set aside
to cool slightly, then transfer to a food
processor and process until smooth.
3 Return the tomato mixture to the pan,
add the marinara mix and simmer for
4 minutes. Add the mussels and herbs and
simmer for another 1–2 minutes, or until
the mussels have opened. Discard any
mussels that do not open.
4 Meanwhile, cook the pasta in a large
saucepan of rapidly boiling salted water
until *al dente*, then drain thoroughly.
Divide the pasta among serving bowls and
spoon the sauce over the top.

NOTE: Marinara mix is a combination
of uncooked seafood available from fish
shops. It usually contains scallops, prawns
(shrimp), mussels and calamari rings. You
can use just one favourite type of seafood,
such as prawns or calamari, instead.

---

red caviar

The roe of various members of the sturgeon
family is known as caviar. There are different
qualities, depending on the fish from which the
roe is extracted, and the colour can be black,
dark brown, grey, golden or salmon. What is
known as red caviar is actually a pale orange. The
eggs should be glossy and firm, and taste neither
too salty nor too fishy.

pappardelle

Pappardelle are long flat noodles, similar to fettuccine but a lot wider at around 2.5 cm (1 inches). They are excellent for sauces that are strong, rich or heavy and are ideal with game and offal. Sometimes one or both sides are crimped, causing confusion with lasagnette, which is only half the width. One can be substituted for the other in most recipes.

pappardelle with roasted salmon and garlic

Preparation time: **10 minutes**
Cooking time: **20 minutes**
Serves **4**

4 small salmon fillets, about 100 g
 (3½ oz) each
80–100 ml (2½–3½ fl oz/⅓ cup) extra
 virgin olive oil
8–10 garlic cloves, peeled
300 g (10½ oz) fresh pappardelle
50 g (1¾ oz) thinly sliced fennel
1½ teaspoons finely grated lime zest
2 tablespoons lime juice
4 fennel fronds, to garnish

1 Preheat the oven to 220°C (425°F/ Gas 7) and lightly oil a ceramic baking dish. Brush the salmon fillets with 2 tablespoons of the olive oil, salt lightly and position in a single layer in the dish.
2 Slice the garlic cloves lengthways and spread them all over the salmon fillets. Brush lightly with olive oil. Bake for 10–15 minutes, or until the salmon is cooked through.
3 Meanwhile, cook the pappardelle in a large saucepan of rapidly boiling salted water until *al dente*. Drain and stir through enough extra virgin olive oil to make it glisten. Toss the fennel and lime zest through the pasta and arrange on warmed serving plates.
4 Top each serving with a salmon fillet, then spoon the pan juices over, with any stray slices of garlic. Drizzle with lime juice. Garnish with fennel fronds and serve accompanied by a simple tomato salad.

spaghettini with salmon

Preparation time: **15 minutes**
Cooking time: **25 minutes**
Serves **6**

500 g (1 lb 2 oz) spaghettini
2 tablespoons olive oil
2 garlic cloves, finely chopped
1 teaspoon chopped fresh chilli
500 g (1 lb 2 oz) very ripe tomatoes,
    chopped
1 teaspoon soft brown sugar
425 g (15 oz) tin pink salmon, drained
    and flaked
30 g (1 oz/½ cup) basil leaves, chopped

1 Cook the spaghettini in a large
saucepan of rapidly boiling salted water
until *al dente*. Drain and return to the pan.
2 While the pasta is cooking, heat the oil
in a medium saucepan and cook the garlic
and chilli for 1 minute over low heat. Add
the tomato with any juices and the sugar.
Stir gently over low heat for 5 minutes,
until the tomato is just warmed through.
3 Add the salmon and basil. Season, then
toss through the pasta before serving.

tagliatelle with octopus

Preparation time: **30 minutes**
Cooking time: **25 minutes**
Serves **4**

500 g (1 lb 2 oz) tagliatelle
1 kg (2 lb 4 oz) baby octopus
2 tablespoons olive oil
1 onion, sliced
1 garlic clove, crushed
425 ml (15 fl oz) tomato passata (puréed
    tomatoes)
125 ml (4 fl oz/½ cup) dry white wine
1 tablespoon bottled chilli sauce
1 tablespoon chopped basil

tagliatelle with octopus

1 Cook the tagliatelle in a large saucepan
of rapidly boiling salted water until
al dente. Drain and return to the pan.
2 Clean the octopus by using a small
sharp knife to remove the guts — either
cut off the head entirely or slice open
the head and remove the guts. Pick up
the body and use your index finger to
push the beak up. Remove the beak and
discard. Clean the octopus thoroughly,
pat dry with paper towels and, if you
prefer, cut in half. Set aside.

3 Meanwhile, heat the oil in a large
frying pan. Add the onion and garlic
and stir over low heat until the onion is
tender. Add the passata, wine, chilli sauce,
basil and salt and pepper, to taste. Bring
to the boil, reduce the heat and simmer
for 10 minutes.
4 Add the octopus to the pan and simmer
for 5–10 minutes, or until tender. Serve
spooned over the pasta.

trout, fettuccine and fennel frittata

Preparation time: 20 minutes
Cooking time: 1 hour 10 minutes
Serves 4

250 g (9 oz) whole smoked trout
200 g (7 oz) fettuccine
250 ml (9 fl oz/1 cup) milk
125 ml (4 fl oz/½ cup) pouring
   (whipping) cream
4 eggs
pinch of freshly grated nutmeg
40 g (1½ oz) thinly sliced fennel
4 spring onions (scallions), sliced
85 g (3 oz/⅔ cup) grated cheddar cheese

1 Preheat the oven to 180°C (350°F/ Gas 4). Remove and discard the skin and bones from the trout.
2 Cook the fettuccine in a large saucepan of rapidly boiling salted water until it is *al dente*. Drain.
3 Combine the milk, cream, eggs and nutmeg in a large bowl and whisk until smooth. Season to taste. Add the trout, fettuccine, fennel and spring onion and toss to distribute evenly. Pour into a lightly greased, 23 cm (9 inch) ovenproof frying pan and sprinkle with the cheese. Bake for about 1 hour, or until set.

fennel

Fennel has an unmistakable aniseed flavour and crunchy texture. Uncooked and sliced, it is used in salads and as antipasto. Cooked, it braises well and is a good companion to seafood and pork. Look for crisp bulbs that are fully formed with many stalks.

The white inner stalks are used as well as the leaves, which are very good chopped and sprinkled on salads and fish, or as a flavouring in seafood sauces. Dried fennel seeds are important in spice mixtures and are used to flavour a diverse range of foods.

tinned salmon

The name 'salmon' is commonly given to several species of fish from the family *Salmonidae*, which also includes trout. Salmon is classified as an oily fish, with flesh that ranges from pale pinkish-orange to red. Tinned salmon often contains skin and bones, which are soft and edible and add calcium and magnesium to the nutrient value of the fish. Salmon is pressure-cooked in the tin to preserve flavour and texture. Red (sometimes called sockeye) salmon has an intense flavour and deep colour, compared with the milder pink salmon.

salmon and pasta frittata

❋ ❋

Preparation time: 25 minutes
Cooking time: 40 minutes
Serves 6

150 g (5½ oz) spaghettini
300 g (10½ oz) frozen broad (fava) beans
30 g (1 oz) butter
1 leek, thinly sliced
415 g (14¾ oz) tinned red salmon, drained, boned and flaked
6 eggs, lightly beaten
125 ml (4 fl oz/½ cup) pouring (whipping) cream
185 ml (6 fl oz/¾ cup) milk

1 Cook the pasta in a large saucepan of rapidly boiling salted water until *al dente*. Drain. Put the broad beans in a bowl, cover with boiling water and set aside for 10 minutes. Drain, then remove and discard the tough outer skins.
2 Melt the butter in a saucepan, add the leek and cook, stirring, over medium heat, until soft. Mix the pasta, broad beans, leek, salmon, egg, cream and milk in a bowl. Season with salt and freshly ground pepper, to taste.
3 Pour the mixture into a lightly greased 25 cm (10 inch) ovenproof frying pan. Cover with a lid and cook over low heat for 25 minutes, or until nearly set.
4 Meanwhile, heat the grill (broiler). Place the frittata under the grill and cook until the top has set. Set aside for 5 minutes, then cut into wedges directly from the pan. Serve with a leafy green salad, if desired.

spaghetti

Spaghetti arrived in Italy via Sicily, where it was introduced by the Arabs after they invaded in 827 AD. Being great wanderers and traders, they needed their pasta in a form that could be stored and easily transported and so their preference for dried spaghetti was passed on. Known then as itriyah (Persian for string), it developed into tria and then trii, a form of spaghetti still popular in Sicily and parts of southern Italy.

spaghetti with creamy garlic mussels

Preparation time: 20 minutes
Cooking time: 15 minutes
Serves 4

500 g (1 lb 2 oz) spaghetti
1.5 kg (3 lb 5 oz) mussels
2 tablespoons olive oil
2 garlic cloves, crushed
125 ml (4 fl oz/½ cup) dry white wine
250 ml (9 fl oz/1 cup) pouring (whipping) cream
2 tablespoons chopped basil

1 Cook the spaghetti in a large saucepan of rapidly boiling salted water until it is *al dente*. Drain.
2 Meanwhile, scrub the mussels and pull out the hairy beards. Discard any open or damaged mussels. Rinse well.
3 Heat the oil in a large saucepan, add the garlic and stir over low heat for 30 seconds. Add the wine and mussels. Simmer, covered, for 5 minutes. Remove the mussels, discarding any that don't open, and set aside.
4 Add the cream and basil to the pan and season to taste. Simmer for 2 minutes, stirring. Serve the sauce and mussels spooned over the spaghetti.

fettuccine with smoked salmon

Preparation time: 10 minutes
Cooking time: 15 minutes
Serves 4

100 g (3½ oz) smoked salmon
35 g (1¼ oz/¼ cup) sun-dried tomatoes
1 tablespoon olive oil
1 garlic clove, crushed
250 ml (9 fl oz/1 cup) pouring (whipping) cream
¼ teaspoon mustard powder
15 g (½ oz/¼ cup) snipped chives, plus extra, to garnish
2 teaspoons lemon juice
375 g (13 oz) fettuccine
2 tablespoons freshly grated parmesan cheese, to serve (optional)

1 Cut the smoked salmon into bite-sized pieces and the sun-dried tomatoes into long, thin strips.

2 Heat the olive oil in a frying pan, add the garlic and stir over low heat for 30 seconds. Add the cream, mustard powder, chives and salt and pepper, to taste. Bring to the boil, then reduce the heat and simmer, stirring, until the sauce begins to thicken. Add the salmon and lemon juice to the pan and stir to combine. Heat gently.

3 While the sauce is cooking, cook the fettuccine in a large saucepan of rapidly boiling salted water until *al dente*. Drain well and return to the pan. Toss the sauce through the hot pasta. Serve immediately topped with the sun-dried tomato, extra chives and parmesan, if desired.

sun-dried tomatoes

These preserved tomatoes are available dry, loosely packed or in jars. They are useful in pasta dishes and salads or on top of pizzas. The flavour is intense and sweet. Some come packed in olive or canola oil and need to be drained. Others are available dry and must be soaked in boiling water for 5 minutes before use. Sun-dried tomatoes combine well with cheese, salad greens, olives, seafood, chicken and meat.

clams

Long thought of as the poor relative in the mollusc family, clams (vongole) are used for their succulent flesh and mild flavour. When bought live in the shells, they are eaten raw or lightly cooked. Shelled, they are preserved in tins or bottles and in this form the flesh is used in sauces and stews. Jars of cooked clams still in their shell are also available, and are an excellent alternative to preparing clams from scratch. The juice in which clams are preserved makes a lightly flavoured seafood stock, good for use in soups and sauces.

spaghetti vongole (spaghetti with clam sauce)

※

Preparation time: 25 minutes
Cooking time: 35 minutes
Serves 4

1 kg (2 lb 4 oz) small clams (vongole) in shell or 750 g (1 lb 10 oz) tin clams in brine
1 tablespoon lemon juice
80 ml (2½ fl oz/⅓ cup) olive oil
3 garlic cloves, crushed
800 g (1 lb 12 oz) tin chopped tomatoes
250 g (9 oz) spaghetti
4 tablespoons chopped flat-leaf (Italian) parsley

1 If using fresh clams, clean thoroughly. Place in a large saucepan with the lemon juice. Cover the pan and shake over medium heat for 7–8 minutes until the shells open, discarding any that don't open. Remove the clam flesh from the shells of the opened clams and set aside; discard the empty shells. If using tinned clams, drain, rinse well and set aside.
2 Heat the oil in a large saucepan. Add the garlic and cook over low heat for 5 minutes. Add the tomatoes and stir to combine. Bring to the boil and simmer, covered, for 20 minutes. Add freshly ground black pepper, to taste, and the clams, and stir until heated through.
3 Meanwhile, cook the spaghetti in a large saucepan of rapidly boiling salted water until *al dente*. Drain and return to the pan. Gently stir in the sauce and the chopped parsley until combined.

gremolata

It is not usual to serve grated cheese with seafood pasta sauces, but for those who can't resist sprinkling a little something on top, there is an alternative! Mix the grated zest of half a lemon with a finely chopped garlic clove and roughly 1 cup of loosely packed chopped parsley. Adjust the proportions to suit your tastes. Called gremolata or gremolada, this mix is traditionally used to accompany osso bucco.

spaghetti and mussels in tomato and herb sauce

Preparation time: **15 minutes**
Cooking time: **30 minutes**
Serves 4

1.5 kg (3 lb 5 oz) mussels
2 tablespoons olive oil
1 onion, thinly sliced
2 garlic cloves, crushed
400 g (14 oz) tin chopped tomatoes
250 ml (9 fl oz/1 cup) white wine
1 tablespoon chopped basil
2 tablespoons chopped parsley
500 g (1 lb 2 oz) spaghetti

1 Scrub the mussels with a stiff brush and pull out the hairy beards. Discard any open or damaged mussels. Rinse well.
2 Heat the olive oil in a large saucepan. Add the onion and garlic and stir over low heat until the onion is translucent. Add the tomatoes, wine, basil, parsley and salt and pepper, to taste. Bring the sauce to the boil, then reduce the heat and simmer for 15–20 minutes, or until it begins to thicken.
3 Add the mussels to the pan and cook, covered, for 5 minutes, shaking the pan occasionally. Discard any mussels that don't open.
4 While the sauce is cooking, add the spaghetti to a large saucepan of rapidly boiling salted water and cook until *al dente*. Drain. Serve the mussels and sauce over the pasta.

pasta with vegetables

The key to great food is freshness. While the Italian cook makes good use of pantry staples such as tinned tomatoes and olive oil, it is the fresh vegetables and herbs that lift the dishes into the sublime. Herbs are generally used fresh, often gathered from the surrounding area in great basketfuls. Tomatoes, capsicums and artichokes ripen under the Mediterranean sun and, tossed together with a bowl of pasta, are as colourful and delicious as they are good for you.

fettuccine with zucchini and crisp-fried basil

Preparation time: **15 minutes**
Cooking time: **15 minutes**
Serves **6**

250 ml (9 fl oz/1 cup) olive oil
1 handful basil leaves
500 g (1 lb 2 oz) fettuccine or tagliatelle
500 g (1 lb 2 oz) zucchini (courgettes)
60 g (2¼ oz) butter
2 garlic cloves, crushed
75 g (2¾ oz/¾ cup) freshly grated
  parmesan cheese

1 To crisp-fry the basil leaves, heat the oil in a small frying pan, add two leaves at a time and cook for 1 minute, or until crisp. Remove with a slotted spoon and drain on paper towels. Repeat with the remaining basil leaves.
2 Cook the fettuccine in a large saucepan of rapidly boiling salted water until *al dente*. Drain and return to the pan.
3 While the pasta is cooking, coarsely grate the zucchini. Heat the butter in a deep heavy-based saucepan over low heat until foaming. Add the garlic and cook for 1 minute. Add the zucchini and cook, stirring occasionally, for 1–2 minutes or until softened. Add to the hot pasta with the parmesan and toss well. Serve the pasta garnished with the crisp basil.

NOTE: The basil leaves can be fried up to 2 hours in advance. Store in an airtight container after cooling.

zucchini

Zucchini, or courgettes, are Italian summer squash. Green or yellow in colour, they should be harvested within 4–6 days of flowering to give a tender rind and crisp flesh. If they are too old or too big, the flesh tends to be bitter. Zucchini require little preparation and only a short cooking time. They can be steamed, boiled, sautéed, baked or deep-fried, and larger zucchini can be stuffed and baked.

olive and mozzarella spaghetti

Preparation time: 20 minutes
Cooking time: 15 minutes
Serves 4

500 g (1 lb 2 oz) spaghetti
50 g (1¾ oz) butter
2 garlic cloves, crushed
60 g (2¼ oz/½ cup) pitted black
   olives, halved
60 ml (2 fl oz/¼ cup) olive oil
20 g (¾ oz/⅓ cup) chopped parsley
150 g (5½ oz) mozzarella cheese,
   cut into small cubes

1 Cook the spaghetti in a large saucepan of rapidly boiling salted water until it is *al dente*. Drain and return to the pan.
2 While the spaghetti is cooking, heat the butter in a small saucepan until it begins to turn nutty brown. Add the garlic and cook over low heat for 1 minute.
3 Add the garlic butter to the pasta with the olives, olive oil, parsley and mozzarella. Toss until well combined.

farfalle with artichoke hearts and olives

Preparation time: 20 minutes
Cooking time: 20 minutes
Serves 4

500 g (1 lb 2 oz) farfalle
400 g (14 oz) marinated artichoke hearts
60 ml (2 fl oz/¼ cup) olive oil
3 garlic cloves, crushed
60 g (2¼ oz/½ cup) pitted black
   olives, chopped
2 tablespoons snipped chives
200 g (7 oz) fresh ricotta cheese

1 Cook the farfalle in a large saucepan of rapidly boiling salted water until *al dente*. Drain and return to the pan.

2 While the pasta is cooking, drain and thinly slice the artichoke hearts. Heat the oil in a large frying pan. Add the garlic and cook over low heat until softened.
3 Add the artichoke and olives to the pan and stir until heated through. Add the chives and ricotta, breaking up the ricotta with a spoon. Cook until the ricotta is heated through.

4 Combine the sauce with the pasta. Season with salt and freshly ground black pepper and serve immediately.

NOTE: This dish is wonderful made with cooked fresh artichoke hearts. Prepare 5 artichoke hearts and then follow the recipe as above.

olive and mozzarella spaghetti

sun-dried tomato sauce on tagliatelle

☀

Preparation time: 20 minutes
Cooking time: 20 minutes
Serves 4

500 g (1 lb 2 oz) tagliatelle
2 tablespoons olive oil
1 onion, chopped

80 g (2¾ oz/½ cup) thinly sliced
   sun-dried tomatoes
2 garlic cloves, crushed
400 g (14 oz) tin chopped
   tomatoes
125 g (4½ oz/1 cup) pitted
   black olives
20 g (¾ oz/⅓ cup) chopped basil
shavings of parmesan cheese, to serve

1   Cook the tagliatelle in a large saucepan
of rapidly boiling salted water until it is
al dente. Drain and return to the pan.

olives

Olives when picked young are
green and hard. They ripen and
darken on the tree. Olives are
preserved in oil, sometimes
with herbs, or in brine. Featured
in a great many Mediterranean
dishes, olives are suitable
for salads and stuffings, are
baked into breads and are an
attractive addition to pasta and
rice dishes. Olives should be
used as soon after purchase as
possible, and it is wisest to buy
the best you can afford. Greek
and Italian olives are thought
to be the finest.

2 Meanwhile, heat the oil in a large frying pan. Add the onion and cook for 3 minutes, stirring occasionally, until soft. Add the sun-dried tomato and garlic and cook for another minute.

3 Add the tomatoes, olives and basil to the pan and season with freshly ground black pepper. Bring to the boil, reduce the heat, and simmer for 10 minutes.

4 Add the sauce to the hot pasta and gently toss through. Serve immediately, topped with parmesan shavings.

NOTE: Sun-dried tomatoes are available dry or loosely packed, or in jars with olive or canola oil. The tomatoes in oil need only to be drained, but the dry tomatoes must be soaked in boiling water for 5 minutes to rehydrate and soften them.

creamy asparagus linguine

✷

Preparation time: **15 minutes**
Cooking time: **15 minutes**
Serves **4**

200 g (7 oz) fresh full-fat ricotta
   cheese
250 ml (9 fl oz/1 cup) pouring (whipping)
   cream
75 g (2¾ oz/¾ cup) freshly grated
   parmesan cheese
freshly grated nutmeg, to taste
500 g (1 lb 2 oz) linguine
500 g (1 lb 2 oz) asparagus spears,
   cut into short lengths
45 g (1½ oz/½ cup) toasted flaked
   almonds, to serve

1 Put the ricotta in a bowl and stir until smooth. Stir in the cream, parmesan and nutmeg and season with salt and freshly ground black pepper, to taste.

2 Cook the linguine in a large saucepan of rapidly boiling salted water until it is not quite tender. Add the asparagus to the pan and cook for another 3 minutes. Drain the pasta and asparagus, reserving 2 tablespoons of the cooking water. Return the pasta and asparagus to the saucepan and keep warm.

3 Add the reserved cooking water to the ricotta mixture, stirring well to combine. Spoon the mixture over the pasta and toss gently to combine. Serve sprinkled with the toasted almonds.

NOTE: To toast flaked almonds, heat them under a medium grill (broiler) for about 2 minutes. Stir them occasionally and be careful to avoid burning them. Alternatively, dry-fry them, stirring occasionally, until lightly browned.

warm vegetable salad

Boil or steam 200 g (7 oz) each of baby carrots, sugar snap peas, yellow baby (pattypan) squash, zucchini (courgettes) and new potatoes until just tender. Do not overcook or the vegetables will lose their bright colours. To make the dressing, combine 2 crushed garlic cloves, 2 tablespoons each of chopped dill and chives, 1 tablespoon lime juice, 1 tablespoon dijon mustard and 80 ml (2½ fl oz/⅓ cup) olive oil. Serve as a side dish.

fettuccine with green olives and eggplant

Preparation time: **20 minutes**
Cooking time: **20 minutes**
Serves **4**

500 g (1 lb 2 oz) fettuccine or tagliatelle
1 large eggplant (aubergine)
2 tablespoons olive oil
2 garlic cloves, crushed
175 g (6 oz) green olives, pitted and sliced
125 ml (4 fl oz/½ cup) lemon juice
2 tablespoons chopped flat-leaf (Italian) parsley
50 g (1¾ oz/½ cup) freshly grated parmesan cheese (optional)

1 Cook the pasta in a large saucepan of rapidly boiling salted water until *al dente*. Drain and return to the pan.
2 While the pasta is cooking, cut the eggplant into small cubes.
3 Heat the oil in a heavy-based frying pan. Add the garlic and cook, stirring, for 30 seconds. Add the eggplant and cook over medium heat, stirring frequently, for 6 minutes, or until tender. Add the olives and lemon juice and season to taste. Add the sauce to the pasta and toss to combine. Serve sprinkled with the parsley and parmesan, if desired.

spaghetti with fresh tomato sauce

Preparation time: 15 minutes
   + 2 hours chilling time
Cooking time: 15 minutes
Serves 4

4 firm ripe tomatoes
8 stuffed green olives
2 tablespoons capers
4 spring onions (scallions), finely chopped
2 garlic cloves, crushed
½ teaspoon dried oregano
20 g (¾ oz/⅓ cup) chopped parsley
80 ml (2½ fl oz/⅓ cup) olive oil
375 g (13 oz) spaghetti or spaghettini

1 Chop the tomatoes into small pieces. Chop the olives and capers. Combine all the ingredients, except the pasta, in a bowl and mix well. Cover and refrigerate for at least 2 hours.
2 Cook the pasta in a large saucepan of rapidly boiling salted water until *al dente*. Drain and return to the pan. Add the cold sauce to the hot pasta and mix well.

NOTE: If you like, you can add 30 g (1 oz/½ cup) shredded basil leaves to the sauce.

linguine with roasted vegetable sauce

Preparation time: 30 minutes
Cooking time: 50 minutes
Serves 4

4 large red capsicums (peppers)
500 g (1 lb 2 oz) firm ripe tomatoes
3 large red onions
1 garlic bulb
125 ml (4 fl oz/½ cup) balsamic vinegar
60 ml (2 fl oz/¼ cup) olive oil
2 teaspoons sea salt
2 teaspoons freshly ground black pepper
500 g (1 lb 2 oz) linguine

linguine with roasted vegetable sauce

100 g (3½ oz) parmesan cheese, shaved
100 g (3½ oz) black olives

1 Preheat the oven to 180°C (350°F/ Gas 4). Cut the capsicums in half and remove the seeds and membrane. Cut the tomatoes and onions in half and separate and peel the garlic cloves.
2 Arrange the vegetables in a single layer over a large ovenproof dish. Pour the vinegar and oil over them and then sprinkle with the sea salt and pepper. Bake for 50 minutes. Allow to cool for 5 minutes before puréeing in a food processor for 3 minutes, or until the mixture is smooth. Taste and adjust the seasoning, if necessary.
3 When the vegetables are almost ready, cook the pasta in a large saucepan of rapidly boiling salted water until *al dente*. Drain. Serve the sauce spooned over the pasta and top with parmesan and olives.

roma tomatoes

Favoured for their high flesh-to-seed ratio, roma tomatoes are ideal for cooking. Also known as plum or egg tomatoes, their colour is a bright, even red and their walls are thick and firm, thus making peeling easy. They are perfect for preserving and are used for tinned tomatoes and sun-dried tomatoes.

grilled vegetables on pasta

Preparation time: **30 minutes**
Cooking time: **20 minutes**
Serves **4**

500 g (1 lb 2 oz) tomato- or
    chilli-flavoured fettuccine or tagliatelle
1 red capsicum (pepper)
1 yellow capsicum (pepper)
250 g (9 oz) roma (plum) tomatoes,
    thickly sliced
2 large zucchini (courgettes), sliced
80 ml (2½ fl oz/⅓ cup) olive oil

3 garlic cloves, finely chopped
10 basil leaves, roughly chopped
4 bocconcini, sliced

1 Cook the pasta in a large saucepan of rapidly boiling salted water until it is *al dente*. Drain and return to the pan. Cut the capsicums into large flat pieces and discard the seeds and membrane. Cook, skin side up, under a hot grill (broiler) for 8 minutes, or until the skin is black and blistered. Transfer to a plastic bag to cool. Peel away the skin and chop the flesh.
2 Sprinkle the tomatoes with salt and brush the zucchini with 1 tablespoon of oil. Cook under a hot grill (broiler) for 10 minutes, or until tender, turning once.

3 Toss the pasta with the vegetables, garlic, basil, the remaining oil and the bocconcini. Season with salt and freshly ground black pepper, to taste.

NOTE: Use plain pasta if flavoured is not available. Add a little chopped chilli to the dish, if you like the spicy taste.

vegetable lasagne

Preparation time: 40 minutes
Cooking time: 1 hour 15 minutes
Serves 6

3 large red capsicums (peppers)
2 large eggplants (aubergines)
2 tablespoons oil
1 large onion, chopped
3 garlic cloves, crushed
1 teaspoon mixed dried herbs
1 teaspoon dried oregano
500 g (1 lb 2 oz) mushrooms, sliced
400 g (14 oz) tin chopped tomatoes
400 g (14 oz) tin red kidney beans,
   rinsed and drained
1 tablespoon sweet chilli sauce
250 g (9 oz) sheets instant lasagne
500 g (1 lb 2 oz) English spinach,
   chopped
30 g (1 oz/1 cup) basil leaves
90 g (3¼ oz) sun-dried tomatoes, sliced
3 tablespoons freshly grated parmesan
   cheese
3 tablespoons grated cheddar cheese

CHEESE SAUCE
60 g (2¼ oz) butter
3 tablespoons plain (all-purpose) flour
500 ml (17 fl oz/2 cups) milk
600 g (1 lb 5 oz) fresh ricotta cheese

1 Preheat the oven to 180°C (350°F/ Gas 4). Brush a 28 x 35 cm (11 x 14 inch) ovenproof baking dish with oil.
2 Cut the capsicums into large flat pieces and remove the seeds and membrane. Cook, skin side up, under a hot grill (broiler) for 8 minutes, or until the skin is black and blistered. Transfer to a plastic

bag to cool. Peel away the skin and cut the flesh into long, thin strips. Set aside.
3 Slice the eggplant into 1 cm (½ inch) rounds and place in a large saucepan of boiling water. Cook for 1 minute, or until just tender. Drain, pat dry with paper towels and set aside.
4 Heat the oil in a large heavy-based frying pan and add the onion, garlic and herbs. Cook over medium heat for 5 minutes, or until the onion is soft. Add the mushrooms and cook for 1 minute.
5 Add the tomatoes, beans, chilli sauce and salt and pepper, to taste. Bring to the boil, then reduce the heat and simmer for 15 minutes, or until the sauce thickens. Remove from the heat and set aside.
6 To make the cheese sauce, heat the butter in a saucepan and stir in the flour over medium heat for 1 minute, or until

smooth. Remove from the heat and gradually stir in the milk. Return to the heat and stir constantly until the sauce boils and begins to thicken. Simmer for another minute. Add the ricotta and stir until smooth.
7 Dip the lasagne sheets, if necessary, in hot water to soften slightly and arrange 4 sheets on the base of the prepared dish. Build up layers on top of the pasta, using half of the eggplant, the spinach, the basil, the grilled capsicum strips, the mushroom sauce and then the sun-dried tomatoes. Top with a layer of pasta and press gently. Repeat the layers, finishing with a layer of lasagne. Top with the cheese sauce and sprinkle with the combined cheeses. Bake for 45 minutes, or until the pasta is soft.

flat-leaf parsley

Also known as Italian or continental parsley, the flat-leafed variety is stronger tasting than curly-leafed and more widely used as a flavouring agent. However, it is mild enough to use in quantity and so can be added to thicken dishes and also to temper other ingredients. The taste of the stems is more delicate and they can be used instead of the leaves for a milder flavour.

chunky spaghetti napolitana

Preparation time: 20 minutes
Cooking time: 1 hour
Serves 6

2 tablespoons olive oil
1 onion, finely chopped
1 carrot, diced
1 celery stalk, diced
500 g (1 lb 2 oz) very ripe tomatoes
125 ml (4 fl oz/½ cup) white wine
2 teaspoons sugar
500 g (1 lb 2 oz) spaghetti

1 tablespoon chopped parsley
1 tablespoon chopped oregano

1 Heat the oil in a heavy-based saucepan. Add the onion, carrot and celery, cover and cook for 10 minutes over low heat, stirring occasionally, taking care not to let the vegetables colour.
2 Chop the tomatoes and add to the vegetables with the wine and sugar. Bring the sauce to the boil, then reduce the heat to low, cover and simmer for 45 minutes, stirring occasionally. Season with salt and pepper. If the sauce becomes too thick, add up to 185 ml (6 fl oz/¾ cup) water.
3 About 15 minutes before serving time, cook the spaghetti in a large saucepan of

rapidly boiling salted water until *al dente*. Drain and return to the pan. Pour about two-thirds of the sauce over the pasta, add the parsley and oregano and gently toss. Serve in bowls or on a platter with the remaining sauce in a jug at the table.

spaghetti with olives and capers

Preparation time: 20 minutes
Cooking time: 20 minutes
Serves 4

170 ml (5½ fl oz/⅔ cup) extra
   virgin olive oil
125 g (4½ oz/1½ cups) fresh white
   breadcrumbs
3 garlic cloves, finely chopped
45 g (1½ oz) tin anchovies, drained
   and finely chopped (optional)
300 g (10½ oz) black olives, pitted
   and roughly chopped
6 roma (plum) tomatoes, peeled and
   chopped
2 tablespoons tiny capers, rinsed
500 g (1 lb 2 oz) spaghetti or
   spaghettini

1 Heat 2 tablespoons of the oil in a frying pan. Add the breadcrumbs and cook, stirring continuously, until golden brown and crisp. Remove from the pan and set aside to cool completely.
2 Heat the remaining oil in the pan. Add the garlic, anchovies and olives and cook over medium heat for 30 seconds. Add the tomato and capers and cook for 3 minutes, or until the tomatoes are soft.
3 Meanwhile, cook the pasta in a large saucepan of rapidly boiling salted water until *al dente*. Drain and return to the pan. Add the tomato mixture and breadcrumbs and toss to combine. Serve immediately, with herbs as a garnish if you like.

capers

Capers are the small, unripe bud of the caper bush. They are preserved in vinegar or salt and their piquant flavour makes them an ideal companion for fish and meat dishes. Salted ones have a more subtle flavour without vinegar overtones, but they need to have the salt rinsed off before use. Tiny capers have a finer flavour and crunchier texture, but are more expensive because of the extra labour required for picking.

linguine with red capsicum

Preparation time: **20 minutes**
Cooking time: **30 minutes**
Serves **6**

3 red capsicums (peppers)
60 ml (2 fl oz/¼ cup) olive oil
1 large onion, sliced
2 garlic cloves, crushed
¼–½ teaspoon chilli powder or flakes
125 ml (4 fl oz/½ cup) pouring
    (whipping) cream
2 tablespoons chopped oregano, plus
    oregano leaves, extra, for garnish
    (optional)
500 g (1 lb 2 oz) linguine or spaghetti
    (plain or spinach)

1 Cut the capsicums into large flat pieces and remove the seeds and membrane. Place, skin side up, under a hot grill (broiler) and cook for 8 minutes, or until black and blistered. Remove from the heat and transfer to a plastic bag to cool. Peel away the skin and cut the flesh into long, thin strips.
2 Heat the oil in a large heavy-based saucepan. Add the onion and stir over low heat for 8 minutes, or until soft. Add the capsicum strips, garlic, chilli and cream and cook for 2 minutes, stirring occasionally. Add the chopped oregano and season, to taste.
3 Meanwhile, cook the pasta in a large saucepan of rapidly boiling salted water until *al dente*. Drain and return to the pan. Add the sauce and toss until well combined. Serve garnished with oregano leaves, if desired.

fusilli with green sauce

Preparation time: **10 minutes**
Cooking time: **15 minutes**
Serves **6**

500 g (1 lb 2 oz) fusilli (spiral pasta)
1 onion
2 zucchini (courgettes)
5–6 large silverbeet (Swiss chard) leaves
2 anchovies (optional)
2 tablespoons olive oil
50 g (1¾ oz) butter
1 tablespoon capers, rinsed
60 ml (2 fl oz/¼ cup) white wine

1 Cook the pasta in a large saucepan of rapidly boiling salted water until *al dente*. Drain and return to the pan.
2 While the pasta is cooking, chop the onion very finely and coarsely grate the zucchini. Remove and discard the stalks from the silverbeet and finely chop or shred the leaves. Roughly chop the anchovies, if using. Heat the oil and butter in a large heavy-based saucepan. Add the onion and zucchini and stir for 3 minutes over medium heat.
3 Add the anchovies, capers, wine and salt and pepper, to taste, and cook, stirring, for 2 minutes. Add the silverbeet and cook for a further 1–2 minutes, or until it has softened. Add to the warm pasta and toss until well combined.

NOTE: If you prefer, you can use 500 g (1 lb 2 oz) English spinach instead of silverbeet. Cut the ends off and shred the leaves into small pieces.

silverbeet

Silverbeet, also known as Swiss chard or seakale spinach, is unusual in that the stalks and leaves are used as separate vegetables. The white stalks, also called ribs, have a sweet and nutty flavour. They are cut from the leaves, then rinsed and trimmed of the stringy outer membrane before being boiled or parboiled for braising. Silverbeet leaves are tougher and not as sweet as those of English spinach, but they can be used in fillings and stuffings and they are strong enough to roll up into parcels for baking or braising.

making fresh breadcrumbs

Fresh breadcrumbs are easily made in a food processor. Discard the crusts, cut the bread into chunks and process until crumbed. For smaller, more even crumbs, simply grate frozen bread and use straight away. Don't use bread that is more than two days old, however, as the flavour of some breads deteriorates with age and their crumbs will carry the stale taste into your dish.

spaghetti with herbs and tomato

Preparation time: 20 minutes
Cooking time: 15 minutes
Serves 4

20 g (¾ oz/¼ cup) fresh white breadcrumbs
500 g (1 lb 2 oz) spaghetti
60 ml (2 fl oz/¼ cup) olive oil
2 garlic cloves, finely chopped
30 g (1 oz) chopped herbs (such as basil, coriander/cilantro, parsley)
4 ripe tomatoes, chopped
30 g (1 oz/¼ cup) chopped walnuts
25 g (1 oz/¼ cup) freshly grated parmesan cheese, plus extra, to serve

1 Heat the grill (broiler) to medium and put the fresh breadcrumbs under for a few seconds, or until slightly golden.
2 Cook the spaghetti in a saucepan of rapidly boiling salted water until *al dente*, then drain and keep warm.
3 Heat 2 tablespoons of the oil in a large frying pan and cook the garlic until soft. Add the remaining oil and the herbs, tomato, walnuts and parmesan. Add the cooked pasta and toss for 1–2 minutes. Top with the crisp breadcrumbs and extra parmesan, if desired.

fettuccine primavera

☀

Preparation time: 35 minutes
Cooking time: 15 minutes
Serves 6

500 g (1 lb 2 oz) fettuccine
155 g (5½ oz) asparagus spears
155 g (5½ oz/1 cup) frozen (or fresh) broad (fava) beans
30 g (1 oz) butter
1 celery stalk, sliced
155 g (5½ oz/1 cup) peas
310 ml (10¾ fl oz/1¼ cups) pouring (whipping) cream
50 g (1¾ oz/½ cup) freshly grated parmesan cheese

1 Cook the pasta in a large saucepan of rapidly boiling salted water until *al dente*. Drain and return to the pan.
2 Meanwhile, cut the asparagus into small pieces. Bring a saucepan of water to the boil, add the asparagus and cook for 2 minutes. Using a slotted spoon, remove the asparagus from the pan and plunge into a bowl of ice-cold water.
3 Cook the beans in a saucepan of boiling water for 1 minute. Use a slotted spoon to remove and transfer to cold water. Drain, then peel and discard the tough outside skin. (If you're using very young, fresh beans, the skin can be left on, but mature and frozen beans should be peeled.) Return the beans to the pan and cook for 2–5 minutes, or until tender.

4 Heat the butter in a heavy-based frying pan. Add the celery and stir for 2 minutes. Add the peas and cream and cook gently for 3 minutes. Add the asparagus, broad beans, parmesan and salt and pepper, to taste. Bring the sauce to the boil and cook for 1 minute. Add the sauce to the cooked fettuccine and toss well to combine.

NOTE: In this classic dish, any vegetables, usually spring vegetables, may be used. Choose your favourites such as leeks, zucchini (courgettes), beans, sugar snap peas or snowpeas (mangetout).

warm broccoli florets with almonds

Cook broccoli florets until tender, then refresh in iced water, sprinkle with toasted flaked almonds and drizzle with a dressing made by mixing melted butter, crushed garlic and lemon juice. Serve as a side dish.

penne with pumpkin and cinnamon sauce

✹

Preparation time: **25 minutes**
Cooking time: **30 minutes**
Serves **4**

340 g (11¾ oz) pumpkin (winter squash)
500 g (1 lb 2 oz) penne
25 g (1 oz) butter
1 onion, finely chopped
2 garlic cloves, crushed
1 teaspoon ground cinnamon
250 ml (9 fl oz/1 cup) pouring
   (whipping) cream
1 tablespoon honey
35 g (1¼ oz/⅓ cup) freshly grated
   parmesan cheese, plus extra, to serve
snipped chives, to garnish

1 Peel the pumpkin, remove the seeds and cut the flesh into small cubes. Boil, steam or microwave the pumpkin until just tender. Drain well.
2 Cook the penne in a large saucepan of rapidly boiling salted water until *al dente*. Drain and return to the pan.
3 While the pasta is cooking, melt the butter in a frying pan and cook the onion over medium heat until soft and golden. Add the garlic and cinnamon and cook for another minute.
4 Pour the cream into the pan, add the pumpkin and honey and simmer for 5 minutes, until the sauce reduces and thickens slightly and is heated through.
5 Add the parmesan and stir until it has melted. Season with salt and freshly ground black pepper, to taste. Pour the sauce over the penne and toss until well combined. Serve sprinkled with chives and extra parmesan.

chickpeas

Chickpeas, garbanzos or ceci originated in the Mediterranean regions and are particularly popular today in Spain, southern Italy and North Africa. Their nut-like taste makes them highly suitable for blending with other flavours and their crunchy texture works well in salads. Chickpea flour (besan) is used in both sweet and savoury pastry making. Dried chickpeas must be soaked overnight before use. Tinned, pre-cooked chickpeas are a time-saving alternative.

conchiglie with chickpeas

Preparation time: **15 minutes**
Cooking time: **20 minutes**
Serves **4**

500 g (1 lb 2 oz) conchiglie (shell pasta)
2 tablespoons extra virgin olive oil
1 red onion, thinly sliced
2–3 garlic cloves, crushed
400 g (14 oz) tin chickpeas, rinsed and
    drained
75 g (2½ oz/½ cup) sun-dried tomatoes,
    drained and thinly sliced
1 teaspoon finely grated lemon zest
1 teaspoon chopped fresh red chilli
2 tablespoons lemon juice
1 tablespoon chopped oregano
1 tablespoon chopped parsley
shavings of parmesan cheese, to serve
    (optional)

1   Cook the conchiglie in a large saucepan
of rapidly boiling salted water until it is
al dente. Drain and return to the pan.
2   While the pasta is cooking, heat the oil
in a frying pan, add the onion and cook
until soft and lightly golden.
3   Add the garlic to the pan and cook
for another minute. Add the chickpeas,
sun-dried tomato, lemon zest and chilli
and cook over high heat until heated
through. Stir in the lemon juice and herbs.
4   Toss the chickpea mixture through
the pasta. Season with salt and pepper
and serve immediately, scattered with
parmesan shavings, if desired.

olives

The sour, pungent taste of these shiny black, green or brown fruits makes a vital contribution to the flavour of the myriad Mediterranean dishes with which we associate them, and many others as well.

The olive tree is the oldest cultivated tree. It originated in Africa and Asia Minor and has been grown in the Mediterranean for over 6000 years. An olive tree takes five years to bear fruit, but its life span is usually over 100 years. There are even trees believed to be over 2000 years old. Known as a symbol of longevity, it is able to withstand harsh climates. The olive branch has long been used as a symbol of peace.

Black and green olives come from the same tree, green is merely the unripe fruit. To preserve fresh olives, soak 1 kg (2 lb 4 oz) black olives in a bucket of cold water for 6 weeks, changing the water every second day. After 6 weeks, drain the olives in a large colander and cover completely with rock salt. Set aside for 2 days. Rinse and set aside to dry thoroughly. Layer the olives in sterilised jars with slivers of preserved lemon skin, slivers of garlic, coriander seeds and sprigs of lemon thyme. Cover with a mixture of oil and white wine vinegar, in equal amounts. Seal and set aside for 2 weeks before using. Store in a cool, dark place for up to 6 months.

sautéed black olives

Soak 500 g (1 lb 2 oz) wrinkled cured black olives in warm water overnight. Rinse and drain. Heat 60 ml (2 fl oz/¼ cup) oil in a large frying pan, add 1 sliced onion and cook over medium heat for 2 minutes. Add the olives and cook for 10 minutes, or until soft. Remove the olives and onion using a slotted spoon and drain in a colander. Add several sprigs of oregano, toss and cool completely. Transfer to a sterilised jar. Refrigerate for up to 3 weeks.

chilli garlic olives

Rinse and drain 500 g (1 lb 2 oz) brined kalamata olives. Make a small incision in the side of each olive. Layer the olives in a sterilised jar with fine strips of orange zest, 1 teaspoon chilli flakes, 4 halved fresh red chillies, 2 thinly sliced garlic cloves and 4 rosemary sprigs. Combine 2 tablespoons lemon juice with 250 ml (9 fl oz/1 cup) olive oil and pour it over the olives. Add extra olive oil to cover, if necessary. Cover and marinate in a cool, dark place for 2 weeks.

olive and tomato tapenade

Soak 3 anchovy fillets in milk for 10 minutes. Rinse and drain. Place in a food processor with 155 g (5½ oz/1 cup) pitted black niçoise olives, 2 garlic cloves, 2 tablespoons chopped capers and the zest of 1 lemon and process for a few seconds, until roughly chopped. Transfer to a bowl and add 80 g (2¾ oz/½ cup) chopped sun-dried tomato, 2 tablespoons lemon juice, 1 tablespoon chopped parsley and 2 tablespoons extra virgin olive oil. Stir to combine and serve with crusty Italian bread.

spaghetti siracusani

spaghetti siracusani

Preparation time: 15 minutes
Cooking time: 25 minutes
Serves 6

1 large green capsicum (pepper)
2 tablespoons olive oil
2 garlic cloves, crushed
2 x 400g (14 oz) tins chopped tomatoes
2 zucchini (courgettes), chopped
2 anchovy fillets, chopped (optional)
1 tablespoon capers, rinsed and chopped
35g (1¼ oz/¼ cup) black olives, pitted
  and halved
2 tablespoons chopped basil leaves
500g (1 lb 2 oz) spaghetti or linguine
50g (1¾ oz/½ cup) freshly grated parmesan
  cheese, to serve

1 Remove the membrane and seeds
from the capsicum. Slice the flesh into
thin strips. Heat the oil in a large deep
saucepan. Add the garlic and stir for
30 seconds over low heat. Add 125 ml
(4 fl oz/½ cup) water along with the
capsicum, tomatoes, zucchini, anchovies,
if using, capers and olives. Cook for
20 minutes, stirring occasionally. Stir in
the basil and salt and pepper, to taste.
2 While the sauce is cooking, cook the
pasta in a large saucepan of rapidly
boiling salted water until *al dente*. Drain.
Serve the sauce over the pasta and
sprinkle with parmesan.

fettuccine boscaiola (fettuccine with mushroom and tomato sauce)

Preparation time: 20 minutes
Cooking time: 25 minutes
Serves 6

500 g (1 lb 2 oz) button mushrooms
1 large onion

warm ginger and sesame carrot salad
Scrub or peel 500 g (1 lb 2 oz) baby carrots and steam or microwave until just
tender. Transfer to a bowl, add 1 tablespoon honey, ¼ teaspoon ground ginger,
50 g (1¾ oz) melted butter, 1 teaspoon lemon thyme leaves and 1 tablespoon
toasted sesame seeds. Toss lightly to coat and serve immediately as a side dish.

2 tablespoons olive oil
2 garlic cloves, finely chopped
2 x 400 g (14 oz) tins tomatoes,
    roughly chopped, juice reserved
500 g (1 lb 2 oz) fettuccine
3 tablespoons chopped parsley

1 Carefully wipe the mushrooms with a damp paper towel and then slice thinly, including the stems.

2 Roughly chop the onion. Heat the oil in a heavy-based frying pan and cook the onion and garlic over medium heat, stirring occasionally, for about 6 minutes, or until the vegetables are light golden. Add the tomatoes, reserved juice, and the mushrooms and bring the mixture to the boil. Reduce the heat, cover the pan and simmer for 15 minutes.

3 While the sauce is cooking, cook the fettuccine in a large saucepan of rapidly boiling salted water until *al dente*. Drain and return to the pan.

4 Stir 2 tablespoons of parsley into the sauce and season with salt and pepper. Toss the sauce through the pasta. Serve sprinkled with the remaining parsley.

NOTE: If you would like a creamy sauce, add 125 ml (4 fl oz/½ cup) of pouring (whipping) cream when adding the parsley (do not reboil or it may curdle).

button mushrooms

Cultivated button mushrooms would have to be the most widely used mushroom today. Because of their mild flavour, clean colour and appearance, and compact size, they are suited to most cooking styles. As well as being good for flavouring sauces and fillings, they can be eaten raw. As they mature, their caps partially open and become known as cap or cup mushrooms. These taste stronger and have more visible and browner gills. Cap mushrooms complement foods of a robust nature and make rich sauces when sautéed in butter or cooked with red wine.

blue cheese and broccoli with rigatoni

☀

Preparation time: **15 minutes**
Cooking time: **15 minutes**
Serves **4**

500 g (1 lb 2 oz) rigatoni
500 g (1 lb 2 oz) broccoli
1 tablespoon vegetable oil
1 onion, sliced
125 ml (4 fl oz/½ cup) dry white wine
250 ml (9 fl oz/1 cup) pouring (whipping)
  cream
½ teaspoon hot paprika
150 g (5½ oz) blue brie cheese, chopped
  into small pieces
2 tablespoons flaked almonds, toasted

1 Cook the rigatoni in a large saucepan of rapidly boiling salted water until *al dente*. Drain and return to the pan.
2 Cut the broccoli into florets and steam or microwave them for 2–3 minutes, until tender, then drain well.
3 Heat the oil in a large saucepan and cook the onion until soft. Add the wine and cream and simmer for 4–5 minutes, until reduced and thickened slightly. Stir in the paprika and cheese, and season with salt and pepper, to taste.
4 Add the broccoli and sauce to the pasta and gently toss over low heat until well mixed and heated through. Serve sprinkled with almonds.

NOTE: You can use a stronger blue cheese, such as gorgonzola, if you like.

crisp zucchini ribbons

Using a sharp vegetable peeler, cut large zucchini (courgettes) into ribbons by running the peeler along them horizontally. Lightly coat the ribbons firstly in beaten egg, then in a mixture of dry breadcrumbs, finely grated parmesan cheese and some chopped herbs. Deep-fry the ribbons, in batches, in hot oil until crisp and golden brown. Serve with a tangy tomato salsa.

pumpkin and pine nut tagliatelle

✻

Preparation time: 25 minutes
Cooking time: 25 minutes
Serves 4

750 g (1 lb 10 oz) butternut pumpkin
   (squash)
30 g (1 oz) butter
1 large onion, chopped
2 garlic cloves, crushed
375 ml (13 fl oz/1½ cups) vegetable stock
¼ teaspoon freshly grated nutmeg
250 ml (9 fl oz/1 cup) pouring
   (whipping) cream

500 g (1 lb 2 oz) fresh tagliatelle
80 g (2¾ oz/½ cup) pine nuts, toasted
   (see Note)
2 tablespoons snipped chives
freshly grated parmesan cheese,
   to serve (optional)

1   Peel the pumpkin, discard the seeds
and cut into small pieces. Melt the butter
in a large saucepan. Add the onion and
cook for 3 minutes, or until soft and
golden. Add the garlic and cook for
another minute. Stir in the stock and
add the pumpkin. Bring to the boil, then
reduce the heat slightly and cook until
the pumpkin is tender. Reduce the heat to
very low and season with the nutmeg and
½ teaspoon freshly ground black pepper.

Stir in the cream until just warmed
through — do not allow the mixture to
boil. Transfer to a food processor and
process for about 30 seconds, just until
the mixture forms a smooth sauce.
2   Meanwhile, cook the tagliatelle in a
large saucepan of rapidly boiling salted
water until *al dente*. Drain and return to
the pan. Return the sauce to the pan and
gently reheat. Add to the pasta with the
pine nuts and toss well. Serve sprinkled
with chives and parmesan, if desired.

NOTE: Toast the pine nuts in a dry frying
pan over medium heat, stirring constantly,
until they are golden brown and aromatic.

pine nuts

These are small, elongated,
creamy white kernels taken
from the nuts of pine trees,
in particular the Pinon and
Stone pines. Sometimes these
trees are called parasol pines
because of their umbrella
shape and they typify the
Mediterranean landscape,
where they are native. The nuts
are always sold shelled and
blanched, and their flavour
can be enhanced by toasting
or roasting them before use.
Pine nuts are used in dessert
and sweet making as well as
in savoury dishes.

spicy penne with capsicum

Preparation time: 30 minutes
Cooking time: 15 minutes
Serves 4

1 large red capsicum (pepper)
1 large green capsicum (pepper)
1 large yellow capsicum (pepper)
500 g (1 lb 2 oz) penne
80 ml (2½ fl oz/⅓ cup) olive oil
2 tablespoons sweet chilli sauce
1 tablespoon red wine vinegar

20 g (¾ oz/⅓ cup) chopped coriander
  (cilantro) leaves
250 g (9 oz) cherry tomatoes, halved
freshly grated parmesan cheese,
  to serve

1 Cut the capsicums into large flat pieces and discard the seeds and membrane. Cook, skin side up, under a hot grill (broiler) for 8 minutes, or until the skin is black and blistered. Transfer to a plastic bag to cool. Peel away the skin and cut the flesh into long, thin strips.
2 Meanwhile, cook the penne in a large saucepan of rapidly boiling salted water until *al dente*. Drain and return to the pan.

3 Whisk together the oil, chilli sauce and vinegar, and season with salt and freshly ground black pepper, to taste.
4 Add the oil mixture, coriander, capsicum and tomato to the pasta. Serve sprinkled with parmesan.

NOTE: This dish can be served warm as a main meal, or at room temperature as a salad. It is an excellent accompaniment for chicken or barbecued meat.

cherry tomatoes

Cherry tomatoes come in a number of varieties including Red Currant, Green Grape, Sweet 100 and Yellow Pear. All are perfect for use in salads and some, such as the Sweet 100, can withstand quick cooking. They are all low in acid and can be extremely sweet. At approximately 5 mm (¼ inch) diameter, Red Currant is the smallest and is often displayed for sale in loose clusters.

fettuccine with snow peas and walnuts

✳

Preparation time: **30 minutes**
Cooking time: **15 minutes**
Serves **4**

500 g (1 lb 2 oz) fettuccine or linguine
60 g (2¼ oz/½ cup) chopped walnuts
30 g (1 oz) butter
1 large onion, chopped
4 bacon slices, chopped (optional)
1 garlic clove, crushed
185 ml (6 fl oz/¾ cup) dry white wine
250 ml (9 fl oz/1 cup) pouring (whipping)
   cream
250 g (9 oz) snow peas (mangetout),
   halved on the diagonal

1   Cook the fettuccine in a large saucepan of rapidly boiling salted water until it is *al dente*. Drain and return to the pan.
2   While the pasta is cooking, scatter the walnuts on a foil-lined grill tray. Cook under a moderately hot grill (broiler) for 2 minutes, or until lightly toasted. Stir after 1 minute and be careful they don't burn. Set aside to cool.
3   Melt the butter in a large saucepan. Add the onion and bacon and cook until the onion is soft and the bacon lightly browned. Add the garlic and cook for another minute.
4   Pour in the wine and cream, bring to the boil and then reduce the heat. Simmer for 4 minutes, add the snow peas and simmer for another minute. Toss the sauce and walnuts through the pasta. Season with salt and pepper, to taste.

NOTE: Don't be tempted to save time by not toasting the nuts. Raw nuts can be bitter and stale in flavour, particularly if they are old or have been stored in the refrigerator.

tagliatelle with tomato and walnuts

Preparation time: 20 minutes
Cooking time: 30 minutes
Serves 6

4 very ripe tomatoes
2 tablespoons oil
1 onion, finely chopped
1 celery stalk, finely chopped
1 carrot, diced
2 tablespoons chopped parsley
1 teaspoon red wine vinegar
60 ml (2 fl oz/¼ cup) white wine
500 g (1 lb 2 oz) tagliatelle or fettuccine
90 g (3 ¼ oz/¾ cup) walnuts, roughly
  chopped
35 g (1¼ oz/⅓ cup) freshly grated
  parmesan cheese, to serve (optional)

1 Score a small cross in the base of each tomato. Place in a bowl of boiling water for 1–2 minutes and then plunge into cold water. Peel the skin away from the cross and roughly chop the flesh.
2 Heat 1 tablespoon of the oil in a large heavy-based saucepan and cook the onion and celery for 5 minutes over low heat, stirring regularly. Add the tomato, carrot, parsley and combined vinegar and wine and simmer for 25 minutes. Season with salt and freshly ground pepper.
3 About 15 minutes before the sauce is ready, cook the pasta in a large saucepan of rapidly boiling water until *al dente*. Drain and return to the pan.
4 Heat the remaining oil in a frying pan, add the walnuts and stir over low heat for 5 minutes. Toss the sauce through the pasta and serve topped with walnuts and sprinkled with parmesan, if desired.

walnuts

Walnuts are encased in a hard, round shell, with two distinct halves. The nut inside consists of two creamy-white, deeply ridged lobes of mild-flavoured flesh. Chopped walnuts are commonly used in pasta sauces as well as fruit cakes, salads, slices and biscuits. Walnuts that are still in their shells can be refrigerated for up to 6 months. Shelled nuts should be bought in airtight containers or tins and stored, after opening, in an airtight glass jar in the refrigerator.

tortellini with eggplant

✳

Preparation time: 10 minutes
Cooking time: 20 minutes
Serves 4

1 red capsicum (pepper)
500 g (1 lb 2 oz) eggplant (aubergine)
500 g (1 lb 2 oz) fresh cheese and
    spinach tortellini
60 ml (2 fl oz/¼ cup) oil
2 garlic cloves, crushed

400 g (14 oz) tin chopped tomatoes
250 ml (9 fl oz/1 cup) vegetable stock
25 g (1 oz) chopped basil

1 Cut the capsicum in half, remove the seeds and membrane and then cut the flesh into small squares. Cut the eggplant into small squares.
2 Cook the tortellini in a large saucepan of rapidly boiling salted water until *al dente*. Drain and return to the pan.
3 While the pasta is cooking, heat the oil in a large frying pan, add the garlic and capsicum and stir over medium heat for 1 minute. Add the eggplant to the pan and stir gently over medium heat for 5 minutes, or until lightly browned.
4 Add the tomatoes and stock to the pan. Stir and bring to the boil, then reduce the heat to low, cover the pan and cook for 10 minutes, or until the vegetables are tender. Add the basil and pasta and stir until mixed through.

NOTE: Cut the eggplant just before using, as it turns brown when exposed to the air.

tortellini

Once, an innkeeper, a local gastronome, had the good fortune of being host to the goddess Venus. Overtaken with curiosity, he couldn't help taking a peek at her through the keyhole of her door. One look at her bellybutton, surrounded by the outline of the keyhole, was enough to inspire him to rush to his kitchen and create something in its image — the tortellini. This tale reflects the love the citizens of Bologna have for one of their most famous pastas (and goddesses!).

creamy pasta

Pasta and cream, a culinary marriage made in heaven. There are times when only the best will do ... when only a bowl of fresh tagliatelle, tossed in a rich creamy sauce and topped with parmesan shavings and cracked black pepper will satisfy your hunger for a taste of decadence. Traditionally, the long thin pastas are served with cream sauces, but these days, the possibilities are limitless.

fusilli with broad bean sauce

✳

Preparation time: **30 minutes**
Cooking time: **25 minutes**
Serves **6**

310 g (11 oz/2 cups) broad (fava) beans
4 bacon slices, rind removed
2 leeks
2 tablespoons olive oil
310 ml (10¾ fl oz/1¼ cups) pouring
   (whipping) cream
2 teaspoons finely grated lemon zest
500 g (1 lb 2 oz) fusilli (spiral pasta)

1 Cook the beans in a saucepan of boiling water for 1 minute. Use a slotted spoon to remove and transfer to cold water. Drain, then peel and discard the tough outside skin. (If you're using very young, fresh beans, the skin can be left on, but mature and frozen beans should be peeled.) Return the beans to the pan and cook for 2–5 minutes, or until tender.
2 Chop the bacon into small pieces. Wash the leeks thoroughly to remove any dirt and grit and then thinly slice.
3 Heat the oil in a heavy-based frying pan. Add the bacon and leek and cook over medium heat, stirring occasionally, for 8 minutes, or until the leek is golden. Add the cream and lemon zest, bring to the boil, then reduce the heat and simmer until the sauce thickens and coats the back of a spoon. Add the broad beans and season with salt and pepper, to taste.
4 While the sauce is simmering, cook the pasta in a large saucepan of rapidly boiling salted water until *al dente*. Drain and return to the pan.
5 Add the sauce to the pasta and toss well to combine. Serve immediately.

NOTE: Broad beans can be cooked and peeled in advance, then refrigerated in a covered container until needed. To peel them, slit or break off the top and then squeeze the beans out. Leaving the tough outside skin on the broad beans will change the delicate texture and flavour of this dish, so it is well worth the extra effort of peeling them.

warm spring vegetable salad

Lightly blanch baby carrots, broccoli, snow peas (mangetout), beans, baby (pattypan) squash and baby corn in boiling water until just tender. Drain and toss through some chopped fresh herbs, melted butter and honey mustard. Serve as a side dish.

mustard

The condiment mustard is made by blending mustard seeds, sometimes ground, with vinegar or wine, food acid, salt and aromatic herbs and spices. The seeds come from various species of the mustard plant and have differing strengths, colours and sizes. Mustard powder is a mix of ground mustard seeds and wheat flour, often flavoured with turmeric and other spices.

tagliatelle with chicken livers and cream

Preparation time: 20 minutes
Cooking time: 15 minutes
Serves 4

375 g (13 oz) tagliatelle
300 g (10½ oz) chicken livers
2 tablespoons olive oil
1 onion, finely chopped
1 garlic clove, crushed
250 ml (9 fl oz/1 cup) pouring (whipping) cream
1 tablespoon snipped chives
1 teaspoon wholegrain mustard
2 eggs, beaten
freshly grated parmesan cheese, to serve
snipped chives, to serve

1 Cook the tagliatelle in a large saucepan of rapidly boiling salted water until it is *al dente*. Drain and return to the pan.

2 While the pasta is cooking, trim any green or discoloured parts from the chicken livers, then slice them. Heat the olive oil in a large frying pan. Add the onion and garlic and stir over low heat until the onion is tender.

3 Add the chicken liver to the pan and cook gently for 2–3 minutes. Remove from the heat and stir in the cream, chives and mustard and season to taste. Return to the heat and bring to the boil. Add the egg and stir quickly to combine. Remove from the heat.

4 Add the sauce to the hot pasta and toss well to combine. Serve sprinkled with parmesan and snipped chives.

black pepper

Peppercorns are the berry of the tropical vine *Piper nigrum*. They are green and soft when immature, and red or yellow when ripe. Black peppercorns are picked when ripe, then sun-dried, which gives them their hard, black, wrinkled appearance. These have the strongest flavour and aroma. Peppercorns lose their sharpness once ground, so it is recommended to keep them whole and grind just before use.

penne with chicken and mushrooms

Preparation time: 30 minutes
Cooking time: 25 minutes
Serves 4

30 g (1 oz) butter
1 tablespoon olive oil
1 onion, sliced
1 garlic clove, crushed
60 g (2¼ oz) prosciutto, chopped
250 g (9 oz) boneless, skinless chicken thighs, trimmed and sliced
125 g (4½ oz) mushrooms, sliced

1 tomato, peeled, halved and sliced
1 tablespoon tomato paste (concentrated purée)
125 ml (4 fl oz/½ cup) white wine
250 ml (9 fl oz/1 cup) pouring (whipping) cream
500 g (1 lb 2 oz) penne
freshly grated parmesan cheese, to serve

1 Heat the butter and oil in a large frying pan. Add the onion and garlic and stir over low heat until the onion is tender. Add the prosciutto and fry until crisp.
2 Add the chicken and cook over medium heat for 3 minutes. Add the mushroom and cook for another 2 minutes. Add the tomato and tomato paste and stir until combined. Stir in the wine and bring to the boil. Reduce the heat and simmer until the liquid is reduced by half.
3 Stir in the cream and season, to taste. Bring to the boil, then reduce the heat and simmer until the sauce begins to thicken.
4 While the sauce is cooking, cook the penne in a large saucepan of rapidly boiling salted water until *al dente*. Drain well and return to the pan. Add the sauce to the pasta and toss to combine. Serve immediately, sprinkled with parmesan.

NOTE: If you prefer, you can use minced (ground) chicken in this recipe instead of the sliced chicken thighs. Follow the recipe as above.

rigatoni with sausage and parmesan

☀

Preparation time: **15 minutes**
Cooking time: **15 minutes**
Serves **4**

2 tablespoons olive oil
1 onion, sliced
1 garlic clove, crushed
500 g (1 lb 2 oz) Italian pork sausage,
    thickly sliced on the diagonal
60 g (2¼ oz) mushrooms, sliced
125 ml (4 fl oz/½ cup) dry white wine
500 g (1 lb 2 oz) rigatoni
250 ml (9 fl oz/1 cup) pouring
    (whipping) cream
2 eggs
50 g (1¾ oz/½ cup) freshly grated
    parmesan cheese
2 tablespoons chopped parsley

1 Heat the oil in a large frying pan.
Add the onion and garlic and stir over
low heat until the onion is tender. Add
the sausage and mushroom and cook
until the sausage is cooked through. Stir
in the wine and bring to the boil. Reduce
the heat and simmer until the liquid is
reduced by half.
2 While the sauce is cooking, cook the
rigatoni in a large saucepan of rapidly
boiling salted water until *al dente*. Drain
and return to the pan.
3 In a large jug, whisk together the
cream, eggs, half the parmesan, the
parsley and salt and pepper, to taste.
Add to the rigatoni with the sausage
mixture and toss. Serve sprinkled with
the remaining parmesan.

NOTE: You can freeze leftover wine for
use in recipes such as this one. You can
also use salami instead of Italian pork
sausage, if you prefer.

bucatini with gorgonzola sauce

bucatini with gorgonzola sauce

Preparation time: **10 minutes**
Cooking time: **20 minutes**
Serves **6**

375 g (13 oz) bucatini or spaghetti
200 g (7 oz) gorgonzola cheese
1 celery stalk
20 g (¾ oz) butter
310 ml (10¾ fl oz/1¼ cups) pouring
   (whipping) cream
250 g (9 oz/1 cup) fresh ricotta cheese,
   beaten until smooth

1   Cook the bucatini in a large saucepan
of rapidly boiling salted water until
al dente. Drain and return to the pan.
2   While the pasta is cooking, chop the
gorgonzola cheese into small cubes and
slice the celery.
3   Heat the butter in a saucepan, add
the celery and stir for 2 minutes. Add the
cream, ricotta and gorgonzola and season
to taste with freshly ground black pepper.
Bring to the boil over low heat, stirring
constantly, then simmer for 1 minute. Add
the sauce to the warm pasta and toss well.

fettuccine with creamy mushroom and bean sauce

Preparation time: **20 minutes**
Cooking time: **20 minutes**
Serves **4**

gorgonzola cheese

Gorgonzola is an Italian
blue-veined cheese. It is
creamy and sweet when
young, and sharp, strong and
slightly crumbly when mature.
As well as being a delicious
table cheese that goes well
with apples and pears, it is a
good companion for cooked
vegetables and meats. It melts
well when heated and makes
a rich, mellow flavouring for
cream-based sauces. It can
be replaced by a creamy mild
blue-vein such as Blue Castello,
or you can use a mixture of half
Blue Castello and half Danish
Blue for a stronger taste.

280 g (10 oz) fettuccine
2 tablespoons oil
1 onion, chopped
2 garlic cloves, crushed
250 g (9 oz) mushrooms, thinly sliced
125 ml (4 fl oz/½ cup) white wine
310 ml (10¾ fl oz/1¼ cups) pouring
   (whipping) cream
125 ml (4 fl oz/½ cup) vegetable stock

1 egg
250 g (9 oz) green beans, trimmed and
   thinly sliced on the diagonal
3 tablespoons chopped basil
100 g (3½ oz/⅔ cup) pine nuts, toasted
   (see Note)
35 g (1¼ oz/¼ cup) sun-dried tomatoes,
   sliced
50 g (1¾ oz) shaved parmesan cheese
herb sprigs, to serve (optional)

1 Cook the pasta in a large saucepan of
rapidly boiling salted water until *al dente*.
Drain, return to the pan and keep warm.

2 Heat the oil in a large heavy-based
frying pan. Add the onion and garlic and
cook over medium heat for 3 minutes, or
until softened. Add the mushroom and
stir for 1 minute. Add the wine, cream
and stock. Bring to the boil, then reduce
the heat and simmer for 10 minutes.

3 Lightly beat the egg in a small bowl.
Add a little of the cooking liquid, stirring
constantly. Pour the egg mixture slowly
into the pan, stirring constantly for
30 seconds over low heat.

4 Add the beans, basil, pine nuts and
sun-dried tomato and stir until heated

through, then season with salt and freshly
ground black pepper, to taste.

5 Serve the sauce spooned over the
pasta. Garnish with parmesan shavings
and sprigs of herbs, if desired.

NOTE: Toast the pine nuts in a dry frying
pan over medium heat, stirring constantly,
until they are golden brown and aromatic.

vegetable stock

A good vegetable stock has
a delicate balance of flavours
suitable for meat and seafood
dishes as well as vegetable
sauces, soups and braises.
Any combination of aromatic,
non-starchy vegetables such as
carrots, onions, leeks, celery or
turnips are simmered for
30 minutes with a bouquet
garni, garlic clove and a little
salt. The result will be a pale
and clear stock with a mild
flavour. A simple alternative
is to use the water in which
vegetables such as carrots or
green beans have been boiled.

anchovy fillets

The most convenient way to buy anchovy fillets is in little tins or jars, preserved in oil. They should be pink, not grey, and have good definable fillets. If they are a little too strong for your taste, drain the amount needed and cover with milk. Leave for 30 minutes before discarding the milk, then pat the fillets dry with paper towel. For a very mild flavour, use only the oil. Also available are anchovy fillets preserved in salt. These have a more delicate flavour, but must be soaked for 30 minutes before use.

conchiglie with broccolini

☀

Preparation time: 15 minutes
Cooking time: 20 minutes
Serves 6

500 g (1 lb 2 oz) conchiglie (shell pasta)
450 g (1 lb) broccolini or broccoli
1 tablespoon oil
1 onion, chopped
1 garlic clove, crushed
3 anchovy fillets, chopped
310 ml (10¾ fl oz/1¼ cups) pouring (whipping) cream
50 g (1¾ oz/½ cup) freshly grated parmesan cheese, to serve

1 Cook the conchiglie in a large saucepan of rapidly boiling salted water until it is *al dente*. Drain and return to the pan.
2 While the conchiglie is cooking, cut the broccolini into short lengths and cook in a saucepan of boiling water for 1 minute. Drain, plunge into cold water and drain again. Set aside.
3 Heat the oil in a frying pan. Add the onion, garlic and anchovies and cook over low heat, stirring, for 3 minutes.
4 Add the cream to the pan and, stirring constantly, bring to the boil. Reduce the heat and simmer for 2 minutes. Add the broccolini and cook for a further 1 minute. Season with salt and freshly ground black pepper. Toss the sauce through the pasta until well combined and serve sprinkled with parmesan.

tagliatelle with asparagus and herbs

Preparation time: **15 minutes**
Cooking time: **15 minutes**
Serves **4–6**

500 g (1 lb 2 oz) tagliatelle
150 g (5½ oz) asparagus spears,
    woody ends trimmed
40 g (1½ oz) butter
1 tablespoon chopped flat-leaf
    (Italian) parsley
1 tablespoon chopped basil
310 ml (10¾ fl oz/1¼ cups) pouring
    (whipping) cream
50 g (1¾ oz/½ cup) freshly grated
    parmesan cheese, plus parmesan
    shavings, to serve

1 Cook the tagliatelle in a large saucepan of rapidly boiling salted water until it is *al dente*. Drain and return to the pan.
2 While the pasta is cooking, cut the asparagus spears into short pieces. Heat the butter in a saucepan, add the asparagus and stir over medium heat for 2 minutes, or until just tender. Add the parsley, basil and cream and season, to taste. Cook for 2 minutes.
3 Add the grated parmesan to the pan and stir well. When thoroughly combined, add the sauce to the warm pasta and toss gently to distribute the ingredients evenly. Serve in warmed pasta bowls with shavings of parmesan cheese.

asparagus

To prepare asparagus for cooking, remove the woody base of the stalk by simply snapping it off. Starting at the base and moving up towards the tip, gently bend the stalk. The tough end will snap off when you reach crisp flesh. Only thick stalks with coarse skins need to be peeled. This is done with a vegetable peeler or a small sharp knife, and the paring should taper off as you near the tip. When these steps are followed, the stalks will cook evenly from top to bottom and it shouldn't be necessary to tie the bunches together for boiling. The cooking time is critical; too short, and the asparagus will be hard and have a metallic taste; too long, and the flesh becomes stringy and water-logged. Asparagus of average thickness takes only 3 minutes to cook. For thick stalks you'll need to add an extra 30–50 seconds.

ravioli with mascarpone and pancetta

ravioli with mascarpone and pancetta

Preparation time: **10 minutes**
Cooking time: **20 minutes**
Serves **4**

500 g (1 lb 2 oz) fresh spinach ravioli
2 teaspoons vegetable oil
90 g (3¼ oz) pancetta, finely chopped
125 ml (4 fl oz/½ cup) chicken stock
185 g (6½ oz) mascarpone cheese
80 g (2¾ oz/½ cup) thinly sliced
    sun-dried tomatoes
2 tablespoons finely shredded basil

1 Cook the ravioli in a large saucepan of rapidly boiling salted water until *al dente*.
2 While the pasta is cooking, heat the oil in a frying pan and cook the pancetta for 2–3 minutes. Stir in the stock, mascarpone and sun-dried tomato.
3 Bring to the boil, reduce the heat and simmer for 5 minutes, until the sauce reduces and thickens. Stir in the basil and ½ teaspoon cracked black pepper.
4 Drain the ravioli and add to the pan with the sauce. Toss together gently to combine. Serve immediately.

fettuccine with smoked cheese and salami

Preparation time: **20 minutes**
Cooking time: **15 minutes**
Serves **4**

375 g (13 oz) tomato fettuccine
200 g (7 oz) sun-dried tomatoes
    in oil
1 large red onion, sliced
2 large garlic cloves, finely chopped
3 bacon slices, finely chopped
150 g (5½ oz) hot or mild salami,
    sliced into strips

tomato and bocconcini salad

Thickly slice 4 large vine-ripened tomatoes and 8 baby bocconcini. Arrange the tomato slices, bocconcini and basil leaves on a serving plate. Drizzle with a little extra virgin olive oil and balsamic vinegar. Sprinkle with cracked black pepper and sea salt. Serve as a side dish.

2 teaspoons plain (all-purpose) flour
1 tablespoon tomato paste (concentrated purée)
375 ml (13 fl oz/1½ cups) evaporated milk
60 g (2¼ oz/½ cup) grated smoked cheese
¼ teaspoon cayenne pepper
2 tablespoons chopped flat-leaf (Italian) parsley
shavings of parmesan cheese, to serve (optional)

1 Cook the fettuccine in a large saucepan of rapidly boiling salted water until it is *al dente*. Drain and return to the pan.
2 Meanwhile, drain the tomatoes, reserving the oil, and cut into strips.

3 Heat the reserved oil in a saucepan and cook the onion for 3 minutes, or until soft and golden. Add the garlic and cook for another minute. Add the sun-dried tomato, bacon and salami and cook for another 2–3 minutes.
4 Stir in the flour, then the tomato paste and cook for 1 minute. Gradually add the evaporated milk, stirring continuously. Bring to the boil and reduce the heat. Add the smoked cheese, cayenne, parsley and black pepper, to taste, and simmer until the cheese melts.
5 Toss the sauce through the hot pasta. Serve immediately, scattered with shavings of parmesan, if desired.

cayenne pepper

Sometimes called Nepal pepper, cayenne pepper is an attractive, bright reddish-orange colour and has a pungency somewhere between that of ground chilli and black pepper. It is named after Cayenne, the main port of French Guiana. Cayenne pepper is made by grinding the dried fruit, minus the seeds, of different members of the capsicum (pepper) family, namely *Capsicum frutescens* and *Capsicum minimum*, and it is favoured because it has a slight sweetness underlying the hot pepper taste. Cayenne pepper can be used as a flavouring in dishes that require long cooking, but it has an intensity that is equally strong when used at the last minute as a condiment.

linguine in honey basil cream

Preparation time: 15 minutes
Cooking time: 20 minutes
Serves 6

500 g (1 lb 2 oz) linguine
240 g (8½ oz) basil leaves
1 small fresh red chilli, chopped
3 garlic cloves, crushed
3 tablespoons pine nuts, toasted
3 tablespoons freshly grated parmesan
  cheese
juice of 1 lemon
125 ml (4 fl oz/½ cup) olive oil
3 tablespoons honey
375 ml (13 fl oz/1½ cups) pouring
  (whipping) cream
125 ml (4 fl oz/½ cup) chicken stock
shavings of parmesan cheese,
  to serve

1 Cook the linguine in a large saucepan of rapidly boiling salted water until *al dente*. Drain and keep warm.

honey

The flavour, consistency, aroma, colour and degree of sweetness in honey is determined by the flowers from which the bees gather their nectar. Most prized for cooking uses is honey from herbs such as thyme and rosemary that have a subtle flavouring and a savoury fragrance. Flowers such as apple blossom give a highly floral perfume and flavour, while others make almost bitter honey.

2 While the pasta is cooking, combine the basil leaves, chilli, garlic, pine nuts, parmesan, lemon juice, oil and honey in a food processor or blender until smooth.
3 Combine the basil mixture, cream and stock in a large saucepan, bring to the boil and simmer for 15–20 minutes, or until the sauce has thickened. Season with cracked black pepper, to taste.
4 Add the pasta to the pan and toss well. Sprinkle with shavings of parmesan.

caramelised onion and blue cheese risoni

✹ ✹

Preparation time: **20 minutes**
Cooking time: **35 minutes**
Serves **4**

500 g (1 lb 2 oz) risoni
30 g (1 oz) butter
60 ml (2 fl oz/¼ cup) olive oil
4 onions, sliced
185 g (6½ oz) blue cheese
100 g (3½ oz) mascarpone cheese
130 g (4½ oz/2 cups) chopped
    English spinach leaves

1 Cook the risoni in a large saucepan of rapidly boiling salted water until *al dente*. Drain well and return to the pan.
2 While the risoni is cooking, heat the butter and the oil in a large heavy-based frying pan. Add the onion and cook over low heat for about 20–30 minutes, until golden brown and caramelised. Remove from the pan with a slotted spoon and drain on paper towels.
3 Mix the blue cheese, mascarpone and onion in a bowl.
4 Add the cheese and onion mixture, as well as the spinach, to the risoni and toss through. Season with salt and freshly ground black pepper before serving.

prosciutto

In Italy, prosciutto simply means ham, and it can be bought cooked, *cotto*, which is similar to boiled hams elsewhere, or raw, *crudo*, which is cured on the bone by salting and air-drying. This is the one referred to in recipes and is known for its versatility and mellow flavour. It is used in salads, on bread and tossed through pasta sauces, or used to add flavour to cooked sauces, stews and soups. It can be mature, with dark ruby flesh, creamy fat and a concentrated flavour and aroma, or younger and more succulent, with pale-pink flesh and white fat.

grilled carbonara

Preparation time: **10 minutes**
Cooking time: **20 minutes**
Serves **4**

250 g (9 oz) linguine
4 eggs
185 ml (6 fl oz/¾ cup) pouring (whipping) cream
6 thin prosciutto slices, chopped
75 g (2½ oz/¾ cup) freshly grated parmesan cheese
2 tablespoons snipped chives, plus extra, for garnish
30 g (1 oz) butter

1 Brush a shallow ovenproof dish with melted butter or oil. Preheat the grill (broiler) to moderately hot.
2 Cook the linguine in a large saucepan of rapidly boiling salted water until *al dente*. Drain and return to the pan.
3 While the pasta is cooking, whisk the eggs and cream together in a bowl, stir in the prosciutto, parmesan (reserving 3 tablespoons) and chives and season with freshly ground black pepper, to taste.
4 Add the egg mixture and the butter to the hot pasta and stir continuously over low heat for 1 minute, or until the egg mixture begins to thicken slightly. Take care not to overcook the mixture, or you will end up with scrambled eggs. The

mixture should be creamy and moist.

5 Pour the pasta into the dish and sprinkle with the reserved parmesan. Place under the grill for a few minutes, until just set and lightly browned on top. Serve with crusty Italian bread.

orecchiette with tuna, lemon and caper sauce

Preparation time: 10 minutes
Cooking time: 20 minutes
Serves 4

500 g (1 lb 2 oz) orecchiette
30 g (1 oz) butter
1 garlic clove, crushed
1 onion, finely chopped
425 g (15 oz) tin tuna in brine, drained
2 tablespoons lemon juice
250 ml (9 fl oz/1 cup) pouring (whipping) cream
2 tablespoons chopped flat-leaf (Italian) parsley
1 tablespoon capers, rinsed and drained
¼ teaspoon cayenne pepper (optional)
caperberries, to garnish (optional)

1 Cook the orecchiette in a large saucepan of rapidly boiling salted water until *al dente*. Drain and return to the pan.
2 Heat the butter in a saucepan and cook the garlic and onion for 1–2 minutes. Add the tuna, lemon juice, cream, half the parsley and the capers. Season with black pepper and cayenne, if using. Simmer over low heat for 5 minutes.
3 Add the tuna sauce to the pasta and toss until thoroughly combined. Serve the pasta sprinkled with the remaining parsley and garnished with caperberries, if desired.

caperberries

When capers, the buds of the caper bush (*Capparis spinosa*), are not picked but left to flower, small berries called caperberries form. These look a little like elongated grapes and are salted and pickled with their stems attached. They have a similar taste to capers (the buds of the plant), but are more often eaten like olives or pickles, or used to garnish a dish. When sliced, they are a good substitute for capers.

creamy seafood ravioli

Preparation time: 1 hour
  + 30 minutes standing time
Cooking time: 30 minutes
Serves 4

PASTA
250 g (9 oz/2 cups) plain (all-purpose)
  flour
3 eggs
1 tablespoon olive oil
1 egg yolk, extra

FILLING
50 g (1¾ oz) butter, softened
3 garlic cloves, finely chopped

2 tablespoons finely chopped flat-leaf
  (Italian) parsley
100 g (3½ oz) scallops, cleaned and
  finely chopped
100 g (3½ oz) raw prawn (shrimp)
  meat, finely chopped

SAUCE
70 g (2½ oz) butter
3 tablespoons plain (all-purpose)
  flour
375 ml (13 fl oz/1½ cups) milk
300 ml (10½ fl oz) pouring
  (whipping) cream
125 ml (4 fl oz/½ cup) dry white
  wine
50 g (1¾ oz/½ cup) freshly grated
  parmesan cheese
2 tablespoons chopped flat-leaf
  (Italian) parsley

1 To make the pasta, sift the flour and a pinch of salt into a bowl and make a well in the centre. Whisk the eggs, oil and 1 tablespoon water in a bowl, then add gradually to the flour and mix to a firm dough. Gather into a ball. Knead the dough on a lightly floured surface for 5 minutes, or until it is smooth and elastic. Transfer to a lightly oiled bowl, cover with plastic wrap and set aside for 30 minutes.

2 To make the filling, mix together the butter, garlic, parsley, scallop and prawn meat. Set aside.

3 Roll out a quarter of the pasta dough at a time until very thin (each portion of dough should be roughly 10 cm/4 inches wide when rolled). Place 1 teaspoonful of filling at 5 cm (2 inch) intervals down one side of the strip. Whisk the extra egg yolk with 60 ml (2 fl oz/¼ cup) water. Brush along one side of the dough and between the filling. Fold the dough over the filling to meet the other side. Press the edges of the dough together firmly to seal. Repeat with the remaining filling and dough.

4 Cut between the mounds with a knife or fluted pastry cutter. Cook, in batches, in a large saucepan of rapidly boiling salted water for 6 minutes each batch. Drain well and when they're all cooked, return them to the pan to keep warm.

5 To make the sauce, melt the butter in a saucepan, stir in the flour and cook over low heat for 2 minutes. Remove from the heat and gradually stir in the combined milk, cream and wine. Cook over low heat until the sauce begins to thicken, stirring constantly to prevent lumps forming. Bring to the boil and simmer gently for 5 minutes. Add the parmesan and parsley and stir until combined. Remove from the heat and spoon over the ravioli.

NOTE: The pasta dough is set aside for 30 minutes to let the gluten in the flour relax. If you don't do this, you run the risk of making tough pasta.

linguine with creamy lemon sauce

Preparation time: 10 minutes
Cooking time: 20 minutes
Serves 4

400 g (14 oz) fresh linguine or spaghetti
¼ teaspoon saffron threads or saffron
   powder (optional)
310 ml (10¾ fl oz/1¼ cups) pouring
   (whipping) cream
250 ml (9 fl oz/1 cup) chicken stock
1 tablespoon finely grated lemon zest, plus
   fine strips of lemon zest, extra, to garnish

1 Cook the linguine or spaghetti in a large saucepan of rapidly boiling salted water until it is *al dente*. Drain and cover to keep warm.

2 If using saffron threads, soak them in a little hot water for 5 minutes. While the pasta is cooking, combine the cream, stock and grated lemon zest in a large frying pan. Bring the mixture to the boil, stirring occasionally.

3 Reduce the heat and simmer for 10 minutes. Season with salt and pepper, to taste. Add the cooked pasta and cook for another 2–3 minutes.

4 Add the saffron threads and liquid, or powder, if using, and stir to combine. Serve garnished with strips of lemon zest.

NOTE: Saffron is available as threads or powder from delicatessens and speciality food stores. If it is unavailable, you could use ¼ teaspoon turmeric.

saffron

Saffron is the dried stamens of the saffron or autumn crocus. Available in threads or as a powdered form, it has a dark orange colour that carries into the food, and a sharp taste that mellows when cooked. Steep the threads in hot water to extract the flavour, or to intensify the flavour, toast until darkened, cool, then crumble to a coarse powder. Saffron is costly because of the labour required to pluck the stamens from each flower.

cheese

Pasta and parmesan are a famous combination, but the Italians produce many other cheeses, from soft creamy-white table cheeses to strong blue-veined varieties, of which they are rightfully proud.

mozzarella

A smooth, matured mild-flavoured cheese, originally made from buffalo's milk, but now sometimes made from cow's milk or a mixture of the two. Manufactured in large quantities around the world, it is available in a variety of shapes, from pear to block, and has a stringy texture when melted. It is famous for its use in pizzas but can be added to sauces or melted over veal steaks.

bocconcini and ovolini

Small mozzarella balls are called bocconcini, although they are sometimes referred to as baby mozzarella. They are fresh, unripened cheeses still made following the traditional method and, unlike matured mozzarella, are enjoyed as a table cheese. Smaller ones are called ovolini. Stored in the refrigerator fully covered in the whey in which they are sold, they will last for up to three weeks. If they show any signs of yellowing, they should be discarded. Serve drained and thinly sliced. Use in salads, as a topping for pizzas or bruschetta, or in baked pasta dishes.

ricotta

A fresh curd cheese made from whey — usually the whey drained off when making mozzarella. It can be made from sheep's (ricotta pecora) or cow's milk (ricotta vaccina) and is usually sold in the basket it is produced in. Ricotta has a short shelf life and should be bought as required. Avoid any that is discoloured or dry. Drain off the excess whey before using. Use in savoury and sweet dishes. Dried ricotta balls are suitable for grating.

gorgonzola

Originally produced in a small village in Milan, gorgonzola is now made throughout the world. It is prized for its rich creamy texture and soft blue flavour. It is less salty than most blue cheeses. Only buy what you need as, like most blues, it has a strong aroma that will permeate other foods. Gorgonzola is delicious as a cream sauce for pasta, in salads, or served with figs or pears. Bring to room temperature before serving.

provolone

Usually sold encased in wax and hanging by a striped red and white string, provolone is often lightly smoked and works well as part of a cheese platter. It is delicious grated in pasta sauces, in fondues or melted over meats. The younger the cheese, the milder the flavour. Refrigerate for up to two weeks.

pecorino

The name given to a range of hard, cooked sheep's-milk curd cheeses. These have a grainy texture, similar to parmesan, and are generally grated for cooking, in the same way as parmesan. Pecorino romano is aged for the longest time and is therefore harder and more suitable for grating. Pecorino pepato has had black peppercorns added to the curd that give it a subtle peppery flavour. Pecorino fresco is the name given to the young fresh cheese. Pecorino will keep in the refrigerator for months. Fully enclose it in plastic wrap as it has a strong aroma that can permeate other foods.

mascarpone

A fresh curd, triple-cream cheese that looks more like cream than cheese. It is very high in fat and has a mild, yet slightly acidic taste. It can be used in a four-cheese sauce or in a baked béchamel sauce topping. It is commonly served with fresh or poached fruit for dessert. Refrigerate for up to five days.

fontina

A sweet, nutty cheese with a soft velvety texture and a few tiny air holes, fontina is sold in wheels, with a golden-brown rind. It is a semi-hard cheese, prized for its melting quality and is the vital ingredient in the Italian-style fondue dish, fonduta. Italian law restricts the use of the name fontina to cheese produced in the Aosta Valley, near Mount Fontin. There are many copies in other regions of Italy and elsewhere. These are known as fontal and are generally softer than fontina. Fontina is delicious melted over polenta or gnocchi, as well as in sauces. It will keep in the refrigerator for up to one week.

parmigiano reggiano

Parmesan derives its name from the Parma region in northern Italy where it is made. It is a hard cheese with a crumbly texture. Parmesan is aged for two to three years in large wooden wheels and can only be stamped 'Parmigiano Reggiano' if it is produced within the provinces of Parma and Reggio, where it is still made using the original method. It is best to buy parmesan in a wedge and grate it yourself, as pre-grated cheese is often dry and lacking flavour. Select parmesan with the rind still attached, with no evidence of whitening at the rim. Parmesan can be served on its own or grated or shaved on top of pasta sauces, in salads or soups. Wrap it in greaseproof paper and foil and store on the bottom shelf of your refrigerator.

grana

Like parmesan, this is a hard grating cheese and, as the name implies, it has a grainy texture. It is easily identified by the imprint on the rind of the cheese that guarantees its authenticity. Grana can be served as a table cheese as it has a more delicate flavour than parmesan.

taleggio

This cheese takes its name from the town where it is produced and can be classified into two varieties. One is the cooked curd, with a thin greyish rind and straw-coloured interior with a mild flavour. The uncooked curd is a surface-ripened cheese with a thin, reddish moulded skin with a pale-yellow buttery interior. It has a delicate sweet flavour with a slightly acidic tang in towards the centre. Taleggio should be purchased only as required. Return to room temperature before serving as a table cheese. Taleggio is also known as stracchino.

asiago

This can either be a table cheese or a grating cheese, depending on how it has been aged and pressed. The younger cheese, asiago d'allevo, has a thin golden rind that darkens to a rusty brown colour as the cheese ripens. The interior is pale yellow with a slightly grainy texture that is scattered with small holes. The flavour sharpens with age. The aged and pressed cheese, asiago pressato has a deep-golden rind and a very pale, straw-coloured interior. It has a pleasant mild flavour and is often used as a dessert cheese.

goat's cheese

Goat's cheese has a distinctive, sharp taste. It varies in texture from a soft, crumbly cheese to a firm chalky cheese, depending on the age and method of production. When young and crumbly it can be spread on bread, served as a table cheese or crumbled over salad and pasta dishes. The firmer cheese can be cut into pieces and marinated in oil and herbs. The cheese should be a clean white with no evidence of drying around the edges. Purchase as required. It should keep for up to two weeks in the refrigerator. Depending on the variety, the rind may vary from black (ash-covered goat's cheese) to off-white. Ashed goat's cheese is made by rolling goat's cheese in fresh herbs that have been cooked in a pan until blackened.

pasta salads

Pasta salads have come about as part of the evolution of pasta. While they are not an authentic Italian creation, the combination of fresh vegetables, finest quality olive oil and cold *al dente* pasta certainly has a Mediterranean flavour. Few foods are so adaptable that they are delicious when served either hot or cold. Pasta is one exception and these salads are guaranteed to leave Italian cooks with just one thought: 'Why didn't we think of that?' Serve these salads as a starter or side dish, or on their own as a light meal.

oregano

Italian oregano (also known as wild marjoram) is closely related to rigani, which is used in Greek kitchens, and to sweet marjoram, common to French and northern Italian cooking. It is milder than rigani but more pungent than sweet marjoram. Oregano is very compatible with tomatoes, garlic and onion and is the herb most often found on pizzas. The plants are hardy and the leaves dry well, ensuring a constant supply.

farfalle salad with sun-dried tomatoes and spinach

☀

Preparation time: **20 minutes**
Cooking time: **15 minutes**
Serves **6**

500 g (1 lb 2 oz) farfalle or fusilli
  (spiral pasta)
3 spring onions (scallions)
50 g (1¾ oz) sun-dried tomatoes,
  cut into strips
1 kg (2 lb 4 oz) English spinach, stalks
  trimmed and leaves shredded
50 g (1¾ oz/⅓ cup) pine nuts, toasted

1 tablespoon chopped oregano
60 ml (2 fl oz/¼ cup) olive oil
1 teaspoon sliced red chilli
1 garlic clove, crushed

1 Cook the pasta in a large saucepan of rapidly boiling salted water until *al dente*. Drain, rinse under cold water and drain again. Allow to cool and then transfer to a large salad bowl.
2 Trim the spring onions and thinly slice on the diagonal. Add to the pasta with the tomato, spinach, pine nuts and oregano.
3 To make the dressing, place the oil, chilli, garlic and salt and freshly ground black pepper in a small screw-top jar and shake well. Pour the dressing over the salad and toss to combine.

spaghetti tomato salad

Preparation time: 25 minutes
Cooking time: 15 minutes
Serves 6

500 g (1 lb 2 oz) spaghetti or bucatini
50 g (1¾ oz/1 cup) basil leaves, shredded
250 g (9 oz) cherry tomatoes, halved
1 garlic clove, crushed
75 g (2¾ oz/½ cup) chopped pitted black
 olives
60 ml (2 fl oz/¼ cup) olive oil
1 tablespoon balsamic vinegar
50 g (1¾ oz/½ cup) freshly grated parmesan
 cheese

1 Cook the pasta in a large saucepan of rapidly boiling salted water until *al dente*. Drain, rinse under cold water and drain again. Set aside.
2 Combine the basil, tomato, garlic, olives, oil and vinegar in a salad bowl. Set aside for about 15 minutes. Mix in the drained pasta.
3 Add the parmesan and salt and pepper, to taste. Toss well and serve immediately.

pumpkin and sage scones

Sift 250 g (9 oz/2 cups) self-raising flour into a bowl with a pinch of salt. Add 250 g cooked and puréed pumpkin and 20 g (¾ oz) butter and rub them into the flour using your fingertips. Add 1 tablespoon chopped sage. Bring the mixture together with a little milk and turn it out onto a baking tray. Shape the mixture into a round and roll it out to about 3 cm (1¼ inches) thick. Lightly mark or cut the scone into segments and then bake in a 180°C (350°F/Gas 4) oven for 15–20 minutes, until lightly browned and cooked through.

tuna, green bean and onion salad

Preparation time: **20 minutes**
Cooking time: **15 minutes**
Serves **4**

200 g (7 oz) green beans, trimmed
   and cut into short lengths
300 g (10½ oz) penne rigate
125 ml (4 fl oz/½ cup) olive oil
250 g (9 oz) tuna steak
1 red onion, thinly sliced
1 tablespoon balsamic vinegar

1 Cook the beans in a large saucepan of boiling water for 1–2 minutes, until tender but still crisp. Remove using a slotted spoon and rinse under cold water. Drain and transfer to a serving bowl.
2 Cook the penne rigate in a large saucepan of rapidly boiling salted water until *al dente*. Drain, rinse under cold water and drain again before adding to the beans.
3 Heat half the oil in a frying pan over high heat. Add the tuna and sear on both sides for 2 minutes. Remove from pan. Reduce heat to medium, add the onion and cook for 3 minutes. Add the vinegar and cook until it has reduced. Cut the tuna into slices, return to the pan and gently stir to coat in the sauce. Transfer the tuna and onion to the serving bowl.
4 Toss the beans, pasta, tuna and onion together gently with the remaining oil and salt and pepper, to taste. Cool to room temperature before serving.

red onions

Red onions are less strongly flavoured than white or brown, which makes them ideal to use raw in salads. Cooking, unfortunately, robs them of their vibrant colour. Cut or chopped onion of any variety soon takes on an unpleasant smell – if you need to chop onion ahead of time, fry it in a little butter or oil and then store it covered in the refrigerator.

pastrami, mushroom and cucumber salad

✳

Preparation time: 20 minutes
  + 7 hours chilling time
Cooking time: 10 minutes
Serves 4

200 g (7 oz) lasagnette, broken into
  quarters
250 g (9 oz) sliced pastrami, cut into strips
1 celery stalk, sliced
2 small tomatoes, cut into wedges
1 Lebanese (short) cucumber, thinly sliced
80 g (2¾ oz) button mushrooms, sliced
1 tablespoon chopped coriander (cilantro)
  leaves

DRESSING
60 ml (2 fl oz/¼ cup) olive oil
2 tablespoons red wine vinegar
½ teaspoon dijon mustard
1 garlic clove, crushed
¼ teaspoon hot chilli oil

1   Cook the lasagnette in a large saucepan
of rapidly boiling salted water until
al dente. Drain, rinse under cold water
and drain again. Allow to cool and
transfer to a large salad bowl.
2   Add the pastrami, celery, tomato,
cucumber and mushroom to the pasta.
3   To prepare the dressing, combine all
the ingredients in a screw-top jar and
shake until well blended.
4   Toss the dressing through the salad and
refrigerate, covered, for several hours.
Adjust the seasoning and sprinkle with
the coriander just before serving.

pastrami

Pastrami is a cured, highly seasoned cut of lean beef made popular in the United States. It is believed to have originated in the Balkans and is closely related to the pastirma of Turkey. Spiced with paprika, pepper, cumin and garlic, and sometimes smoked, it is delicious sliced and eaten cold.

polenta bread

Preheat the oven to 200°C (400°F/Gas 6). Add some freshly grated parmesan cheese, chopped herbs (basil, parsley, oregano and/or sage), a crushed garlic clove and a little pouring (whipping) cream to soft cooked polenta. Mix well and season, to taste. Pour into a greased and lined baking dish and bake in the oven until the crust is golden and the polenta is set. Cut into slices and serve warm.

artichokes

Artichokes are a thistle and the edible part of a globe artichoke is the flower head. In the centre of this is the choke, a mass of hairs which is, in fact, the flower, and this sits on a tender cup-like base. It is surrounded by fleshy leaves, of which the tough, outer ones are discarded to reveal the heart, the lower section of delicate inner leaves surrounding the choke and bottom cup. Tinned or bottled artichoke hearts retain a good flavour and are a time-saving substitute for fresh ones.

italian-style chicken and pasta salad

Preparation time: 30 minutes
  + 3 hours marinating time
Cooking time: 10 minutes
Serves 8

3 boneless, skinless chicken breasts
60 ml (2 fl oz/¼ cup) lemon juice
1 garlic clove, crushed
2 tablespoons seasoned lemon pepper
2 tablespoons olive oil
135 g (4¾ oz/1½ cups) penne, cooked
1 Lebanese (short) cucumber, halved lengthways and thinly sliced
100 g (3½ oz) prosciutto, cut into thin strips
80 g (2¾ oz/½ cup) thinly sliced sun-dried tomatoes
70 g (2½ oz/½ cup) pitted black olives, halved
110 g (3¾ oz/½ cup) halved bottled artichoke hearts
50 g (1¾ oz/½ cup) parmesan cheese shavings (optional)

CREAMY BASIL DRESSING
80 ml (2½ fl oz/⅓ cup) olive oil
1 tablespoon white wine vinegar
¼ teaspoon seasoned pepper
1 teaspoon dijon mustard
3 teaspoons cornflour (cornstarch)
170 ml (5½ fl oz/⅔ cup) pouring (whipping) cream
20 g (¾ oz/⅓ cup) shredded basil

1 Remove the excess fat and sinew from the chicken. Flatten the chicken slightly with a mallet or rolling pin.
2 Combine the lemon juice and garlic in a bowl. Add the chicken and stir until coated. Cover and refrigerate for at least 3 hours or overnight, turning occasionally.
3 Drain the chicken and coat in the seasoned pepper. Heat the oil in a large heavy-based frying pan. Cook the chicken for 4 minutes each side, or until lightly browned and cooked through. Remove from the heat, allow to cool and then cut into small pieces.

4 To make the creamy basil dressing, combine the oil, vinegar, pepper and mustard in a medium saucepan. Blend the cornflour with 80 ml (2½ fl oz/⅓ cup) water in a small bowl or jug until smooth. Add to the pan. Whisk over medium heat for 2 minutes, or until the sauce boils and thickens. Add the cream, basil and salt, to taste. Stir until heated through.

5 Combine the pasta, chicken, cucumber, prosciutto, tomato, olives and artichoke hearts. Pour over the warm creamy basil dressing and toss gently to combine. Serve warm or cold, scattered with parmesan shavings, if desired.

creamy seafood salad

Preparation time: 30 minutes
Cooking time: 15 minutes
Serves 8 as an entrée, 4 as a main meal

400 g (14 oz) medium-sized conchiglie (shell pasta)
250 g (9 oz/1 cup) whole-egg mayonnaise (see Note)
3 tablespoons fresh or 2 tablespoons dried tarragon
1 tablespoon finely chopped flat-leaf (Italian) parsley
cayenne pepper, to taste
1 teaspoon lemon juice, or to taste
1 kg (2 lb 4 oz) cooked shellfish meat (such as prawns/shrimp, lobster, crab — any one of these or a combination, cut into bite-sized pieces)
2 mild red radishes, thinly sliced
1 small green capsicum (pepper), julienned

1 Cook the conchiglie in a large saucepan of rapidly boiling salted water until it is al dente. Drain, then rinse under cold water and drain again. Place in a large bowl and stir through 1–2 tablespoons of the mayonnaise. Cool to room temperature, stirring occasionally to prevent it from sticking.

2 If using dried tarragon, simmer it in 60 ml (2 fl oz/¼ cup) milk for 3–4 minutes and then drain. Combine the tarragon, parsley, cayenne and lemon juice with the remaining mayonnaise.

3 Add the shellfish meat, radishes and capsicum to the pasta and season with salt and pepper, to taste. Mix in the tarragon mayonnaise, tossing gently to coat. Cover and chill before serving, adding more mayonnaise or extra lemon juice if the mixture is a little dry.

NOTE: If you prefer, you can make your own mayonnaise. Whisk together 2 egg yolks, 1 teaspoon dijon mustard and 2 teaspoons lemon juice for 30 seconds, until light and creamy. Add 250 ml (9 fl oz/1 cup) light olive oil, about a teaspoon at a time, whisking continuously. Increase the amount of oil as the mayonnaise thickens. When all the oil has been added, stir in an extra 2 teaspoons lemon juice and season with salt and ground white pepper, to taste. Alternatively, you can use a food processor. Use the same ingredients, but process the yolks, mustard and juice for 10 seconds. With the motor running, slowly add the oil until combined.

rocket, cherry tomato and
spicy salami pasta salad

rocket, cherry tomato and spicy salami pasta salad

✹

Preparation time: 15 minutes
Cooking time: 20 minutes
Serves 6

350 g (12 oz) short pasta of your choice
50 g (1¾ oz) spicy Italian salami slices, cut
    into thin strips
150 g (5½ oz) rocket (arugula)
200 g (7 oz) cherry tomatoes, halved
80 ml (2½ fl oz/⅓ cup) olive oil
60 ml (2 fl oz/¼ cup) white wine vinegar
1 teaspoon sugar

1 Cook the pasta in a large saucepan of
rapidly boiling salted water until *al dente*.
Drain, rinse under cold water and drain
again. Allow to cool.
2 Heat a frying pan over medium heat,
add the salami and cook until crisp. Drain
well on paper towels.
3 Combine the salami, pasta, rocket and
tomato in a large bowl.
4 In a small food processor, blend the oil,
vinegar, sugar and ¼ teaspoon each of
salt and pepper, for 1 minute. Drizzle over
the salad just before serving.

chicken, pear and pasta salad

✹

Preparation time: 35 minutes
Cooking time: 15 minutes
Serves 6

350 g (12 oz) gemelli or fusilli (spiral pasta)
200 g (7 oz) boneless, skinless chicken
    breasts
2 ripe pears
3 spring onions (scallions), thinly sliced,
    plus extra, for garnish (optional)
2 tablespoons toasted slivered almonds
100 g (3½ oz) creamy blue-vein cheese
3 tablespoons sour cream

damper

Sift 500 g (1 lb 2 oz/4 cups) self-raising flour with 1 teaspoon salt and 1 teaspoon
caster (superfine) sugar into a large bowl. Use a knife to mix in enough milk,
about 375 ml (13 fl oz/1½ cups), to make a fairly stiff dough that leaves the side
of the bowl. Knead the dough for about 1 minute on a floured surface, and shape
into a ball. Place on a greased baking tray, flatten slightly, cut 2 slits across the top
and brush with milk. Bake at 210°C (415°F/Gas 6–7) for 15 minutes, then reduce
the temperature to 180°C (350°F/Gas 4) and bake for a further 20 minutes, or
until the damper is golden and the base sounds hollow when tapped.

1 Cook the pasta in a large saucepan of rapidly boiling salted water until *al dente*. Drain, rinse under cold water and drain again. Allow to cool.

2 Meanwhile, place the chicken in a frying pan, cover with cold water and simmer gently for 8 minutes, or until tender, turning it occasionally. Remove the chicken from the pan and set aside to cool. Thinly slice the chicken and place in a bowl with the cooled pasta.

3 Halve the pears, remove the cores and thinly slice. Add to the chicken with the spring onion and almonds.

4 Mix the cheese and the sour cream with 60 ml (2 fl oz/¼ cup) ice-cold water and ¼ teaspoon each of salt and pepper, in a food processor until smooth. Pour the mixture over the salad and stir to combine. Transfer the salad to a serving dish and garnish with the extra spring onion, if desired.

pears

The pear is a very versatile fruit. It can be eaten fresh, used in desserts and sweets, or cooked in savoury dishes. The crisp, firm texture reacts well to heat and the flavour is compatible with many other foods. Poultry, cheeses, salad greens and strangely enough, olive oil, make particularly good companions. There is a huge selection of local varieties grown. They can be categorised into dessert pears, those with a clear, crisp sweet flesh intended for eating fresh, and cooking pears, which have a firm, often granular flesh and a more tart taste.

barbecued chicken and pasta salad

Preparation time: **15 minutes**
Cooking time: **15 minutes**
Serves **6**

1 barbecued chicken
500 g (1 lb 2 oz) penne
60 ml (2 fl oz/¼ cup) olive oil
2 tablespoons white wine vinegar
200 g (7 oz) cherry tomatoes, halved
20 g (¾ oz/⅓ cup) chopped basil
75 g (2¾ oz/1½ cup) sliced pitted
    black olives

1 Pull the meat from the barbecued chicken. Discard the skin and finely shred the meat using your fingers.
2 Cook the penne in a large saucepan of rapidly boiling salted water until it is *al dente*. Drain thoroughly and transfer to a serving bowl. Combine the oil and vinegar and toss through the pasta while it is still warm.
3 Add the chicken, tomato, basil and olives to the pasta, and toss thoroughly to combine. Season with freshly ground black pepper. Serve warm, as a main meal, or at room temperature as part of a selection of salads.

NOTE: The salad can be prepared up to 2 hours in advance. Refrigerate the chicken until close to serving time and add it to the salad at the last minute. Chop and add the basil close to serving time as well, as it discolours when cut.

lemon and vegetable pasta salad

Preparation time: **20 minutes**
Cooking time: **15 minutes**
Serves **4**

250 g (9 oz) farfalle
80 ml (2½ fl oz/⅓ cup) olive oil
250 g (9 oz) broccoli, cut into
    small florets
125 g (4½ oz) snow peas (mangetout),
    topped and tailed
150 g (5½ oz) baby (pattypan) squash,
    cut into quarters
2 tablespoons sour cream
1 tablespoon lemon juice
2 teaspoons finely grated lemon zest
1 celery stalk, thinly sliced
1 tablespoon chopped chervil, plus chervil
    sprigs, to garnish

1 Cook the farfalle in a large saucepan of rapidly boiling salted water until *al dente*. Drain well, toss with 1 tablespoon of the olive oil and set aside to cool.

barbecued chicken and pasta salad

chervil

An umbelliferous plant cultivated as a pot-herb, chervil has a delicate, slightly aniseed flavour. It has stiff stems and dainty, curly leaves, which can be chopped for use but are often left whole, like little petals. Its aroma evaporates quickly, so the leaves are best used fresh or added to hot dishes at the last minute. Chervil is folded through omelettes, sprinkled over soup and used as a garnish.

2 Combine the broccoli, snow peas and squash in a large bowl, cover with boiling water and leave for 2 minutes. Drain, plunge into iced water, drain again and pat dry with paper towels.

3 Put the sour cream, lemon juice and zest and the remaining oil in a screw-top jar and shake for 30 seconds, or until combined. Season with salt and pepper.

4 Combine the cooled pasta, celery and drained vegetables in a large bowl and sprinkle with chopped chervil. Pour over the dressing and toss to combine. Garnish with chervil sprigs, if desired, and serve at room temperature.

bread

Crusty and fresh, in all its delightful varieties, bread is the perfect accompaniment to most meals. Serve it plain, or dress it up with garlic, cheese, basil, parsley and other fresh herbs.

garlic grissini sticks

Preheat the oven to 200°C (400°F/Gas 6). Combine 2 crushed garlic cloves with 1 tablespoon olive oil. Brush over 1 packet of grissini sticks and wrap each in paper-thin strips of prosciutto. Bake for 5 minutes, until the ends crisp. Cool on trays before serving. Makes about 25.

cheesy herb rolls

Preheat the oven to 220°C (425°F/Gas 7). Combine 125 g (4½ oz) softened butter with 1 tablespoon each of chopped basil, parsley and chives and 30 g (1 oz/¼ cup) grated cheddar cheese. Season with salt and pepper. Cut 4 crusty rosetta rolls into thin slices, but don't cut all the way through. Spread each side of each slice with the flavoured butter. Bake for 15 minutes, or until the rolls are crisp and golden. Serves 4.

crisp focaccia toasts with pesto

Cut a square of focaccia, about 20 cm (8 inches) in half horizontally. Combine 50 g (1¾ oz/1 cup) basil leaves, 2 garlic cloves, 3 tablespoons toasted pine nuts and 4 tablespoons freshly grated parmesan cheese in a food processor until roughly chopped. With the motor running, gradually add 60 ml (2 fl oz/¼ cup) olive oil and process until the mixture forms a smooth paste. Brush the focaccia squares with olive oil and toast both sides until golden brown. Spread the pesto over the focaccia and cut into small rectangles. Makes 16–20.

roasted capsicum bruschetta

Cut 1 red and 1 yellow capsicum (pepper) in half, removing the seeds and membrane. Place, skin side up, under a hot grill (broiler) until the skin is black and blistered. Transfer to a plastic bag to cool. Peel away the skin and cut the flesh into thin strips. Cut 1 loaf of woodfired Italian bread into thin slices and toast lightly until golden. Rub each side of the bread slices with halved garlic cloves and brush lightly with extra virgin olive oil. Top with a little of the capsicum and sprinkle with fresh lemon thyme. Makes about 30 slices.

anchovy and tomato crostini

Cut a baguette into thick slices. Brush lightly with olive oil and toast until golden. Spread with 250 g (9 oz/1 cup) sun-dried tomato pesto and top with 50 g (1¾ oz) chopped black olives, 50 g (1¾ oz) drained, thinly sliced anchovy fillets and some shredded basil. Makes about 15 pieces.

pasta with mediterranean-style vegetables

Preparation time: 30 minutes
Cooking time: 15 minutes
Serves 6

350 g (12 oz) macaroni
200 g (7 oz) fried and marinated
  eggplant (aubergine) slices (see Note)
100 g (3½ oz) sun-dried or semi-dried
  (sun-blushed) tomatoes

60 g (2¼ oz) kalamata olives, pitted
200 g (7 oz) sliced or shaved double-
  smoked ham
2 tablespoons sweet chilli sauce
1 tablespoon white wine vinegar
1 tablespoon olive oil
2 tablespoons chopped flat-leaf (Italian)
  parsley

1 Cook the macaroni in a large saucepan of rapidly boiling salted water until it is *al dente*. Drain, rinse under cold water and drain again. Cool, then place in a bowl.
2 Slice the eggplant, tomatoes, olives and ham and add to the pasta. (If using

shaved ham

Ham that is very finely sliced is known as shaved ham. It should be wafer-thin, but still in discernible pieces that fall into a loosely bulky heap. This method of preparation gives the ham a delicate texture. Shaved ham is widely available and should be eaten as soon as possible, as it spoils more quickly than unshaved.

shaved ham, simply separate it into smallish pieces.)

3 Whisk together the sweet chilli sauce, vinegar, oil and salt and pepper, to taste, until well combined. Drizzle the dressing over the pasta and vegetables and toss well. Serve scattered with the parsley.

NOTE: Marinated vegetables are available from delicatessens. If preferred, red or green capsicums (peppers) or zucchini (courgettes) can be used.

smoked salmon, dill and egg pasta salad

Preparation time: **20 minutes**
Cooking time: **15 minutes**
Serves **4–6**

350 g (12 oz) farfalle or fusilli (spiral pasta)
2 eggs
200 g (7 oz) smoked salmon, cut into
    thin strips
1 tablespoon finely chopped dill
3 tablespoons sour cream
2 tablespoons lemon juice
1 tablespoon chopped flat-leaf (Italian)
    parsley, to garnish

1 Cook the pasta in a large saucepan of rapidly boiling salted water until *al dente*. Drain, rinse under cold water and drain again. Allow to cool.

2 While the pasta is cooking, cook the eggs for 12 minutes, or until hard-boiled. Allow to cool and then peel, finely grate or chop, and set aside.

3 Divide the pasta among serving bowls and scatter the smoked salmon and dill over the top.

4 In a small bowl, whisk together the sour cream, lemon juice, salt and pepper. Drizzle the dressing over the pasta. Sprinkle the egg and parsley over the top and serve immediately.

dill

Dill is a native of the Mediterranean and has been used since ancient times for its medicinal properties and culinary flavours. All of the upper plant is aromatic, but the delicate leaves have the most subtle taste and aroma. Their bittersweet flavour complements dairy produce and enhances fish and seafood particularly well. Because its essential oil is extremely volatile, it quickly evaporates in temperatures above 30°C (86°F), and for this reason dill should be added to a cooked dish just before serving.

conchiglie salad with bocconcini, asparagus and oregano

Preparation time: 25 minutes
Cooking time: 15 minutes
Serves 4–6

350 g (12 oz) conchiglie (shell pasta)
155 g (5½ oz) asparagus spears
200 g (7 oz) bocconcini cheese, thinly sliced
100 g (3½ oz) cherry tomatoes, quartered
2 tablespoons oregano leaves
80 ml (2½ fl oz/⅓ cup) walnut oil
1 tablespoon white wine vinegar
1 tablespoon balsamic vinegar

1 Cook the conchiglie in a large saucepan of rapidly boiling salted water until *al dente*. Drain, rinse under cold water and drain again. Allow to cool.
2 Cut the asparagus into short lengths. Bring a small saucepan of water to the boil, add the asparagus and blanch for 1 minute. Drain, transfer to a bowl of iced water to cool and then drain again.
3 In a large bowl, combine the conchiglie, asparagus, bocconcini, tomato and oregano. In a small bowl, whisk together the walnut oil, vinegars and salt and pepper until well combined.
4 Drizzle the dressing over the salad and toss thoroughly before serving.

balsamic vinegar

Balsamic vinegar, aceto balsamico, is a speciality of the area around Modena in central northern Italy. It is made from the newly pressed juice of selected white grapes, which is slowly boiled down to one-third of its volume. The resulting syrup is aged over a number of years, in a series of wooden casks, until it becomes concentrated, mellow and highly aromatic. It is a dense, almost black sauce which is used sparingly not as a regular vinegar, but as a condiment. A good balsamic vinegar should be sweet and syrupy but not cloying, with an intense aroma and flavour. There are many imitations being manufactured and a cheap copy bears little resemblance to the real thing. This is an instance where it is truly worth spending extra for the genuine article.

warm garlic prawn and fettuccine salad

✳ ✳

Preparation time: 30 minutes
Cooking time: 25 minutes
Serves 4–6

300 g (10½ oz) fettuccine
2 tablespoons olive oil
4 garlic cloves, crushed
300 g (10½ oz) raw prawns (shrimp), peeled
    and deveined, tails intact
2 tablespoons whisky
125 ml (4 fl oz/½ cup) pouring (whipping)
    cream
3 spring onions (scallions), thinly sliced

1 Cook the pasta in a large saucepan of rapidly boiling salted water until *al dente*. Drain, rinse under cold water and drain again. Allow to cool and set aside.
2 Heat the oil in a heavy-based frying pan. Add the garlic and cook, stirring, for 30 seconds. Add the prawns and stir-fry over high heat until they change colour. Add the whisky and cook until it evaporates. Add the cream and spring onion and simmer for 2 minutes.
3 Drizzle the sauce over the pasta. Season with plenty of salt and pepper.

parmesan biscuits

Sift 250 g (9 oz/2 cups) plain (all-purpose) flour with 1 teaspoon baking powder, ¼ teaspoon paprika and ½ teaspoon salt into a bowl. Rub in 60 g (2¼ oz) butter. Add 25 g (¾ oz/¼ cup) finely grated parmesan cheese and 185 ml (6 fl oz/¾ cup) milk and bring the mixture together. Roll out the mixture to about 2 cm (¾ inch) thick and cut out the biscuits. Sprinkle with some more parmesan and bake in a 220°C (425°F/Gas 7) oven for 15 minutes.

rigatoni with tomato, haloumi and spinach

Preparation time: 30 minutes
Cooking time: 1 hour
Serves 6

6 roma (plum) tomatoes
sugar, to sprinkle
4 garlic cloves, chopped
400 g (14 oz) rigatoni
60 ml (2 fl oz/¼ cup) lemon juice
60 ml (2 fl oz/¼ cup) olive oil
200 g (7 oz) haloumi cheese,
    very thinly sliced
100 g (3½ oz/2 cups) baby spinach

1 Preheat the oven to 180°C (350°F/ Gas 4). Cut the tomatoes in half and put on a non-stick baking tray, lined with foil if you like, and sprinkle generously with sugar, salt, pepper and the garlic. Bake for 1 hour, or until quite dehydrated and shrunken. Leave to cool and then cut in half again.

2 While the tomatoes are cooking, cook the rigatoni in a large saucepan of rapidly boiling salted water until *al dente*. Drain, rinse under cold water and drain again. Allow to cool.

3 Combine the lemon juice and oil and season, to taste. Toss the lemon dressing through the pasta and then toss through the tomato, haloumi and spinach. Serve sprinkled with freshly ground pepper.

haloumi

Originating in Cyprus, this salty, semi-hard sheep's milk cheese is a popular table cheese. It is often served sprinkled with mint or thickly sliced and grilled or fried, then served with a squeeze of lemon juice.

lemon and date ziti

Preparation time: 20 minutes
Cooking time: 25 minutes
Serves 4–6

360 g (12¾ oz/2 cups) dried pitted
    dates, halved
375 ml (13 fl oz/1½ cups) port
375 g (13 oz) ziti
60 ml (2 fl oz/¼ cup) balsamic vinegar
125 ml (4 fl oz/½ cup) olive oil
150 g (5½ oz) rocket (arugula), trimmed
rind from 3 preserved lemons (see Note),
    finely chopped

1   Place the dates and port in a small
saucepan. Bring to the boil, then reduce
the heat and simmer for 10 minutes.
Strain the dates, reserving the port.
Set aside to cool.
2   Cook the ziti in a large saucepan of
rapidly boiling salted water until *al dente*.
Drain, rinse in cold water and drain again.
Allow to cool.
3   Combine the vinegar, reserved port
and oil in a bowl. Taste and season with a
little sugar, if necessary.
4   Toss the dressing through the pasta
with the dates, rocket and lemon zest.

NOTE: Preserved lemons can be
purchased at any good delicatessen or
speciality food store. They are available
either per lemon or bottled.

dates

Date palms grow in desert
regions and have been
cultivated for thousands of
years. Fresh dates have a fruity,
moist pulp and are an excellent
source of iron, folic acid and
vitamin B6, as well as having
a high fibre content. There are
hard and soft dates, the latter
being preferred for table use.
Both dry well, with soft dates
maintaining succulent, soft
flesh. Fresh and soft dried
dates are interchangeable in
recipes, however dried are
sweeter and have a slightly
more concentrated flavour.

grilled capsicum and anchovy salad

✺

Preparation time: **15 minutes**
Cooking time: **25 minutes**
Serves **6**

500 g (1 lb 2 oz) spaghetti
2 large red capsicums (peppers)
1 small red onion, finely chopped
1 large handful flat-leaf (Italian) parsley
2–3 anchovy fillets, chopped
60 ml (2 fl oz/¼ cup) olive oil
2 tablespoons lemon juice

1 Cook the pasta in a large saucepan of rapidly boiling salted water until *al dente*. Drain, rinse under cold water, drain again.
2 Cut the capsicums in half and remove the seeds and membrane. Place, skin side up, under a hot grill (broiler) and cook for 8 minutes, or until the skin is black and

salt

There are two sources of salt, or sodium chloride: rock salt, found in crystalline form in the ground, and sea salt, extracted from sea water. Refined sea salt is available in pure crystal form, which must be ground, in thin flakes ready to use, or already ground. This free-running table salt has had products such as phosphate of lime added to prevent the pure salt reverting to crystal form when in humidity. Pure salt provides the best flavour.

warm pasta and crab salad

blistered. Transfer to a plastic bag to cool, then peel away the skin and cut the flesh into long, thin strips.

3 In a large salad bowl, combine the pasta, capsicum, onion, parsley, anchovies, oil and lemon juice, and season to taste. Toss until well combined and serve immediately.

warm pasta and crab salad

Preparation time: **20 minutes**
Cooking time: **10 minutes**
Serves **6**

200 g (7 oz) spaghetti
2 tablespoons olive oil
30 g (1 oz) butter, melted
3 x 200 g (7 oz) tins crabmeat, drained
1 large red capsicum (pepper), cut into
  thin strips
2 teaspoons finely grated lemon zest
3 tablespoons freshly grated parmesan cheese
2 tablespoons snipped chives
3 tablespoons chopped flat-leaf (Italian)
  parsley

1 Break the spaghetti in half and cook in a large saucepan of rapidly boiling salted water until *al dente*. Drain.

2 Place the spaghetti in a large serving bowl and toss with the combined oil and butter. Add all the remaining ingredients and toss to combine. Sprinkle with cracked black pepper and serve warm.

NOTE: Substitute 500 g (1 lb 2 oz) fresh crab meat for the tinned, if you prefer.

tuscan warm pasta salad

Preparation time: **15 minutes**
Cooking time: **15 minutes**
Serves **6**

tuscan warm pasta salad

500 g (1 lb 2 oz) rigatoni
80 ml (2½ fl oz/⅓ cup) olive oil
1 garlic clove, crushed
1 tablespoon balsamic vinegar
400 g (14 oz) tin artichoke hearts, drained
  and quartered
8 thin prosciutto slices, chopped
80 g (2¾ oz/½ cup) sun-dried tomatoes
  in oil, drained and thinly sliced
15 g (½ oz/¼ cup) basil, shredded
70 g (2½ oz) rocket (arugula) leaves,
  washed and drained well
40 g (1½ oz/¼ cup) pine nuts, toasted
  (see Note)
45 g (1½ oz/¼ cup) small black olives

1 Add the rigatoni to a large saucepan of rapidly boiling water and cook until *al dente*. Drain and transfer to a bowl.

2 Meanwhile, whisk together the oil, garlic and balsamic vinegar. Toss the dressing through the hot pasta. Allow the pasta to cool slightly. Add the artichoke, prosciutto, sun-dried tomato, basil, rocket, pine nuts and olives.

3 Toss all the ingredients together until well combined. Season to taste.

NOTE: To toast the pine nuts, cook in a dry frying pan over medium heat for 1–2 minutes, until lightly golden.

gnocchi

Simplicity and adaptability are the two characteristics to which gnocchi owes its popularity. While making your own spaghetti may be a daunting task, making gnocchi is a skill anyone can master. Once you've perfected the basic potato recipe, you can experiment with other vegetables, such as pumpkin, carrot, spinach or parsnip. Gnocchi also lends itself to buttery, creamy or tomato sauces. Whatever the combination, these little dumplings are simply divine.

gnocchi romana

Preparation time: 20 minutes
 + 1 hour chilling time
Cooking time: 40 minutes
Serves 4

750 ml (26 fl oz/3 cups) milk
½ teaspoon freshly grated nutmeg
85 g (3 oz/⅔ cup) semolina
1 egg, beaten
150 g (5½ oz/1½ cups) freshly grated
  parmesan cheese
60 g (2¼ oz) butter, melted
125 ml (4 fl oz/½ cup) pouring
  (whipping) cream
75 g (2¾ oz/½ cup) freshly grated
  mozzarella cheese

1 Line a deep Swiss roll (jelly roll) tin
with baking paper. Combine the milk and
half the nutmeg in a saucepan and season.
Bring to the boil, reduce the heat and
slowly stir in the semolina. Cook, stirring
often, for 5–10 minutes, or until very stiff.
2 Remove the pan from the heat, add
the egg and 100 g (3½ oz/1 cup) of the
parmesan. Stir to combine, then spread
the mixture in the tin. Refrigerate for
1 hour, or until the mixture is firm.
3 Preheat the oven to 180°C (350°F/
Gas 4). Lightly grease a shallow casserole
dish. Cut the semolina into rounds using a
floured 4 cm (1½ inch) pastry cutter and
arrange in the dish.
4 Pour the melted butter over the top,
followed by the cream. Combine the
remaining parmesan with the mozzarella

semolina

Semolina is a term that
describes a particular meal
milled from grain. Usually
applied to wheat, it has a
coarse, discernible bead,
unlike flour which is fine and
powdery. It is higher in protein
than flour and has a firmer
texture that gives 'bite' to the
pasta or dough it goes into.
Different grades are milled,
with fine semolina preferred
for the making of gnocchi
and a medium grain for baked
desserts and puddings.

and sprinkle over the rounds. Sprinkle with the remaining nutmeg. Bake for 20–25 minutes, or until golden.

potato gnocchi with tomato and basil sauce

✳ ✳

Preparation time: **1 hour**
Cooking time: **50 minutes**
Serves **4–6**

TOMATO SAUCE
1 tablespoon olive oil
1 onion, chopped
1 celery stalk, chopped
2 carrots, chopped
800 g (1 lb 12 oz) tin chopped tomatoes
1 teaspoon sugar
30 g (1 oz/½ cup) chopped basil
freshly grated parmesan cheese,
    to serve

POTATO GNOCCHI
1 kg (2 lb 4 oz) all-purpose
    potatoes
30 g (1 oz) butter
250 g (9 oz/2 cups) plain (all-purpose)
    flour
2 eggs, beaten

1 To make the tomato sauce, heat the oil in a large frying pan, add the onion, celery and carrot and cook for 5 minutes, stirring regularly. Add the tomatoes and sugar and season with salt and pepper, to taste. Bring to the boil, reduce the heat to very low and simmer for 20 minutes. Cool slightly and process, in batches, in a food processor until smooth. Add the basil and set aside.
2 To make the potato gnocchi, peel the potatoes, chop roughly and steam or boil until very tender. Drain thoroughly and mash until smooth. Using a wooden spoon, stir in the butter and flour, then beat in the egg. Cool.
3 Turn the gnocchi mixture onto a floured surface and divide into two

potatoes for gnocchi

The best potatoes for gnocchi are old, starchy ones with a low water content. Their mealy flesh results in tender and light gnocchi. If the potatoes hold a lot of moisture, more flour will be required for the dough, which in turn will cause the gnocchi to be rubbery. The potatoes are best baked, steamed or boiled, and they should not be puréed in a processor as this results in a gluey texture.

portions. Roll each into a long sausage shape. Cut into short pieces and press each piece with the back of a fork.
4 Cook the gnocchi, in batches, in a large saucepan of boiling salted water for about 2 minutes, or until they rise to the surface. Using a slotted spoon, drain the gnocchi and transfer to serving bowls. Serve with the tomato sauce spooned over and sprinkled with the parmesan.

gnocchi

Gnocchi are little dumplings, sometimes as tiny as peas, but never bigger than a mouthful. Traditionally based on semolina flour, ricotta cheese or potato, they are now made with different grains such as buckwheat, and vegetables including pumpkin (winter squash) and artichokes. Although nearly always served with a sauce as an entrée, they also make a good accompaniment. Once made, they should be cooked and eaten as quickly as possible.

gnocchi
cheese bake

gnocchi cheese bake

Preparation time: 10 minutes
Cooking time: 15 minutes
Serves 4

500 g (1 lb 2 oz) fresh potato gnocchi
30 g (1 oz) butter, chopped
1 tablespoon chopped Italian (flat-leaf)
    parsley
100 g (3½ oz) fontina cheese, sliced
100 g (3½ oz) provolone cheese, sliced

1   Preheat the oven to 200°C (400°F/ Gas 6). Cook the gnocchi, in batches, in a large saucepan of boiling salted water for about 2 minutes, or until they rise to the surface. Carefully remove from the pan using a slotted spoon and drain well.
2   Put the gnocchi in a lightly greased ovenproof dish. Scatter with the butter and parsley. Lay the fontina and provolone cheeses over the top of the gnocchi. Season with sea salt and cracked black pepper. Bake for 10 minutes, or until the cheese has melted and is golden. Serve immediately.

gnocchi with tomato and fresh basil

Preparation time: 10 minutes
Cooking time: 20 minutes
Serves 4

1 tablespoon olive oil
1 onion, finely chopped
2 garlic cloves, crushed
400 g (14 oz) tin chopped tomatoes
2 tablespoons tomato paste
    (concentrated purée)
250 ml (9 fl oz/1 cup) pouring (whipping)
    cream
40 g (1½ oz/¼ cup) chopped sun-dried
    tomatoes
375 g (13 oz) fresh potato gnocchi
1 tablespoon finely chopped basil
60 g (2¼ oz) pepato cheese, grated

1   Heat the oil in a saucepan and cook the onion for 2 minutes, or until softened. Add the garlic and cook for another minute. Stir in the tomatoes and tomato paste and cook for about 5 minutes.

2 Reduce the heat, add the cream and sun-dried tomatoes and stir through. Simmer gently for another 3 minutes.
3 Meanwhile, cook the gnocchi in batches in a large saucepan of boiling salted water. Cook for about 2 minutes, or until they rise to the surface. Drain using a slotted spoon and add to the sauce with the basil. Season with salt and freshly ground black pepper. Transfer to an ovenproof dish and sprinkle with the pepato cheese. Cook under a hot grill (broiler) for 5 minutes, until bubbling. Garnish with herbs, if you like.

NOTE: Pepato cheese is quite a pungent pepper cheese. You can use a milder cheese, if you prefer.

pumpkin gnocchi with sage butter

✹

Preparation time: **45 minutes**
Cooking time: **1 hour 30 minutes**
Serves **4**

500 g (1 lb 2 oz) pumpkin (winter squash), unpeeled
185 g (6½ oz/1½ cups) plain (all-purpose) flour
50 g (1¾ oz/½ cup) freshly grated parmesan cheese
1 egg, beaten
100 g (3½ oz) butter
2 tablespoons chopped sage, plus sage leaves, to garnish

1 Preheat the oven to 160°C (315°F/ Gas 2–3). Brush a baking tray with oil or melted butter.
2 Cut the pumpkin into large pieces, leaving the skin on, and put on the tray. Bake for 1¼ hours, or until very tender. Cool slightly. Scrape the flesh from the skin, avoiding any tough or crispy parts, and transfer to a large bowl. Sift the flour into the bowl, add half the parmesan, the egg and a little ground black pepper. After mixing thoroughly, turn onto a lightly

floured surface and knead for 2 minutes, or until smooth.
3 Divide the dough in half. Using floured hands, roll each half into a sausage shape about 40 cm (16 inches) long. Cut into 16 equal pieces and form each into an oval shape. Press firmly with the floured prongs of a fork to make an indentation.
4 Cook the gnocchi in batches in a large saucepan of boiling salted water for

about 2 minutes, or until they rise to the surface. Drain using a slotted spoon and keep warm.
5 To make the sage butter, melt the butter in a small frying pan, remove from the heat and stir in the chopped sage.
6 Divide the gnocchi among serving bowls and drizzle with sage butter. Sprinkle with the remaining parmesan and garnish with sage leaves.

pumpkin gnocchi with sage butter

pumpkin for gnocchi

Hard, richly coloured pumpkin (winter squash) is best for making gnocchi. The moist flesh and sweetness of a butternut, for instance, is not suitable. The best pumpkin is dry and vibrant orange and will give a light gnocchi full of flavour and colour. Work the dough quickly and lightly, and use as little flour as possible, to avoid toughness. Wherever practical, bake or steam the pumpkin, rather than boiling it, and mash it with a fork or a ricer, not a processor.

making gnocchi

Today, our favourite gnocchi are potato-based but variations can be made using other vegetables such as pumpkin or parsnip, or semolina or ricotta cheese.

Gnocchi are little dumplings. No matter what they are based on, the consistency of the dough should always be soft and light. When cooking vegetables to be used for gnocchi, ensure that the cooking process doesn't result in soggy vegetables, otherwise you will have to add more flour, thus making the dough too heavy. Work quickly so the dough doesn't become too sticky or soft. Gnocchi are best eaten as soon after cooking as possible and you should have any accompanying sauce ready before you cook the dumplings.

traditional potato gnocchi

When making potato gnocchi, it is important to use floury potatoes, preferably old boiling potatoes, because they have a low moisture content. Traditionally, the potatoes are prepared by baking in their skins, thus keeping the potato dry. However, as this is quite time-consuming, most people prefer to steam or boil them. If you do this, make sure you don't overcook the potatoes or they will break up and absorb too much moisture. Also, drain them thoroughly.

Many recipes for potato gnocchi include eggs, to make the gnocchi easier to handle. However, eggs also require the addition of more flour to absorb the extra moisture, thus making the gnocchi a little tougher. Experiment to find which way you prefer to work. Here is the traditional method. To make enough for 4–6 people, you'll need 1 kg (2 lb 4 oz) floury old potatoes, unpeeled, and about 200 g (7 oz) plain (all-purpose) flour.

1 Prick the unpeeled potatoes all over with a fork and bake in a 200°C (400°F/Gas 6) oven for 1 hour, or until tender. Don't wrap in foil. When cool enough to handle but still hot, peel and mash using a masher, or put through a ricer or food mill.

2 Add three-quarters of the flour and gradually work it in with your hands. When a loose dough forms, transfer it to a lightly floured surface and knead gently. Work in the remaining flour as you knead, but only enough to give a soft, light dough that does not stick to your hands or the work surface, but is still damp to touch. Stop kneading at this stage. Lightly flour the work surface and dust the inside tines of a fork with flour. Take a portion of the dough, about one-fifth, and roll it with your hands on the floured surface to form a long, even sausage the thickness of your ring finger. Cut it into 2 cm (¾ inch) pieces.

3 Put a piece on the tines of the fork and press down with your finger, flipping the gnocchi as you do so. It will be rounded into a concave shell shape, ridged on the outer surface. Form a hollow in the centre to allow the gnocchi to cook evenly and hold the sauce more easily. Continue with the remaining dough.

4 Cook the gnocchi in batches, about 20 at a time, in a large saucepan of boiling salted water. The gnocchi are cooked when they all rise to the surface, after 2–3 minutes cooking. Remove each batch using a slotted spoon and keep them warm while cooking the remainder. Sauce, and serve.

Potato gnocchi can be frozen, shaped but uncooked, for up to two months. They will need to be first frozen in a single layer, not touching, before being stored in airtight containers. When you are ready to use them, lower them gently, in batches, into boiling water straight from the freezer.

fontina cheese

A semi-hard cheese from the Italian Alps, fontina has a creamy texture and sweet, nutty flavour. It is eaten as a table cheese, but is also ideal for cooking because it melts completely to give a thick, rich cream. It is used in sauces for pasta and vegetables, and is the star ingredient of the famous *fonduta*, the Piedmontese version of fondue.

gnocchi with fontina sauce

Preparation time: **10 minutes**
Cooking time: **15 minutes**
Serves **4**

200 g (7 oz) fontina cheese, finely chopped
125 ml (4 fl oz/½ cup) pouring (whipping) cream
80 g (2¾ oz) butter
2 tablespoons freshly grated parmesan cheese
400 g (14 oz) fresh potato gnocchi

1 Combine the cheese, cream, butter and parmesan in a bowl over a saucepan of simmering water. Heat, stirring occasionally, for 6–8 minutes, or until the cheese has melted and the sauce is smooth and hot.
2 Meanwhile, cook the gnocchi, in batches, in a large saucepan of boiling salted water for about 2 minutes, or until they rise to the surface.
3 Drain the gnocchi using a slotted spoon and serve with the sauce poured over the top. Garnish with oregano leaves or other fresh herbs, if you like.

herbed potato gnocchi with chunky tomato

✳ ✳

Preparation time: **1 hour**
Cooking time: **30 minutes**
Serves **4**

500 g (1 lb 2 oz) floury potatoes, peeled
　and chopped
1 egg yolk
3 tablespoons freshly grated parmesan
　cheese, plus extra, for garnish
3 tablespoons chopped herbs (such as
　parsley, basil and chives)
125 g (4½ oz/1 cup) plain (all-purpose) flour
1 tablespoon olive oil
2 garlic cloves, crushed
1 onion, chopped
4 bacon slices, roughly chopped
150 g (5½ oz) sun-dried tomatoes,
　roughly chopped
400 g (14 oz) tin chopped tomatoes
1 teaspoon soft brown sugar
2 teaspoons balsamic vinegar
1 tablespoon shredded basil

1 To make the gnocchi, steam or boil the
potato until just tender. Drain thoroughly,
cool and mash. Transfer 2 cups of the
potato to a large bowl. Add the egg yolk,
grated parmesan and herbs and mix until
combined. Gradually add enough flour
to form a slightly sticky dough. Knead
gently for 5 minutes, adding more flour if
necessary, until smooth.
2 Divide the dough into four portions.
Roll each portion on a lightly floured
surface to form a sausage 2 cm (¾ inch)
thick. Cut into 2.5 cm (1 inch) pieces.
Roll each piece into an oval shape and roll
carefully over lightly floured prongs on
the back of a fork. Put on a lightly floured
tray and cover until ready to use.
3 To make the sauce, heat the oil in
a large frying pan, add the garlic and
onion and cook over medium heat for
5 minutes, or until the soft and golden.
4 Add the bacon to the pan and cook,
stirring occasionally, for 5 minutes, or

until the bacon is browned and crisp. Stir
in the sun-dried tomato, tomatoes, sugar
and vinegar and bring to the boil. Reduce
the heat and simmer, stirring occasionally,
for 15 minutes, or until the sauce has
thickened. Stir the basil through the sauce
or use as a garnish, if you prefer.

5 Cook the gnocchi, in batches, in a
large saucepan of boiling salted water for
about 2 minutes, or until they rise to the
surface. Drain well and serve topped with
the tomato sauce and extra parmesan.

feta cheese

Feta originated in Greece where it was made in the mountains from sheep's milk. It is a semi-hard, pure white cheese with a crumbly texture, not matured but preserved in a liquid made up of its whey and brine. Its flavour is fresh, mild and slightly salty and this intensifies as the cheese gets older. Feta cheese is an essential ingredient in the Greek salad and is used in fillings for stuffed vegetables, and in pies and tarts.

spiced carrot and feta gnocchi

Preparation time: 45 minutes
Cooking time: 40 minutes
Serves 6–8

1 kg (2 lb 4 oz) carrots
200 g (7 oz) feta cheese, crumbled
280 g (10 oz/2¼ cups) plain
   (all-purpose) flour
¼ teaspoon freshly grated nutmeg
¼ teaspoon garam masala
1 egg, lightly beaten

MINTED CREAM SAUCE
30 g (1 oz) butter
2 garlic cloves, crushed
2 spring onions (scallions), sliced
250 ml (9 fl oz/1 cup) pouring
   (whipping) cream
2 tablespoons shredded mint

1   Cut the carrots into large pieces and steam, boil or microwave until tender. Drain and set aside to cool

slightly before transferring to a food processor. Add the feta and process together until smooth.

2 Transfer the mixture to a large bowl. Stir in the sifted flour, spices and egg, and mix to form a soft dough. Lightly coat your fingertips with flour and shape teaspoons of the mixture into flat circles.

3 To make the minted cream sauce, melt the butter in a frying pan, add the garlic and spring onion and cook over medium heat for 3 minutes, or until the garlic is soft and golden. Add the cream and bring to the boil, then reduce the heat and simmer for 3 minutes, or until the cream has thickened slightly. Remove from the heat and stir through the mint.

4 Meanwhile, cook the gnocchi, in batches, in a large saucepan of boiling salted water for about 2 minutes, or until they float to the surface. Use a slotted spoon to transfer to warmed serving plates. Drizzle the minted cream sauce over the gnocchi and serve.

NOTE: This mixture is quite soft. Make sure the work surface is lightly floured and keep your fingertips coated in flour when shaping the gnocchi.

spinach and ricotta gnocchi

✻ ✻

Preparation time: 45 minutes
  + 1 hour chilling time
Cooking time: 30 minutes
Serves 4–6

4 slices white bread, crusts removed
125 ml (4 fl oz/½ cup) milk
500 g (1 lb 2 oz) frozen spinach, thawed
250 g (9 oz/1 cup) fresh ricotta cheese
2 eggs
50 g (1¾ oz/½ cup) freshly grated parmesan cheese
melted butter, to serve (optional)
shavings of parmesan cheese, to serve

1 Place the bread in a bowl, add the milk and set aside for 10 minutes to soak, then squeeze out the excess liquid. Squeeze out the excess liquid from the spinach.

2 Combine the bread in a bowl with the spinach, ricotta, eggs and parmesan, and season. Use a fork to mix thoroughly. Cover and refrigerate for 1 hour.

3 Lightly dust your hands in flour. Roll heaped teaspoonsful of the mixture into dumplings. Cook the gnocchi, in batches, in a large saucepan of boiling salted water for about 2 minutes, or until they rise to the surface. Serve drizzled with foaming melted butter, if you wish, and topped with the parmesan shavings.

frozen spinach

Of all the frozen vegetables, spinach stands out as one of the best. Fresh spinach starts to lose nutrients the moment it is picked, so the immediate processing of frozen spinach gives it an advantage. Its flavour is comparable, and, best of all, it's ready to use. Simply defrost, squeeze out the excess moisture, and add to frittatas, omelettes, sauces, fillings, soups and casseroles, or cook with a little butter and serve as a vegetable.

parsnip gnocchi

Preparation time: 45 minutes
Cooking time: 45 minutes
Serves 4

500 g (1 lb 2 oz) parsnips
185 g (6½ oz/1½ cups) plain (all-purpose) flour
50 g (1¾ oz/½ cup) freshly grated parmesan cheese

GARLIC HERB BUTTER
100 g (3½ oz) butter
2 garlic cloves, crushed
3 tablespoons chopped lemon thyme
1 tablespoon finely grated lime zest

1 Cut the parsnips into large pieces. Cook in a large saucepan of boiling water for 30 minutes, or until very tender. Drain thoroughly and leave to cool slightly.
2 Mash the parsnip in a bowl until smooth. Sift the flour into the bowl and

parsnips

Although parsnips are root vegetables, they belong to the umbelliferae or parsley family. They are cultivated for their large, tapering ivory taproots, which have a fruity taste and smell. The starchy flesh purées well and whole parsnips add flavour to stews and casseroles. If the parsnip has developed a tough core, remove it before use.

add half of the parmesan. Season with salt and pepper and mix to a soft dough.

3 Divide the dough in half. Using floured hands, roll each half of the dough out on a lightly floured surface into a sausage shape 2 cm (¾ inch) wide. Cut into short pieces, shape each piece into an oval and roll gently over lightly floured prongs on the back of a fork.

4 Cook the gnocchi, in batches, in a large saucepan of boiling salted water for about 2 minutes, or until they rise to the surface. Use a slotted spoon to transfer them to serving plates.

5 To make the garlic herb butter, combine all the ingredients in a small saucepan and cook over medium heat for 3 minutes, or until a nutty brown colour.

6 To serve, drizzle the garlic herb butter over the gnocchi and sprinkle with the remaining parmesan cheese.

red capsicum gnocchi with goat's cheese

☀ ☀

Preparation time: **1 hour**
Cooking time: **40 minutes**
Serves **6–8**

1 large red capsicum (pepper)
500 g (1 lb 2 oz) sweet potatoes, chopped
500 g (1 lb 2 oz) floury potatoes, peeled and chopped
1 tablespoon sambal oelek
1 tablespoon finely grated orange zest
340 g (11¾ oz/2¾ cups) plain (all-purpose) flour
2 eggs, lightly beaten
500 ml (17 fl oz/2 cups) bottled tomato pasta sauce, warmed
100 g (3½ oz) goat's cheese
2 tablespoons finely shredded basil

1 Cut the capsicum in half and discard the seeds and membrane. Put, skin side up, under a hot grill (broiler) and cook for 8 minutes, or until the skin is black and blistered. Remove from the heat and transfer to a plastic bag to cool. Peel away

the skin and process the flesh in a food processor to form a smooth purée.

2 Steam or boil the sweet potato and potato in a large saucepan until they are very soft. Drain thoroughly, then transfer to a large bowl and mash until smooth. Allow to cool slightly.

3 Add the capsicum purée, sambal oelek, orange zest, flour and eggs, and mix to form a soft dough. Using floured hands, roll heaped teaspoonsful of the dough into oval shapes. Press gently with the lightly floured prongs on the back of a fork.

4 Cook the gnocchi, in batches, in a large saucepan of boiling salted water for about 2 minutes, or until they rise to the

surface. Use a slotted spoon to transfer to warmed serving plates. Top with the warmed pasta sauce. Crumble the goat's cheese and scatter over the top, then sprinkle with the shredded basil.

nasturtium and watercress salad

Combine 1 bunch watercress, the petals from 10 nasturtium flowers, 20 small nasturtium leaves and the separated leaves of 1 witlof (chicory/Belgian endive). Drizzle with a light caesar salad dressing. Sprinkle with chopped pecans. Serve as a side dish.

filled pasta

Make your own pasta dough, shape it into delicate pillows of ravioli, wrap it around your finger to make horseshoe tortellini, or roll it out into cannelloni tubes. You can fill tiny parcels of pasta with just about any of your favourite ingredients, from puréed vegetables, spinach and ricotta, to robust meat sauces. In some parts of Italy, just wrapping leftovers in pasta is part of the heritage, so there are no limitations. Of course, if time is short, you can buy the pasta and simply add your own sauce ... but that's not half as much fun.

ravioli with chicken filling

Preparation time: 1 hour
  + 30 minutes standing time
Cooking time: 45 minutes
Serves 4

PASTA
250 g (9 oz/2 cups) plain (all-purpose) flour
3 eggs
1 tablespoon olive oil
1 egg yolk

FILLING
125 g (4½ oz) minced (ground) chicken
75 g (2¾ oz) fresh ricotta or cottage cheese
60 g (2¼ oz) chicken livers, trimmed and chopped
30 g (1 oz) prosciutto, chopped
1 salami slice, chopped
2 tablespoons freshly grated parmesan cheese
1 egg, beaten
1 tablespoon chopped flat-leaf (Italian) parsley
1 garlic clove, crushed
¼ teaspoon mixed (pumpkin pie) spice

TOMATO SAUCE
2 tablespoons olive oil
1 onion, finely chopped
2 garlic cloves, crushed
800 g (1 lb oz) tin tomatoes, chopped
3 tablespoons chopped basil
½ teaspoon dried mixed herbs
herb sprigs, to garnish (optional)

1 To make the pasta, sift the flour and a pinch of salt into a large bowl and make a well in the centre. Whisk together the eggs, oil and 1 tablespoon water, add gradually to the flour and combine until the mixture forms a ball. Knead on a floured surface for 5 minutes, or until smooth and elastic. Transfer to an oiled bowl, cover with plastic wrap and set aside for 30 minutes.
2 To make the filling, mix all the filling ingredients with salt and pepper, to taste, in a food processor until finely chopped.
3 To make the tomato sauce, heat the oil in a saucepan, add the onion and garlic and stir over low heat until the onion is tender. Increase the heat, add the tomatoes, basil, dried herbs and salt and pepper, to taste. Bring to the boil, then reduce the heat and simmer for 15 minutes. Remove from the heat and set aside.
4 Roll out half the pasta dough until 2 mm (1/16 inch) thick. Cut with a knife or fluted pastry wheel into 10 cm (4 inch) wide strips. Place teaspoonsful of filling at 5 cm (2 inch) intervals down one side of each strip. Whisk the egg yolk with

60 ml (2 fl oz/¼ cup) water and brush along one side of the dough and between the filling. Fold the dough over the filling to meet the other side. Repeat with the remaining filling and dough. Press the edges of the dough together firmly to seal. Cut between the mounds with a knife or a fluted pastry wheel. Cook, in batches, in a large saucepan of rapidly boiling salted water for 10 minutes. Reheat the sauce in a large pan. Add the ravioli and stir until heated through. Season with freshly ground pepper and serve.

chicken mezzelune with cream sauce

✹ ✹

Preparation time: 45 minutes
Cooking time: 15 minutes
Serves 4–6 as an entrée

250 g (9 oz) packet gow gee wrappers

CHICKEN AND HAM FILLING
250 g (9 oz) boneless, skinless chicken
    breast, trimmed and roughly chopped
1 egg, beaten
pinch of ground white pepper
90 g (3¼ oz) ham or prosciutto
2 teaspoons finely snipped chives
2 teaspoons chopped marjoram

CREAM SAUCE
30 g (1 oz) butter
2 spring onions (scallions), finely chopped
2 tablespoons white wine
375 ml (13 fl oz/1½ cups) pouring
    (whipping) cream

1 To make the filling, chop the chicken in a food processor. Add the egg, pepper and ½ teaspoon of salt and process until finely chopped. Transfer to a bowl. Finely chop the ham or prosciutto and stir into the chicken with the herbs.
2 Lay the gow gee wrappers on a work surface, six at a time, and put a teaspoonful of chicken filling in the centre of each. Brush the edges with cold water,

fold in half to form a half-moon shape (mezzelune), and press the edges together firmly to seal. Place on a tea towel (dish towel) and fill the remaining wrappers.
3 If making your own pasta, roll the dough as thinly as possible, or use a pasta machine and pass the dough through 5–6 settings. Cut into circles with an 8 cm (3¼ inch) cutter, fill and seal as above.

4 To make the cream sauce, heat the butter, add the spring onion and cook for 2–3 minutes. Add the wine and cream and simmer until reduced. Season, to taste.
5 Cook batches of mezzelune in rapidly boiling salted water for 2–3 minutes, until the chicken is just cooked through. Drain and serve with the sauce spooned over. Garnish with chives, if you like.

ricotta cheese

Ricotta is an unsalted, unripened cheese made from the whey of sheep's or cow's milk. It has a limited shelf life and can only be used when fresh. When kept too long it sours and develops an acid flavour. It has a delicate, creamy flavour and a light, crumbly texture that blends well with other ingredients, especially other dairy produce. Ricotta, literally recooked, takes its name from the method by which it is made. In ordinary cheese-making there is leftover hot whey of milk. When this is heated again and the solid milk parts skimmed off and drained, ricotta results.

spinach and ricotta shells

Preparation time: **20 minutes**
Cooking time: **15 minutes**
Serves **4**

20 giant conchiglie (shell pasta)
1 tablespoon olive oil
2 bacon slices, finely chopped
1 onion, finely chopped
500 g (1 lb 2 oz) English spinach, chopped
750 g (1 lb 10 oz) fresh ricotta cheese
35 g (1¼ oz/⅓ cup) freshly grated parmesan cheese
250 ml (9 fl oz/1 cup) bottled tomato pasta sauce

1 Cook the conchiglie in a large saucepan of rapidly boiling salted water until it is *al dente*. Drain.
2 Meanwhile, heat the oil in a saucepan, add the bacon and onion and stir over medium heat for 3 minutes, or until lightly browned. Add the spinach and stir over low heat until wilted. Add the ricotta cheese and stir until combined.
3 Spoon the mixture into the pasta shells and sprinkle with the parmesan. Put the shells on a cold, lightly oiled grill (broiler) tray. Cook under medium–high heat for 3 minutes, or until lightly browned and heated through.
4 Warm the pasta sauce in a small saucepan over high heat for 1 minute, or until heated through. Spoon onto serving plates and top with the shells.

prawn tortelloni

✳ ✳

Preparation time: 40 minutes
Cooking time: 30 minutes
Serves 4

300 g (10½ oz) raw prawns (shrimp)
20 g (¾ oz) butter
1 garlic clove, crushed
2 spring onions (scallions), chopped
125 g (4½ oz) fresh ricotta cheese
1 tablespoon chopped basil
200 g (7 oz) packet gow gee wrappers

SAUCE
100 ml (3½ fl oz olive oil
1 garlic clove, crushed
2 spring onions (scallions), including green
    part, finely sliced
1 dried red chilli, crumbled
1 firm tomato, finely diced, or 1 tablespoon
    diced sun-dried tomato

1 Peel the prawns, reserving the heads
and shells to flavour the sauce, then
remove and discard the dark vein and
roughly chop the prawns.
2 Heat the butter and gently cook the
garlic and spring onion until soft and
golden. Cool, then mix with the prawn
meat, ricotta and basil and season, to
taste. Put a teaspoonful of the mixture on
each gow gee wrapper, moisten the edges
with water, fold over to form a semi-circle
and press firmly to seal. Press the corners
together to make a tortelloni shape. For a
large circular shape, use more filling and
cover with another circle of pasta.
3 To make the sauce, heat 60 ml (2 fl oz/
¼ cup) of the oil in a large frying pan.
When hot, add the shells and heads of the
prawns and toss over high heat until they
turn red. Lower the heat and cook for a
few minutes, pressing on the heads to
extract as much flavour as possible. Add
125 ml (4 fl oz/½ cup) water, cover and
cook over low heat for 5 minutes. Remove
the shells and heads from the pan using
a slotted spoon, pressing out as much of
the flavoured liquied as possible before
discarding them.

4 In another saucepan, heat the
remaining oil, then add the garlic, spring
onion and chilli and stir over low heat
until the garlic is pale golden. Add the
prawn stock and tomato and cook until
heated through.
5 Bring a large saucepan of salted water
to the boil. Drop the tortelloni into the
boiling water and cook for 3–4 minutes.

Drain, then add to the sauce and toss until
the pasta is well coated.

NOTE: Tortelloni are large tortellini.

lasagne bows

pumpkin and herb ravioli

✳ ✳

Preparation time: 50 minutes
+ 30 minutes standing time
Cooking time: 1 hour 15 minutes
Serves 6

500 g (1 lb 2 oz) pumpkin (winter squash), seeded, peeled and cut into chunks
220 g (7¾ oz/1¾ cups) plain (all-purpose) flour
3 eggs, lightly beaten
¼ teaspoon freshly grated nutmeg
15 sage leaves
15 flat-leaf (Italian) parsley leaves
125 g (4½ oz) butter, melted
60 g (2¼ oz) freshly grated parmesan cheese

1 Preheat the oven to 180°C (350°F/ Gas 4). Place the pumpkin on an oiled baking tray and bake for 1 hour or until tender, then allow to cool. Remove the skin. Place the flour and eggs in a food processor. Process for 30 seconds, or until the mixture forms a dough. Transfer to a lightly floured surface and knead for 3 minutes, or until the dough is smooth and elastic. Cover with a clean tea towel (dish towel) and set aside for 30 minutes.
2 Mash the pumpkin and nutmeg. Roll out half the dough to form a rectangle about 2 mm (¹⁄₁₆ inch) thick. Roll out the remaining half to form a rectangle slightly larger than the first.
3 On the smaller rectangle, place heaped teaspoonsful of pumpkin mixture in straight rows, at intervals about 5 cm (2 inches) apart. Flatten each mound of pumpkin slightly and place a sage or parsley leaf on top of each.
4 Lightly brush water between the mounds of filling. Place the larger sheet of dough on top, then press down gently between the pumpkin mounds to seal. Cut into squares with a knife or fluted cutter. Bring a large saucepan of water to the boil and cook the ravioli, a few at a time, for 4 minutes, or until just tender. Drain

thoroughly. Serve sprinkled with salt and pepper and gently tossed with the melted butter and parmesan.

NOTE: Ravioli can be made several hours in advance. Refrigerate in layers between sheets of baking paper to prevent them sticking together. Cook just before serving.

lasagne bows

✳ ✳

Preparation time: 20 minutes
Cooking time: 20 minutes
Serves 4

four 16 x 24 cm (6¼ x 9½ inch) fresh lasagne sheets
400 g (14 oz) fresh ricotta cheese
1 egg, lightly beaten
¼ teaspoon freshly grated nutmeg
50 g (1¾ oz/1 cup) chopped herbs
30 g (1 oz) butter, chopped
300 ml (10½ fl oz) bottled tomato pasta sauce
freshly grated parmesan cheese, to serve
shredded basil leaves, to garnish

1 Preheat the oven to 200°C (400°F/ Gas 6). Cook the lasagne sheets in a large saucepan of rapidly boiling salted water until al dente, stirring frequently to ensure they do not stick together.
2 While the pasta is cooking, combine the ricotta, egg, nutmeg and herbs in a bowl. Drain the pasta and carefully lay one sheet on a flat surface. Place 2–3 tablespoons of the ricotta mixture in the centre of the sheet. Fold the top third of the lasagne sheet over the filling, then the bottom third over the top. Gently twist the ends of the roll to make a shape that resembles a bow. Repeat with the remaining sheets and filling.
3 Lightly brush a large rectangular ovenproof dish with melted butter or oil. Place the bows in the dish, dot with the butter and pour the pasta sauce over the centre of the bows, leaving the ends exposed. Cover and bake for 5 minutes,

or until the bows are heated through. Serve immediately, sprinkled generously with the parmesan and basil.

spinach ravioli with sun-dried tomato sauce

✳ ✳

Preparation time: 20 minutes
Cooking time: 15 minutes
Serves 4

150 g (5½ oz/¾ cup) firmly packed, chopped, cooked English spinach
250 g (9 oz/1 cup) fresh ricotta cheese, well drained
2 tablespoons freshly grated parmesan cheese
1 tablespoon snipped chives
1 egg, lightly beaten
200 g (7 oz) packet gow gee wrappers

SAUCE
100 g (3½ oz) sun-dried tomatoes
80 ml (2½ fl oz/⅓ cup) extra virgin olive oil
40 g (1½ oz/¼ cup) pine nuts

1 Combine the spinach, ricotta, parmesan, chives and half the egg in a bowl. Mix well and season to taste. Place 1½ teaspoons of the mixture in the centre of a gow gee wrapper. Brush the edge of the wrapper lightly with some of the remaining egg, then cover with another wrapper. Repeat until all the wrappers are used. Press the edges firmly to seal. Using a 7 cm (2¾ inch) plain scone cutter, cut the ravioli into circles.
2 Cook the ravioli, in batches, in a large saucepan of rapidly boiling salted water for 4 minutes, or until al dente. Don't crowd the pan. Keep each batch warm while cooking the remainder.
3 To make the sauce, slice the sun-dried tomatoes and combine with the other ingredients in a large saucepan. Heat slowly until warm. Carefully drain the ravioli, add to the sauce and toss very gently. Serve immediately.

filling pasta

The benefits of making your own filled or stuffed pasta are many. You can determine the pasta flavour, size and shape, as well as the taste and texture of the filling.

fillings

Ingredients for filled pasta are fresh and interesting. Some, such as cheeses and mashed pumpkin, are smooth, while foods such as shellfish are better in small, discernible pieces. As a general rule, the finer the filling, the smaller the shape.

A binding ingredient is generally needed. This is often a soft cheese such as ricotta, but can be cream, sauce or gravy. The moisture content can be controlled by the addition of a little grated parmesan cheese, breadcrumbs or even mashed potato.

Within a short time, any moisture in the filling will begin to seep through the pasta, causing it to become soggy. Therefore, the filling should be quite dry, particularly if the pasta isn't going to be cooked immediately. Fresh filled pasta should be eaten soon after being made.

equipment

You will need a long sharp knife, a pastry brush and, ideally, a fluted pastry wheel, to give a good seal. A cutter-crimper wheel gives an excellent seal, but can be less manoeuvrable on curved edges. Ravioli stamps or cutters are sometimes available. Moulded ravioli trays give a uniform shape and enable you to make a lot of ravioli quickly, once the technique is mastered.

ravioli

To serve four to six, you will need one batch of basic pasta dough (page 16), about 1½ cups of filling and a beaten egg, for sealing the edges. There are two ways of hand-shaping ravioli: by cutting out the dough and individually folding each one over the filling, or by covering one sheet of dough and the filling with another sheet and cutting shapes from this. The folded method is very simple and has the advantage of a better seal, with only three cut edges that are firmly joined together by hand. The double-sheeted method is quicker, but results in a ravioli with all cut edges, increasing the likelihood of them opening up.

double-sheeted method

1 Lightly dust a large work surface with flour. Divide the dough into four. Roll two portions out into very thin (about 2.5 mm/ ⅛ inch, or less) sheets, using a hand-cranked pasta machine, or with a rolling pin on the work surface. Roll one sheet slightly bigger than the other and cover with a tea towel (dish towel).

2 Spread the smaller sheet out on the work surface. In one corner, lightly mark out two or three ravioli squares for size. Spoon some filling into the centre of each and flatten slightly with the back of the spoon. This will help you determine the amount of filling per square and the spacing between each. The filling should cover about two-thirds of the area of each square. Spoon equal amounts of filling, evenly spaced, over the sheet. Flatten lightly with the back of the spoon.

3 Brush beaten egg between the filling along the cutting lines. Take the larger sheet and, starting at one end, place it over the first, matching the sides and pressing it here and there so that it sticks to the bottom layer without slipping. Don't stretch it, but let it settle into position naturally.

4 Run your fingers along the cutting lines to press them together, or use the fine edge of a ruler, which will mark the lines as well as seal them. Now, cut along these lines using a sharp knife or pastry wheel.

5 Transfer to a lightly floured baking tray or large platter and refrigerate while you work the remaining dough and filling. Don't put them on top of one another or they'll stick together. They can be refrigerated, covered, for up to 3 hours, depending on the moisture content of the filling. The cooking time varies according to the thickness of the pasta and type of filling.

tortellini

These small rounds of pasta dough are filled with anything from cooked meat, chicken and fish, to vegetables and soft cheeses, and then sealed and shaped into rings. To make tortellini for four to six people, you will need one batch of basic pasta dough (page 16), 1½ cups of smooth-textured filling and a beaten egg for sealing.

1 Lightly dust a large work surface with flour. Divide the dough into four, keeping all portions covered until needed. Using a hand-cranked pasta machine or with a rolling pin on the prepared surface, roll out one portion of dough very thinly, about 2.5 mm (⅛ inch) or less.
2 Spread the pasta out on a lightly floured work surface and avoid flouring it from now on. With a 6 cm (2½ inch) cutter or an upturned glass, cut out circles.
3 Lightly brush the edge of each circle with beaten egg or water, then spoon about ½ teaspoonful of filling onto the centre of each circle.
4 Working with one circle at a time, fold one side over the other to encase the filling. The cut sides should not match up exactly, but overlap slightly. Press the edges firmly together, slightly easing the filling along the length of the half-moon as you do so. Roll the rim of the cut edge back over itself, with the taller side uppermost. Now, with the folded rim on the outside, wrap the shape around your index finger and press the two ends together. A dab of water might be needed to help seal them.
5 Place the tortellini on a lightly floured baking tray or large platter and keep chilled while you work the remaining pasta and filling. Depending on the dryness of the filling used, they will keep, covered, in the refrigerator for up to 6 hours.

cannelloni

These tubes of pasta have various fillings, such as cooked meat with cheese, spinach with ricotta or mashed pumpkin with pine nuts. As a rough guide, depending on the size of cannelloni you choose to make and the amount of filling you want to use, one batch of basic plain dough (page 16) will make about 20 tubes that are 10 cm (4 inches) long. Cut the pasta for cannelloni wide enough to wrap comfortably around the filling you want to use. Allow for a 2.5 cm (1 inch) overlap at the seam on larger tubes, down to half that on small, finger-sized tubes. Too little overlap and the cannelloni may expand and open when baked, making serving difficult; too much and the pasta will be too thick. Cut one or two extra sheets in case some tear during cooking. To fill 20 tubes, you will need about 4 cups of filling.

1 Roll out fresh pasta sheets to about 2.5 mm (⅛ inch) thick using a hand-cranked pasta machine or rolling pin.
2 Bring a large saucepan of water to the boil and grease a shallow ovenproof dish.
3 Cut the pasta into sheets of the size you require, bearing in mind that they will increase slightly during cooking. The length of the tube runs with the grain of the pasta.
4 Keeping the uncooked sheets covered, drop 3 or 4 pasta sheets at a time, depending on their size, into the water and boil for 1½–2 minutes. Fish them out with a wide strainer or sieve and spread on dry tea towels (dish towels) while you cook the rest of the sheets. Turn the sheets over once when partially dry. Do not allow to dry too much as the edges crack when rolling. Trim if necessary. You might like to cut out a paper template to use as a guide so they will be the same size.
5 Arrange some filling down the centre of each sheet, running it in the same direction as the grain. Roll the pasta tightly around the filling to form a tube. Place the tubes side by side, seam side down, in the prepared dish, with the overlapping joins on the bottom. Cannelloni are nearly always dressed with sauce and topped with cheese before being finished off in the oven, or under the grill (broiler).

freezing

Filled pastas freeze well and must be cooked straight from the freezer, not defrosted. To freeze filled or stuffed pasta, do so in a single layer or, if necessary, between baking paper. Cover with a tea towel (dish towel). When frozen, transfer to an airtight container.

spinach and ricotta cannelloni

❋ ❋ ❋

Preparation time: **1 hour**
Cooking time: **1 hour 15 minutes**
Serves 4

375 g (13 oz) fresh lasagne sheets
2 tablespoons olive oil
1 large onion, finely chopped
1–2 garlic cloves, crushed
1 kg (2 lb 4 oz) English spinach,
    finely chopped
650 g (1 lb 7 oz) fresh ricotta cheese,
    beaten
2 eggs, lightly beaten
¼ teaspoon freshly grated nutmeg

TOMATO SAUCE
1 tablespoon olive oil
1 onion, chopped
2 garlic cloves, finely chopped
500 g (1 lb 2 oz) very ripe tomatoes,
    chopped
2 tablespoons tomato paste
    (concentrated purée)
1 teaspoon soft brown sugar
150 g (5½ oz/1 cup) grated
    mozzarella cheese

1 Cut the lasagne sheets into 16 evenly sized pieces and trim lengthways so they will fit neatly into a deep-sided, rectangular ovenproof dish when filled. Bring a large saucepan of water to a rapid boil and cook 1–2 lasagne sheets at a time until just softened. The amount of time will differ, depending on the type and brand of lasagne, but is usually about 2 minutes. Remove the sheets carefully with a wide strainer or sieve and lay flat on a clean, damp tea towel (dish towel). Repeat with the remaining lasagne sheets.
2 Heat the oil in a heavy-based frying pan. Cook the onion and garlic until golden, stirring regularly. Add the spinach, cook for 2 minutes, cover with a tight-fitting lid and steam for 5 minutes. Drain, removing as much liquid as possible. The spinach must be quite dry

cannelloni

Cannelloni are simply rectangles of pasta rolled around a filling. The pasta can be sheets of fresh egg dough, or fresh lasagne sheets, which need to be blanched before filling, or instant tubes. The dried product is also available in a form that requires no pre-cooking. Once the tubes are filled they may be sauced and then baked with cheese scattered over the top.

or the pasta will be soggy. Combine the spinach with the ricotta, eggs, nutmeg and salt and pepper. Set aside.
3 To make the tomato sauce, heat the oil in a frying pan and cook the onion and garlic for 10 minutes over low heat, stirring occasionally. Add the tomatoes, including the juice, the tomato paste, sugar, 125 ml (4 fl oz/½ cup) water and salt and pepper. Bring the sauce to the boil, then reduce the heat and simmer for 10 minutes. If a smoother sauce is preferred, purée in a food processor until the desired consistency is reached.

4 Preheat the oven to 180°C (350°F/ Gas 4). Lightly brush the ovenproof dish with melted butter or oil. Spread about one-third of the tomato sauce over the base of the dish. Working with one sheet of lasagne at a time, spoon 2½ tablespoons of the spinach mixture down the centre of the sheet, leaving a border at each end. Roll up and place, seam side down, in the dish. Repeat with the remaining pasta sheets and filling. Spoon the remaining tomato sauce over the cannelloni and scatter the mozzarella evenly over the top.

5 Bake for 30–35 minutes, or until golden brown and bubbling. Set aside for 10 minutes before serving. Garnish with sprigs of herbs, if desired.

NOTE: Dried cannelloni tubes can be used instead of lasagne sheets.

conchiglie with chicken and pesto

❋ ❋

Preparation time: 45 minutes
Cooking time: 30 minutes
Serves 4

20 giant conchiglie (shell pasta)
2 tablespoons olive oil
2 leeks, thinly sliced
500 g (1 lb 2 oz) minced (ground) chicken
1 tablespoon plain (all-purpose) flour
250 ml (9 fl oz/1 cup) chicken stock
4 tablespoons chopped pimiento
50 g (1¾ oz/½ cup) freshly grated
    parmesan cheese

PESTO
50 g (1¾ oz/1 cup) basil leaves
3 tablespoons pine nuts
2 garlic cloves, crushed
60 ml (2 fl oz/¼ cup) olive oil

1 Preheat the oven to 180°C (350°F/ Gas 4). Brush a shallow baking dish with melted butter or oil. Cook the conchiglie in a large saucepan of rapidly boiling salted water until *al dente*. Drain well.
2 Heat the oil in a heavy-based saucepan, add the leek and stir-fry over medium heat for 2 minutes. Add the chicken and stir until well browned and all the liquid has evaporated. Use a fork to break up any lumps as the mince cooks. Add the flour and stir for 1 minute. Add the stock and pimiento and stir over medium heat until boiling. Reduce the heat and simmer for 1 minute, or until the mixture has reduced and thickened.
3 To make the pesto, blend the basil, pine nuts, garlic and oil in a food

processor or blender for 30 seconds, or until smooth. Spoon into a small bowl and press plastic wrap over the surface to exclude any air.
4 To assemble, spoon the chicken mixture into the cooled pasta shells, then transfer to the prepared baking dish and cover with foil. Bake for 15 minutes, or until heated through. Serve topped with a dollop of the pesto and sprinkled with the grated parmesan.

caramelised leeks and crisp bacon

Trim leeks, cut in half lengthways and then into long pieces, taking care to keep the leaves together. Cook over low heat in butter and a little soft brown sugar, turning occasionally, until very tender and caramelised. Take care not to overcook the leek or it will fall apart. Top with pieces of crisp bacon and roughly chopped flat-leaf (Italian) parsley. Serve as a side dish.

chicken ravioli with buttered sage sauce

✳

Preparation time: **15 minutes**
Cooking time: **10 minutes**
Serves 4

500 g (1 lb 2 oz) fresh or dried chicken-filled
    ravioli or agnolotti
60 g (2¼ oz) butter
4 spring onions (scallions), chopped
2 tablespoons sage leaves, chopped, plus
    extra whole leaves, to garnish
50 g (1¾ oz/½ cup) freshly grated
    parmesan cheese, to serve

1 Cook the ravioli in a large saucepan
of rapidly boiling salted water until
al dente. Drain and return to the pan.
2 While the ravioli is cooking, melt
the butter in a heavy-based saucepan.
Add the spring onion and sage and stir
for 2 minutes. Season with salt and
pepper, to taste.
3 Add the sauce to the pasta and toss
well. Spoon into warmed serving bowls
and sprinkle with the parmesan. Serve
immediately, garnished with sage leaves.

sage

Once believed to enhance longevity and give
wisdom, this strongly flavoured, fragrant herb is
commonly paired with pork, chicken and veal as
it was traditionally used to counteract rich, oily
meats. Use sage, especially in its dried form, with
discretion, as a heavy hand will cause its pungent
flavour to overpower rather than complement the
food with which it is being cooked.

cream

Cream results from allowing milk to settle. Fats rise to the top and when skimmed off are a pourable single cream with a fat content of 10–20%, or in some countries 35%. Thick (double/heavy) cream, which contains at least 30% fat, has to be separated mechanically, to give a spoonable cream. Other natural creams, thick and stiff, will contain as much as 60% fat. Thickened (whipping) cream has had a starch or gelatine added to it.

tortellini with mushroom sauce

Preparation time: 15 minutes
Cooking time: 10 minutes
Serves 4

500 g (1 lb 2 oz) tortellini
60 g (2¼ oz) butter
185 g (6½ oz) button mushrooms, sliced
1 garlic clove, crushed
310ml (10¾ fl oz/1¼ cups) pouring (whipping) cream
1 small lemon, zest finely grated
pinch of freshly grated nutmeg
3 tablespoons freshly grated parmesan cheese

1 Cook the tortellini in a large saucepan of rapidly boiling salted water until *al dente*. Drain, return to the pan and keep warm.

2 Meanwhile, melt the butter in a saucepan and cook the mushrooms for 2 minutes over medium heat. Add the garlic, cream, lemon zest, nutmeg and freshly ground black pepper. Stir over low heat for 1–2 minutes. Stir in the grated parmesan and cook gently for 3 minutes.

3 Add the sauce to the tortellini and stir gently to combine. Spoon into serving dishes, sprinkle with pepper and garnish with fresh herbs, if desired.

fresh chillies

There are many different types of fresh chilli, ranging from small and fiery to fat and mildly hot. The seeds and the membrane, which are the hottest parts, are generally removed from all but the tiniest. Where a recipe simply calls for fresh chilli, use your experience to select which type. The most fiery are usually small chillies such as bird's eye, available in red or green. Serranos, which are red, green or yellow, are also small and very hot. Jalapeños are plump, green or red, and as hot as the serranos weight for weight. Correctly identifying chillies is quite difficult, especially since even growers disagree and the names vary internationally.

tortellini with bacon and tomato sauce

Preparation time: **15 minutes**
Cooking time: **20 minutes**
Serves **4**

500 g (1 lb 2 oz) fresh or dried
   tortellini

1 tablespoon olive oil
4 bacon slices, chopped
2 garlic cloves, crushed
1 medium onion, chopped
1 teaspoon chopped red chillies
400 g (14 oz) tin chopped tomatoes
125 ml (4 fl oz/½ cup) pouring
   (whipping) cream
2 tablespoons chopped basil

1 Cook the tortellini in a large saucepan of rapidly boiling salted water until it is *al dente*. Drain thoroughly and then return to the pan.

2 Meanwhile, heat the oil in a medium heavy-based saucepan. Add the bacon, garlic and onion and cook for 5 minutes over medium heat, stirring often.

3 Add the chilli and tomatoes to the pan. Reduce the heat and simmer for 10 minutes. Stir in the cream and basil and cook for a further 1 minute. Add the sauce to the pasta and toss well. Serve immediately.

green beans with garlic and cumin

Fry a sliced onion and crushed garlic clove in a little olive oil and add a 400 g (14 oz) tin of chopped tomatoes and a pinch of ground cumin. Cook until reduced by half, then add 300 g (10½ oz) sliced green beans. Cook the beans in the tomato mixture until tender but still bright green. Sprinkle with toasted cumin seeds. Serve as a side dish.

mushroom ravioli

Preparation time: **30 minutes**
Cooking time: **15 minutes**
Serves **4 as a starter**

70 g (2½ oz/½ cup) hazelnut kernels, toasted and skinned
90 g (3¼ oz) unsalted butter
150 g (5½ oz) mushrooms
1 tablespoon olive oil
200 g (7 oz) packet won ton wrappers

1 Chop the hazelnuts in a food processor. Heat the butter in a frying pan over medium heat until it sizzles and turns nutty brown. Remove from the heat, stir in the hazelnuts and season with salt and freshly ground black pepper, to taste.
2 Wipe the mushrooms with paper towel. Finely chop the stems and caps. Heat the oil in a saucepan, add the mushrooms and stir until soft. Season with salt and pepper, to taste, and cook until the liquid has evaporated. Allow to cool.
3 Lay 12 won ton wrappers on a work surface and put a small teaspoonful of the mushroom filling on six of them. Brush the edges of the wrappers with water and place another wrapper on top. Press firmly to seal. If desired, trim the edges with a pasta cutter. Lay the ravioli on a tray lined with a clean tea towel (dish towel) and cover with another tea towel.

Repeat with 12 more squares. Filling and sealing a few at a time prevents the ravioli from drying out.
4 When all the ravioli are made, cook in batches in a large saucepan of rapidly boiling salted water. Don't crowd the pan. Very thin pasta will be done in about 2 minutes after the water returns to the boil, so lift out with a slotted spoon and drain in a colander while the next batch is cooking. Serve with the hazelnut sauce.

NOTE: Won ton wrappers made with egg are best. If you can't get toasted and skinned hazelnuts from your health food store, spread the nuts on a baking tray and roast in a 180°C (350°F/Gas 4) oven for 10–12 minutes. Cool, then rub in a tea towel (dish towel) to remove as many of the skins as possible.

ravioli

It is thought that ravioli originated in the seaport of Genoa, when thrifty housewives used pasta to wrap around little spoonfuls of leftovers in the hope of disguising them. The sailors happily took their *rabiole* to sea, unaware of the origins of the filling. Today, we are more discerning about the fillings we put in ravioli, and they are stuffed with carefully considered combinations of meats, cheeses or vegetables.

baked pasta

Sheets of pasta layered with ragu or rich tomato sauce and a smooth, creamy béchamel, then finished with freshly grated parmesan cheese and left in the oven to bubble and melt until the smell becomes irresistible, lasagne is undoubtedly the most famous (and perhaps the favourite) baked pasta dish of our times. But what about pasticcio, cannelloni and macaroni cheese? If you've perfected your lasagne, it could be time to try another little bit of baked pasta magic.

macaroni eggplant cake

Preparation time: 1 hour
Cooking time: 1 hour 20 minutes
Serves 6

115 g (4 oz/¾ cup) macaroni
2–3 eggplants (aubergines), thinly sliced
　lengthways
2–3 tablespoons olive oil
1 onion, chopped
1 garlic clove, crushed
500 g (1 lb 2 oz) minced (ground) pork,
　beef or chicken
400 g (14 oz) tin chopped tomatoes
2 tablespoons tomato paste (concentrated
　purée)
80 g (2¾ oz/½ cup) frozen peas
150 g (5½ oz/1 cup) freshly grated
　mozzarella cheese
60 g (2¼ oz/½ cup) freshly grated
　cheddar cheese
1 egg, beaten
50 g (1¾ oz/½ cup) freshly grated
　parmesan cheese

1　Lightly brush a deep 23 cm (9 inch) spring-form tin with oil or butter and line with baking paper. Cook the macaroni in a large saucepan of rapidly boiling salted water until *al dente*. Drain and set aside.

2　Spread the eggplant on trays, sprinkle with salt and set aside for 20 minutes. Rinse and pat dry with paper towels. Heat 2 tablespoons of oil in a frying pan and cook the eggplant, in batches, in a single layer, until golden on each side. Add more oil as required. Drain on paper towels.

3　Add the onion and garlic to the same pan and stir over low heat until the onion is tender. Add the mince and brown, breaking up any lumps with a spoon or fork as it cooks. Add the tomatoes, tomato paste and salt and pepper, to taste, and stir well. Bring to the boil. Reduce the heat and simmer for 15–20 minutes.

4　Meanwhile, mix together the peas, macaroni, mozzarella, cheddar, egg and half the parmesan. Set aside.

5　Preheat the oven to 180°C (350°F/ Gas 4). Place a slice of eggplant in the centre of the base of the prepared tin. Arrange three-quarters of the eggplant in an overlapping pattern to cover the base and side of the tin. Sprinkle with half the remaining parmesan.

6　Combine the mince mixture and macaroni mixture. Carefully spoon the filling into the eggplant case, packing down well. Arrange the remaining eggplant slices, overlapping, on top. Sprinkle with the remaining parmesan.

7　Bake, uncovered, for 25–30 minutes, or until golden. Allow to rest for 5 minutes before unmoulding onto a serving plate. Serve with salad, if desired.

NOTE: You can omit the minced pork and add chopped cooked Italian sausage and chopped cooked chicken to the tomato mixture, if you prefer. Extra tomato sauce can be served with this dish. Make it by simmering tinned chopped tomatoes with a little crushed garlic, pepper and chopped basil until thickened.

ricotta lasagne

✳ ✳

Preparation time: **1 hour**
Cooking time: **1 hour 30 minutes**
Serves **8**

500 g (1 lb 2 oz) fresh spinach lasagne
   sheets
30 g (1 oz/½ cup) basil leaves, chopped
2 tablespoons fresh breadcrumbs
3 tablespoons pine nuts
2 teaspoons paprika
1 tablespoon freshly grated parmesan
   cheese

RICOTTA FILLING
750 g (1 lb 10 oz) fresh ricotta cheese
50 g (1¾ oz/½ cup) freshly grated
   parmesan cheese
pinch of freshly grated nutmeg

TOMATO SAUCE
1 tablespoon olive oil
2 onions, chopped
2 garlic cloves, crushed
800 g (1 lb 12 oz) tin chopped tomatoes
1 tablespoon tomato paste (concentrated
   purée)

BÉCHAMEL SAUCE
60 g (2¼ oz) butter
60 g (2¼ oz/½ cup) plain (all-purpose) flour
500 ml (17 fl oz/2 cups) milk
2 eggs, lightly beaten
35 g (1¼ oz/⅓ cup) freshly grated parmesan
   cheese

1 Lightly brush a 25 x 33 cm (10 x 13 inch) baking dish with melted butter or oil. Cut the pasta sheets into large pieces and cook, 2–3 at a time, in boiling water for 3 minutes. Drain and spread on damp tea towels (dish towels) until needed.
2 To make the ricotta filling, mix the ricotta, parmesan, nutmeg and a little freshly ground black pepper in a bowl.
3 To make the tomato sauce, heat the oil in a frying pan, add the onion and cook for 10 minutes, stirring occasionally, until very soft. Add the garlic and cook for another minute. Add the tomatoes

and tomato paste and stir until well combined. Stir until the mixture comes to the boil, then reduce the heat and simmer, uncovered, for 15 minutes, or until thickened, stirring occasionally.
4 To make the béchamel sauce, heat the butter in a small saucepan. Add the flour and stir for about 1 minute, until golden and smooth. Remove from the heat and gradually stir in the milk. Return to the heat and stir until the sauce boils and begins to thicken. Remove from the heat and stir in the eggs. Return to medium heat and stir until almost boiling, but do not boil. Add the cheese and season, to taste. Put plastic wrap on the surface to

prevent a skin forming. Preheat the oven to 200°C (400°F/Gas 6).
5 Put a layer of lasagne sheets in the prepared dish. Spread with a third of the ricotta filling, sprinkle with basil, then top with a third of the tomato sauce. Repeat the layers, finishing with pasta.
6 Pour the béchamel sauce over the top and spread until smooth. Sprinkle with the combined breadcrumbs, pine nuts, paprika and parmesan. Bake for 45 minutes, or until browned. Set aside for 10 minutes before serving.

NOTE: Allowing the lasagne to stand before serving makes it easier to cut.

paprika

Ground paprika is the dried and pounded form of sweet red capsicums (peppers), *Capsicum annuum*. It is bright reddish-orange and gives a rosy hue to dishes when used in any quantity. With its slightly pungent taste, paprika is the distinctive flavour in the Hungarian classic, goulash, and it benefits from slow cooking to maximise its impact. Paprika is available in varying strengths, from very sweet and mild to fully flavoured and highly aromatic.

seafood with pasta

Preparation time: 30 minutes
Cooking time: 45 minutes
Serves 6

250 g (9 oz) instant lasagne sheets
500 g (1 lb 2 oz) boneless white fish fillets
125 g (4½ oz) scallops, cleaned
500 g (1 lb 2 oz) raw prawns (shrimp),
    peeled and deveined
125 g (4½ oz) butter

1 leek, chopped
85 g (3 oz/⅔ cup) plain (all-purpose)
    flour
500 ml (17 fl oz/2 cups) milk
500 ml (17 fl oz/2 cups) dry white wine
125 g (4½ oz/1 cup) freshly grated
    cheddar cheese
125 ml (4 fl oz/½ cup) pouring
    (whipping) cream
50 g (1¾ oz/½ cup) freshly grated
    parmesan cheese
2 tablespoons chopped flat-leaf
    (Italian) parsley

cheddar cheese

Cheddar, the best loved of all
English cheeses, originated in
the small Somerset village of
Cheddar. It is a hard cow's milk
cheese that is matured to give
well-balanced flavours with a
mellow aftertaste.

1 Preheat the oven to 180°C (350°F/ Gas 4). Line a greased deep lasagne dish, approximately 30 x 30 cm (12 x 12 inch) with lasagne sheets, breaking them to fill any gaps. Set aside.

2 Chop the fish, scallops and prawns into even-sized pieces.

3 Melt the butter in a large saucepan. Add the leek and cook, stirring, for 1 minute. Add the flour and cook, stirring, for 1 minute. Gradually blend in the milk and wine, stirring until the mixture is smooth. Cook, stirring constantly, over medium heat until the sauce boils and thickens. Reduce the heat and simmer for 3 minutes. Remove from the heat and stir in the cheddar cheese and salt and pepper, to taste. Return to the heat, add the seafood and simmer for 1 minute.

4 Spoon half the seafood mixture over the lasagne sheets. Top with a layer of lasagne sheets. Continue layering, finishing with lasagne sheets.

5 Pour the cream over the top. Sprinkle with the combined parmesan and parsley. Bake, uncovered, for 30 minutes, or until bubbling and golden.

NOTE: Lasagne sheets are available in straight or ridged sheets.

pasta pie

✹ ✹

Preparation time: **20 minutes**
Cooking time: **1 hour**
Serves **4**

250 g (9 oz) macaroni
1 tablespoon olive oil
1 onion, sliced
125 g (4½ oz) pancetta, chopped
125 g (4½ oz) ham, chopped
4 eggs
250 ml (9 fl oz/1 cup) milk
250 ml (9 fl oz/1 cup) pouring (whipping) cream
2 tablespoons snipped chives
125 g (4½ oz/1 cup) grated cheddar cheese
125 g (4½ oz) bocconcini (about 4), chopped

1 Preheat the oven to 180°C (350°F/ Gas 4). Cook the macaroni in a large saucepan of rapidly boiling salted water until *al dente*. Drain.

2 Heat the oil in a large saucepan, add the onion and stir over low heat until just tender. Stir in the pancetta and cook for 2 minutes. Add the ham and stir well. Remove from the heat and allow to cool.

3 In a bowl, whisk together the eggs, milk, cream, chives and salt and pepper, to taste. Mix in the cheddar, bocconcini, pancetta mixture and drained pasta, and mix to combine well. Spread evenly over the base of a greased casserole dish. Bake for 35–40 minutes, or until the mixture is set.

durum wheat

Durum wheat is a hard wheat with high levels of protein and therefore more gluten. It is considered the best wheat for pasta making and by law, all dried pasta made in Italy must be made from 100% pure durum wheat semolina, pasta di semola di grano duro. As well as the nutritional benefits it provides, it gives pasta a good colour, from pale lemon to golden, and more flavour. Durum wheat is necessary for the resilient texture of quality pasta and its presence helps to achieve the desired cooked state that is known as *al dente*.

pasta soufflé

pasta soufflé

✹ ✹

Preparation time: 35 minutes
Cooking time: 1 hour
Serves 4

2 tablespoons freshly grated parmesan
   cheese
60 g (2¼ oz) butter
1 small onion, finely chopped
2 tablespoons plain (all-purpose) flour
500 ml (17 fl oz/2 cups) milk
125 ml (4 fl oz/½ cup) chicken stock
3 eggs, separated
115 g (4 oz/¾ cup) small macaroni, cooked

210 g (7½ oz) tin salmon, drained
   and flaked
1 tablespoon chopped flat-leaf
   (Italian) parsley
finely grated zest of 1 lemon

1 Preheat the oven to 210°C (415°F/
Gas 6–7). Brush a 1.5 litre (52 fl oz/
6 cup), 18 cm (7 inch) soufflé dish with
oil. Coat the base and side with parmesan.
Shake off any excess.
2 To collar the dish, cut a piece of foil or
baking paper 5 cm (2 inches) longer than
the circumference of the soufflé dish. Fold
the foil in half lengthways. Wrap the foil
around the outside of the dish; it should
extend 5 cm (2 inches) above the rim.
Secure the foil with string.
3 Heat the butter in a large saucepan.
Add the onion and cook over low heat
until tender. Add the flour and stir for
2 minutes, or until the mixture is lightly
golden. Remove from the heat. Gradually
blend in the milk and stock, stirring until
the mixture is smooth. Return to the heat.
Stir constantly over medium heat until
the mixture boils and thickens. Reduce
the heat and simmer for 3 minutes. Add
the egg yolks and whisk until smooth. Add
the macaroni, salmon, parsley, lemon zest
and salt and pepper. Stir until combined.
Transfer the mixture to a large bowl.
4 Using electric beaters, beat the egg
whites in a small, dry mixing bowl until
stiff peaks form. Using a metal spoon,
fold gently into the salmon mixture.
Spoon into the prepared dish and bake
for 40–45 minutes, or until well risen
and browned. Serve immediately.

NOTE: Hot soufflés should be made just
before you want to serve them as they
will collapse very quickly after removal
from the oven. The base mixture can be
prepared, up to the end of Step 3, well
in advance. Soften the mixture before
folding in the beaten egg whites. Whites
should be folded into the mixture just
before cooking.

classic lasagne

✹ ✹ ✹

Preparation time: 40 minutes
Cooking time: 1 hour 40 minutes
Serves 8

2 tablespoons olive oil
30 g (1 oz) butter
1 large onion, finely chopped
1 carrot, finely chopped
1 celery stalk, finely chopped
500 g (1 lb 2 oz) minced (ground) beef
150 g (5½ oz) chicken livers, trimmed and
   finely chopped
250 ml (9 fl oz/1 cup) tomato passata
   (puréed tomatoes)

250 ml (9 fl oz/1 cup) red wine
2 tablespoons chopped flat-leaf
   (Italian) parsley
375 g (13 oz) fresh lasagne sheets
100 g (3½ oz/1 cup) freshly grated
   parmesan cheese

BÉCHAMEL SAUCE
60 g (2¼ oz) butter
40 g (1½ oz/⅓ cup) plain (all-purpose) flour
560 ml (19¼ fl oz/2¼ cups) milk
½ teaspoon freshly grated nutmeg

1 Heat the oil and butter in a large heavy-based frying pan and cook the onion, carrot and celery over medium heat until softened, stirring constantly. Increase the heat, add the beef and brown well, breaking up any lumps with a fork. Add the chicken livers and cook until they change colour. Add the tomato passata, wine and parsley, and season, to taste. Bring to the boil, then reduce the heat and simmer for 45 minutes. Set aside.

2 To make the béchamel sauce, melt the butter in a saucepan over low heat. Add the flour and stir for 1 minute. Remove from the heat and gradually stir in the milk. Return to the heat and stir constantly until the sauce boils and begins to thicken. Simmer for another minute. Add the nutmeg and season, to taste. Cover the surface with plastic wrap to prevent a skin forming, and set aside.

3 Cut the lasagne sheets to fit into a deep, rectangular ovenproof dish.

4 Preheat oven to 180°C (350°F/Gas 4). Grease the ovenproof dish. Spread a thin layer of meat sauce over the base and follow with a thin layer of béchamel. If the béchamel has cooled and become too thick, warm it gently to make spreading easier. Lay lasagne sheets on top, gently pressing to push out any air. Continue the layers, finishing with béchamel. Sprinkle with the parmesan and bake for 35–40 minutes, or until golden brown. Allow to cool for 15 minutes before cutting.

NOTE: Instant lasagne can be used instead of fresh. Follow the manufacturer's instructions. If you prefer, you can leave out the chicken livers and increase the amount of minced beef by 150 g (5½ oz).

béchamel sauce

Béchamel is known today as a white sauce made by adding milk to a roux, although originally it was produced by adding cream to a thick velouté. The sauce owes its name to a certain Marquis Louis de Béchameil, a rich handsome gourmet who acted as chief steward to Louis XIV. It is unlikely that he created the sauce, but more probable that one of the King's cooks named it in his honour.

cinnamon

The best quality cinnamon comes from the Sri Lankan cinnamon tree, *Cinnamomum zeylanicum*, which has the most wonderfully aromatic scent and a delicate and fresh flavour. It is made from the dried inner bark of young shoots where, once exposed, thin layers curl up into a cylinder as they dry. These are slipped together in rolls of 10, then cut into quills of equal length. It is more costly than Chinese cinnamon, commonly known as cassia, in which older, outer bark is collected for drying. Cinnamon is used whole, broken into pieces or ground to flavour sweet dishes and baked foods, and it is an ingredient of curry powder and garam masala.

macaroni cheese

Preparation time: **20 minutes**
Cooking time: **50 minutes**
Serves **4**

500 ml (17 fl oz/2 cups) milk
250 ml (9 fl oz/1 cup) pouring (whipping) cream
1 bay leaf
1 whole clove
½ cinnamon stick
60 g (2¼ oz) butter
2 tablespoons plain (all-purpose) flour
250 g (9 oz/2 cups) freshly grated cheddar cheese
50 g (1¾ oz/½ cup) freshly grated parmesan cheese
375 g (13 oz) elbow macaroni
80 g (2¾ oz/1 cup) fresh breadcrumbs
2 rindless bacon slices, chopped and fried until crisp

1 Preheat the oven to 180°C (350°F/ Gas 4). Pour the milk and cream into a medium saucepan with the bay leaf, clove and cinnamon stick. Bring to the boil, then remove from the heat and set aside for 10 minutes. Strain into a jug; remove and discard the flavourings.

2 Melt the butter in a medium saucepan over low heat. Add the flour and stir for 1 minute. Remove from the heat and gradually add the milk and cream mixture, stirring until smooth. Return to the heat and stir constantly until the sauce boils and thickens. Simmer for 2 minutes, then remove from the heat and add half the cheddar, half the parmesan and salt and pepper, to taste. Set aside.

3 Cook the macaroni in a large saucepan of rapidly boiling salted water until it is *al dente*. Drain, return to the pan and mix in the sauce. Spoon into a casserole dish. Sprinkle with the combined breadcrumbs, bacon and remaining cheeses. Bake for 15–20 minutes, or until golden. Serve.

NOTE: You can add chopped cooked chicken to the white sauce before mixing with the pasta.

minced chicken

Good minced (ground) chicken will be made of meat from all parts of the chicken. It will have a good proportion of fat and include white and dark meat. Use it soon after it is made as it will spoil more quickly than regular cuts of meat. Avoid buying pre-minced chicken that looks grey and patchy.

conchiglie with chicken and ricotta

✷ ✷

Preparation time: **15 minutes**
Cooking time: **1 hour 10 minutes**
Serves 4

500 g (1 lb 2 oz) conchiglie (shell pasta)
2 tablespoons olive oil
1 onion, chopped
1 garlic clove, crushed
60 g (2¼ oz) prosciutto, chopped
125 g (4½ oz) mushrooms, chopped
250 g (9 oz) minced (ground) chicken
2 tablespoons tomato paste
  (concentrated purée)
400 g (14 oz) tin chopped tomatoes
125 ml (4 fl oz/½ cup) dry white wine
1 teaspoon dried oregano
3 tablespoons freshly grated parmesan
  cheese

250 g (9 oz/1 cup) fresh ricotta cheese
150 g (5½ oz/1 cup) grated mozzarella
  cheese
1 teaspoon snipped chives
1 tablespoon chopped flat-leaf (Italian)
  parsley

1 Cook the conchiglie in a large saucepan of rapidly boiling salted water until it is *al dente*. Drain well.
2 Meanwhile, heat the oil in a large frying pan. Add the onion and garlic and stir over low heat until the onion is tender. Add the prosciutto and stir for 1 minute. Add the mushrooms and cook for 2 minutes. Add the chicken and brown well, breaking it up with a fork as it cooks. Stir in the tomato paste, tomatoes, wine and oregano. Season, to taste. Bring to the boil, then reduce the heat and simmer for 20 minutes.
3 Preheat the oven to 180°C (350°F/ Gas 4). Combine half the parmesan with

the ricotta, mozzarella, chives and parsley. Spoon a little cheese mixture into each shell. Spoon some of the chicken sauce into a casserole dish. Arrange the shells on top and top with the remaining sauce. Sprinkle with the remaining parmesan and bake for 25–30 minutes, until golden.

NOTE: Use medium or large (giant) conchiglie for this dish.

baby spinach, walnut and cheddar salad

Combine baby spinach leaves, toasted walnut halves and shavings of vintage cheddar cheese in a salad bowl. Drizzle with a good-quality French dressing. Serve as a side dish.

baked spaghetti frittata

✹ ✹

Preparation time: **30 minutes**
Cooking time: **35 minutes**
Serves **4**

30 g (1 oz) butter
125 g (4½ oz) mushrooms, thinly sliced
1 green capsicum (pepper), seeded
  and chopped
125 g (4½ oz) ham, sliced
80 g (2¾ oz/½ cup) frozen peas
6 eggs
250 ml (9 fl oz/1 cup) pouring (whipping)
  cream, or milk
100 g (3½ oz) spaghetti, cooked and
  chopped
2 tablespoons chopped flat-leaf (Italian)
  parsley
5 g (¾ oz/¼ cup) freshly grated parmesan
  cheese

1 Preheat the oven to 180°C (350°F/
Gas 4). Lightly brush a 23 cm (9 inch)
flan (tart) tin with oil or melted butter.
2 Melt the butter in a frying pan, add the
mushrooms and cook over low heat for
2–3 minutes. Add the capsicum and cook
for 1 minute. Stir in the ham and peas.
Remove the pan from the heat and allow
the mixture to cool slightly.
3 In a small bowl, whisk the eggs, cream
and salt and pepper. Stir in the spaghetti,
parsley and mushroom mixture and pour
into the prepared dish. Sprinkle with
parmesan and bake for 25–30 minutes.

NOTE: Serve with chargrilled vegetables
and leafy salad greens.

baked cannelloni milanese

✳

Preparation time: 40 minutes
Cooking time: 1 hour 35 minutes
Serves 4

500 g (1 lb 2 oz) minced (ground) pork
    and veal
50 g (1¾ oz/½ cup) dry breadcrumbs
2 eggs, beaten
1 teaspoon dried oregano
100 g (3½ oz/1 cup) freshly grated
    parmesan cheese
12–16 instant cannelloni tubes
375 g (13 oz/1½ cups) fresh ricotta cheese
60 g (2¼ oz/½ cup) freshly grated
    cheddar cheese

TOMATO SAUCE
425 ml (15 fl oz) tomato passata (puréed
    tomatoes)
400 g (14 oz) tin chopped tomatoes
2 garlic cloves, crushed
3 tablespoons chopped basil

1 Preheat the oven to 180°C (350°F/
Gas 4). Lightly grease a rectangular
casserole dish.
2 In a bowl, combine the mince,
breadcrumbs, egg, oregano, half the
parmesan and salt and pepper. Use a
teaspoon to stuff the cannelloni tubes
with the mixture. Set aside.
3 To make the tomato sauce, bring the
tomato passata, tomatoes and garlic to
the boil in a saucepan. Reduce the heat
and simmer for 15 minutes. Add the basil
and pepper, to taste, and stir well.
4 Spoon half the tomato sauce over the
base of the prepared dish. Arrange the
stuffed cannelloni tubes on top. Cover
with the remaining sauce. Spread with
the ricotta cheese. Sprinkle with the
combined remaining parmesan and the
cheddar cheese. Bake, covered with foil,
for 1 hour. Uncover and bake for another
15 minutes, or until golden. Cut into
squares to serve.

tomato passata

Also known as puréed tomatoes, tomato passata
is a pantry staple. Keep a bottle on hand and you
can make myriad pasta sauces at a moment's
notice, adding other stand-bys such as capers,
olives, tuna, herbs and so on. Many passatas have
flavourings added, such as herbs or vegetables,
so experiment with different ones to find those
that you like. You can easily make your own (the
end of summer is a perfect time, when there's
a glut of fresh tomatoes), by blanching, peeling
and passing them through a food mill or sieve.
Discard the seeds and skin as they will give a
bitter taste.

pasta and spinach timbales

100 g (3½ oz) spaghetti or tagliolini, cooked
60 g (2¼ oz/½ cup) grated cheddar cheese
50 g (1¾ oz/½ cup) freshly grated parmesan cheese

1 Preheat the oven to 180°C (350°F/ Gas 4). Brush six 250 ml (9 fl oz/1 cup) dariole moulds or ramekins with melted butter or oil. Line the bases with baking paper. Heat the butter and oil together in a frying pan. Add the onion and stir over low heat until tender. Add the spinach and cook for 1 minute. Remove from the heat and allow to cool. Stir through the eggs and cream. Stir in the pasta, grated cheeses, and salt and pepper, to taste. Spoon into the prepared moulds.
2 Place the moulds in a baking dish. Pour enough boiling water into the baking dish to come halfway up the sides of the moulds. Bake for 30–35 minutes, or until set. Halfway through cooking, you may need to cover the tops with a sheet of foil to prevent excess browning. Near the end of cooking time, test the timbales with the point of a knife. When cooked, the knife should come out clean.
3 Allow to rest for 15 minutes before turning them out of the moulds. Run the point of a knife around the edge of each mould and invert onto serving plates.

rigatoni gratin

✳ ✳

Preparation time: **20 minutes**
Cooking time: **30 minutes**
Serves **4**

375 g (13 oz) rigatoni
60 m (2 fl oz/¼ cup) light olive oil
300 g (10½ oz) slender eggplants (aubergines), chopped
4 small zucchini (courgettes), thickly sliced
1 onion, sliced
400 g (14 oz) tin chopped tomatoes
1 teaspoon chopped oregano
pinch of cayenne pepper

pasta and spinach timbales

✳ ✳

Preparation time: **25 minutes**
Cooking time: **45 minutes**
Serves **6**

30 g (1 oz) butter
1 tablespoon olive oil
1 onion, chopped
500 g (1 lb 2 oz) English spinach, trimmed, steamed and well drained
8 eggs, beaten
250 ml (9 fl oz/1 cup) pouring (whipping) cream

8–10 black olives, pitted and sliced
250 g (9 oz) mozzarella cheese, cut into
   small cubes
2 tablespoons freshly grated parmesan
   cheese

1 Preheat the oven to 180°C (350°F/
Gas 4). Cook the rigatoni in a large
saucepan of rapidly boiling salted water
until *al dente*. Drain the pasta thoroughly
and transfer to an oiled, shallow
ovenproof dish.
2 While the pasta is cooking, heat the oil
in a large frying pan and fry the eggplant,
zucchini and onion for 5 minutes, or until
lightly browned.
3 Add the tomatoes, oregano, cayenne
pepper and olives and simmer gently
for 5 minutes. Pour the vegetable sauce
over the pasta and toss through with
one-third of the mozzarella. Season with
freshly ground black pepper, to taste.
Sprinkle with parmesan and distribute the
remaining mozzarella evenly over the top.
4 Bake for 10 minutes, or until the
cheese has melted and the top is lightly
browned. Serve.

baked creamy
cheesy pasta

※

Preparation time: **15 minutes**
Cooking time: **50 minutes**
Serves **4**

500 g (1 lb 2 oz) fusilli (spiral pasta)
625 ml (21½ fl oz/2½ cups) pouring
   (whipping) cream
3 eggs
250 g (9 oz) feta cheese, crumbled
2 tablespoons plain (all-purpose) flour
2 teaspoons freshly grated nutmeg
125 g (4½ oz/1 cup) grated cheddar
   or mozzarella cheese

1 Cook the fusilli in a large saucepan of
rapidly boiling salted water until *al dente*.
Drain, reserving 250 ml (9 fl oz/1 cup) of
the cooking water. Set the pasta aside.

2 Preheat the oven to 180°C (350°F/
Gas 4) and brush a 1.75 litre (61 fl oz/
7 cup) ovenproof dish with olive oil.
3 Whisk the cream, eggs and reserved
water in a large bowl until thoroughly
combined. Stir in the feta, flour, nutmeg
and salt and freshly ground black pepper,
to taste, until well combined.

4 Transfer the pasta to the prepared dish.
Pour the cream mixture over the top and
sprinkle with the grated cheese. Bake for
30–35 minutes, or until the mixture is just
set and the top is lightly golden.

mozzarella

Most mozzarella made outside Italy today is intended for cooking, to be sprinkled over pizzas and put into lasagnes and baked dishes. It is a matured, sometimes processed cheese with a rubbery texture, but with great melting qualities. When heated, it breaks down completely and becomes smooth and runny, and forms long strands when stretched, much to the delight of children. It is not eaten as a table cheese, unlike fresh mozzarella (bocconcini) which is pure white with a creamy taste and is ideal for salads and antipasto. In Italy, it is sometimes still made from the milk of buffaloes, as it has been for centuries.

meatballs and pasta

✷ ✷

Preparation time: 40 minutes
Cooking time: 1 hour 20 minutes
Serves 4

100 g (3½ oz/⅔ cup) macaroni
500 g (1 lb 2 oz) minced (ground) beef
1 onion, finely chopped
80 g (2¾ oz/1 cup) fresh breadcrumbs
2 tablespoons freshly grated parmesan cheese
1 tablespoon chopped basil
1 egg, beaten
2 tablespoons olive oil
150 g (5½ oz/1 cup) freshly grated mozzarella cheese

SAUCE
1 onion, sliced
1 garlic clove, crushed
1 red capsicum (pepper), seeded and sliced
125 g (4½ oz) mushrooms, sliced
60 g (2 oz/¼ cup) tomato paste (concentrated purée)
125 ml (4 fl oz/½ cup) red wine

1 Cook the macaroni in a large saucepan of rapidly boiling salted water until *al dente*. Drain thoroughly and set aside.
2 Meanwhile, combine the beef, onion, half the breadcrumbs, the parmesan, basil and egg until well mixed. Form heaped teaspoonsful into small balls.
3 Heat the oil in a large frying pan. Add the meatballs and cook until well

browned. Drain on paper towels. Transfer to an ovenproof dish. Preheat the oven to 180°C (350°F/Gas 4).

4 To make the sauce, add the onion and garlic to the same pan and stir over low heat until the onion is tender. Add the capsicum and mushroom and cook for 2 minutes. Stir in the tomato paste, then wine and 250 ml (9 fl oz/1 cup) water. Bring to the boil, stirring continuously. Mix in the macaroni and season, to taste. Pour over the meatballs.

5 Bake, uncovered, for 30–35 minutes. Sprinkle with the combined mozzarella cheese and remaining breadcrumbs. Bake for another 10 minutes, or until golden.

pasta-filled capsicums

✸ ✸

Preparation time: 40 minutes
Cooking time: 1 hour
Serves 6

150 g (5½ oz) risoni
1 tablespoon olive oil
1 onion, finely chopped
1 garlic clove, crushed
3 rindless bacon slices, finely chopped
150 g (5½ oz/1 cup) freshly grated
   mozzarella cheese
50 g (1¾ oz/½ cup) freshly grated
   parmesan cheese
2 tablespoons chopped flat-leaf (Italian)
   parsley
4 large red capsicums (peppers), halved
   lengthways and seeded
400 g (14 oz) tin chopped tomatoes
125 ml (4 fl oz/½ cup) dry white wine
1 tablespoon tomato paste (concentrated
   purée)
½ teaspoon dried oregano
2 tablespoons shredded basil

1 Cook the risoni in a large saucepan of boiling salted water until *al dente*. Drain.
2 Preheat the oven to 180°C (350°F/ Gas 4). Lightly oil a large, shallow ovenproof dish.
3 Heat the oil in a frying pan. Add onion and garlic and stir over low heat until onion is tender. Add the bacon and stir until crisp. Transfer to a bowl and combine with risoni, cheeses and parsley. Spoon the mixture into the capsicum halves and arrange in a single layer in the dish.
4 In a bowl, combine the tomatoes, wine, tomato paste, oregano and salt and pepper, to taste. Spoon over the risoni mixture and bake for 35–40 minutes. Serve sprinkled with the basil.

risoni

Risoni is dried pasta in the shape of rice. It is good in soups and is perfect for stuffing vegetables. Used in stews, it contributes body and substance without bulk and for this reason it is also ideal as an ingredient of stuffing for poultry.

cannelloni

✵ ✵

Preparation time: 45 minutes
Cooking time: 1 hour 10 minutes
Serves 6

12–15 instant cannelloni tubes
150 g (5½ oz/1 cup) freshly grated
    mozzarella cheese
50 g (1¾ oz/½ cup) freshly grated
    parmesan cheese

BEEF AND SPINACH FILLING
1 tablespoon olive oil
1 onion, chopped
1 garlic clove, crushed
500 g (1 lb 2 oz) minced (ground) beef
250 g (9 oz) packet frozen spinach,
    thawed
3 tablespoons tomato paste (concentrated
    purée)
125 g (4½ oz/½ cup) fresh ricotta cheese
1 egg
½ teaspoon dried oregano

BÉCHAMEL SAUCE
250 ml (9 fl oz/1 cup) milk
1 parsley sprig
5 black peppercorns
30 g (1 oz) butter
1 tablespoon plain (all-purpose) flour
125 ml (4 fl oz/½ cup) pouring (whipping)
    cream

TOMATO SAUCE
425 ml (15 fl oz) tomato passata (puréed
    tomatoes)
2 tablespoons chopped basil
1 garlic clove, crushed
½ teaspoon sugar

1 Preheat the oven to 180°C (350°F/
Gas 4). Lightly oil a large shallow
ovenproof dish. Set aside.
2 To make the beef and spinach filling,
heat the oil in a frying pan, add the onion
and garlic and stir over low heat until the
onion is tender. Add the beef and brown
well, breaking up with a fork as it cooks.
Add the spinach and tomato paste. Stir
for 1 minute and then remove from the
heat. In a small bowl, mix the ricotta, egg,
oregano and salt and pepper, to taste.
Stir the mixture through the beef until
combined. Set aside.
3 To make the béchamel sauce, combine
the milk, parsley and peppercorns in
a small saucepan. Bring to the boil.
Remove from the heat and allow to stand
for 10 minutes. Strain, discarding the
flavourings. Melt the butter in another
small saucepan, add the flour and stir for
1 minute, or until smooth. Remove from
the heat and gradually stir in the milk.
Return to the heat and stir constantly
over medium heat until the sauce boils
and begins to thicken. Reduce the heat,
simmer for another minute, then stir in
the cream and salt and pepper, to taste.
4 To make the tomato sauce, stir all the
ingredients in a saucepan until combined.
Bring to the boil, then reduce the heat
and simmer for 5 minutes. Season with
salt and pepper, to taste.
5 Spoon the beef and spinach filling into
a piping (icing) bag and fill the cannelloni
tubes or fill using a teaspoon.

garlic

How garlic is prepared depends
upon the degree of flavour
required for the intended
dish. If the cloves are finely
chopped or mashed, they will
be the most intense as more
oils are released this way. For
a mild taste without garlicky

undertones, the cloves are used
whole, often unpeeled, and
then discarded before the dish
is eaten. A stronger flavour
without pungency comes from
cloves that are peeled and
halved. Roasted garlic has a
sweeter, more mellow flavour.

6 Spoon a little tomato sauce in the base of the dish. Arrange the cannelloni on top. Pour the béchamel sauce over the cannelloni, followed by the remaining tomato sauce. Sprinkle the combined cheeses over the top. Bake, uncovered, for 35–40 minutes, or until golden.

NOTE: Serve with a mixed green salad or steamed vegetables, such as broccoli or green beans, if desired.

italian omelette

Preparation time: 20 minutes
Cooking time: 15 minutes
Serves 4

2 tablespoons olive oil
1 onion, finely chopped
125 g (4½ oz) ham, sliced
6 eggs
60 ml (2 fl oz/¼ cup) milk
150 g (5½ oz) fusilli (spiral pasta), cooked
    and drained
3 tablespoons freshly grated parmesan
    cheese
2 tablespoons chopped parsley
1 tablespoon chopped basil
60 g (2¼ oz/½ cup) freshly grated cheddar
    cheese

1 Heat half the oil in a frying pan. Cook the onion over low heat until softened. Add the ham to the pan and stir for 1 minute. Transfer to a plate and set aside.
2 In a bowl, whisk the eggs, milk and salt and pepper, to taste. Stir in the pasta, parmesan, herbs and onion mixture.
3 Heat the remaining oil in the same pan. Pour the egg mixture into the pan and sprinkle with the cheddar cheese. Cook over medium heat until the mixture begins to set around the edges. Place under a hot grill (broiler) to complete the cooking. Cut into wedges and serve with a crisp green or mixed salad, if desired.

pasticcio

Preparation time: 1 hour
Cooking time: 1 hour 50 minutes
Serves 6

250 g (9 oz/2 cups) plain (all-purpose) flour
125 g (4½ oz) butter, chilled and chopped
55 g (2 oz/¼ cup) caster (superfine) sugar
1 egg yolk
150 g (5½ oz) bucatini or penne

FILLING
2 tablespoons olive oil
1 onion, chopped
2 garlic cloves, finely chopped
500 g (1 lb 2 oz) minced (ground) beef
150 g (5½ oz) chicken livers, trimmed
    and chopped
2 tomatoes, chopped
125 ml (4 fl oz/½ cup) red wine
125 ml (4 fl oz/½ cup) rich beef stock
1 tablespoon chopped oregano
¼ teaspoon freshly grated nutmeg
50 g (1¾ oz/½ cup) freshly grated
    parmesan cheese

BÉCHAMEL SAUCE
60 g (2¼ oz) butter
2 tablespoons plain (all-purpose) flour
375 ml (13 fl oz/1½ cups) milk

1   Put the flour, butter, sugar and egg
yolk in a food processor with 1 tablespoon
water. Process lightly until the mixture
forms a ball, adding more water if
necessary. Lightly knead the dough on
a floured surface until smooth. Wrap in
plastic wrap and refrigerate.
2   To make the filling, heat the oil in
a heavy-based saucepan and cook the
onion and garlic until softened and lightly
golden. Increase the heat, add the beef
and cook until browned, breaking up any
lumps with a fork. Add the livers, tomato,
wine, stock, oregano and nutmeg, then
season well. Bring to the boil over high
heat, then reduce the heat and simmer,
covered, for 40 minutes. Allow to cool
and then stir in the parmesan.
3   To make the béchamel sauce, heat

the butter in a saucepan over low heat.
Add the flour and stir for 1 minute, or
until the mixture is golden and smooth.
Remove from the heat and gradually stir
in the milk. Return to the heat and stir
constantly until the sauce boils and begins
to thicken. Simmer for another minute.
Season, to taste.
4   Cook the pasta in a saucepan of rapidly
boiling salted water until it is *al dente*.
Drain and cool.
5   Preheat the oven to 160°C (315°F/
Gas 2–3). Lightly grease a 23 cm (9 inch)

deep pie dish. Divide the dough into two
portions and roll out one piece to fit the
base of the dish, overlapping the sides.
Spoon half of the filling into the dish, top
with the bucatini and then slowly spoon
the béchamel sauce over the top, allowing
it to seep down and coat the bucatini.
Spoon the remaining filling over the top.
Roll out the remaining dough and cover
the pie. Trim the edges and pinch lightly to
seal. Bake for 50–55 minutes, or until the
pastry is dark golden brown and crisp. Set
aside for 15 minutes before cutting.

pastitsio

✳ ✳

Preparation time: 1 hour
Cooking time: 1 hour 40 minutes
Serves 8

2 tablespoons olive oil
4 garlic cloves, crushed
3 onions, chopped
1 kg (2 lb 4 oz) minced (ground) lamb
800 g (1 lb 12 oz) tin chopped tomatoes
250 ml (9 fl oz/1 cup) red wine
250 ml (9 fl oz/1 cup) chicken stock
3 tablespoons tomato paste (concentrated purée)
2 tablespoons oregano leaves
2 bay leaves
350 g (12 oz) ziti
2 eggs, lightly beaten
750 g (1 lb 10 oz/3 cups) Greek-style yoghurt
3 eggs, extra, lightly beaten
200 g (7 oz) kefalotyri or manchego cheese, grated
½ teaspoon freshly grated nutmeg
50 g (1¾ oz/½ cup) freshly grated parmesan cheese
80 g (2¾ oz/1 cup) fresh breadcrumbs

1 Preheat the oven to 200°C (400°F/Gas 6). Heat the olive oil in a large heavy-based saucepan and cook the garlic and onion over low heat for 10 minutes, or until the onion is soft and golden.
2 Add the lamb and cook over high heat until browned, stirring constantly and breaking up any lumps. Add the tomatoes, wine, stock, tomato paste, oregano and bay leaves. Bring to the boil, then reduce the heat and simmer, covered, for 15 minutes. Remove the lid and cook for 30 minutes. Season with salt and pepper.
3 While the meat is cooking, cook the ziti in a large saucepan of rapidly boiling salted water until *al dente*. Drain well. Transfer to a bowl and stir the eggs through. Spoon into a lightly greased 4 litre (140 fl oz/16 cup) ovenproof dish. Top with the meat sauce.
4 Place the yoghurt, extra eggs, cheese and nutmeg in a bowl and whisk to

pasticcio and pastitsio

It is easy to be confused by the terms pasticcio and pastitsio (pastizio, or pastetseo). In Italian cooking, pasticcio is a generic term used to describe a pie in which the composite parts such as meat, pasta and vegetables are baked in layers. Lasagne is, in fact, one type of pasticcio, and some have a pastry crust. Pasticcio is made for special occasions and can be plain and simple, or quite elaborate in its composition and the ingredients used. It is eaten as a main course and is traditionally served unaccompanied, with a salad or vegetable course following. Pastitsio is the Greek version, and the two are often so similar that it's hard to tell from the recipe which country the cook hails from. Pastitsio is likely to be made with lamb instead of beef, and often favourite Greek ingredients such as olives and Greek-style yoghurt will feature.

combine. Pour the yoghurt mixture evenly over the meat sauce. Sprinkle evenly with the combined parmesan and breadcrumbs. Bake for 30–35 minutes, or until the top is crisp and golden brown. Allow the pastitsio to stand for 20 minutes before serving. Serve with a mixed green salad, if desired.

NOTE: Kefalotyri and manchego are firm, grating cheeses. You can substitute parmesan if they are unavailable.

butternut pumpkin

Butternut pumpkins or squash are well named, for they have a sweet, buttery and slightly nutty taste. When young, they should be evenly firm, with no cracks or blemishes on the skin. The flesh inside will be crisp, with a good bright colour and a low water content.

butternut pumpkin filled with pasta and leeks

✳ ✳

Preparation time: 30 minutes
Cooking time: 1 hour 15 minutes
Serves 2 as a light meal, or 4 as an
  accompaniment

1 medium butternut pumpkin
  (squash)

20 g (¾ oz) butter
1 leek, thinly sliced
125 ml (4 fl oz/½ cup) pouring (whipping)
  cream
pinch of freshly grated nutmeg
60 g (2¼ oz) cooked linguine or stellini
60 ml (2 fl oz/¼ cup) olive oil

1 Preheat the oven to 180°C (350°F/ Gas 4). Cut off the top quarter of the pumpkin (where the stalk attaches) to make a lid. Level off the other end so that it stands evenly. Scrape out the seeds and sinew from the pumpkin and discard. Hollow out the centre to make room for the filling. Sprinkle salt and pepper over the cut surfaces and then stand the pumpkin in a small greased baking dish.

2 Melt the butter in a small frying pan and gently cook the leek until softened. Add the cream and nutmeg and cook over low heat for 4–5 minutes, or until thickened. Season with salt and pepper, to taste, and stir in the pasta.

3 Fill the butternut pumpkin with the pasta mixture, place the lid on top and drizzle with the olive oil. Bake for 1 hour, or until tender. Test by inserting a skewer into the thickest part of the pumpkin.

NOTE: Choose a butternut that is round and fat, not one with a long stem of flesh.

chicken, veal and mushroom loaf

✹ ✹

Preparation time: **20 minutes**
Cooking time: **1 hour 15 minutes**
Serves **6**

100 g (3½ oz) pappardelle
20 g (¾ oz/¼ cup) fresh breadcrumbs
1 tablespoon dry white wine
375 g (13 oz) minced (ground) chicken
375 g (13 oz) minced (ground) veal
2 garlic cloves, crushed
100 g (3½ oz) button mushrooms,
    finely chopped
2 eggs, lightly beaten
pinch of freshly grated nutmeg
pinch of cayenne pepper
60 g (2¼ oz/¼ cup) sour cream
4 spring onions (scallions), finely chopped
2 tablespoons chopped flat-leaf (Italian)
    parsley

1 Grease a 1.5 litre (52 fl oz/6 cup) loaf (bar) tin. Cook the pappardelle in a large saucepan of rapidly boiling salted water until *al dente*. Drain.

2 Preheat the oven to 200°C (400°F/ Gas 6). Soak the breadcrumbs in the wine. Mix the soaked crumbs in a bowl with the chicken, veal, garlic, mushroom, egg, nutmeg and cayenne, and season with salt and pepper. Mix in the sour cream, spring onion and parsley.

3 Press half the chicken mixture into the prepared tin with your hands.

4 Form a deep trough along the length of the chicken mixture and fill it with pasta.

Press the remaining chicken mixture over the top. Bake for 50–60 minutes, draining the excess fat and juice from the tin twice during cooking. Cool slightly, then slice.

NOTE: The mushrooms can be chopped in a food processor, but don't prepare them too far in advance or they will discolour and darken the loaf.

giant conchiglie with ricotta and rocket

Preparation time: 50 minutes
Cooking time: 1 hour
Serves 6

40 giant conchiglie (shell pasta)
600 ml (21 fl oz) bottled tomato pasta sauce

2 tablespoons oregano leaves, chopped
2 tablespoons basil leaves

FILLING
185 g (6½ oz) marinated artichokes
500 g (1 lb 2 oz/12 cups) fresh ricotta
  cheese
100 g (3½ oz/1 cup) freshly grated
  parmesan cheese
150 g (5½ oz) rocket (arugula),
  finely shredded

80 g (2¾ oz) sun-dried tomatoes, finely
  chopped
95 g (3¼ oz) sun-dried capsicum (pepper),
  finely chopped
1 egg, lightly beaten

CHEESE SAUCE
60 g (2¼ oz) butter
30 g (1 oz/¼ cup) plain (all-purpose)
  flour
750 ml (26 fl oz/3 cups) milk
100 g (3½ oz) gruyère cheese,
  grated
2 tablespoons chopped basil

1 Cook the conchiglie in a large saucepan of rapidly boiling salted water until *al dente*. Drain and arrange the shells in a single layer on two non-stick baking trays to prevent them sticking together. Cover lightly with plastic wrap.

2 To make the filling, finely chop the artichokes. Combine with the remaining ingredients in a large bowl. Spoon the filling into the shells, taking care not to overfill them or they will split.

3 To make the cheese sauce, melt the butter in a small saucepan over low heat. Add the flour and stir for 1 minute, or until golden and smooth. Remove from the heat and gradually stir in the milk. Return to the heat and stir constantly until the sauce boils and begins to thicken. Simmer for a further minute. Remove from the heat and stir in the gruyère cheese and basil. Season, to taste.

4 Preheat the oven to 180°C (350°F/ Gas 4). Spread 250 ml (9 fl oz/1 cup) of the cheese sauce over the base of a 3 litre (105 fl oz/12 cup) ovenproof dish. Arrange the filled conchiglie in the dish, top with the remaining sauce and bake for 30 minutes, or until the sauce is golden.

5 Pour the bottled pasta sauce into a saucepan and add the oregano. Cook over medium heat for 5 minutes, or until heated through. To serve, divide the sauce among the warmed serving plates, top with the filled conchiglie and sprinkle with the basil leaves.

green olive paste

When the pulp of green olives is mixed with olive oil, salt and herbs, the resulting purée is known as green olive paste or pâté. As is, it makes an excellent dip or spread for bread and it can be used to dress pasta and vegetables. Stirred through soups and sauces, it adds flavour and colour, and it is delicious rubbed into the skin of poultry.

pasta with green olive paste and three cheeses

Preparation time: 10 minutes
Cooking time: 35 minutes
Serves 4

400 g (14 oz) mafalda (mini lasagne) or pappardelle
2 tablespoons olive oil
2 garlic cloves, crushed
125 g (4 oz/½ cup) green olive paste
80 ml (2½ fl oz/⅓ cup) pouring (whipping) cream
50 g (1¾ oz/½ cup) freshly grated parmesan cheese
60 g (2¼ oz/½ cup) grated cheddar cheese
50 g (1¾ oz/½ cup) grated jarlsberg cheese

1 Preheat the oven to 200°C (400°F/ Gas 6). Lightly brush a deep ovenproof dish with oil. Cook the pasta in a large saucepan of rapidly boiling salted water until *al dente*. Drain and return to the pan.
2 Toss the olive oil, garlic and green olive paste through the pasta and then mix in the cream. Season with ground black pepper. Transfer to the prepared dish.
3 Sprinkle with the cheeses and bake, uncovered, for 20 minutes, or until the top is crisp and the cheeses have melted.

pasta pronto

Forget packet meals and take-aways: pasta is the ultimate convenience food. All of these dishes can be ready in around 30 minutes, some of them so fast they are on the table before the family's had time to sit down. Who knows when friends might call in unexpectedly? A good hoard of dried pasta is the key to quick, fuss-free meals and should be part of every well-stocked pantry. Was that the doorbell? Start grating the parmesan cheese.

linguine with anchovies, olives and capers

Ready to eat in **30 minutes**
Serves 4

500 g (1 lb 2 oz) linguine
2 tablespoons olive oil
2 garlic cloves, crushed
2 very ripe tomatoes, peeled and chopped
3 tablespoons capers, rinsed
75 g (2½ oz/½ cup) pitted black olives,
    finely chopped
55 g (2 oz/¼ cup) pitted green olives,
    finely chopped
60 ml (2 fl oz/¼ cup) dry white wine
3 tablespoons chopped parsley or basil
90 g (3¼ oz) tin anchovies, drained and
    chopped

1 Cook the linguine in a large saucepan of rapidly boiling salted water until *al dente*. Drain and return to the pan.
2 While the pasta is cooking, heat the oil in a large frying pan. Add the garlic and stir over low heat for 1 minute. Add the tomato, capers and olives and cook for 2 minutes, stirring often.
3 Stir in the wine, parsley or basil, and freshly ground black pepper, to taste. Bring to the boil, then reduce the heat and simmer for about 5 minutes. Remove from the heat. Add the anchovies and stir gently to combine.
4 Add the sauce to the warm pasta and toss well to distribute the sauce evenly.

NOTE: For a variation or on special occasions, you may like to serve this dish with the following topping. Heat a little olive oil in a small saucepan, add some fresh white breadcrumbs and a crushed garlic clove. Toss over the heat until crisp and golden and sprinkle over the top with freshly grated parmesan cheese.

green olives

As the name suggests, green olives are the unripe fruit of the olive tree. When olives begin forming they contain no oil, just sugars and organic acids and it is these that give green olives their tangy flavour. As olives mature, they change from pale green through to bright green, rose, deep purple and black, and the oil content increases. The flesh goes from being hard and crisp, to soft and slightly spongy. For these reasons, green olives need to be treated differently from black olives to become edible, and it also helps explain why there is such a contrast in flavour and texture between them.

pasta with fragrant lime and smoked trout

Ready to eat in **30 minutes**
Serves **4**

500 g (1 lb 2 oz) spinach and plain linguine
1 tablespoon extra virgin olive oil
3 garlic cloves, crushed
1 tablespoon finely grated lime zest
2 tablespoons poppy seeds
250 g (9 oz) smoked trout, skin and
 bones removed
400 g (14 oz) camembert cheese,
 chopped
2 tablespoons chopped dill
lime wedges, to serve

1 Cook the linguine in a large saucepan of rapidly boiling salted water until *al dente*. Drain and return to the pan.
2 Heat the oil in a large, heavy-based frying pan. Add the garlic and cook over low heat for 3 minutes or until aromatic. Add the lime zest and poppy seeds to the pan and toss to coat.
3 Fold the trout, camembert and dill through the mixture and cook over low heat until the camembert begins to melt. Toss gently through the pasta and serve immediately with a squeeze of lime.

fettuccine with spinach and prosciutto

Ready to eat in **20 minutes**
Serves **4–6**

500 g (1 lb 2 oz) spinach or plain
 fettuccine
2 tablespoons olive oil
8 thin prosciutto slices, chopped
3 spring onions (scallions), chopped
500 g (1 lb 2 oz) English spinach
1 tablespoon balsamic vinegar

½ teaspoon caster (superfine) sugar
50 g (1¾ oz/½ cup) freshly grated
 parmesan cheese

1 Cook the pasta in a large saucepan of rapidly boiling salted water until just *al dente*. Drain and return to the pan.
2 Meanwhile, heat the oil in a large saucepan. Add the prosciutto and spring onion and cook, stirring occasionally, over medium heat for 5 minutes or until crisp.
3 Trim the stalks from the spinach, roughly chop the leaves and add them to the pan. Stir in the vinegar and sugar, cover and cook for 1 minute or until the spinach has softened. Season, to taste.
4 Add the sauce to the pasta and toss well to distribute the sauce evenly. Sprinkle with the grated parmesan and serve immediately.

fettuccine with spinach and prosciutto

limes

The lime is a tropical citrus tree. The fruit are small and a distinctive yellowish-green. They are almost perfectly rounded with a thin skin. The taste is pleasantly sharp, with tropical overtones. Slices of the unpeeled fruit make an attractive garnish, while the juice and zest are used to enhance both sweet and savoury dishes. Lime juice works well as a curing agent and is particularly effective on fresh seafood.

chicken ravioli with lime balsamic dressing

Ready to eat in **30 minutes**
Serves **4**

250 g (9 oz) minced (ground) chicken
1 egg, lightly beaten
1 teaspoon finely grated orange zest
50 g/1¾ oz/½ cup) freshly grated
   parmesan cheese

1 tablespoon finely shredded basil
275 g (9¾ oz) won ton wrappers
2 tablespoons lime juice
2 tablespoons balsamic vinegar
½ teaspoon honey
1 tablespoon olive oil
finely snipped chives, to garnish

1 Combine the chicken, egg, orange zest, parmesan and basil in a bowl. Place a heaped tablespoon of chicken mixture in the centre of a won ton wrapper, lightly brush the edges with water and top with another wrapper. Press the edges

firmly together to seal. Repeat with the remaining filling and wrappers. (This is a quick way to make ravioli.)

2 Cook the ravioli in a large saucepan of rapidly boiling salted water for 5 minutes.

3 Meanwhile, combine the lime juice, vinegar, honey and oil in a small bowl and whisk to combine. Drain the ravioli and serve drizzled with the dressing and sprinkled with the chives.

ziti with roasted tomatoes and ovolini

☀

Ready to eat in **30 minutes**
Serves **4**

200 g (7 oz) yellow teardrop tomatoes
200 g (7 oz) red cherry tomatoes
500 g (1 lb 2 oz) ziti
200 g (7 oz) ovolini cheese (see Note)
100 g (3½ oz) capers
3 tablespoons marjoram leaves
3 tablespoons lemon thyme leaves
2 tablespoons extra virgin olive oil
3 tablespoons balsamic vinegar

1 Preheat the oven to 200°C (400°F/ Gas 6). Cut all the tomatoes in half and bake, cut side up, for 15 minutes.

2 Meanwhile, cook the ziti in a large saucepan of rapidly boiling salted water until *al dente*. Drain and return to the pan.

3 Add the tomatoes and remaining ingredients to the drained pasta and toss thoroughly. Serve immediately.

NOTE: Ovolini is a type of small fresh cheese available from speciality stores and some supermarkets. Use bocconcini cut into small pieces, if ovolini is unavailable. You can use smaller quantities of herbs if you prefer.

herb salad

Combine basil leaves, rocket (arugula), flat-leaf (Italian) parsley leaves, coriander (cilantro) leaves and baby spinach leaves in a bowl. Drizzle with a dressing made of crushed garlic, lemon juice, honey and olive oil. Toss well and serve immediately with loads of freshly cracked black pepper. Serve as a side dish.

mixed tomato salad

Combine cherry, teardrop and sliced plum (roma) tomatoes in a bowl with chopped red onion and loads of finely shredded basil. Toss in a little red wine vinegar and olive oil. Serve as a side dish.

penne with rocket

penne with rocket

Ready to eat in **20 minutes**
Serves **4**

500 g (1 lb 2 oz) penne
100 g (3½ oz) butter
200 g (7 oz) rocket (arugula), roughly
   chopped
3 tomatoes, finely chopped
45 g (1½ oz/½ cup) freshly grated
   pecorino cheese
shavings of parmesan cheese,
   to serve

1 Cook the penne in a large saucepan of
rapidly boiling salted water until *al dente*.
Drain and return to the pan. Place over
low heat and add the butter, tossing it
through until it melts and coats the pasta.
2 Add the rocket and tomato to the
pasta. Toss through to wilt the rocket.
Stir in the pecorino and season, to taste.
Serve topped with the parmesan.

farfalle with peas

Ready to eat in **20 minutes**
Serves **4**

500 g (1 lb 2 oz) farfalle
235 g (8½ oz/1½ cups) frozen baby peas
8 thin pancetta slices, chopped
60 g (2¼ oz) butter
2 tablespoons each shredded basil and mint

1 Cook the farfalle in a large saucepan of
rapidly boiling salted water until *al dente*.
Drain and return to the pan.
2 While the pasta is cooking, steam,
microwave or boil the peas until just
tender; drain. Melt the butter in a
saucepan and cook the pancetta over
medium heat for 2 minutes. Toss the
butter and pancetta through the pasta
with the peas, basil and mint. Season
with cracked black pepper and serve.

tomato, egg and olive salad

Thickly slice 6 ripe tomatoes and arrange on a large serving platter. Top with
1 thinly sliced red onion, 6 peeled and sliced hard-boiled eggs, 90 g (3¼ oz/
½ cup) marinated black olives and scatter a few torn basil leaves over the top.
Drizzle with extra virgin olive oil and sprinkle generously with sea salt and
freshly cracked black pepper. Serve as a side dish.

penne and pistachio pesto

Ready to eat in **20 minutes**
Serves **4**

500 g (1 lb 2 oz) penne
125 g (4½ oz) unsalted pistachio nuts
4 garlic cloves
1 tablespoon green peppercorns
2 tablespoons lemon juice
150 g (5½ oz) pitted black olives
150 g (5½ oz/1½ cups) freshly grated
   parmesan cheese
125 ml (4 fl oz/½ cup) light olive oil
sprigs of parsley, to garnish

1 Cook the penne in a large saucepan of rapidly boiling salted water until *al dente*. Drain and return to the pan.
2 Meanwhile, combine the pistachios, garlic, peppercorns, lemon juice, olives and grated parmesan in a food processor for 30 seconds, or until roughly chopped.
3 With the motor running, gradually pour in the olive oil in a thin stream. Blend until the mixture is smooth. Toss the pesto through the hot pasta and serve garnished with parsley.

red wine

Where a richer, more mellow taste is called for in a dish, red wine is used. Its earthy, robust flavours make it a good companion to red meats and game and the colour makes it better suited to tomato-based sauces and gravies. The red wine best suited for cooking is young, full-bodied and well balanced, one that would be enjoyed as a table wine. When used with dairy produce, such as in a cream sauce, port or other sweet, fortified wines are preferable.

spaghetti with rich beef and mushroom sauce

Ready to eat in **30 minutes**
Serves **6**

1 tablespoon light olive oil
1 large onion, finely chopped
2 garlic cloves, crushed
500 g (1 lb 2 oz) minced (ground) lean beef

350 g (12 oz) button mushrooms, halved
1 tablespoon mixed dried herbs
½ teaspoon paprika
800 g (1 lb 12 oz) tin chopped tomatoes
125 g (4½ oz/½ cup) tomato paste (concentrated purée)
125 ml (4 fl oz/½ cup) dry red wine
125 ml (4 fl oz/½ cup) beef stock
500 g (1 lb 2 oz) spaghetti
freshly grated parmesan cheese, to serve

1 Heat the oil in a large, deep saucepan. Add the onion, garlic and beef and cook for 5 minutes, using a fork to break up any lumps. Add the mushroom, herbs, paprika and cracked black pepper. Reduce the heat to low and stir in the tomatoes, tomato paste, wine and stock. Cover and simmer for 15 minutes.

2 While the sauce is cooking, cook the spaghetti in a large saucepan of rapidly boiling salted water until *al dente*. Drain. Spoon the sauce over the spaghetti and serve with the parmesan to sprinkle over.

penne with roasted capsicum

✳

Ready to eat in **30 minutes**
Serves **4**

1 red capsicum (pepper)
1 green capsicum (pepper)
1 yellow or orange capsicum (pepper)
1 tablespoon olive oil
2 garlic cloves, crushed
6 anchovy fillets, finely chopped
1 teaspoon cracked black pepper
80 ml (2½ fl oz/⅓ cup) dry white wine

250 ml (9 fl oz/1 cup) vegetable stock
2 tablespoons tomato paste (concentrated purée)
500 g (1 lb 2 oz) penne
1 tablespoon chopped flat-leaf (Italian) parsley

1 Cut the capsicums into large flat pieces and discard the seeds and membrane. Grill (broil), skin side up, for 8 minutes, or until the skin is black and blistered. Transfer to a plastic bag to cool. Peel the skin away and cut into long, thin strips.
2 Heat the oil in a large saucepan, add the garlic and anchovy and cook over low heat for 2–3 minutes. Add the capsicum, seasoned pepper and wine. Bring to the boil, then reduce the heat and simmer for 5 minutes. Stir in the stock and tomato paste and simmer for 10 minutes.
3 While the sauce is cooking, cook the penne in a large saucepan of rapidly boiling water until *al dente*. Drain, add to the capsicum sauce and toss until well combined. Stir in the parsley and serve immediately with crusty Italian bread.

NOTE: If you can't find yellow capsicums, use an extra red one, as they are sweeter than the green.

the difference between capsicums

Red, yellow, green and purple capsicums belong to the same capsicum (pepper) family but have different characteristics. Colour is the most obvious, but texture, flavour and digestive properties also vary. Red capsicums have a sweeter flavour and softer flesh, properties that change when subjected to heat. This makes them the best for roasting or grilling. Gold and yellow come next, with green and purple capsicums chosen where a crisp flesh and clean taste are required, such as for use in salads and stir-fries.

spaghettini with garlic and chilli

Ready to eat in **20 minutes**
Serves 4–6

500 g (1 lb 2 oz) spaghettini or spaghetti
125 ml (4 fl oz/½ cup) extra virgin olive oil
2–3 garlic cloves, finely chopped
1–2 fresh red chillies, seeded and finely chopped
3 tablespoons chopped flat-leaf (Italian) parsley
freshly grated parmesan cheese, to serve

1 Cook the spaghettini in a large saucepan of rapidly boiling salted water until *al dente*. Drain and return to the pan.
2 Meanwhile, heat the oil in a large frying pan. Add the garlic and chilli, and cook over very low heat for 2–3 minutes, or until the garlic is golden. Take care not to burn the garlic or chilli as this will make the sauce bitter.
3 Toss the parsley and warmed oil, garlic and chilli mixture through the pasta. Season with salt and pepper, to taste. Serve sprinkled with parmesan.

fusilli with sage and garlic

Ready to eat in **20 minutes**
Serves 4

500 g (1 lb 2 oz) fusilli (spiral pasta)
60 g (2¼ oz) butter
2 garlic cloves, crushed
10 g (¼ oz/½ cup) sage leaves
2 tablespoons pouring (whipping) cream
freshly grated parmesan cheese, to serve

1 Cook the fusilli in a large saucepan of rapidly boiling salted water until *al dente*. Drain and return to the pan.
2 Meanwhile, melt the butter in a frying pan. Add the garlic and sage, and cook over low heat for 4 minutes, stirring often.
3 Stir in the cream and season with salt and freshly ground black pepper. Stir the sauce through the pasta until thoroughly coated. Serve sprinkled with parmesan.

spaghettini with garlic and chilli

bacon

Bacon is meat from the side and back of a pig. It is cured by dry-salting and then smoked to give a distinctive taste. Bacon is usually sold in thin slices called rashers. The middle cut — sometimes called the prime cut — contains the least fat and most meat. Streaky bacon is cut from the tail end of the loin and is streaked with more fat.

ruote with lemon, olives and bacon

Ready to eat in **25 minutes**
Serves 4

500 g (1 lb 2 oz) ruote (see Note)
6 bacon slices
125 g (4½ oz/1 cup) black olives, pitted and sliced
80 ml (2½ fl oz/⅓ cup) lemon juice
2 teaspoons finely grated lemon zest
80 ml (2½ fl oz/⅓ cup) olive oil
4 tablespoons chopped flat-leaf (Italian) parsley

1 Cook the ruote in a large saucepan of rapidly boiling salted water until *al dente*. Drain and return to the pan.

2 While the pasta is cooking, discard the bacon rind and cut the bacon into thin strips. Cook in a frying pan until lightly browned and crisp.

3 In a bowl, combine the olives, lemon juice, lemon zest, olive oil, parsley and bacon. Gently toss the olive and bacon mixture through the pasta until it is evenly distributed. Sprinkle with freshly ground black pepper, to taste.

NOTE: Ruote is a pasta resembling wagon wheels. Small chunks of sauce become trapped between the spokes.

parsley

Curly-leaf and flat-leaf (Italian) parsley are commonly used in everyday cooking. Parsley adds flavour as well as colour to a dish, is equally at home fresh or cooked, and is ideal as a garnish for savoury foods. If you don't grow your own, buy parsley with unwilted leaves and firm stems. For storage, immerse the stalks in cold water for up to a week, or put the parsley in the vegetable section of the refrigerator, wrapped in paper towels. Parsley is a rich source of iron as well as vitamins A, B and C.

spaghetti puttanesca

Ready to eat in **30 minutes**
Serves 6

80 ml (2½ fl oz/⅓ cup) olive oil
2 onions, finely chopped
3 garlic cloves, finely chopped
½ teaspoon chilli flakes
6 large ripe tomatoes, diced
4 tablespoons capers, rinsed

8 anchovy fillets in oil, drained and chopped
150 g (5½ oz) kalamata olives
3 tablespoons chopped flat-leaf (Italian) parsley
375 g (13 oz) spaghetti

1 Heat the olive oil in a saucepan, add the onion and cook over medium heat for 5 minutes. Add the garlic and chilli flakes and cook for 30 seconds. Add the tomato, capers and anchovy. Simmer over low heat for 10–15 minutes, or until the sauce is thick and pulpy. Stir the olives and parsley through the sauce.

2 While the sauce is cooking, cook the spaghetti in a large saucepan of rapidly boiling salted water until *al dente*. Drain and return to the pan.

3 Stir the sauce through the pasta, season, to taste, and serve immediately.

spaghetti with peas and onions

Ready to eat in **25 minutes**
Serves 4–6

500 g (1 lb 2 oz) spaghetti or vermicelli
1 kg (2 lb 4 oz) baby onions
1 tablespoon olive oil
4 bacon slices, chopped
2 teaspoons plain (all-purpose) flour
250 ml (9 fl oz/1 cup) chicken stock
125 ml (4 fl oz/½ cup) white wine
155 g (5½ oz/1 cup) shelled fresh peas

1 Cook the pasta in a large saucepan of rapidly boiling salted water until *al dente*. Drain and return to the pan.

2 While the pasta is cooking, trim the outer skins and ends from the onions, leaving only a small section of the green stem attached.

3 Heat the oil in a large heavy-based saucepan. Add the bacon and onions and stir over low heat for 4 minutes or until golden. Sprinkle the flour lightly over the top and stir for 1 minute.

4 Add the combined stock and wine and stir until the mixture boils and thickens slightly. Add the peas and cook for 5 minutes or until the onions are tender. Season with freshly ground black pepper, to taste. Add the mixture to the pasta and toss gently to combine. Garnish with fresh herbs, such as basil, if you like.

baby onions

Also known as salad, pearl or bulb spring onions, these have a small white onion bulb at the end of a long green stem. They do not need to be peeled, only the stem and ends trimmed before cooking. They have a milder onion taste than mature onions and are slightly sweet. You can use the bulb and also the green stems in cooked savoury dishes or salads, either raw or cooked. Choose baby onions with firm green stems with no black or yellow tinges, and pure-white bulbs. Remove rubber bands or string, then wrap in paper towels and store in a sealed plastic bag in the refrigerator.

spicy sausage and fennel rigatoni

Ready to eat in **25 minutes**
Serves **4–6**

500 g (1 lb 2 oz) rigatoni
30 g (1 oz) butter
1 tablespoon olive oil
500 g (1 lb 2 oz) chorizo sausage, thickly
   sliced on the diagonal
1 fennel bulb, thinly sliced
2 garlic cloves, crushed
80 ml (2½ fl oz/⅓ cup) lime juice
400 g (14 oz) tin red pimientos,
   thickly sliced
100 g (3½ oz) rocket (arugula)
shavings of fresh parmesan, to serve
   (optional)

1 Cook the rigatoni in a large saucepan of rapidly boiling salted water until *al dente*. Drain and return to the pan.
2 Meanwhile, heat the butter and oil in a large frying pan. Add the chorizo and cook over medium heat until well browned. Add the fennel and cook, stirring occasionally, for 5 minutes.
3 Add the garlic and stir for 1 minute. Stir in the lime juice and pimientos and bring to the boil, then reduce the heat and simmer for another 5 minutes.
4 Add the sausage mixture and rocket to the pasta and toss to combine. Top with shavings of parmesan, if desired.

NOTE: Chorizo is a spicy dried sausage, heavily flavoured with garlic and chilli. It is similar to salami, which can be substituted if chorizo is not available.

fusilli with vegetables

Ready to eat in **30 minutes**
Serves **4–6**

500 g (1 lb 2 oz) fusilli (spiral pasta)
60 ml (2 fl oz/¼ cup) olive oil
6 baby (pattypan) squash, sliced
3 zucchini (courgettes), sliced
2 garlic cloves, crushed
3 spring onions (scallions), chopped
1 red capsicum (pepper), cut into strips
65 g (2¼ oz/⅓ cup) fresh corn kernels
4 tomatoes, chopped
2 tablespoons chopped flat-leaf (Italian)
   parsley

1 Cook the fusilli in a large saucepan of rapidly boiling salted water until *al dente*. Drain and return to the pan.
2 Meanwhile, heat 2 tablespoons of the oil in a wok or frying pan, add the squash and zucchini and stir-fry for 3 minutes, or until the vegetables are just tender. Add the garlic, spring onion, capsicum and corn kernels to the wok and stir-fry for another 2–3 minutes. Add the tomato and stir until combined.
3 Add the remaining olive oil and the parsley to the pasta and toss until well combined. Serve the pasta topped with the vegetable mixture.

NOTE: This is a good recipe to use up any vegetables you have on hand. Mushrooms, broccoli, snow peas (mangetout) and asparagus are all suitable, and other herbs such as chives, basil or coriander (cilantro) can be added.

cream of onion pasta

Ready to eat in **30 minutes**
Serves **4**

500 g (1 lb 2 oz) fettuccine or linguine
50 g (1¾ oz) butter
6 onions, thinly sliced
125 ml (4 fl oz/½ cup) beef stock
125 ml (4 fl oz/½ cup) pouring (whipping)
  cream
shavings of parmesan cheese, to serve
spring onion (scallion), sliced, to garnish
  (optional)

1 Cook the fettuccine in a large saucepan
of rapidly boiling salted water until
al dente. Drain and return to the pan.
2 Meanwhile, melt the butter, add the
onion and cook over medium heat for
10 minutes, until soft. Stir in the stock
and cream and simmer for 10 minutes.
Season with salt and pepper, to taste.
3 Stir the sauce through the fettuccine
and serve topped with the parmesan
shavings. Garnish with spring onion,
if you wish.

spaghetti with creamy lemon sauce

Ready to eat in **20 minutes**
Serves **4**

500 g (1 lb 2 oz) spaghetti
250 ml (9 fl oz/1 cup) pouring (whipping)
  cream
185 ml (6 fl oz/¾ cup) chicken stock
1 tablespoon finely grated lemon zest, plus
  shredded zest, for garnish
2 tablespoons finely chopped flat-leaf
  (Italian) parsley
2 tablespoons snipped chives

1 Cook the spaghetti in a large saucepan
of rapidly boiling salted water until
al dente. Drain and return to the pan.

2 Meanwhile, combine the cream,
stock and lemon zest in a saucepan over
medium heat. Bring to the boil, stirring
occasionally. Reduce the heat and simmer
gently for 10 minutes, or until the sauce
has reduced and thickened slightly.
3 Toss the sauce and herbs through the
spaghetti. Serve immediately, garnished
with shredded lemon zest.

asparagus and parmesan salad

Cook 300 g (10½ oz) asparagus in
a saucepan of boiling water until
bright green and tender but still
crisp. Refresh in iced water and
drain well. Arrange the asparagus
on a plate and top with shavings
of parmesan cheese. Drizzle with
a little balsamic vinegar and
extra virgin olive oil and sprinkle
generously with cracked black
pepper. Serve as a side dish.

sorrel

Sorrel is a bitter leaf vegetable rich in vitamins A and C, as well as in essential minerals. Young, glossy leaves are simply rinsed and trimmed of their tough stems before being tossed in a green salad. Sorrel's clean, sharp flavour makes it a good companion to fish and rich poultry such as goose and duck, and it is used to flavour stews and sauces. When subjected to prolonged heat, it breaks down to a pulp, so it is good for puréeing. Avoid iron or aluminium pans when cooking with sorrel, as the chemical reaction that results leaves the sorrel acrid.

tortellini broth

Ready to eat in **20 minutes**
Serves **4**

250 g (9 oz) tortellini
1 litre (35 fl oz/4 cups) good-quality beef stock
60 g (2¼ oz/½ cup) sliced spring onions (scallions), plus extra, for garnish

1 Cook the tortellini in a large saucepan of rapidly boiling salted water until *al dente*. Drain and divide among deep, warmed soup bowls.
2 Meanwhile, bring the stock to the boil in a saucepan. Add the spring onion and simmer for 3 minutes.
3 Ladle the stock over the tortellini and garnish with the extra spring onion. Serve immediately.

artichoke, egg and sorrel pasta

Ready to eat in **25 minutes**
Serves **4**

500 g (1 lb 2 oz) conchiglie (shell pasta)
2 tablespoons olive oil
3 garlic cloves, crushed
315 g (11 oz) marinated artichoke hearts,
 halved
3 tablespoons chopped flat-leaf (Italian)
 parsley
160 g (5¾ oz) sorrel leaves, roughly
 chopped
4 hard-boiled eggs, chopped
shavings of fresh parmesan, to serve

1 Cook the conchiglie in a large saucepan
of rapidly boiling salted water until it is
al dente. Drain and keep warm.
2 Meanwhile, heat the oil in a frying
pan, add the garlic and cook over medium
heat until golden. Add the artichoke
and parsley and cook over low heat for
5 minutes, or until heated through.
3 Transfer the pasta to a large bowl. Add
the sorrel, egg and artichoke and toss to
combine. Serve immediately, topped with
the parmesan and cracked black pepper.

cheesy buckwheat and bean pasta

Ready to eat in **30 minutes**
Serves **4**

500 g (1 lb 2 oz) buckwheat fusilli
 (spiral pasta)
1 tablespoon olive oil
2 garlic cloves, crushed
1 onion, chopped
300 ml (10½ fl oz) bottled tomato pasta
 sauce
80 ml (2½ fl oz/⅓ cup) orange juice
400 g (14 oz) tin kidney beans, rinsed and
 drained

125 g (4½ oz/1 cup) grated cheddar cheese,
 plus extra, for serving
3 tablespoons chopped mixed herbs

1 Cook the fusilli in a large saucepan of
rapidly boiling salted water until *al dente*.
Drain and return to the pan.
2 Meanwhile, heat the oil in a frying pan.
Add the garlic and onion and cook over
medium heat for 3 minutes, or until the
onion is golden but not brown.
3 Add the pasta sauce, orange juice and
kidney beans to the pan. Bring to the
boil, then reduce the heat and simmer
gently for 5 minutes, or until the sauce is
heated through.
4 Add the sauce to the pasta with the
cheddar cheese and herbs. Stir until the
cheese melts and serve immediately,
topped with extra grated cheddar.

cheesy buckwheat and bean pasta

gorgonzola and toasted walnuts on linguine

Ready to eat in **25 minutes**
Serves **4**

75 g (2¾ oz/¾ cup) walnut halves
500 g (1 lb 2 oz) linguine
75 g (2½ oz) butter
150 g (5½ oz) gorgonzola cheese, chopped
    or crumbled
2 tablespoons pouring (whipping) cream
155 g (5½ oz/1 cup) shelled fresh peas

1 Preheat the oven to 180°C (350°F/ Gas 4). Spread the walnuts on a baking tray and bake for about 5 minutes, until lightly toasted. Set aside to cool.
2 Cook the linguine in a large saucepan of rapidly boiling water until *al dente*. Drain and return to the pan.
3 While the pasta is cooking, melt the butter in a small saucepan over low heat and add the gorgonzola, cream and peas. Stir gently for 5 minutes, or until the sauce has thickened. Season with salt and pepper, to taste. Add the sauce and walnuts to the pasta and toss until well combined. Serve immediately, sprinkled with freshly ground black pepper.

NOTE: You can use frozen peas if you prefer. Don't bother to thaw them, just add them as directed in the recipe. Use a milder blue cheese such as Blue Castello in place of the gorgonzola, if you don't like really strong blue cheese.

preparing and cooking black mussels

Black mussels are a variety of bivalve mollusc with a rounded black shell and plump, succulent flesh. Like all shellfish, they must be bought and eaten fresh and they must be thoroughly cleaned before cooking. First, discard those that are open or damaged. Scrub the unopened mussels with a stiff brush and remove the hairy beard. If the mussels are gritty, they can be soaked in clean, salted water for one to two hours to make them expel grit and sand. After a final rinse, put them in a saucepan to steam open. By the time they have all opened, they will be cooked. Before using, discard any unopened mussels and any with flat and dried-out flesh.

tomato mussels on spaghetti

❋ ❋

Ready to eat in **30** minutes
Serves **4**

16 black mussels
500 g (1 lb 2 oz) spaghetti
80 ml (2½ fl oz/⅓ cup) olive oil
1 large onion, finely chopped
2 garlic cloves, crushed

800 g (1 lb 12 oz) tin chopped tomatoes
125 ml (4 fl oz/½ cup) white wine

1 Scrub the mussels thoroughly and remove the hairy beards. Discard any open or damaged mussels.
2 Cook the spaghetti in a large saucepan of rapidly boiling salted water until *al dente*. Drain, return to the pan and toss with half the olive oil.
3 Meanwhile, heat the remaining olive oil in a pan, add the onion and cook until soft, but not brown. Add the garlic

and cook for another minute. Stir in the tomatoes and wine and bring to the boil. Reduce the heat and simmer gently.
4 Meanwhile, put the mussels in a large saucepan and just cover with water. Cook over high heat for a few minutes, until the mussels have opened. Shake the pan often and discard any mussels that have not opened after 5 minutes.
5 Add the mussels to the tomato sauce and stir to combine. Serve the pasta with mussels and sauce over the top. Garnish with sprigs of thyme, if desired.

spaghetti with herbs

spaghetti with herbs

Ready to eat in **20 minutes**
Serves 4

500 g (1 lb 2 oz) spaghetti
50 g (1¾ oz) butter
30 g (1 oz/½ cup) shredded basil
10 g (¼ oz/⅓ cup) chopped oregano
20 g (¾ oz/⅓ cup) snipped chives
freshly garted parmesan, to serve

1 Cook the spaghetti in a large saucepan
of rapidly boiling salted water until
al dente. Drain and return to the pan.
2 Add the butter to the pan, tossing until
it melts and coats the strands of spaghetti.
Add the basil, oregano and chives to
the pan and toss the herbs through the
buttery pasta until well distributed.
Season, to taste, and serve immediately.

pasta with pesto and parmesan

Ready to eat in **15 minutes**
Serves 4

500 g (1 lb 2 oz) linguine or taglierini
40 g (1½ oz/¼ cup) pine nuts
100 g (3½ oz/2 firmly packed cups)
    basil leaves
2 garlic cloves, chopped
25 g (¾ oz/¼ cup) freshly grated parmesan
    cheese, plus shavings, to garnish
125 ml (4 fl oz/½ cup) extra virgin olive oil

1 Cook the pasta in a large saucepan of
rapidly boiling salted water until *al dente*.
Drain and return to the pan.
2 Meanwhile, finely chop the pine nuts,
basil leaves, garlic and parmesan in a
food processor. With the motor running,
add the olive oil in a slow stream to form
a smooth paste. Season, to taste. Toss
the pesto through the hot pasta until it
is thoroughly distributed. Garnish with
shavings of fresh parmesan.

calabrian spaghetti

Ready to eat in **20 minutes**
Serves **4**

500 g (1 lb 2 oz) spaghetti
80 ml (2½ fl oz/⅓ cup) olive oil
3 garlic cloves, crushed
50 g (1¾ oz) anchovy fillets,
  finely chopped, plus extra, to serve
1 teaspoon thinly sliced red chillies, plus
  extra, to serve (optional)
3 tablespoons chopped flat-leaf (Italian)
  parsley

1 Cook the spaghetti in a large saucepan of rapidly boiling salted water until *al dente*. Drain and return to the pan.
2 Meanwhile, heat the oil in a small saucepan. Add the garlic, anchovy and chilli and cook over low heat for 5 minutes, being careful not to brown the garlic too much or it will be bitter. Add the parsley and cook for a few more minutes. Season with salt and ground black pepper, to taste.
3 Add the sauce to the pasta and toss through until thoroughly coated. Serve immediately, garnished with a little extra chopped anchovy and chilli, if desired.

pesto

When a pesto (including the cheese) is stored for any length of time, the composition of the ingredients alters. The cheese component reacts with other ingredients, in particular the basil, and starts to turn rancid. It will keep, at best, for five to seven days, if refrigerated in an airtight jar with a layer of olive oil or plastic wrap covering the exposed surface. A more successful option when making pesto to put away is to leave out the cheese and stir it through when the sauce is ready to be used. In this way, your pesto will keep for two to three months refrigerated, or five to six months frozen.

ravioli with peas and artichokes

Ready to eat in **30 minutes**
Serves **4**

650 g (1 lb 7 oz) fresh cheese
    and spinach ravioli
1 tablespoon olive oil
8 marinated artichoke hearts,
    quartered

2 large garlic cloves, finely chopped
125 ml (4 fl oz/½ cup) dry white wine
125 ml (4 fl oz/½ cup) chicken stock
310 g (11 oz/2 cups) frozen peas
125 g (4½ oz) thinly sliced prosciutto,
    chopped
7 g (¼ oz/¼ cup) chopped flat-leaf
    (Italian) parsley
½ teaspoon cracked black pepper

1 Cook the ravioli in a large saucepan of rapidly boiling salted water until *al dente*. Drain and keep warm.

sambal oelek

This is a simple hot paste traditionally made from red chillies, sugar and salt. It is used as a relish in Indonesian and Malaysian cooking and can be used as a substitute for fresh chillies in most recipes. Covered, it will keep for months in the refrigerator.

2 Meanwhile, heat the oil in a saucepan and cook the artichoke and garlic over medium heat for 2 minutes, stirring frequently. Add the wine and stock and stir until well mixed. Bring to the boil, reduce the heat slightly and simmer for 5 minutes. Add the peas (they don't need to be thawed first) and simmer for another 2 minutes.

3 Stir the prosciutto, parsley and pepper into the artichoke mixture. Serve the ravioli topped with the sauce.

NOTE: You can buy marinated artichoke hearts in jars from supermarkets and also from delicatessen counters.

brandied cream and salmon fusilli

Ready to eat in **30 minutes**
Serves **2**

375 g (13 oz) fusilli (spiral pasta)
45 g (1½ oz) butter
1 leek, thinly sliced
1 large garlic clove, crushed
60 ml (2 fl oz/¼ cup) brandy
½ teaspoon sambal oelek
2 tablespoons finely chopped dill
1 tablespoon tomato paste (concentrated purée)
250 ml (9 fl oz/1 cup) pouring (whipping) cream
250 g (9 oz) smoked salmon, thinly sliced
red caviar or lumpfish roe, to garnish (optional)

1 Cook the fusilli in a large saucepan of rapidly boiling salted water until *al dente*. Drain and keep warm.

2 Heat the butter in a large saucepan and cook the leek over medium heat for a few minutes, until soft. Add the garlic and cook for another minute. Add the brandy and cook for another minute. Stir in the sambal oelek, dill, tomato paste and cream. Simmer gently for 5 minutes, until the sauce reduces and thickens slightly.

3 Add the pasta and smoked salmon to the sauce. Toss until well combined and season with a little salt and freshly ground black pepper, to taste. Divide the pasta between two warmed serving bowls. Garnish with a spoonful of caviar, if you like, and serve immediately.

NOTE: Wash the leek thoroughly, as dirt and grit can sometimes be caught in the inner layers.

garlic bucatini

pasta niçoise

Ready to eat in **25 minutes**
Serves **4**

500 g (1 lb 2 oz) farfalle
350 g (12 oz) green beans
80 ml (2½ fl oz/⅓ cup) olive oil
60 g (2¼ oz) sliced anchovy fillets
2 garlic cloves, finely sliced
250 g (9 oz) cherry tomatoes, halved
freshly grated parmesan cheese, to serve
   (optional)

1 Cook the farfalle in a large saucepan of rapidly boiling salted water until *al dente*. Drain and return to the pan.
2 Meanwhile, place the beans in a heatproof bowl and cover with boiling water. Set aside for 5 minutes, drain and rinse under cold water.
3 Heat the oil in a frying pan and stir-fry the beans and anchovy for 2–3 minutes. Add the garlic and cook for 1 minute. Add the tomatoes and stir through.
4 Add the sauce to the pasta, toss well and warm through. Serve with the grated parmesan, if desired.

garlic bucatini

Ready to eat in **15 minutes**
Serves **4**

500 g (1 lb 2 oz) bucatini
80 ml (2½ fl oz/⅓ cup) olive oil
8 garlic cloves, crushed
2 tablespoons chopped flat-leaf (Italian)
   parsley
freshly grated parmesan cheese, to serve

1 Cook the bucatini in a large saucepan of rapidly boiling water until *al dente*. Drain and return to the pan.
2 When the pasta is almost finished cooking, heat the olive oil over low heat in a frying pan and add the garlic. Cook for 1 minute before removing from the heat. Add the garlic oil and the parsley to the pasta and toss to distribute thoroughly. Serve sprinkled generously with grated parmesan.

spaghetti mediterranean

Ready to eat in **30 minutes**
Serves 4–6

500 g (1 lb 2 oz) spaghetti
750 g (1 lb 10 oz) tomatoes
125 ml (4 fl oz/½ cup) extra virgin olive oil
2 garlic cloves, crushed
4 spring onions (scallions), finely sliced
6 anchovy fillets, chopped

½ teaspoon finely grated lemon zest
1 tablespoon thyme leaves
12 stuffed green olives, thinly sliced
shredded basil, to serve

1 Cook the spaghetti in a large saucepan of rapidly boiling salted water until *al dente*. Drain and return to the pan.
2 While the pasta is cooking, score a small cross in the base of each tomato. Cover with boiling water for 1–2 minutes, then drain and plunge into cold water. Peel the skin away from the cross and cut the tomatoes in half. Place a sieve over a small bowl and squeeze the tomato seeds and juice into it; discard the seeds. Chop the tomatoes roughly and set aside.
3 In a bowl, combine the oil, garlic, spring onion, anchovy, lemon zest, thyme and olives. Add the tomato and tomato juice, mix well and season with salt and freshly ground black pepper, to taste. Add the sauce to the pasta, toss to combine and sprinkle with basil.

thyme

There are many different types of thyme used in cooking, ranging from grey-green leaves and a pungent scent, to tiny bright-green leaves with a more evasive perfume. In fact, the aroma that thyme imparts to a dish is just as important as the flavour. Wild thyme is refined and aromatic while lemon thyme gives off a subtle lemony aroma when heated. With small leaves of low moisture content, thyme is easy to dry.

tomato paste

Tomato paste, also known as tomato purée or concentrated purée, is made by simmering whole tomatoes until very thick, dark and no longer liquid. Only salt is added, and sometimes a little sugar. The resulting paste has an intense flavour that is used sparingly in sauces, stocks, stews and soups. The many commercial brands have varying degrees of concentration, so it is a matter of trying different ones until you find one that best suits your needs. Italian tomato paste is graded, so look for doppio concentrato (double concentrate), or triplo concentrato (triple concentrate) on the label.

spaghetti carbonara with mushrooms

Ready to eat in **25 minutes**
Serves **4**

500 g (1 lb 2 oz) spaghetti
8 bacon slices
180 g (6¼ oz/2 cups) button mushrooms
2 teaspoons chopped oregano
4 eggs, lightly beaten
250 ml (9 fl oz/1 cup) pouring (whipping) cream
65 g (2¼ oz/⅔ cup) freshly grated parmesan cheese

1 Cook the spaghetti in a large saucepan of rapidly boiling salted water until it is *al dente*. Drain and return to the pan.
2 Meanwhile, trim the bacon and cut into small pieces. Thinly slice the mushrooms. Fry the bacon until lightly browned, then set aside on paper towels. Add the mushroom to the pan and fry for 2–3 minutes, until soft.
3 Add the mushroom, bacon, oregano and the combined egg and cream to the drained spaghetti. Cook over low heat, stirring, until the mixture starts to thicken slightly. Remove from the heat and stir in the parmesan cheese. Season with salt and cracked black pepper, to taste. Serve with crusty bread, if desired.

spaghetti with tomato sauce

Ready to eat in **30 minutes**
Serves **4**

500 g (1 lb 2 oz) spaghetti
1 tablespoon olive oil
1 onion, finely chopped
2 garlic cloves, crushed
800 g (1 lb 12 oz) tin chopped tomatoes
1 teaspoon dried oregano
2 tablespoons tomato paste (concentrated purée)
2 teaspoons sugar
shavings of fresh parmesan cheese, to serve (optional)

1 Cook the spaghetti in a large saucepan of rapidly boiling salted water until *al dente*. Drain and return to the pan.
2 Heat the oil in a saucepan, add the onion and cook for 3 minutes, until soft. Add the garlic and cook, stirring, for another minute.
3 Add the tomatoes and bring to the boil. Add the oregano, tomato paste and sugar, reduce the heat and simmer for 15 minutes. Season, to taste. Serve the pasta topped with the tomato sauce and parmesan, if desired.

ricotta and basil with tagliatelle

Ready to eat in **25 minutes**
Serves **4**

500 g (1 lb 2 oz) tagliatelle
20 g (¾ oz/1 cup) flat-leaf (Italian) parsley leaves
50 g (1¾ oz/1 cup) basil leaves
1 teaspoon olive oil
50 g (1¾ oz/⅓ cup) chopped sun-dried capsicum (pepper)
250 g (9 oz/1 cup) sour cream
250 g (9 oz/1 cup) fresh ricotta cheese

25 g (¾ oz/¼ cup) freshly grated parmesan cheese

1 Cook the tagliatelle in a large saucepan of rapidly boiling salted water until *al dente*. Drain and return to the pan.
2 While the pasta is cooking, process the parsley and basil in a food processor or blender until just chopped. Set aside.
3 Heat the oil in a frying pan, add the capsicum and fry for 2–3 minutes. Stir in the sour cream, ricotta and parmesan and stir over low heat for 4 minutes, or until heated through. Do not allow to boil.
4 Add the herbs and sauce to the pasta, toss to combine and serve.

ricotta and basil with tagliatelle

farfalle with peas, prosciutto and mushrooms

☀

Ready to eat in **20 minutes**
Serves **4**

375 g (13 oz) farfalle
60 g (2¼ oz) butter
1 onion, chopped
200 g (7 oz) mushrooms, thinly sliced
250 g (9 oz) frozen peas
3 prosciutto slices, roughly chopped
250 ml (9 fl oz/1 cup) pouring (whipping) cream
1 egg yolk
fresh parmesan cheese, to serve (optional)

1 Cook the farfalle in a large saucepan of rapidly boiling salted water until *al dente*. Drain and return to the pan.
2 While the pasta is cooking, heat the butter in a pan, add the onion and mushroom and stir over medium heat for 5 minutes or until tender.
3 Add the peas and prosciutto to the onion and mushroom. Combine the cream and egg yolk in a bowl and pour into the pan. Cover and simmer for 5 minutes or until heated through.
4 Mix the sauce through the pasta or serve the sauce spooned over the top of the pasta. Can be topped with shaved or grated fresh parmesan.

fennel, orange and almond salad

Finely slice 1 or 2 fennel bulbs. Peel 3 oranges, taking care to remove all of the bitter white pith, and cut into segments. Toast 100 g (3½ oz) flaked almonds in a frying pan until golden. Combine the fennel, oranges and almonds in a bowl. Add 150 g (5½ oz) crumbled creamy blue vein cheese and 50 g (1¾ oz) thinly sliced sun-dried capsicum (pepper). Make a dressing by combining 60 ml (2 fl oz/ ¼ cup) orange juice, 1 teaspoon sesame oil and 1 tablespoon red wine vinegar. Drizzle over the salad and serve as a side dish.

penne with sun-dried tomatoes and lemon

Ready to eat in **25 minutes**
Serves **4**

250 g (9 oz) penne
60 ml (2 fl oz/¼ cup) olive oil
3 bacon slices, chopped
1 onion, chopped
80 ml (2½ fl oz/⅓ cup) lemon juice
1 tablespoon thyme leaves
50 g (1¾ oz/⅓ cup) chopped sun-dried
   tomatoes
80 g (2¾ oz/½ cup) pine nuts, toasted

1 Cook the pasta in a large saucepan of rapidly boiling salted water until *al dente*. Drain and return to the pan.
2 Meanwhile, heat the oil in a large saucepan, add the bacon and onion and stir over medium heat for 4 minutes or until the the onion has softened.
3 Add the pasta to the pan with the lemon juice, thyme, sun-dried tomato and pine nuts. Stir over low heat for 2 minutes, or until heated through.

NOTE: You can use pancetta instead of bacon, if preferred.

farfalle with pink peppercorns and sugar snap peas

Ready to eat in **30 minutes**
Serves **4**

400 g (14 oz) farfalle
250 ml (9 fl oz/1 cup) white wine
250 ml (9 fl oz/1 cup) pouring (whipping)
   cream
100 g (3½ oz) pink peppercorns in vinegar,
   drained
300 g (10 oz) crème fraîche
200 g (7 oz) sugar snap peas, topped
   and tailed

1 Cook the farfalle in a large saucepan of rapidly boiling salted water until *al dente*. Drain and return to the pan.
2 While the pasta is cooking, pour the wine into a large saucepan and bring to the boil, then reduce the heat and simmer until reduced by half.
3 Add the cream to the wine and bring to the boil again, then reduce the heat and simmer until reduced by half.
4 Remove from the heat and stir in the pink peppercorns and crème fraîche. Return to the heat and add the sugar snap peas, simmering until they turn bright green. Season with salt, if necessary. Stir through the pasta and serve immediately.

penne with sun-dried tomatoes and lemon

index

Page numbers in *italics* refer to photographs. Page numbers in **bold** refer to margin notes.